CRITICAL INSIGHTS

Ernest Hemingway

CRITICAL INSIGHTS

Ernest Hemingway

Editor
Eugene Goodheart
Brandeis University

Salem Press
Pasadena, California   Hackensack, New Jersey

Cover photo: Time & Life Pictures/Getty Images

Published by Salem Press

© 2010 by EBSCO Publishing
Editor's text © 2010 by Eugene Goodheart
"The *Paris Review* Perspective" © 2010 by Petrina Crockford for *The Paris Review*

∞ The paper used in these volumes conforms to the American National Standard for Permanence of Paper for Printed Library Materials, Z39.48-1992 (R1997).

Library of Congress Cataloging-in-Publication Data
Ernest Hemingway / editor, Eugene Goodheart.
    p. cm. — (Critical insights)
Includes bibliographical references and index.
ISBN 978-1-58765-630-9 (one volume : alk. paper)
    1. Hemingway, Ernest, 1899-1961--Criticism and interpretation. I. Good-heart, Eugene.
  PS3515.E37Z586555 2010
  813'.52—dc22

                  2009026438

PRINTED IN CANADA

Contents_____

Career, Life, and Influence_____

Critical Contexts_____

Critical Readings_____

Resources

About This Volume_____

Eugene Goodheart

Ernest Hemingway's public persona and reputation, literary style, affinity with modern painting, and conception of character are among the subjects of these commentaries on the author's life and work. Following my general introduction, R. Baird Shuman introduces us to Hemingway's life. In her contribution for *The Paris Review*, Petrina Crockford speaks of his "adventurous life as brash and uncompromising as that of his greatest characters."

Jennifer Banach Palladino, in her essay on the cultural and historical contexts of Hemingway's work, reminds us of the cataclysmic events of the early twentieth century (World War I and the Spanish Civil War) in which Hemingway was both participant and observer, and Robert C. Evans traces the vicissitudes of his extraordinary reputation. Matthew Bolton contrasts William Faulkner's Baroque style with Hemingway's pared-down prose, noting, however, the capacity of each writer to employ the other's style when necessary. These opening essays provide contexts for close readings of Hemingway's major works.

A chapter from Carlos Baker's landmark 1963 study *Hemingway: The Writer as Artist* points up the "half-symbolic" resonances of his deceptively plain style. In a close reading of "Hills Like White Elephants," an elusive and elliptical short story about an impending abortion, Hilary K. Justice adjudicates between conflicting interpretations of the story. Following the lead of Lillian Ross's interview of Hemingway, Ron Berman demonstrates the writer's affinity with Paul Cézanne in his use of reiteration, revealing Hemingway's naturalism to be a version of abstract art. Neil Heims's essay on *The Sun Also Rises* shows how the other characters in the novel are projections of conflicts within the protagonist and narrator, Jake Barnes. Heims addresses the role of anti-Semitism in the novel and attempts to answer the vexed question of whether anti-Semitic attitudes should be attributed to Hemingway as well as to the characters in the novel.

George Cheatham takes up Scott Donaldson's controversial view that the moral code of *The Sun Also Rises* consists in the exact and equal "exchange of values." He argues to the contrary that value in Jake Barnes's behavior emerges from a generosity of spirit that rises above the transactive (money) language that figures human relationships in the novel. Frederic Henry, the wounded protagonist of Hemingway's World War I novel *A Farewell to Arms*, emerges from Scott Donaldson's account, or, as Donaldson might say, from Henry's own narrative, as less a man of action than a character absorbing the blows of fate. It is his lover Catherine Barkley who, in her willingness to sacrifice herself for him, is the moral hero of the novel. Mark Spilka has a similar view of Frederic Henry. In a detailed argument, he sets the evolution of the Hemingway hero from the apparent stoic manliness of Jake Barnes in *The Sun Also Rises* to the feminine vulnerability of Henry, already foreshadowed in Jake Barnes, against the background of Hemingway's relationships with his wives.

Viewing *A Farewell to Arms* through the feminist lens of *Regeneration*, Pat Barker's novel of World War I, Diane Price Herndl sees what Hemingway's masculine ethos prevents him from seeing: "the self-destructiveness of wartime masculinity." Acknowledging flaws in *For Whom the Bell Tolls*, A. Robert Lee nevertheless makes a detailed and forceful case for the artistic integrity of the novel.

With the sensitivity of a literary critic, Philip Melling provides an anthropological perspective on *The Old Man and the Sea*. Turning his back on his own culture, the protagonist Santiago has internalized the values of American popular culture, invoking his hero Joe DiMaggio in his heroic struggle with the fish, in effect failing to appreciate what Hemingway appreciates, the knowledge of the sea contained in Cuban folklore and witchcraft and the historical legacy of slavery. In the concluding essay, Louis A. Renza moves back and forth between the two "bookends" of Hemingway's career, *In Our Time* and *A Moveable Feast*, in his reflections on the tension between "the self-referential act of writing" and "the perceptual immediacy of the referential scene." He also addresses Hemingway's need for isolation and the ambiguous effects of his immense public persona on his writing.

CAREER, LIFE, AND INFLUENCE

On Ernest Hemingway

Eugene Goodheart

Ernest Hemingway is to American and English literary culture in the first half of the twentieth century what Byron was to English and European literary culture in the early nineteenth century. These writers fashioned for themselves heroic—though, to be sure, differing—self-images. In the second half of the twentieth century Norman Mailer reenacted Hemingway's role. "Literary culture" is too modest a phrase to represent the extent of their charismatic appeal. What is it in Hemingway's literary achievement that gave rise to the public persona, and does the public persona enhance or detract from it?

Jennifer Banach Palladino's essay in this collection reminds us of the cataclysmic events of the early twentieth century (World War I and the Spanish Civil War, a prelude to World War II) in which Hemingway was both participant and observer as journalist and novelist. Set in Italy during World War I, *A Farewell to Arms* is a love story between Frederic Henry (a Hemingway surrogate?), a soldier wounded in the war, and Catherine Barkley. The hero of *For Whom the Bell Tolls*, Robert Jordan (another Hemingway surrogate?), is an American volunteer on the antifascist Loyalist side in the Spanish Civil War who gives his life on the battlefield. Writing is a lonely and sedentary activity. We do not usually think of writers as men of action. In a time when the prototypical protagonist of modern fiction is the antihero, Hemingway is the rare writer drawn to the life of violent action. This is part of the explanation of his public persona. But the life of action alone doesn't explain Hemingway's charismatic appeal. What has fascinated both readers and nonreaders alike is his discovery or invention of a style, at once literary and moral, that represents the actions of both his heroes and himself.

Hemingway describes the style best in a splendid metaphor: "The dignity of movement of an iceberg is due to only one-eighth of it being above water." Words like "plain," "crisp," and "spare" have been used to characterize the prose. (See Matthew Bolton's essay on the Hemingwayesque and the Faulknerian.) The metaphor of the iceberg asks us to keep in mind the emotional charge that lies below the spare prose. The Hemingway hero suffers like the rest of us, maybe more than the rest of us. He knows fear and humiliation in the face of violence, but he will not allow suffering, fear, and humiliation to subvert his manhood. His code is expressed in the phrase "grace under pressure." The prose is a kind of manual of conduct. Thus in the description of a fishing trip in the story "Big Two-Hearted River," Nick Adams, the hero of Hemingway's first collection of stories, *In Our Time*, displays expertness in baiting a hook, in making a fire, and in his confident knowledge of the environment. There is correspondence between the precision of the prose and Adams's expert competence. The prose is distinguished not only by what is said but also by what is suggested in what is unsaid. We are meant to admire the tight-lipped silence of the matador as he faces the charge of the bull or the resolve of the soldier facing gunfire. It is hardly a leap to see the Hemingway ethos in the verbal reserve and swagger of the Western hero of the cinema confronting danger.

We may have our doubts about what lies beneath the surface. Rather than containing a rich emotional charge, the laconic hero may be emotionally detached and remote from the experience, in a word, hollow or numb inside. Hemingway, a proto-existentialist, suspects that what underlies our experience of the world is *nada*, or nothingness. Meursault, the sociopathic narrator of Albert Camus's *L'Étranger*, a master of spare and crisp prose, must have been an admiring reader of Hemingway's prose. We discern Hemingway's influence on the behavior of the American adolescent, who, even without knowing anything about the writer and his work, learns to conceal his fear and anxiety by affecting a cool and indifferent exterior. Could it be that Hemingway's obsession with manly behavior betrays the embarrassment of the American male at the expression of emotion, a fear of the threat of the feminine within? Women like Lady Brett in *The Sun Also Rises* are Circe-like in their dangerous attractiveness.

In a generally admiring essay, Robert Penn Warren expresses a reservation about Hemingway's heroic pose: "We never see a story in which honor calls for slow, grinding, day to day conquest of nagging difficulties. In other words, the [heroic] idea is submitted to the test of a relatively small area of experience, to experience of a hand-picked sort, and to characters of a limited range." Warren has in mind the scene of battle, the matador's encounter with the bull, the old man with the fish. In *The Old Man and the Sea*, the aging fisherman Santiago engages in what he considers to be a life and death struggle with a large fish: "You are killing me, fish, the old man thought. But you have a right to. Never have I seen a greater or more beautiful, or a calmer or more noble thing than you, brother. Come on and kill me. I do not care who kills who." The old man speaks to the fish as if it had human consciousness to match his own. The speech is overblown, even a little absurd, an old man's straining for heroic effect. (By contrast, Herman Melville was able to raise Moby Dick to a virtual supernatural presence because of the way Ahab demonized him. Santiago's adversary is not endowed with the White Whale's advantages.) Behind Warren's judgment is a conception of the novel as traditionally concerned with ordinary life, "the dull spaces," in D. H. Lawrence's surprising phrase. Rather than a novelist of ordinary life, Hemingway appears to be a throwback to the ancient idea of epic heroism. For me, the problem does not lie so much in the limited province in which the heroic will is exercised, as Warren has it, but rather in the authenticity of the heroic pose.

What has not been sufficiently remarked upon in the commentary on Hemingway is a dissonance between the heroic pose and his deflationary rhetoric. He was not alone among writers who, having experienced the ravages of World War I, turned against the high rhetoric of patriotism and romantic love. His antidote was the plain English of ordinary speech. There is, I think, another kind of admirable behavior, if not exactly heroism, in Hemingway that is compatible with his plain style to be found in *The Sun Also Rises*. The novel is set in Paris after World War I. The protagonist, Jake Barnes, an American expatriate, has been made sexually impotent in the war. He is one among a number of expatriates who are impotent in other ways. (Hemingway's imagination crosses the seas from the rootedness of Nick Adams in the landscape of the American Midwest to the rootlessness of Jake Barnes and his fellow expatriates.) The emasculation of the male characters, from one perspective, reflects the ravages of the war. But in Jake's case, it has a paradoxical force as an expression of an inward withdrawal from the corrupt world in which he finds himself. Impotence is a way of keeping one's integrity virginal and clean. In a drunken state, an unexpected circumstance for self-knowledge, Jake realizes what has happened to him and what he has become. He has turned accident into essence in a stoic renunciation of the world.

> Women made such swell friends. Awfully swell. In the first place, you had to be in love with a woman to have a basis for friendship. I had been having Brett for a friend. I had not been thinking of her side of it. I had been getting something for nothing. That only delayed the presentation of the bill. The bill always came. That was one of the swell things you could count on.
>
> I thought I had paid for everything. Not like the woman pays and pays and pays. No idea of retribution or punishment. Just exchange of values. You gave up something and got something else. Or you worked for something. You paid someway for something that was good.

It is worth remarking that, for all his vaunted spareness of style, economy of words is not one of Hemingway's "virtues." (The spareness of style is in the short sentence and the absence of qualifying adjectives, as in the following sentences in the story "The Three-Day Blow": "There was the cottage, the porch bare, smoke coming from the chimney. In back was the chicken coop and the second-growth timber like a hedge against the woods behind.") In his essay on Hemingway and Cézanne, Ron Berman notes that Hemingway found inspiration in Cézanne's use of "reiteration." Note the almost incantatory repetition of the words "pay" and "something" in Jake Barnes's reflections. The idea of the passage could have been expressed simply and economically: "You gave up something and got something in return." But such economy would not have adequately represented Jake's state of mind. What the repetition of words does represent is what Warren says is missing in Hemingway's heroic pose, "the nagging difficulties" that confront lives, whether ordinary or extraordinary. Like repetitions of physical exercise, the repetitions of language strengthen mind and will in their resolve. They make possible Jake's achievement of stoic grace under pressure. Hemingway admired the soldier, the matador, the fisherman, the hunter, and the outdoorsman. Each of these characters depends on the repetitive exercise of his skills. In his devotion to the craft of writing, Hemingway is himself a character of the type he wrote about. What distracts and detracts from his achievement is the straining for the epic heroic effect that became part of his personal legend. As a writer, a creator of character, story, and language, he is most compelling in representing the disciplined containment of the inner struggles and reflections of a man of integrity such as Jake Barnes.

Biography of Ernest Hemingway_____

R. Baird Shuman

Early Life

Born on July 21, 1899, into a conservative, upper-middle-class family in Oak Park, Illinois, an affluent suburb of Chicago, Ernest Hemingway spent much of his life and early literary career trying to break away from the constraints of his youth. Ernest's father, Clarence Edmonds Hemingway, was a physician who had a great interest in hunting and fishing. The young Hemingway, whose father hoped that his son would eventually join him in his medical practice, became an avid outdoorsman at an early age. Grace Hall Hemingway, Ernest's mother, was a cultivated woman, with a strong interest in music. She was a forceful woman, and Ernest came to believe early on that his father was henpecked.

Hemingway completed high school in 1917, just as the United States was being drawn into World War I. He had no wish to go to college and was eager to serve his country. His defective vision precluded his serving in the armed forces, so after a summer at Walloon Lake, Hemingway, drawing on his experience in writing for his high school newspaper in Oak Park, went to Kansas City as a reporter for the *Star*, a celebrated daily newspaper of that era. He was to return to Oak Park only five or six times in his entire life after he made the initial break. In Kansas City, Hemingway served an intense journalistic apprenticeship for seven months before he left for Italy as a Red Cross ambulance driver in May, 1918. He had been in Italy for less than six weeks when he was wounded at Fossalta di Piave on Italy's boundary with Austria. Despite his wounds, he dragged an injured solider from the front line to safety. For this act of heroism, he was decorated.

After spending some time in an Italian hospital near Milan recovering from his wounds, Hemingway was sent home, where he was looked upon as a hero. He reveled in his newly won celebrity. After he regained his strength at Lake Walloon, Hemingway went to Chicago, where he held a variety of menial jobs. Soon he married Hadley Richardson, eight years older than he, and sailed with her for France, where he served as a foreign correspondent for the *Toronto Star*. He arrived in Paris just as the city was reaching a postwar zenith of intellectual ferment and literary activity, and there he was to remain for the better part of the next decade, living and working among such influential literary figures as F. Scott Fitzgerald, Gertrude Stein, Ford Madox Ford, Ezra Pound, and James Joyce.

Hemingway, handsome with animated eyes, a ready smile, and a dark mustache, was soon the darling of Parisian literary society. His good looks and amiability won for him a legion of friends, many of whom ultimately came to see the darker side of his highly complex and often bewildering personality. Aside from his journalistic commitments, he began in Paris to work assiduously on his short stories and a novel about the postwar expatriates who lived somewhat aimless existences in France and Spain. On a personal level, Hemingway was able to give purpose to his own life by writing about the aimlessness that characterized many of the Americans of his generation who lived in Europe at that time. He came to deplore the term he had popularized (borrowed from Gertrude Stein): the "lost generation."

Hemingway's first book, a collection of short stories interspersed with imagistic reflections, *In Our Time* (1924, 1925), was recognized by the literati as a work of considerable promise. Although the book was not a resounding commercial success, it was clearly the work of a serious author who had begun to master his craft.

Life's Work

Hemingway's first novel, *The Sun Also Rises* (1926), established him as an author of considerable significance, just as *In Our Time* had established him as an author of considerable promise. *The Sun Also Rises*, a book that was right for its time, depicts the dislocated members of the postwar generation. Set in Paris and Pamplona, Spain, it featured

Hemingway's first extended treatment of one of his lifelong fascinations: the art of the bullfight. It was not merely the timeliness of *The Sun Also Rises* that established Hemingway as a serious artist; it was also the meticulous control that he exercised over his material and the care and authenticity of his spare descriptions that made both readers and literary critics realize that he was an author of extraordinary stature.

The Sun Also Rises was followed by *A Farewell to Arms* (1929), which was published in the year that Hemingway divorced his first wife, Hadley, who had borne him one son, John. The protagonist of *A Farewell to Arms* is an American disenchanted with a society that could let something such as World War I happen. He finally deserts the disordered Italian army in which he has been serving. His disenchantment is intensified by the death of his lover, who dies while giving birth to their child.

In the years following *A Farewell to Arms*, Hemingway became an increasingly romantic figure, a rugged outdoorsman who spent much time attending bullfights in Spain, hunting big game in Africa, and fishing the waters off Key West, Florida, where he resided when he was not traveling. Out of this period were to come such books as *Death in the Afternoon* (1932), an extended discourse on bullfighting in which Hemingway gives valuable insights into his own creative processes; and *Green Hills of Africa* (1935), which remains one of the most sensitively written books about big game and those who hunt it.

Out of Hemingway's Key West experience came his novel *To Have and Have Not* (1937), a mediocre book set in Cuba and Key West during the Great Depression. Hemingway's next book, *For Whom the Bell Tolls* (1940), was an optimistic novel that called for the unity of humankind. The book is set in Spain during the Civil War, which Hemingway had seen at first hand as a correspondent with strong Loyalist sympathies. *For Whom the Bell Tolls* was to be Hemingway's last novel for ten years, after which he published *Across the River and into the Trees* (1950), an overly sentimental novel of little distinction.

Meanwhile, in 1940, Hemingway divorced Pauline Pfeiffer, his second wife and the mother of his sons Patrick and Gregory, after thirteen years of marriage. He married Martha Gellhorn, a writer, almost immediately, then divorced her in 1945. He then married Mary Welsh, also a writer, to whom he remained married until the end of his life.

When Hemingway returned from covering the Spanish Civil War, he bought Finca Vigía, a quite modest estate not far from Havana, Cuba. It would be his home until 1959, when the Fidel Castro regime forced him out of the country. He then bought a home in Ketchum, Idaho, where he was to spend the remaining years of his life.

During World War II, Hemingway first served as a correspondent in China, then, from 1944 until the end of the war, as a correspondent in Europe, crossing the English Channel on D-Day with the Twenty-second Regiment of the Fourth Infantry Division. With the regiment he saw considerable combat in Normandy and later at the Battle of the Bulge. He also devised the Crook Factory, which, in 1943, undertook some ill-conceived and abortive missions on his boat, *The Pilar*, to attempt to destroy German submarines in the waters off Cuba.

Hemingway's excursion into drama was with a play about the Spanish Civil War, *The Fifth Column* (1938). It was published in *"The Fifth Column" and the First Forty-nine Stories* (1938), a collection that includes such celebrated stories as "The Killers," "The Snows of Kilimanjaro," and "The Short Happy Life of Francis Macomber."

Hemingway had a writing slump after World War II that plagued him for the remainder of his life. *Across the River and into the Trees* brought vitriolic reviews, and some critics thought that this book marked the end of Hemingway's literary career. He published *The Old Man and the Sea* (1952) two years later, however, and this short, tightly controlled novel about Santiago, an old fisherman who almost dies during a three-day encounter with a marlin, helped to salvage his deteriorating reputation. The book won the Pulitzer Prize in 1953 and was also instrumental in Hemingway's being awarded the Nobel Prize in Literature in 1954.

The Old Man and the Sea was Hemingway's last novel, although two earlier, unfinished novels, *Islands in the Stream* (1970) and *The Garden of Eden* (1986), were published posthumously. The last of these was constructed by Scribner's editor Tom Jenks from more than fifteen hundred manuscript pages that Hemingway left on his death. Also published posthumously was *A Moveable Feast* (1964), a memoir that details Hemingway's life in Paris during the 1920's and has much of the power and grace of his early work.

Hemingway began to suffer increasingly from depression and anxiety after World War II, and he was twice hospitalized at the Mayo Clinic for electric shock therapy. On July 2, 1961, after returning to Ketchum from his second hospitalization, Hemingway ended his life with a shotgun blast.

From *Dictionary of World Biography: The 20th Century.* Pasadena, CA: Salem Press, 1999. Copyright © 1999 by Salem Press, Inc.

Bibliography

Benson, Jackson J., ed. *New Critical Approaches to the Short Stories of Ernest Hemingway.* Durham, N.C.: Duke University Press, 1990. Section 1 covers critical approaches to Hemingway's most important long fiction; section 2 concentrates on story techniques and themes; section 3 focuses on critical interpretations of the most important stories; section 4 provides an overview of Hemingway criticism; section 5 contains a comprehensive checklist of Hemingway short fiction criticism from 1975 to 1989.

Berman, Ronald. *Fitzgerald, Hemingway, and the Twenties.* Tuscaloosa: University of Alabama Press, 2001. An explication of the cultural context of the era and how the works of these two American writers are imbued with the attitudes and icons of their day.

_____. "Vaudeville Philosophers: 'The Killers.'" *Twentieth Century Literature* 45 (Spring, 1999): 79-93. Discusses the influence of the modernist reevaluation of vaudeville on Ernest Hemingway's short story; notes that Hemingway's interest in vaudeville resulted from its pervasive presence in society and its acceptance in the intellectual world; argues that vaudeville scripts inspired Hemingway's interest in the juxtaposition of urban sophistication and rural idiocy.

Bloom, Harold, ed. *Ernest Hemingway.* Broomall, Pa.: Chelsea House, 2000. Includes articles by a variety of critics who treat topics such as Hemingway's style, unifying devices, and visual techniques.

Burgess, Anthony. *Ernest Hemingway*. New York: Thames and Hudson, 1999. Originally published in 1978 as *Ernest Hemingway and His World*. Includes bibliographical references and an index.

Dubus, Andre. "A Hemingway Story." *The Kenyon Review* 19 (Spring, 1997): 141-147. Dubus, a respected short-story writer himself, discusses Hemingway's "In Another Country." States that, whereas he once thought the story was about the futility of cures, since becoming disabled he has come to understand that it is about healing.

Flora, Joseph M. *Ernest Hemingway: A Study of the Short Fiction*. Boston: Twayne, 1989. An introduction to Hemingway's short fiction that focuses on the importance of reading the stories within the literary context Hemingway creates for them in the collections *In Our Time*, *Winner Take Nothing*, and *Men Without Women*. Argues that Hemingway devises an echo effect in which one story reflects another.

Hays, Peter L. *Ernest Hemingway*. New York: Continuum, 1990. A brief but instructive overview of Hemingway's life and his achievement as a writer. Offers brief critical summaries of the novels and many short stories. Contains a useful chronology.

Hotchner, A. E. *Papa Hemingway: A Personal Memoir*. New ed. New York: Carroll & Graf, 1999. Written by one of Hemingway's close friends, an editor, novelist, playwright, and biographer. Originally published in 1966, this Hemingway Centennial Edition features a new introduction.

Lamb, Robert Paul. "The Love Song of Harold Krebs: Form, Argument, and Meaning in Hemingway's 'Soldier's Home.'" *The Hemingway Review* 14 (Spring, 1995): 18-36. Claims that the story concerns both war trauma and a conflict between mother and son. Discusses the structure of the story; argues that by ignoring the story's form, one misses the manner of Hemingway's narrative argument and the considerable art that underlies it.

Leonard, John. "'A Man of the World' and 'A Clean, Well-Lighted Place': Hemingway's Unified View of Old Age." *The Hemingway Review* 13 (Spring, 1994): 62-73. Compares the two Hemingway stories in terms of the theme of age. Notes also the themes of aloneness, consolation of light, loss of sexuality and physical prowess, depression, violence, and the need for dignity.

Mellow, James R. *Hemingway: A Life Without Consequences*. Boston: Houghton Mifflin, 1992. A well-informed, sensitive handling of the life and work by a seasoned biographer.

Nolan, Charles J., Jr. "Hemingway's Complicated Enquiry in *Men Without Women*." *Studies in Short Fiction* 32 (Spring, 1995): 217-222. Examines the theme of homosexuality in "A Simple Enquiry" from Hemingway's *Men Without Women*. Argues that the characters in the story are enigmatic, revealing their complexity only after one has looked carefully at what they do and say.

Reynolds, Michael. *Hemingway: The American Homecoming*. New York: W.W. Norton, 1992.

_____. *Hemingway: The Final Years*. New York: W.W. Norton, 1999.

_____. *Hemingway: The 1930's*. New York: W.W. Norton, 1997. Reynolds's multivolume, painstaking biography is devoted to the evolution of Hemingway's life and writing.

_____. *Hemingway: The Paris Years*. New York: Blackwell, 1989.

_____. *The Young Hemingway*. New York: Blackwell, 1986.

Tetlow, Wendolyn E. *Hemingway's "In Our Time": Lyrical Dimensions*. Lewisburg, Pa.: Bucknell University Press, 1992. Argues that the collection is a "coherent, integral work" unified by such elements as the character Nick Adams, image patterns, symbols, and recurrent themes. Claims the book is analogous to a poetic sequence, a group of works that tend to interact as an organic whole. Discusses the lyrical elements in Hemingway's self-conscious juxtaposition of stories and interchapters.

Wagner-Martin, Linda. *Ernest Hemingway: A Literary Life*. New York: Palgrave Macmillan, 2007. Hemingway's life is examined here, especially his troubled relationship with his parents. Wagner-Martin makes insightful connections between his personal life, his emotions, and his writing.

_____, ed. *Hemingway: Seven Decades of Criticism*. East Lansing: Michigan State University Press, 1998. A collection of essays ranging from Gertrude Stein's 1923 review of Hemingway's stories to recent responses to *The Garden of Eden*. Includes essays on "Indian Camp," "Hills Like White Elephants," and *In Our Time* as self-begetting fiction.

The *Paris Review* Perspective_____

Petrina Crockford for *The Paris Review*

Ernest Hemingway believed that the duty of the fiction writer is to convey the truth about the world. "A writer's problem," he said, "is always how to write truly and having found what is true, to project it in such a way that it becomes part of the experience of the person who reads it." And the most immediate way to get into the head and heart of the reader, Hemingway thought, was with ruthlessly pared-down prose. This style is evident in a vignette from *In Our Time*:

> The first German I saw climbed up over the garden wall. We waited till he got one leg over and then potted him. He had so much equipment on and looked awfully surprised and fell down into the garden. Then three more came over further down the wall. We shot them. They all came just like that.

With his deadpan tone and simple diction, Hemingway refused to embroider his prose with needless verbiage. The passage is affecting all the same. In his memoir *A Moveable Feast*, he explains how he honed his technique: "If I started to write elaborately, or like someone introducing or presenting something, I found that I could cut that scrollwork or ornament out and throw it away and start with the first true simple declarative sentence I had written."

Some of this simplifying instinct came from his early training as a journalist; he began his writing career as a cub reporter for the *Kansas City Star*. But it would be a mistake to think Hemingway was concerned with mere word count; more than any reporter, he wanted to im-

_____
The *Paris Review* Perspective   **15**

plicate the reader in his stories at the deepest emotional level. He used omission—eliminating a character's backstory or referring to important plot points only elliptically—to encourage readers to fill in these missing pieces using their own reserves of experience. He believed strongly in the power of the unstated. He likened the effect to an iceberg: "The dignity of movement of an iceberg is due to only one-eighth of it being above water," he wrote in *Death in the Afternoon*. He fleshed this metaphor out in his 1958 interview with *The Paris Review*, saying, "I always try to write on the principle of the iceberg . . . to eliminate everything unnecessary to conveying experience to the reader so that after he or she has read something it will become a part of his or her experience and seem actually to have happened." In the sparse landscape of Hemingway's prose, it is the reader's intuitive inclusion of detail that completes the story. Rather than telling us how to feel, Hemingway nudges us toward our own conclusions. We are required to read something of ourselves into his stories—a distinctly American and democratic view of writing.

Just as he sought to overwhelm the reader with his stories, writing consumed Hemingway, so that drawing a line between the man and his novels becomes nearly impossible. Details from his life appear frequently in his work. His earliest published stories, written mostly in Paris, recall childhood summers spent hunting and fishing at his family's cottage in Michigan; his first novel, *The Sun Also Rises*, is anchored in his time spent among Paris's postwar "lost generation"; *The Old Man and the Sea* (which helped win him the Nobel Prize in 1954) tracks closely his own experiences deep-sea fishing off the coast of Cuba. His service with the Red Cross during World War I and his war reporting on the Spanish Civil War and World War II also profoundly influenced his fiction. In novels such as *A Farewell to Arms* and *For Whom the Bell Tolls*, Hemingway used these wartime experiences as a vehicle to explore his long-standing preoccupation with themes of violence and manhood. As his career progressed, he settled comfortably into the role of the brusque, patriarchal writer, often overplaying it for effect. In a 1950 interview with Lillian Ross of *The New Yorker*, for example, he spoke without articles ("He read book all way up on plane"), as if in parodic defense of his prose. He lived a vigorous, adventurous life as brash and uncompromising as that of his greatest characters, inhabiting a male-dominated, solitary, and stoic world. In his *Paris Review* interview, he confessed that he had no use for a life in which this vitality, both physical and mental, would be diminished: "People who know what they are doing should last as long as their heads last."

Ernest Hemingway committed suicide in July 1961. He was sixty-two years old. He had not only transformed American writing, he became an embodiment of it. "I almost wouldn't trust a young novelist," Norman Mailer said, "who doesn't imitate Hemingway in his youth." His influence looms large to this day. As he said of writing, if "you make it alive, and if you make it well enough, you give it immortality."

Bibliography

Baker, Carlos. *Ernest Hemingway: A Life Story*. New York: Charles Scribner's Sons, 1969.

_____. *Hemingway: The Writer as Artist*. Princeton: Princeton University Press, 1972.

Hemingway, Ernest. *The Complete Short Stories of Ernest Hemingway: The Finca Vigía Edition*. New York: Charles Scribner's Sons, 1987.

_____. *Death in the Afternoon*. 1932. New York: Charles Scribner's Sons, 1960.

_____. *A Farewell to Arms*. 1929. New York: Charles Scribner's Sons, 1969.

_____. "Fascism Is a Lie." Speech given to the 1937 American Writers' Congress. New York, 4 June 1937. Rpt. in *Conversations with Ernest Hemingway*. Ed. Matthew J. Bruccoli. Jackson: University Press of Mississippi, 1986.

_____. *For Whom the Bell Tolls*. 1940. New York: Collier Books, 1987.

_____. *In Our Time*. 1925. New York: Scribner Paperback Fiction, 1996.

_____. *A Moveable Feast*. New York: Charles Scribner's Sons, 1964.

_____. *The Old Man and the Sea*. 1952. New York: Scribner Paperback Fiction, 1995.

_____. *Selected Letters, 1917-1961*. Ed. Carlos Baker. New York: Charles Scribner's Sons, 1981.

_____. *The Sun Also Rises*. 1926. New York: Charles Scribner's Sons, 1954.

_____, and George Plimpton. "The Art of Fiction No. 21." *The Paris Review* 18 (1958).

Mailer, Norman. "The Art of Fiction No. 193." *The Paris Review* 181 (2007).

Ross, Lillian. "How Do You Like It Now, Gentlemen?" *New Yorker* 13 May 1950: 36-62. Rpt. in *Portrait of Hemingway*. New York: The Modern Library, 1999.

CRITICAL
CONTEXTS

Ernest Hemingway:
A Cultural and Historical Context_____

Jennifer Banach Palladino

In April of 1917, after attempts at diplomacy by President Woodrow Wilson, a hesitant United States entered World War I as a self-proclaimed associate power, assisting the Allied Powers of Britain, France, Russia, and Italy in the fight against the Central Powers of Germany, Austria-Hungary, and their empires. The war had been precipitated by the assassination of the Archduke Franz Ferdinand, heir to the Austro-Hungarian throne, by a Bosnian Serb citizen commonly thought to be a member of the Serbian secret society Black Hand, an offshoot of the Young Bosnia movement, which sought unification of the Slavic people via the creation of an independent state. As Austria-Hungary retaliated against the Serbian kingdom, countries began to form alliances and declare war against each other. International tensions caused by arms races and military buildup due to the presumed desire for preservation of a balance of power in Europe, as well as economic and trade conflicts, contributed significantly to the swift escalation of events, which erupted into a global war. Countries all over the globe were now entangled in a conflict that had been nicknamed "The War to End All Wars."

The United States had attempted to remain removed from the conflict, seeking to mediate and initiate diplomatic resolutions, but the country joined the war a short time later after diplomatic efforts failed. Germany had continued to pursue unrestricted submarine warfare long after warnings were issued following the 1915 sinking of the *Lusitania*, a British liner carrying American passengers. Equipped with only a modest army consisting largely of volunteers, the United States began drafting, increasing its reserve of soldiers until they numbered in the millions. When the soldiers arrived in Europe, they were faced with unspeakable terrors. New technologies increased the horrors of war, and soldiers were now exposed to gunfire, cannon fire, chemical warfare, and even aircraft strikes. Despite new technology, battles were often fought in trenches on the fronts around the continent of Europe. This kind of warfare, which was primarily defensive, resulted in an extraordinary number of casualties and deaths, still recognized as the largest numbers in world history. Soldiers fought for several years until armistices and treaties were signed in 1918 and 1919, including the well-known Treaty of Versailles, and many American servicemen remained abroad until the war came to a close with a final peace treaty in 1923.

Among the Americans in Europe was a young volunteer named Ernest Miller Hemingway. He had been born on July 21, 1899, in Oak Park, Illinois, and remained in the Chicago suburb throughout his childhood and adolescence. He attended the local public high school, Oak Park and River Forest Township High School, where he became interested in writing, and graduated in 1917. Rather than attend college, Hemingway took to journalism, writing as a cub reporter for the *Kansas City Star*, but a few months after his writing career had begun, he attempted to join the U.S. Army in an effort to serve his country abroad. He failed the medical exam owing to his inadequate vision and joined the Red Cross as an ambulance driver instead. In France and Italy, Hemingway witnessed firsthand the horrors of war as the Central Powers consistently attacked the Allied forces in the areas where he was stationed. On July 8, 1918, he was wounded by a mortar shell and machine-gun fire while delivering supplies to soldiers. He was awarded a medal of valor from the Italian government for saving a soldier's life while hurt, sustaining injuries that were significant enough that they prevented him from serving further as an ambulance driver. Instead Hemingway began working at an Italian hospital run by the American Red Cross.

When the war concluded, he returned to Oak Park and a short time later moved to Toronto, Ontario, where he resumed work as a reporter, this time for the *Toronto Star* newspaper. In 1920, he moved to Chicago for a brief period, continuing to write for the Toronto newspaper until

1921, when he moved to Paris with his first wife, Hadley Richardson. The psychological impact of the war on soldiers and civilians had been immense. Soldiers suffered from post-traumatic disorders and had difficulty adapting to civilian life. Many people became disillusioned by nationalism, which seemed to have contributed to the atrocities, and believed in the significance of fostering better international relations. With this in mind, many American citizens moved abroad throughout the 1920s. In the literary world, these expatriates included writers such as Sherwood Anderson, Gertrude Stein, Ezra Pound, James Joyce, and Hemingway—writers who would later be recognized as primary figures in the initiation of the modernist movement in literature. While Hemingway would return to Toronto in 1923, his first book, *Three Stories and Ten Poems*, would not be published in Canada or in the United States, but rather in Paris.

Hemingway's experience of the war and his subsequent experience of life as an expatriate in Paris had a profound impact on him, affecting his writing long after the war had concluded and he had left Paris. The influence of the events and atrocities he witnessed throughout the war and his romances during this time (which were, in essence, failed romances) was evident as early as 1925, when Hemingway made his American publishing debut with a collection of short stories appropriately titled *In Our Time*. The collection, which had appeared in Paris in a somewhat altered, more compact form a year earlier, introduced Hemingway's most famous protagonist, Nick Adams, a young man from the Midwest who becomes a soldier. It was the first of many Hemingway books that would tell stories that took place in the years surrounding World War I, depicting the grave effects of the war on those who had witnessed it. *The Torrents of Spring*, a novella published in 1926, tells the story of World War I veterans, physically and mentally diminished by the war, in search of the perfect woman. The theme of war and the often failed search for redemption through love would reappear in Hemingway's works until his death, although they would be most prominent in Hemingway's works of the late 1920s: the novel

The Sun Also Rises, the story of a group of American expatriates in Paris and Spain, including the impotent veteran Jake Barnes, and the short-story collection *Men Without Women*, which contains stories such as "Now I Lay Me," in which Nick Adams has almost been killed on the front in Italy and undergoes therapy that includes imagining marriages to the women he knows, and "In Another Country," in which soldiers are afflicted with injuries that affect them most ironically.

In 1929, Hemingway published *A Farewell to Arms*, a novel that tells the story of the tragic romance of American soldier Frederic Henry and British nurse Catherine Barkley during World War I. The book catapulted Hemingway to fame and granted him financial security. Speaking of the novel, author and critic Robert Penn Warren stated, "It told a truth about the First World War and a truth about the generation who had fought it and whose lives, because of the war, had been wrenched from the expected pattern and old values" (35). The statement was applicable to the great majority of the author's works. Hemingway's 1933 collection of short stories *Winner Take Nothing* and works written as late as the 1950s, such as *Across the River and into the Trees*, would reveal Hemingway's ongoing preoccupation with this period in time and its profound and lasting effects.

In writing about the experience of World War I, Hemingway became the representative voice of his generation—a generation that writer Gertrude Stein had nicknamed the "lost generation," a phrase originally said to have been uttered by a car mechanic that now came to embody those men and women whose way of living had been irreversibly altered by the war. Hemingway's stories and novels captured the loss of innocence and happiness that were characteristic of the times and revealed the difficult contradictions of faith experienced by many during this era. His experience of the war, his romances, and the dislocation that resulted became lasting fodder for the author's stories and novels, showing up even in posthumous works such as *A Moveable Feast*.

In the ensuing years, Hemingway would become preoccupied with at least two other wars—the Spanish Civil War and World War II.

When civil war broke out in Spain in 1936 following an attempted coup d'état against the Second Spanish Republic, the author traveled to Spain as a reporter for the North American Newspaper Alliance. Hemingway favored the leftist Republicans, and posthumous writings on the war have raised questions regarding the possibility of Hemingway's direct involvement with the Republic. The war concluded in 1939 with the founding of a dictatorship by Nationalist general Francisco Franco. One year later, Hemingway published *For Whom the Bell Tolls*, a story about an American Republican soldier who falls in love with a young Spanish woman in the midst of the country's civil war.

On December 8, 1941, the United States entered World War II. While the full details of Hemingway's involvement in this war are cloudy, it is believed that Hemingway again wanted to be a part of the fight, and reports have him boarding a ship that was sinking German submarines. Other accounts have him informally commanding troops. What is known for certain is that Hemingway later resumed work as a war correspondent, observing the events of D-Day from a landing craft. At the end of the war he traveled to Cuba. Hemingway had a difficult time working during this period. He began writing various works, including *The Garden of Eden* and *Islands in the Stream*, but did not complete any during this time, and many of the works he began would not be published until after his death. However, it was during these years that Hemingway also began work on what would eventually become his most well-known work, *The Old Man and the Sea*.

In 1950 Hemingway published *Across the River and into the Trees*, the story of an old American colonel who falls in love with a young Italian woman. The book was considered a failure, with critics noting that it did not capture the feelings surrounding World War II the way that his other books had captured the essence of World War I and the Spanish Civil War. The failure was short-lived. Hemingway's critical and popular standing turned dramatically in 1952, when he published the now-completed novella *The Old Man and the Sea*, on which he had begun work more than a decade earlier. It appeared in the September issue of *Life* magazine and was a commercial and critical success, earning Hemingway the Pulitzer Prize in 1953 and leading to an American Academy of Arts and Letters Award of Merit and the Nobel Prize in Literature in 1954. The novella, which tells the story of Santiago, an old Cuban fisherman who struggles to catch the greatest fish of his life only to lose it to sharks before reaching shore, has invited a wide variety of interpretations, with some claiming that the old man and the boy in the story are based on real people that Hemingway had met in Cuba and others claiming they could see in the work the reconstructed passion of Christ. Perhaps most interesting is that some have seen it as an analogy for Hemingway's own struggles as a man and as a writer. Although it may never be possible to know Hemingway's intention, this reading in particular illuminates one of the defining factors of the author's work.

By the 1930s, it seemed that Hemingway was revealing more of himself in his works. His main characters were reminiscent of himself, and minor characters resembled his real-life acquaintances. The male characters embodied a masculinity that Hemingway came to characterize in his own life, and in bestowing them with these features, he made it difficult for readers and critics to separate his persona from his work. Hemingway's father had taken his son hunting, fishing, and camping in northern Michigan when he was a child. In high school Hemingway took up boxing and played football. Later he added to the list his experiences as a soldier and participant in world wars, and, finally, he became interested in bullfighting and safaris in Africa. His characters enjoyed the same masculine pursuits. Robert Penn Warren provides countless examples:

As for the typical characters, they are usually tough men, experienced in the hard worlds they inhabit, and not obviously given to emotional display or sensitive shrinking—men like Rinaldi or Frederic Henry of *A Farewell to Arms*, Robert Jordan of *For Whom the Bell Tolls*, Harry Morgan of *To*

Have and Have Not, the big-game hunter of "The Snows of Kilimanjaro," the old bullfighter of "The Undefeated," or the pugilist of "Fifty Grand." Or if the typical character is not of this seasoned order, he is a very young man, or boy, first entering the violent world and learning his first adjustment to it. (39)

If there was any suspicion that this was somehow subconscious or even accidental, one had only to consider the follow-up to *A Farewell to Arms*. In 1931 Hemingway had moved to Key West, Florida, where he continued to write in between his travels through the 1950s. In 1932 he published a compilation titled *Death in the Afternoon*, which examines the tradition of bullfighting and addresses themes of fear and courage in the face of death. Edmund Wilson made an important observation about the work:

> With *Death in the Afternoon* . . . a new development for Hemingway commences. He writes a book not merely in the first person, but in the first person in his own character as Hemingway, and the results are unexpected and disconcerting. *Death in the Afternoon* has its value as an exposition of bullfighting; and Hemingway is able to use the subject as a text for an explicit statement of his conception of man eternally pitting himself—he thinks the bullfight a ritual of this—against animal force and the odds of death. (22)

Hemingway continued this trend with his 1935 book *Green Hills of Africa*, a work based on a safari that the author had taken with his wife a few years earlier. Posthumous works such as *A Moveable Feast* and *The Dangerous Summer* revealed this same penchant for autobiographical revelation. Wilson's observation of Hemingway's shift to an autobiographical text is, therefore, a significant one because it is, in large part, the answer to the question of what has driven the success of Hemingway's work and secured his place in the canon of literature. Numerous works of fiction and nonfiction about the wars and similar cultural and political events were being published during Hemingway's time. Why has Hemingway's work survived among the rest as representative? Wilson points out that the answer lies not simply in Hemingway's choice of subject matter but also in his intimate approach to the work and, correspondingly, the distinct style in which he wrote. Hemingway draws his readers' attention to this himself in the foreword to *Green Hills of Africa*:

> Unlike many novels, none of the characters or incidents in this book is imaginary. Any one not finding sufficient love interest is at liberty, while reading it, to insert whatever love interest he or she may have at the time. The writer has attempted to write an absolutely true book to see whether the shape of a country and the pattern of a month's action can, if truly presented, compete with a work of the imagination.

In other words, Hemingway's stories are not simply representative of the era and its emotional atmosphere; they are autobiographical, revealing Hemingway's own feelings, experiences, and failures. This uninhibited revelation of self, which would be resurrected in the fiction of Norman Mailer and many other contemporary authors years later, while perhaps not a new device (evidenced in the works of Marcel Proust, D. H. Lawrence, and James Joyce, among others), was rather undisguised and more central a component than in previous works of literature. Earl Rovit and Gerry Brenner point out the social significance of this, that "more often than not, Hemingway's fiction seems rooted in journeys into himself much more clearly and obsessively than is usually the case with major fictional writers. Indeed, the subject of his fiction is almost always the exposition of his dynamic relation to the world at the time he is writing" (143).

The trend of writing about cultural issues through autobiographical text continued to be evidenced in Hemingway's later works, with his works mirroring his own experiences and the political scenery at the time he was writing. As a result, modern fiction was now entangled with journalism and with autobiography—in essence, fiction was now inextricably linked to reality, straying from the imaginative musings of the works that had preceded this period. Hemingway's famous protagonist Nick Adams was much like the author himself, a veteran profoundly affected by war, obsessed with masculine pursuits, seeking romance as a redeeming experience, and—like Hemingway, who had numerous failed marriages—not succeeding. The relationship between Frederic and Catherine in *A Farewell to Arms* and Catherine's death in childbirth were based on Hemingway's own romance with Agnes von Kurowsky, a nurse who worked at the Milan hospital where Hemingway was stationed following his injury in 1918, and on his second wife's difficult birthing of the couple's son Patrick in 1928, while the romances presented in *The Sun Also Rises* are said to be related to the author's own romances during his time in France. The suicide of Robert Jordan's father in *For Whom the Bell Tolls* is also reminiscent of the suicide of Hemingway's own father in 1928. Hemingway's inclusion of his own life and the events that characterized his lifetime in his works would become integral and defining components of his oeuvre. This intimate inclusion had its disadvantages as well. Rovit and Brenner explain:

> In the attempt to assess Hemingway's ultimate significance as a major twentieth-century writer, another factor intrudes to make his work more important than the intrinsic value that his finely wrought short stories and novels possess. Hemingway's legendary personality, as he lived it in the newspapers and the public eye, is inextricably intertwined with his fictional themes and images. . . . In Hemingway's case, his life and literary efforts were so much of a single piece and his public life was so romantically close to the heroic derring-do of his fictional heroes that this mergence of life and literature cannot be dismissed by literary criticism. (151)

The most intimate details of Hemingway's own life, including his struggle with depression, his failed marriages, and his countless injurics and near-death accidents, seemed to belong to the public along with his works. Despite this intrusion, Hemingway continued to feature themes relevant to his own life and to the social and political climate of the times, including failed romance, confrontation with death, the drive to overcome obstacles in a difficult and unforgiving world, and the difficulty of maintaining faith. Robert Penn Warren made a critical observation, noting that this was not out of necessity, but rather by his deliberate choosing:

> A writer may write about that special world merely because he happens to know that world, but he may also write about that special world because it best dramatizes for him the issues and questions that are his fundamental concerns—because, in other words, that special world has a kind of symbolic significance for him. (39)

As if Hemingway's willingness to divulge the deepest parts of himself and his ability to capture the essence of his era were not enough, as he addressed war, failed romance, and death as major themes, he seemed to recognize that a new style was also necessary. The old romantic style, which included fantasy, symbolism, and metaphor, no longer seemed relevant or effective in the postwar world. Instead Hemingway applied the concise and direct stylings of journalism to his works. He provided only the information that he considered to be wholly necessary. He pruned metaphors and overt symbols from the great majority of his work, relying on reality to communicate information and evoke emotional response. A typical exchange went something like this:

> "Wouldn't you like me to read?" she asked. She was sitting on a canvas chair beside a cot. "There's a breeze coming up."
> "No thanks."
> "Maybe the—Maybe the truck will come."
> "I don't give a damn about the truck."
> "I do."

"You give a damn about so many things that I don't."

"Not so many, Harry."

"What about a drink?"

"It's supposed to be bad for you. It said in Black's to avoid all alcohol. You shouldn't drink."

"Molo!" he shouted.

"Yes Bwana."

"Bring whiskey-soda." ("The Snows of Kilimanjaro" 5)

Sentences were simple, and dialogue was understated and brief. The spare text seemed to represent properly the atmosphere of the era. It seemed that there was no more appropriate way to present the difficult themes inherent in Hemingway's work. Critic Edmund Wilson pronounced:

The condition of life is pain; and the joys of the most innocent surface are somehow tied to its stifled pangs. The resolution of this dissonance in art made the beauty of Hemingway's stories. He had in the process tuned a marvelous prose. Out of the colloquial American speech, with its simple declarative sentences and its strings of Nordic monosyllables, he got effects of the utmost subtlety. (18)

However, while Hemingway's style may have included simple sentences and monosyllables, it was not plain or lacking. Instead, while it was used to create short stories and novels, it evoked the flavor of poetry itself. Literary critic Harold Bloom has noted that no other short story writer or novelist in the history of American literature is so akin in style to that of the greatest poets. "What seems unique," he says, "is that Hemingway is the only American writer of prose fiction in this century who, as a stylist, rivals the principal poets: Stevens, Eliot, Frost, Hart Crane, aspects of Pound, W. C. Williams, Robert Penn Warren and Elizabeth Bishop" (2). He goes on to outline the author's proximity to the work of other well-known American poets such as Walt

Whitman and Emily Dickinson. It is an interesting insight when we recall that we are discussing not a poet but a novelist and short-story writer.

Hemingway's influence has been evident in great abundance, and countless authors have attempted to duplicate his style. "If one measure of an artist's success is the influence he exerts on his contemporaries and successors, then Hemingway is certainly the most important twentieth-century writer in this respect," say Rovit and Brenner (149). His embrace of the masculine is perhaps embodied most closely in the works of Norman Mailer, while his application of journalism in fiction is embodied not only in the works of Mailer but in the works of Truman Capote and Joan Didion. He influenced the writers of the Beat generation and many authors who followed. He influenced popular fiction, such as crime fiction and pulp fiction, and literary fiction alike, but his influence has extended far beyond the realm of literature. The combination of his unique style, his ability to reveal the world in its true form, and his larger-than-life persona transformed Hemingway into a legend. Bloom addresses this idea from a revealing perspective: "Hemingway now is myth, and so is permanent as an image of American heroism, or perhaps more ruefully the American illusion of heroism" (5). While it may seem at first that this statement has everything to do with the mode of Hemingway's demise, upon further consideration one may realize that this would have been Hemingway's legacy regardless of his tragic end. It is, after all, a legacy tethered to the steadfast and sometimes dark pursuit of unveiling truth.

Works Cited

Bloom, Harold, ed. *Ernest Hemingway*. New York: Chelsea House, 1985.

Hemingway, Ernest. *Green Hills of Africa*. 1935. New York: Simon & Schuster, 1996.

_____. *The Snows of Kilimanjaro, and Other Stories*. New York: Charles Scribner's Sons, 1970.

Rovit, Earl, and Gerry Brenner. *Ernest Hemingway*. Rev. ed. Boston: Twayne, 1986.

Warren, Robert Penn. "Ernest Hemingway." *Ernest Hemingway*. Ed. Harold Bloom. New York: Chelsea House, 1985. (Rpt. from *Robert Penn Warren: Selected Essays*. New York: Vintage Books, 1966.)

Wilson, Edmund. "Hemingway: Gauge of Morale." *Ernest Hemingway*. Ed. Harold Bloom. New York: Chelsea House, 1985. (Rpt. from *The Wound and the Bow*. New York: Oxford University Press, 1947.)

In His Time (and Later):
Ernest Hemingway's Critical Reputation_____

Robert C. Evans

Ernest Hemingway (1899-1961) is widely considered one of the handful of the most significant American authors of the twentieth century; some critics would even place him among the top two or three (with William Faulkner and F. Scott Fitzgerald). Certainly Hemingway has been one of the most influential American writers of any era; his distinctive but accessible style, along with his interest in issues of universal and enduring relevance (such as love, war, death, friendship, and the value of "grace under pressure"), make him a major author who writes comprehensible prose about matters that many people can relate to. Although he began as a "modernist" author who was championed by the likes of Ezra Pound and Gertrude Stein, his work rarely seems forbidding, self-indulgent, or arcane. He is not as obviously allusive, as obsessively intellectual, or as self-consciously "literary" as Pound, nor is he especially inscrutable or given to off-putting technical gimmicks, as is so often true of Stein. A master both of the short story and of the novel, he has had a profound impact on later writers, and he was one of the few authors who enjoyed the respect of his peers as well as the loyalty of a broad popular audience. His novels (and even some of his stories) were inevitably turned into successful films; his public life, covered widely in the mass media, took on mythic proportions; and indeed any distinction between his art and his life often seemed (as it often was) nonexistent. When he committed suicide, his death was mourned around the world—by writers and by millions of his readers.

Probably Hemingway's chief importance is as a stylist. He wrote in a lean, clean, stripped-down style that seems much simpler than it really is. Difficult to imitate but often mimicked, easy to parody but hard to reproduce, it is obviously indebted to Hemingway's youthful, no-nonsense training as a newspaper reporter, even as it also reflects the precise but suggestive "imagism" of the early poetry of Ezra Pound. One short sample—a complete "chapter" taken from his brief book of sketches titled *in our time* (1924)—illustrates many of the traits that analysts have pointed to over the decades as highly typical of Hemingway's prose:

> We were in a garden at Mons. Young Buckley came in with his patrol from across the river. The first German I saw climbed up over the garden wall. We waited until he got one leg over and then potted him. He had so much equipment on and looked awfully surprised and fell down into the garden. Then three more came over further down the wall. We shot them. They all came just like that.

This passage epitomizes many of the most characteristic aspects of Hemingway's phrasing. The words are simple and the sentences tend to be short. Hemingway avoids unnecessary adjectives and adverbs, focusing on straightforward nouns and unsurprising verbs. There is no obvious straining after eloquence or grandiloquence; the sentence structure tends to be as simple as the diction. Here, as in much of his later writing, Hemingway tends to avoid similes and metaphors. The phrasing is declarative, understated, and unemotional. More is implied than is actually stated, and emphasis is gained by repetition rather than by elaborate development or abstract explanation. The imagery is economical, precise, and vivid; the tone is laconic and hard-boiled. Short statements are strung together with "ands," and extreme violence is reported matter-of-factly, with no hint of sentimentality. The general plainness enhances the impact of any unusual words (such as "potted"); the characterization of the narrator is indirect and implicit (as in the implied youthfulness of the phrase "awfully surprised"). Symbolism and irony are suggested rather than overtly stressed: death occurs in a garden; the invader of the garden is "potted"; the narrator seems mildly surprised by the surprise of the dead man; deaths are reported just as unemotionally as the return of a friendly patrol. Readers are left to make up their own minds about the significance of the events described; the narrator doesn't preach or pontificate. The tone is dry and objective; the manner is reticent. One of the few standard features understandably missing from this quick and cryptic passage is Hemingway's frequent emphasis on dialogue, a trait more often found in his stories and novels than in his sketches.

The passage cited above, however, is typical of Hemingway's writing not only in its style but also in its themes. Critics have often commented on Hemingway's frequent emphasis on men in groups and on men without women, and war is, of course, also a frequent topic of much of his writing. Here, as so often elsewhere, Hemingway emphasizes men (almost always men) at the moment of death as well as men doing their duty—duties that often involve killing either other men or animals, often in ways that seem highly ritualistic and unemotional. Hemingway's world is frequently violent and brutal, and the attitudes of his characters are often emotionally detached. The world is as it is and has to be faced without illusions. Rarely does Hemingway psychologize or explore, explicitly, the mental or emotional depths of his characters; their morals and values mostly have to be inferred from their behavior. Death is the ultimate fact of life; life may have no larger, transcendent meaning or purpose; God is noticeable mostly by his absence; the capacity to live successfully is often the capacity to endure; and if heroes exist, they are the men (usually men) who can exhibit grace under pressure. In this passage, as so often in his other works, Hemingway writes about a topic (war) he knew from firsthand experience or from personal observation, which is one of the reasons that his writings—whether they describe fishing, bullfighting, big-game hunting, or explorations of the West, the Midwest, Europe, Africa, or Cuba—often seem so credible and convincing. His life was packed full of "manly" activities, and his writing reflects that fact. His male characters have often been considered more believable than his females, and his female characters are often seen and evaluated, in his fiction, from male perspectives. Male friendship is important in Hemingway's works, but so is conflict between men. Nature can be beautiful (as the garden setting here implies), but nature is also, ultimately, indifferent to human beings. Survival is sometimes a matter of skill but is also often merely a matter of luck. In all these ways, then, this brief passage from one of Hemingway's earliest books reflects stylistic and thematic traits that his work exhibited throughout his long career.

Most of the comments made so far about Hemingway's characteristic style and themes reflect the general consensus of modern criticism, as can be seen from a perusal of the various items tabulated in this essay's list of works consulted. Hemingway's career, however, was never as simple or straightforward as his style seemed to be, and his standing among critics has risen, fallen, risen, fallen, and risen again over the decades, especially as each new work (especially each new novel) made its first appearance. Jeffrey Meyers, compiler of one of the richest collections of reactions to Hemingway, has helpfully summarized the evolution of Hemingway's reputation by arguing that it

has had five distinct phases and has fluctuated wildly during each decade of his career. He received almost universal praise in the 1920s and reached the peak of his contemporary reputation with 'A Farewell to Arms' in 1929. His books of the 1930s—'Death in the Afternoon,' 'Winner Take Nothing,' 'The Green Hills of Africa,' 'To Have and Have Not'—were severely criticized by disenchanted reviewers; but he made a major recovery with 'For Whom the Bell Tolls' in 1940. He published no significant work in the 1940s, which culminated in the almost universally condemned novel, 'Across the River and into the Trees' (1950). But two years later he achieved an astonishing critical triumph with 'The Old Man and the Sea.' He brought out no books during the last nine years of his life, but regained his reputation with the posthumously published 'A Moveable Feast' in 1964. Though most critics found 'Islands in the Stream' [1970] disappointing, the retrospective review of his entire career has now placed him securely with the leading novelists of his time. (Meyers 9)

Meyers wrote too early to include the posthumous works *The Dangerous Summer* (1985) and the highly provocative (and controversial) *The Garden of Eden* (1986), but most scholars would agree with Meyers's assessment of the trajectory of Hemingway's career. Most analysts would argue that, in addition to some of his best stories, the works on which his reputation most depends are *in our time* (1924), the expanded and slightly retitled *In Our Time* (1925), and especially the novels *The Sun Also Rises* (1926), *A Farewell to Arms* (1929), *For Whom the Bell Tolls* (1940), and *The Old Man and the Sea* (1952). It is these novels, in particular, that have commanded by far the most critical attention and respect, and in the pages that remain it seems worthwhile to sketch briefly the kinds of commentary and controversies they have elicited.

The Sun Also Rises focuses on a young but impotent American veteran and journalist named Jake Barnes and the hard-drinking, hard-partying American and British friends and hangers-on with whom he spends (some would say "wastes") his time in Paris and Spain in the years following World War I. Nearly all the men in the book, including Jake, are attracted to a highly sexed, highly attractive, and somewhat cynical British woman named Lady Brett Ashley. She is engaged to a Scotsman named Mike Campbell, has a brief fling (while engaged) with a desperate and persistent Jewish American admirer named Robert Cohn, and becomes infatuated (while still engaged) with a handsome young Spanish bullfighter named Pedro Romero. She ultimately decides not to continue her affair with Romero, since she does not want to be a "bitch that ruins children." This novel is often considered Hemingway's best, and it had a major impact when first published. Many critics have argued that the book satirizes the empty lives of its generally superficial characters, but many initial readers were intrigued by the hedonistic lifestyle the novel describes, and many young women tried to model their conduct and appearance on that of the boyish, shapely, and vivacious Lady Brett. Most critics agree that Robert Cohn is the chief butt of the novel's satire, partly because he is so needy, partly because he is so obstinate, and partly because he lacks the grace and quiet dignity that Hemingway admired in his heroes. Cohn's character has been part of the debate over anti-Semitic overtones in Hemingway's work, though a few commentators have tried to suggest that Cohn is not much worse (and is perhaps even better) than most of the other characters. Practically everyone, however, agrees that Pedro Romero, the young and courageous bullfighter, provides the standard by which the conduct and values of most of the other characters can be measured and found wanting. Cohn, an ex-boxer, has physical strength, and in fact he pummels Jake, Mike, and even Romero, but it is Romero who has the combination of inner and outer fortitude that Hemingway most admires. Brett admires it, too, and some critics find it disturbing that Jake allegedly pimps for Brett by introducing her to Romero. Most commentators, however, find Jake a sympathetic figure. He is a man who wants to love Brett (and whom Brett claims to love, insofar as Brett is capable of really loving), but he cannot fulfill her sexual demands.

The novel has been praised for its effective (often "witty") dialogue, its understated style, and its credible depictions of expatriate life in Paris, the bullfighting festival at Pamplona, and the pleasures of fishing in the Spanish countryside. Some early critics saw it as Hemingway's treatment of themes first made famous in T. S. Eliot's poem *The Waste Land*, although that argument is not as widely accepted now as it once was. Nevertheless, most commentators still tend to read the book as an implied indictment of the sterility and vacuousness of a society that had only recently become "modern" in the fullest senses of that word. Brett strikes some as an ultimately admirable figure who eventually demonstrates a capacity for moral maturity and self-denial; others see her as a shallow, somewhat pathetic temptress who is more to be pitied than respected. The novel ends with no one feeling especially happy or fulfilled, but perhaps Jake has become more mature, less fixated on Brett, and so more capable of eventual (if limited) happiness. *The Sun Also Rises* has often been seen as the classic depiction of the so-called lost generation—the group of young men and women whose lives were forever scarred by the wasteful and pointless slaughter of World War I. The book's title, which comes from Ecclesiastes, has been interpreted by some (including Hemingway himself) as implying that while each generation passes away, the permanent things (especially nature and basic moral values) endure. People like Romero are the people who ultimately matter; values like his are the ones most worthy of admiration and imitation. And yet many young women who first read the book began to drink, smoke, curse, dress, and wear their hair like their vacuous heroine, Lady Brett.

Hemingway's next major novel, *A Farewell to Arms*, deals even more directly than his first with the impact of World War I. The book is actually set during the war and focuses on the experiences, in conflict and love, of a young American ambulance driver named Frederic Henry, who is serving with a group of Italians, including a lively, good-humored, and memorable young doctor named Rinaldi. Through Rinaldi, Frederic meets an attractive British nurse named Catherine Barkley. At first Frederic's interest in her is mainly physical, but they soon fall in love. Frederic is wounded in the war; Catherine becomes pregnant; Frederic decides to desert during a wholesale retreat by Italian forces; the lovers manage to escape to Switzerland, but then Catherine and their baby die in childbirth, leaving Frederic even more wounded and alone. Much of the critical controversy generated by this novel centers on the two main characters. Frederic is sometimes seen as immature, selfish, and self-pitying from beginning to end, whereas other critics argue that he grows emotionally and deepens psychologically through his relationship with Catherine. According to this reading, then, although the book ends with a death and a stillbirth, Frederic himself is nevertheless in a sense reborn, becoming a better, deeper person through his months-long involvement with his pregnant lover. For some readers, indeed, Catherine is the true hero of the novel; it is she (these readers claim) who displays the wisdom, grace, common sense, and final courage that Hemingway admires. Other readers, however, find her childish and clingy; to them she seems a perfect example of Hemingway's alleged inability to create credible female characters. Some readers see Catherine as a pathetic doormat, but increasingly there is a tendency to find her admirably mature and generous—a heroine who lives up to the Hemingway "code" of stoic fortitude.

Most early readers of *A Farewell to Arms* found the love story moving and the war story (especially the Italian retreat) highly convincing in its depiction of the chaos and pointlessness of modern warfare. Some readers felt that Hemingway had insufficiently integrated the two plots: some wanted more emphasis on the war, and a few were offended by the relatively frank (for its time) depiction of the lovemaking of Frederic and Catherine. Subsequent analysts have praised the book for its use of symbolism (especially in depicting different landscapes and the different seasons), its vivid dialogue, its occasional experiments in stream-of-consciousness technique, and its skill in showing how huge public events can affect individual private lives. Early readers and critics alike felt that in writing this novel, Hemingway had made good on the promise displayed in his previous works—a fact that made his relative failures in the 1930s all the more disappointing. Many analysts during this later decade felt that Hemingway had become too addicted to describing macho men and pointless blood sports; he was also censured for a lack of clear political commitment during the decade of the Great Depression and the rise of fascism. By the end of the 1930s, however, his sympathies were clearly (if not dogmatically) with the left, and he took a special interest in supporting the antifascist cause during the Spanish Civil War.

These interests are reflected in the plot, characters, and themes of *For Whom the Bell Tolls*, the most explicitly political of Hemingway's great novels and also the longest of his important books. The book describes the efforts of Robert Jordan, an American college professor who comes to Spain to assist the ragtag Republican forces in their battle against native and foreign fascists. Jordan links up with a group of Spanish guerrillas in the mountains; his main objective is to blow up an important bridge. While living with the peasants, he falls in love with a beautiful Spanish girl named Maria, who had earlier been raped by some fascists. Despite conflict within the group of peasants, Jordan succeeds in destroying the bridge, but he dies in the process. This novel was strongly praised when it first appeared (although some communists disliked its depiction of leftist atrocities), and a few critics even argued that it is better than either *The Sun Also Rises* or *A Farewell to Arms*. Other readers, however, have found it too long, too sentimental, too lax in its structure, and too hard to believe in its depiction of the love of Jordan and Maria. Its dialogue (especially its heavy emphasis on Spanish colloquialisms) has been both praised and condemned, and indeed one famous review by a Spaniard complained that Hemingway had botched his depiction of the Spanish people and his use of the Spanish language. (Jordan, for instance, often calls Maria "rabbit" as a term of affectionate tenderness, but in Spanish slang that word has vulgar connotations.)

One of the most memorable and inventive aspects of the book is the way Hemingway manages to have his characters curse without actually using curse words (as in "go obscenity yourself"), and many readers have found his depiction of the colorful old peasant woman Pilar especially masterful. On the other hand, various critics have complained that many of the characters are too stereotypical, that the pace of the book is too leisurely, that the details are often too profuse, and that in general the book would have been more effective if it had also been shorter. Jordan is generally seen as an exemplar (perhaps a bit too predictably) of Hemingway's stoic heroic code, and Maria has often been viewed as one more example of Hemingway's tendency to depict women sentimentally, especially when those women prove useful and pleasurable to men. It should be said, however, that many readers did find—and still find—the love story beautiful and compelling.

In its length and in its general wordiness, *For Whom the Bell Tolls* is a far cry from the kind of fiction with which Hemingway began (especially from the vignettes of *in our time*). It is an ambitious work on a grand and epic scale, and it deals with war and politics directly in a way that is true of none of the other great Hemingway novels. Some readers found it a more conventional, less pathbreaking book than the best of Hemingway's earlier efforts, but others welcomed the undeniable improvement it represented over the work that had disappointed so many readers and critics in the 1930s. Finally, it seemed, Hemingway was back on track, and some early critics considered it his best book so far. And then, of course, the United States found itself, by the very end of 1941, involved in World War II (which had already started in Europe in September 1939), and Hemingway in turn found himself involved in the war as a self-appointed submarine hunter (in the waters off Cuba) and then as a war correspondent and eyewitness to the final days of the conflict in 1944-45. By this time he had become a conspicuous public figure, and his life seemed almost more interesting than his recent prose. The novel he produced in 1950—*Across the River and into the Trees*—was widely regarded as a major disappointment, but he redeemed his reputation undeniably with the publication, in 1952, of a brief, moving novel whose very title—*The Old Man and the Sea*—suggested its function as a kind of mythic parable. In no time at all the book helped win Hemingway the Nobel Prize, which served to confirm his status as one of the most significant writers in the world.

Set in Cuba (where Hemingway himself was living), *The Old Man and the Sea* depicts the epic battle between an elderly deep-sea fisherman, Santiago, and a huge and vigorous marlin. Santiago has gone for months without a catch, and so, when he snags the gigantic fish and successfully battles it for two days, he assumes that his luck has changed. Unfortunately, however, a swarm of sharks attack and consume the dead fish, leaving only its head strapped to Santiago's boat. When the old man finally manages to return to shore, he is respected— despite his apparent failure—not only by the community in general but especially by Manolin, the boy who acts almost as his grandson and disciple. Indeed, some readers saw the book as resembling an almost Christian parable of victory through defeat, while others saw the tale as a kind of allegory of Hemingway's own literary career, with Santiago representing Hemingway, the struggle for the marlin representing his efforts to reel in a great work, and the attack of the sharks representing the vicious attacks of the critics. More generally, readers were inspired by this apparently simple tale of man in conflict (but also in harmony) with nature. The old man's humble but dignified courage in the struggle both to survive and to prevail was taken to symbolize the kind of courage demanded in any person's struggles with life. The novel seemed to imply an inspiring lesson that a man might be defeated in practical or worldly terms while still triumphing spiritually and as a person. The book seems to suggest that what matters is not (to use an old cliché) whether one wins or loses but how one plays the game. Santiago and Manolin, in fact, are both keenly interested in American baseball, and the mutual affection between the old man and the young boy is typical of Hemingway's general emphasis on friendship between males. No woman appears as a major character in this book, and no romantic encounters are described; by excising these elements, Hemingway automatically removed two major sources of problems that had prompted some of the strongest objections to some of his earlier work.

Not everyone, of course, admired the new book. Some critics felt that both the story and the prose were too sentimental, and some felt that the work was an exercise in self-pity, with Manolin offering Santiago the kind of hero worship that Hemingway himself so obviously desired. Others complained that the Christian symbolism was too blatant and too trite (Santiago battles the fish for three days, and near the end of the book he lies exhausted on his back with outstretched arms). By far, however, most of the early reviewers felt that Hemingway had produced not only his best work in years but perhaps also the best work of his career. No less a judge than William Faulkner suggested that *The Old Man and the Sea* might prove to be the most important American novel of its era. The book was praised for its simple prose, its suggestive symbolism, its inspiring message, and its implied rejection of the nihilism that had allegedly darkened so much of Hemingway's previous work. The book was seen as an affirmation of such fundamental human values as love, humility, courage, and the bond between the old and the young, and the work was celebrated for its economy, its straightforward three-part structure, and its tight focus on an admirable central character. Santiago was sometimes compared to the protagonists of Homeric epics, and the book was at other times seen as a rewriting of Herman Melville's *Moby Dick*, with Santiago as a kind of anti-Ahab—a simple, humble man (not an obsessed monomaniac) capable of respecting and valuing the creature he pursued, a creature he saw not merely as an antagonist but as a kind of friend. Santiago respects and admires the marlin with whom he struggles, and both the man and the beast have won the respect and admiration of most of Hemingway's readers. Both the fisherman and the fish are ultimately defeated, but each wins a more important victory by exhibiting strength, determination, courage, and the fundamental will to survive.

It is sad to realize, when reading *The Old Man and the Sea*, that Hemingway himself would die by his own hand less than a decade after this novel appeared. Hemingway, unhealthy both in body and in mind, was apparently unable to survive and endure as Santiago does, but at the time of his death his stature as one of the two or three most important American writers of his era was secure. In the decades since his death, his reputation has only continued to grow as the critics of each succeeding generation have found new traits to admire or explore in his fiction. Formalist critics (who value the craftsmanship of good writing) have always appreciated the careful artistry of his works. Archetypal critics (who focus on basic human desires and fears and on the most universal kinds of stories) have always been intrigued by the "mythic" elements of Hemingway's texts. Meanwhile, his life and writings have offered plenty of fodder to psychoanalytic critics, and his work has been both censured and admired by generations of Marxists. Feminist criticism, which became especially prominent during and after the 1970s, was often initially troubled by Hemingway's apparently macho ethics and aesthetic, but more recently feminists have begun to make a strong case for the virtues of some of his heroines (especially Catherine Barkley). More broadly, critics interested in matters of gender in general have found much to intrigue them in Hemingway's works (especially his posthumous novel *The Garden of Eden*), while multicultural critics have begun to explore Hemingway's depictions of various nationalities (such as the Spanish, Italians, and Cubans), ethnic groups (such as blacks and Jews), and sexual minorities (such as gays and even cross-dressers). And, of course, the myth of Hemingway the man has made him the subject (or target) of numerous biographers, who have interpreted his life in ways that have been both countless and often controversial. At the beginning of the twenty-first century, then, Hemingway seems to be one of the twentieth-century American writers who is most likely not only to endure but also to prevail, at least in the sense of remaining the focus of constantly renewed attention and debate.

Bibliographical Overview

The secondary literature on Hemingway is now so vast that it seems pointless to list individual works. Instead, the list of works consulted below lists the best guides to such secondary commentary. The annotated "reference guides" prepared by Wagner and Larson are good places to begin; they briefly describe contemporary reviews and scholarly studies (mostly American) from the beginning of Hemingway's career up until 1989. The compilations edited by Stephens and Meyers are invaluable because they actually reprint many contemporary reviews, while the overviews by Hoffman and Stark not only survey but also evaluate modern Hemingway scholarship from the beginnings to the late 1980s. The volume edited by Asselineau is particularly interesting because it reports responses from reviewers and scholars in England, France, Germany, Italy, Norway, Sweden, and the Soviet Union. Meanwhile, Bakker's book not only reports Dutch reactions but also draws heavily on the American reviews reprinted by Stephens, so that Bakker provides much more information than his main title might suggest. Among recent surveys of academic criticism, the one by Beegel is especially lively and valuable, while anyone seriously interested in keeping up with Hemingway studies should consult the surveys included in each volume of the annual series *American Literary Scholarship* (which first appeared in 1963).

Works Consulted

Asselineau, Roger. "Hemingway's Reputation in France Since His Death in 1961." *The Hemingway Review*, Special European Issue (1992): 75-80.

_____, ed. *The Literary Reputation of Hemingway in Europe*. New York: New York University Press, 1965.

Axton, Marie. "Hemingway's Literary Reputation in England." *The Hemingway Review*, Special European Issue (1992): 4-13.

Bakker, J. *Ernest Hemingway in Holland, 1925-1981: A Comparative Analysis of the Contemporary Dutch and American Reception of His Work*. Amsterdam: Rodopi, 1986.

Baldwin, Dean, and Gregory L. Morris. *The Short Story in English: Britain and North America—An Annotated Bibliography*. Metuchen, NJ: Scarecrow Press, 1994.

Beegel, Susan F. "Conclusion: The Critical Reputation of Ernest Hemingway." *The Cambridge Companion to Hemingway*. Ed. Scott Donaldson. Cambridge: Cambridge University Press, 1996. 269-99.

Benson, Jackson J., ed. *The Short Stories of Ernest Hemingway: Critical Essays*. Durham, NC: Duke University Press, 1975.

Hoffman, Frederick J. "Ernest Hemingway." Supplement by Melvin J. Friedman. *Sixteen Modern American Authors: A Survey of Research and Criticism*. Ed. Jackson R. Bryer. Durham, NC: Duke University Press, 1973. 367-416.

Larson, Kelli A. "Bibliographical Essay: Lies, Damned Lies, and Hemingway Criticism." *A Historical Guide to Ernest Hemingway*. New York: Oxford University Press, 2000. 213-34.

_____. *Ernest Hemingway: A Reference Guide, 1974-1989*. Boston: G. K. Hall, 1991.

_____. "Stepping into the Labyrinth: Fifteen Years of Hemingway Scholarship." *The Hemingway Review* 11.2 (1992): 19-24.

Meyers, Jeffrey, ed. *Hemingway: The Critical Heritage*. London: Routledge & Kegan Paul, 1982.

Monteith, Moira. "A Change in Emphasis: Hemingway Criticism in Britain over the Last Twenty-five Years." *The Hemingway Review* 1.2 (1982): 2-19.

Smith, Paul. *A Reader's Guide to the Short Stories of Ernest Hemingway*. Boston: G. K. Hall, 1989.

Stark, Bruce. "Ernest Hemingway." *Sixteen Modern American Authors: A Survey of Research and Criticism*, vol. 2. Ed. Jackson R. Bryer. Durham, NC: Duke University Press, 1990. 404-79.

Stephens, Robert O., ed. *Ernest Hemingway: The Critical Reception*. New York: Burt Franklin, 1977.

Wagner, Linda Welshimer. *Ernest Hemingway: A Reference Guide*. Boston: G. K. Hall, 1977.

_____, ed. *Hemingway: Seven Decades of Criticism*. East Lansing: Michigan State University Press, 1998.

Toward a Definition of the Hemingwayesque and the Faulknerian_____

Matthew J. Bolton

Reviewing Cormac McCarthy's 2005 novel *No Country for Old Men* for *The New York Times*, Michiko Kakutani observes: "Mr. Mc-Carthy has always vacillated between clean, Hemingwayesque prose and pseudo-Faulknerian eloquence." The terms "Hemingwayesque" and "Faulknerian" serve as a remarkable sort of shorthand for talking about prose, evoking not merely each respective author's recurring themes and preoccupations but also his distinctive and instantly recognizable style. It would be hard to find two American novelists whose names so immediately speak to a particular way of constructing a sentence than Ernest Hemingway and William Faulkner, and it would be even harder to find two whose styles can be so readily placed at opposite ends of a spectrum, such that any subsequent writer might be measured as tending more toward the concentration of the former or the expansiveness of the latter. As Norman Mailer said of Hemingway's "restraint" and Faulkner's "excess": "Between the two, it's almost as if you've now been given your parameters. This is the best of one extreme and this is the best of another. And somewhere between the two you may be able to find your style in time to come." Mailer and McCarthy belong to two of several generations of men and women to find their styles by steering a course between Hemingway's and Faulkner's respective poles. One of the best ways to understand Hemingway, therefore, is to read Faulkner, and vice versa. In comparing the two authors' styles, one will inevitably begin to touch on their larger themes and preoccupations, for how each author constructs a line or a paragraph is predicated on how he sees the world and man's place in it.

Yet the paradox of reading Hemingway and Faulkner against each other is that the more familiar one becomes with the obvious differences between their respective styles and materials, the greater is the capacity of each man's work to surprise us with passages written in a mode we tend to associate with the other. The terms "Hemingway-esque" and "Faulknerian" have come to stand for a broad set of cultural assumptions and generalities—some more accurate than others—about how and what each man wrote. The more portable and widely applicable these terms become, the less accurately they reflect the two novelists' work itself. For reducing two shelves of novels and short stories into the abstract terms "Hemingwayesque" and "Faulknerian" is a quasi-parodic act; it involves selecting and exaggerating certain characteristics of each author's distinctive voice and subject matter while ignoring or eliding others. The frequency with which these authors are imitated and with which their styles are invoked speaks less to the incisiveness of their readers than to the distinctiveness of their voices. We recognize their styles viscerally and immediately, just as it takes only a word or two for us to recognize the timbre of an old friend's voice on the telephone or across a room. It is because of this familiarity that we recognize echoes of Hemingway and Faulkner's prose styles in other authors, whether those authors are writing in a parodic vein—like the participants in the annual Bad Hemingway and Faux Faulkner contests—or in earnest.

As a point of comparison, consider F. Scott Fitzgerald. *The Great Gatsby* was published, to great acclaim, within two years of *The Sun Also Rises* and *The Sound and the Fury*. Yet while one might use the term "Fitzgeraldesque" to speak of a certain mood (perhaps, the elegiac) or of a set of themes (say, the unacknowledged sacrifice of the innocent, or the dark underbelly of the American dream, or the tragic nature of memory), it would not speak of a particular way of constructing sentences and using adjectives to anyone other than a Fitzgerald scholar. This is not to say that the language of *The Great Gatsby* is less powerful or beautiful than that of *The Sun Also Rises* or *The Sound and the Fury*. It is, however, less idiosyncratic and therefore less identifiable and less "imitate-able." A Fitzgerald parody contest would not generate the response that the Hemingway and Faulkner contests do. To parody Fitzgerald, one would have to do so thematically, writing a spoof set in the gilded, Art Deco New York of the 1920s, for those elements that can be readily identified and exaggerated in Fitzgerald are not to be found on the level of his language itself.

Hemingway and Faulkner therefore have made their marks not only on the formal and thematic conventions of the novel but also on the English language. Malcolm Cowley, only a few years after *The Sun Also Rises* had been published, commented that "bright young men from the Middle West were trying to be Hemingway heroes, talking in tough understatements from the sides of their mouths" (in Meyers 16). It is hard for a casual reader to finish two or three Hemingway novels without finding him- or herself thinking and speaking in the pared-down, telegraphic mode of his narrators and characters. It is even harder, one might argue, for a serious writer to come away from Hemingway and Faulkner without sounding something like one or the other—or like both, as Kakutani claims Cormac McCarthy does. As the Nobel Prize committee wrote of Hemingway in awarding him the 1954 prize in literature (five years after Faulkner received the award), Hemingway had "set a standard as easy to imitate as it is difficult to obtain." This is why countless aficionados not only cannot touch on Hemingway or Faulkner's power but also cannot through their imitations diminish that power. The long-standing tradition of authors writing in the shadow of Hemingway and Faulkner has only served to render these two figures that much more central to American literature, for in the years between World War I and World War II, Hemingway and Faulkner redefined the scope and purpose of the novel, and by extension the resources of the language.

* * *

It would be legitimate to approach Hemingway and Faulkner from a biographical vantage point, noting that these close contemporaries both began their careers as poets, both published some of their earliest work in the same issue of a literary magazine called *The Double*

Dealer, and both initially benefited from and later publicly rejected—by printing parodies of his work—the mentorship of the older writer Sherwood Anderson. One could note that Faulkner and Hemingway were in Paris at the same time in the 1920s, both living the garret life and haunting the gardens and cafés, but never met in person. Or one could trace the public ripostes between the two men in the 1940s and 1950s—the catalyst of which was Faulkner's comment in a University of Mississippi lecture hall that Hemingway was a "coward" as an artist—or repeat the accolades with which Faulkner greeted the publication of *The Old Man and the Sea* and the scorn with which Hemingway greeted that of *A Fable* (Rovit and Waldhorn 157; Baker 337). But to understand the relationship between their disparate styles, a reader would be better served by closing Hemingway's and Faulkner's biographies and opening their books instead. To draw some initial generalizations about each man's style, and by so doing to approach a definition of the inherently reductive terms "Hemingwayesque" and "Faulknerian," one need only compare passages of dialogue or narration from the canonical novels or short stories of each.

As a metonymy of their work, take what are perhaps their two most-frequently anthologized short stories: Faulkner's "A Rose for Emily" and Hemingway's "Hills Like White Elephants." As these stories often appear within a few pages of each other in short-story anthologies and literature textbooks, they are often read and taught as being representative of each author's larger body of work. These stories are therefore worth discussing not because they are the authors' best work (in fact, each might reasonably be characterized as driven by a cheap gimmick) but because the frequency with which they are anthologized suggests that they are considered prototypical examples of each author's style and themes. Comparing these stories on the level of diction and syntax—the choice of words and the arrangement of words into clauses and sentences—casts light on the broad cultural assumptions regarding the Hemingwayesque and the Faulknerian.

"A Rose for Emily" begins with a one-sentence paragraph that, while not overly long or overly complex, sets the discursive tone that will mark the story as a whole:

> When Miss Emily Grierson died, our whole town went to her funeral: the men through a sort of respectful affection for a fallen monument, the women mostly out of curiosity to see the inside of her house, which no one save an old manservant—a combined gardener and cook—had seen in at least ten years. (*Portable Faulkner* 392)

The line builds through a series of coordinated clauses and asides, providing more and more detail about why the townspeople attended Miss Emily's funeral and how Miss Emily had been living in the decade before her death. The dashes that set off a parenthetical aside are typical of Faulkner and will be used a half dozen times in "A Rose for Emily." The effect is distinctly conversational, as if the dash were a tap on the reader's shoulder and the clause that it offsets a muttered piece of information the narrator thought the reader ought to have. We see these dashes several times in Part IV of the story. When Emily is carrying on with Homer Barron, for example, "the ladies forced the Baptist minister—Miss Emily's people were Episcopal—to call on her" (398). It is as if there is always more to say about these characters and their histories than a single grammatical sentence can contain. The complex structure of Faulkner's sentences, therefore, reflects the complex social context the narrator is attempting to convey. The dashes and the parenthetical asides, like the colons, semicolons, and coordinating conjunctions that stud this brief story, make meaning through a dizzying accretion of clauses. "A Rose for Emily" is a story that hinges on who knows what when, and indeed it relies for its overall effect on withholding a telling piece of information until its very end. One might therefore think of the narrator of "A Rose for Emily"—a plural narrator who always refers to "we" and "us" rather than "I" and "me," as if he speaks for the whole town of Jefferson—as employing the grammar of gossip.

Compare Faulkner's discursive mode to the hard immediacy with which "Hills Like White Elephants" begins:

> The hills across the valley of the Ebro were long and white. On this side there was no shade and no trees and the station was between two lines of rails in the sun. Close against the side of the station there was the warm shadow of the building and a curtain, made of strings of bamboo beads, hung across the open door into the bar, to keep out flies. The American and the girl with him sat at a table in the shade, outside the building. It was very hot and the express from Barcelona would come in forty minutes. It stopped at this junction for two minutes and went on to Madrid. (*The Complete Stories* 211)

Hemingway's description of this setting is photorealistic, conveying what the eyes can see rather than what the collective consciousness can remember. Whereas the first sentence of Faulkner's story is complex, Hemingway's sentences here are simple or compound, linking clauses through "and" rather than "which" or "that." While this unnamed Spanish town and its sleepy train station must each have its own history, that history will not make its way into a narrative that is so attuned to the present moment. It is as if the building in the shadow of which the story unfolds will exist only for the forty minutes during which the travelers wait for their train. The narrator, and hence the reader, tacitly assumes the American travelers' perspective on the place as being immediately present but entirely inconsequential.

Compare this sense of the fleeting present with the historicizing gaze of the Faulkner narrator, whose description of Emily's house is as rooted in the past as it is in the present: "It was a big squarish frame house that had once been white, decorated with cupolas and spires and scrolled balconies in the heavily lightsome style of the seventies, set on what had once been our most select street" (392). One can imagine how differently the bare reportage of the Hemingway narrator would render this same house, describing its present condition and perhaps its state of dilapidation, but not setting that condition in the context of the last fifty years of local history. The narrators of "A Rose for Emily" and "Hills Like White Elephants" seem to have fundamentally different senses of time.

Faulkner's expansion into the historical and Hemingway's concentration on the immediate are evident not only in their syntax (the way in which they order words in relation to each other) but also in their very diction (their actual choice of words). Faulkner tends to describe people and places through long lists of abstract, Latinate adjectives. Consider his narrator's description of Emily's position in town in the decades after the disappearance of her fiancé, Homer: "Thus she passed from generation to generation—dear, inescapable, impervious, tranquil, and perverse" (400). Most novelists would choose the single best adjective to describe Emily. Perhaps they would even choose two or three. But very few could list five adjectives without sounding foolish, and still fewer could effectively deploy two adjectives that share a root ("impervious" and "perverse," which may suggest a third word: Emily's sexual "perversion"). For Faulkner, such a list speaks both to multiplicity (a single person or object containing a great many aspects) and to singularity—for no one has possessed exactly this combination of qualities before, and no author has used these words in this combination before. It is as if the accumulation of a great number of abstract adjectives reaches at once for the universal and the particular. Again such abstraction speaks to a long view of history. How many years must one live around a neighbor before characterizing her as "inescapable"? How many encounters must one have with that neighbor before describing her as both "dear" and "perverse"? Faulkner's adjectives speak not only of the origins of the language, looking back as they do to the classical world, but also to the years of quotidian encounters and back-fence gossip in Jefferson society that they sum up.

Hemingway takes the opposite approach, using the simplest of adjectives or, where he can, avoiding such modifiers altogether. Most of the adjectives in the narration of "Hills Like White Elephants" are concrete descriptors of temperature and size: "warm," "hot," "big," "white," "cool," "dry," "damp." The characters' dialogue, on the other hand, is full of subjective measures of quality and pleasure, such as "fine," "bright," "lovely," "nice," "simple," and "natural." Again the effect is to keep the narrative focused on the objective and the external. Nothing is described that cannot be immediately apprehended or overheard. This difference is apparent in the naming of characters, too. Whereas Miss Emily is named in the first paragraph of her story, Hemingway's protagonists are marked only by the most obvious of descriptors, "the American and the girl." Their identity as Americans is as readily apparent from their clothes and manner and language as anything else in or around the train station, and so even the generic labeling of the characters ultimately partakes of the concrete and the visual. The girl's pet name, Jig, makes its way into the text only through the direct address of the young man. As in his description of the valley and the station, the narrator limits himself to describing what he can objectively see and hear rather than drawing on some well of local knowledge or authorial insight.

Faulkner's and Hemingway's radically different approaches to syntax and diction—and, by extension, description and narration—in these two stories therefore speak to a larger epistemological divide. Faulkner's complex sentences and accumulated Latinate descriptors and Hemingway's declarative sentences and concrete diction represent not merely two different ways to communicate information but also two different beliefs about the nature of information. Style, in this case, is substance. For the Faulkner narrator, truth is to be found not only in a faithful rendering of the present moment but also in a constant commerce between the present moment and the remembered past. If "A Rose for Emily" presents any challenge to an inexperienced reader, it is that of following the narrator as he moves backward and forward in time. The story, while not much longer in word count than Hemingway's, spans more than fifty years of history, and its telling draws on the collective memories of the whole community. As the narrator shuttles about in time, the reader must constantly put the events he relates into chronological—and hence causal—order. This is a demand that Faulkner placed again and again on his readers, perhaps most notably in the Benjy section of *The Sound and the Fury*, and it may speak to his larger vision of personal and communal history. Faulkner summed up his sense of time in a phrase that appears in several of his novels, attributed sometimes to his narrator and sometimes to his authorial stand-in, Gavin Stevens: "The past is never dead. It is not even past." One might see Homer Barron's preserved and unburied body, shrouded in "that even coating of the patient and biding dust" (402), as a *reductio ad absurdum* symbol of the enduring presence of the past.

If Faulkner's narrative is rooted in memory, Hemingway's is rooted in perception. The paradigmatic Hemingway narrator's role is to perceive and report, but not to editorialize. Whereas "A Rose for Emily" presents the reader with a dizzying, fractured narrative, "Hills Like White Elephants" moves forward as relentlessly and unerringly as a train. There are no reversals, no flashbacks, no embedded narratives, no subordinate clauses or asides that might convey to the reader privileged information about these characters and their histories. Yet as the story moves forward in something resembling "real time," the reader may find that this mode of purely externalized, linear reportage presents as many challenges as does Faulkner's achronological historicizing. Where the reader of "A Rose for Emily" must give order to an overabundance of information, the reader of "Hills Like White Elephants" must draw inferences from spare description and laconic dialogue to piece together the backstories of these two nameless characters and to make informed predictions about what their future will hold. Inexperienced or inattentive readers might miss the unnamed subject of the couple's conversation—abortion—entirely. By the same token, the inexperienced reader may miss the tonal subtleties of the characters' dialogue. Their mounting annoyance with each other, their fears and resentments that flash out at the slightest provocation, their memories of better times together and their awareness of how far they have fallen—all of this accumulated history may be gleaned from their exchanges. The unborn child—and the possibility of aborting it—is this story's "elephant in the room," and much of the couple's bickering over drinks and landscapes represents a desperate form of avoidance.

"Hills Like White Elephants" is, quite literally, a textbook definition of Hemingway's much-repeated iceberg analogy. In his disquisition on bullfighting, *Death in the Afternoon*, Hemingway writes:

> If a writer of prose knows enough about what he is writing about he may omit things that he knows and the reader, if the writer is writing truly enough, will have a feeling of those things as strongly as though the writer had stated them. The dignity of movement of an iceberg is due to only one-eighth of it being above water. The writer who omits things because he does not know them only makes hollow places in his writing.

What makes "Hills Like White Elephants" so effective is the degree to which Hemingway has sunk these characters' history below the surface of their conversation and their mannerisms. The reader is able to infer so much about their situation precisely because Hemingway himself knows the situation.

There is, then, to judge from these two stories, an essential difference between the relative weight that Faulkner and Hemingway give to the historic and the present, to memory and perception, and to the depths of the conscious mind and the surfaces of the visible world. This difference in form intersects with a difference in theme and setting, such that it becomes difficult to distinguish among these three elements. So many of Hemingway's protagonists are American expatriates, living away from the complex web of familial and societal relationships that drive and doom Faulkner's characters. Like the American and the girl waiting for the train to Madrid, most Hemingway protagonists have uprooted themselves from family and native soil to live abroad. Most of Faulkner's characters, on the other hand, are residents of the fictional Yoknapatawpha County, and their lives are inextricably bound up with those of their countrymen and their ancestors. Hemingway's laconic concentration and Faulkner's baroque expansiveness are integrally related to the people and places about whom they write.

Of course, one might object that these stories employ different points of view—Faulkner's first-person narrator to Hemingway's third-person narration—and that any such comparisons are therefore moot. Yet reading a Faulkner novel that is told from the third-person point of view, such as *Light in August* or the last section of *The Sound and the Fury*, and a Hemingway novel told from the first person, such as *The Sun Also Rises* or *A Farewell to Arms*, suggests just the opposite. Faulkner tends to be just as expansive when writing in the third person, while Hemingway tends to keep to his spare reportage even when a narrator is relaying events from his own life. In *The Sound and the Fury*, for example, the sections narrated by Benjy and Jason Compson are marked by Anglo-Saxon diction, declarative sentences and concrete descriptions, while it is in the final, third-person section that Faulkner's prose is at its most stately and magisterial (the Quentin section will be considered subsequently). Consider the first line of that last, third-person section:

> The day dawned bleak and chill, a moving wall of gray light out of the northeast which, instead of dissolving into moisture, seemed to disintegrate into minute and venomous particles, like dust that, when Dilsey opened the door of the cabin and emerged, needled laterally into her flesh, precipitating not so much a moisture as a substance partaking of the quality of thin, not quite congealed oil. (265)

In a contrary-to-fact construction that is characteristic of his prose, Faulkner builds toward a description of what *is* by passing through a description of what is *not*. If the sentences of "A Rose for Emily" swell and branch in order to include the past and the historic, passages like this one do so in order to include the conditional and the hypothetical. The paired clauses "instead of . . . seemed to . . ." and "not so much . . . as . . ." describe first the potential or typical and then follow that description with one of the actual or singular. The rain is "not so much moisture" but rather a substance like "not quite congealed oil." While the folksy gossiping and muttered asides of "A Rose for Emily" are not to be found here, this more formal narrator nevertheless shares in that narrator's mode of building power and import through a baroque accumulation of details and descriptors.

By the same token, Hemingway's first-person narratives show the laconic restraint that marks the reportage of the featureless narrator of "Hills Like White Elephants." The stoicism and detachment of the Hemingway narrator stems from his scrupulous attention to action and surface detail rather than to reaction and underlying emotion. Even in telling his own story, he focuses on what he has seen and done rather than what he feels and remembers. Think of Jake Barnes in *The Sun Also Rises*, whose relationship with Brett Ashley is doomed by the war injury that has left him impotent and the impetuous life that has left her emotionally stunted. He will admit to his friend Bill Gorton, who during an unguarded moment on a fishing trip asks Jake whether he has ever been in love with Brett, that he has been so "on and off for a hell of a long time" (123). Yet it is only under direct questioning that Jake reveals the depths of his emotions, and indeed this confession makes its way into the narrative only because it has been spoken and therefore must be reported. In the context of other emotionally fraught scenes, Jake keeps his focus on external action rather than inner reaction. On the night before Brett leaves Paris for a tryst with Robert Cohn, Jake describes their parting in these two paragraphs, which close the novel's first book:

> "Good night, Jake. Good night, darling. I won't see you again." We kissed standing at the door. She pushed me away. We kissed again. "Oh, don't!" Brett said.
>
> She turned quickly and went into the hotel. The chauffeur drove me around to my flat. I gave him twenty francs and he touched his cap and said: "Good night, sir," and drove off. I rang the bell. The door opened and I went up-stairs and went to bed. (65)

The reader may infer what Jake is thinking and feeling as he makes his way back to his apartment and climbs into bed, but Jake will not admit to it himself—at least not in this scene. Jake's silence regarding his own inner life creates a void that the reader rushes to fill, feeling on Jake's behalf what he himself will not admit to feeling.

The difference between Hemingway's and Faulkner's distinctive styles may not therefore be reduced to a difference in person or in how each author positions his narrators in relation to the stories they tell. It is more than stylistic and more than strategic. Rather, the striking and immediate difference between the sorts of words each chooses and the sorts of sentences each constructs speaks to a larger divide between how the two authors see man's place in time and the world.

* * *

It is easy enough to set up a dichotomy between Hemingway's and Faulkner's distinctive styles, and easy enough in so doing to draw larger distinctions between their characteristic ways of constructing a line, a paragraph, or a story. What is far more interesting, however, is to challenge this dichotomy by finding instances in which each author writes in a mode that we tend to associate with the other. These instances resist the notion that Hemingway's and Faulkner's works can be fully contained by the terms "Hemingwayesque" and "Faulknerian." Constructing the dichotomy between these two authors requires one level of familiarity with their work; deconstructing it requires the next. For it is through this process of deconstruction that one sees Hemingway and Faulkner as being bound up with the larger forces of modernism and as taking different routes around some of the same obstacles and toward some of the same goals.

One way to challenge the Hemingway and Faulkner dichotomy is to ask who speaks most directly for Faulkner in *The Sound and the Fury*. The novel presents readers with four very different narrators. Each of the three Compson brothers—the man-child Benjy, the doomed and hypersensitive Quentin, and the monstrously narcissistic Jason—narrates a section, while an omniscient third-person narrator relates the last section. The unpunctuated stream-of-consciousness prose of the Quentin section is often considered to be prototypical Faulkner. By eliminating punctuation and clausal construction, Faulkner creates the impression of fluidity and speed, as if the text on the page were a transcript of Quentin's mind at work. Quentin recalls, for example, an aphorism of his father's: ". . . was the saddest word of all there is nothing else in the world its not despair until time its not even time until it was . . ." (197). The reader must make meaning of this, silently punctuating and slowing the passage to produce something like the following: "[The word] 'was' [is] the saddest word of all. There is nothing else in the world. It's not despair until time. It's not even time until it was." This section is a bravura performance, one that places as many demands on its reader as does a chapter of James Joyce's *Ulysses*.

The comparison to *Ulysses* holds true in another respect as well: like Joyce's young artist Stephen Dedalus, Quentin Compson is aware of the processes of his own thought and revises the language of his internal monologues. Watching a classmate boating, Quentin thinks of the youth as "still pulling upstream majestical in the face of god gods. Better. Gods" (111). This instance of metaconsciousness—what Victorian poet and critic Matthew Arnold called "the dialogue of the mind with itself"—suggests that Quentin takes an active role in shaping and directing the movement of his thought processes. Other passages likewise show the mind of an artist at work, such as here: "*A face reproachful tearful an odor of camphor and of tears a voice weeping steadily and softly beyond the twilit door the twilight-colored smell of honeysuckle*" (95). This repetition and refining of words suggests a poet drafting verse or a painter layering one shade over another. Because Quentin is an emerging artist, one who has access to the full range of Faulkner's lexicon and habitually refines his choice of words and images with the sensitive inner ear of the poet, there is a temptation to read him as a stand-in for Faulkner himself and to read his fevered monologues as Faulkner speaking in his "true" voice.

Yet how would our definition of the "Faulknerian" change were we to accept the Benjy section as being no less prototypical of the author's style than is the Quentin section? A mute man-child with no sense of the passage of time, Benjy scrupulously reports what he sees and hears, but not his responses to these perceptions. Consider this description of walking across a pasture: "Our shadows were on the grass. They got to the trees before we did. Mine got there first" (54). Joseph Blotner, Faulkner's biographer, notes of these lines: "Benjy can record, like a camera eye, but he cannot interpret. For him there is no causal relationship between the movement of his body and the movement of his shadow" (211). Like a camera eye, Benjy's gaze often fixes itself on a single object to the exclusion of everything else. He records a childhood fight between his sister Caddy and his brother Jason this way, "She fought. Father held her. She kicked at Jason. He rolled into the corner, out of the mirror. Father brought Caddy to the fire. They were all out of the mirror. Only the fire was in it. Like the fire was in a door" (65). Benjy's eyes are fixed on the mirror, and so he relates only those images that the mirror reflects. Not only does he fail to comment on his emotional response to the fight, he also fails even to follow the fight during those instances when its participants are no longer reflected in the mirror into which he has been gazing.

This narrative emphasis on recording physical actions rather than emotional reactions begins to sound rather like the laconic objectivity commonly denoted by the term "Hemingwayesque." As in many of Hemingway's narratives, readers can gauge much of Benjy's inner life only by his own physical actions and by the verbal reactions of the people around him. Benjy's crying, for example, is generally conveyed not by Benjy himself but through the reactions of Luster, the African American boy charged with keeping him. A memory of Benjy's lost sister Caddy comforting him gives way to chastisement from Luster:

Caddy knelt and put her arms around me and her cold bright face against mine. She smelled like trees.

"You're not a poor baby. Are you. Are you. You've got your Caddy. Haven't you got your Caddy."

Cant you shut up that moaning and slobbering, Luster said. Aint you shamed of yourself, making all this racket. (9)

Just as only Bill Gorton's insistent questioning leads Jake to admit that he once loved Brett, so only Luster's comment alerts the reader that Benjy's memories of his sister have moved him to tears. One might recall a line from the dying Catherine Barkley's monologue: "Don't mind me darling. Please don't cry. Don't mind me" (330). It is through Catherine's observation, not through Frederic's narration, that the reader can gauge Frederic's emotional state. When Benjy does say he has been crying, he generally does not give the reason. When he gets undressed for the night, Benjy, who had been castrated some years before, reports, "*I got undressed and I looked at myself, and I began to cry. Hush, Luster said. Looking for them aint going to do no good. They're gone*" (73). Like the reader of "Hills Like White Elephants," the reader here must make a causal connection between action and reaction and between past and present.

Compare this last scene to a similar one in *The Sun Also Rises*, in which Jake Barnes, rendered impotent by a war injury, gets ready for bed: "Undressing, I looked at myself in the mirror of the big armoire beside the bed. That was a typically French way to furnish a room. Practical, too, I suppose. Of all the ways to be wounded" (30). Jake tries to report on the armoire as a means of staying focused on the concrete and the external, but his emotional response to his injury overcomes his ability to maintain a clinical detachment. He describes, for once, not what he sees, but how he feels. Thus it is not a description of his injury that appears in the text, but a wave of regret for that injury.

When Jake gets into bed a moment later, he finds that the regretful mood that undressing occasioned has not left him:

I lay awake thinking and my mind jumping around. Then I couldn't keep away from it, and I started to think about Brett and all the rest of it went away. I was thinking about Brett and my mind stopped jumping around and started to go in sort of smooth waves. Then all of a sudden I started to cry. Then after a while it was better and I lay in bed and listened to the heavy trams go by and way down the street, and then I went to sleep. (31)

The process by which Jake's thoughts become less agitated as he lies in bed may remind one of Benjy's description of sleep. Benjy's entire narrative is predicated by his "mind jumping around," to use Jake's term, as he muddles his memories of what has happened with his perceptions of what is happening. Yet both men find at night that lying in bed brings a sort of peace. Benjy says:

Caddy held me and I could hear us all, and the darkness, and something that I could smell. And then I could see the windows, where the trees were buzzing. Then the dark began to go in smooth bright shapes, like it always does, even when Caddy says I have been asleep. (75)

Both men experience the processes of their own minds kinesthetically: Jake says that his mind "started to go in sort of smooth waves," while for Benjy it is the darkness itself, as he slips into unconsciousness, that "began to go in smooth bright shapes." To create a character for whom the past is always present, Faulkner employs a mode of concrete reportage and direct sensual apprehension that seems to partake of the Hemingwayesque. The distinction between the historicizing gaze of the narrator in "A Rose for Emily" and the objectifying gaze of that of "Hills Like White Elephants" collapses in the figure of Benjy, for whom, to use a phrase from T. S. Eliot's *Four Quartets*, "all time is eternally present."

Just as one can find the Hemingwayesque in Faulkner's work, so can one find the Faulknerian in Hemingway. When Hemingway's characters become overtired, or drunk, or injured, they have a tendency to lapse into a mode of unguarded stream-of-consciousness narration that seems closer to the Quentin section of *The Sound and the Fury* than to the declaratives of "Hills Like White Elephants." In *A Farewell to Arms*, Frederic Henry retreats on foot from Caporetto and escapes execution as a deserter by jumping into a fast-moving, cold river. Exhausted, he stows aboard a freight train, crawling under a canvas tarp to lie atop a load of guns. With his body finally at rest, his mind begins to race. He thinks of where he is now and where he would rather be, in the arms of Catherine Barkley:

> You did not love the floor of a flat-car nor guns with canvas jackets and the smell of vaselined metal or a canvas that rain leaked through, although it is very fine under a canvas and pleasant with guns; but you loved some one else whom now you knew was not even to be pretended there; you seeing now very clearly and coldly—not so coldly as clearly and emptily.

This contrary-to-fact construction—building toward what something is by passing through what something is not—is more closely associated with Faulkner than with Hemingway. And like Stephen Dedalus or Quentin Compson, Frederic here revises his own thoughts: "clearly and coldly" becomes "not so coldly as clearly and emptily." Recall Quentin's self-correction: "majestical in the face of god gods. Better. Gods" (111). The casting of this whole passage in the second person further suggests the workings of an exhausted mind.

This passage, and similar ones in *The Sun Also Rises*, *For Whom the Bell Tolls*, and other first-person narratives, suggest that the laconic restraint that often characterizes the Hemingway narrator is more deliberate and affected than it may appear. When they are weakened or disabled, these tight-lipped stoics lose their restraint and begin to sound as expansive and verbose as a Quentin Compson. Just as the occasional moments where Quentin revises and recrafts his phrases suggest that he has some measure of control over his stream-of-consciousness narrative, so do the moments where the Hemingway narrators lose their restraint suggest that such restraint is cultivated. The Hemingway narrator's tight focus on the external and the active represents a conscious disciplining of thought and memory. As Catherine cautions Henry before his surgical operation: "When you're going under the ether just think about something else—not us. Because people get very blabby under an anaesthetic" (103). In Hemingway's fiction, ether is only one of the means by which the body may be made to betray the mind. His narrators get "blabby" under other traumatic circumstances, and their sudden flow of words in such situations demonstrates the degree of conscious effort that goes into maintaining their objectivity and restraint.

Once a reader thinks to look for Hemingwayesque constructions in Faulkner and Faulknerian constructions in Hemingway, he or she finds them with ease. From the clean-lined prose of Benjy to the racing thoughts of an exhausted Frederic Henry, words and lines and scenes in the actual work of Hemingway and Faulkner resist the facile oversimplifications that the terms "Faulknerian" and "Hemingwayesque" have come to represent. To be culturally literate, one should recognize the sort of dichotomy that Kakutani and Mailer construct in discussing these two writers.

Works Cited

Baker, Carlos. *Hemingway: The Writer as Artist*. Princeton, NJ: Princeton University Press, 1952.

Blotner, Joseph. *Faulkner: A Biography*. New York: Random House, 1984.

Faulkner, William. *Absalom, Absalom!* 1936. New York: Random House, Vintage International, 1991.

_____. *The Portable Faulkner*. Ed. Malcolm Cowley. New York: Viking Press, 1977.

_____. *The Sound and the Fury*. 1929. New York: Random House, Vintage International, 1990.

Hemingway, Ernest. *The Complete Stories: The Finca Vigía Edition*. New York: Charles Scribner's Sons, 1987.

_____. *Death in the Afternoon*. New York: Charles Scribner's Sons, 1932.

_____. *A Farewell to Arms*. New York: Charles Scribner's Sons, 1929.

_____. *The Sun Also Rises*. New York: Charles Scribner's Sons, 1926.

Kakutani, Michiko. "On the Loose in Badlands: Killer with a Cattle Gun." *The New York Times*, July 28, 2005.

Meyers, Jeffrey, ed. *Hemingway: The Critical Heritage*. London: Routledge & Kegan Paul, 1982.

Rovit, Earl, and Arthur Waldhorn. *Hemingway and Faulkner in Their Time*. New York: Continuum, 2005.

CRITICAL
READINGS

The First Forty-five Stories _____

Carlos Baker

"A man should find things he cannot lose."
—A major in Milan[1]

I. Under the Iceberg

"The dignity of movement of an iceberg," Hemingway once said, "is due to only one-eighth of it being above water." His short stories are deceptive somewhat in the manner of an iceberg. The visible areas glint with the hard factual lights of the naturalist. The supporting structure, submerged and mostly invisible except to the patient explorer, is built with a different kind of precision—that of the poet-symbolist. Once the reader has become aware of what Hemingway is doing in those parts of his work which lie below the surface, he is likely to find symbols operating everywhere, and in a series of beautiful crystallizations, compact and buoyant enough to carry considerable weight.

Hemingway entered serious fiction by way of the short story. It was a natural way to begin. His esthetic aims called for a rigorous self-discipline in the presentation of episodes drawn, though always made over, from life. Because he believed, firmly as his own Abruzzian priest, that "you cannot know about it unless you have it,"[2] a number of the stories were based on personal experience, though here again invention of a symbolic kind nearly always entered into the act of composition.

The early discipline in the short story, and it was rarely anything but the hardest kind of discipline, taught Hemingway his craft. He learned how to get the most from the least, how to prune language and avoid waste motion, how to multiply intensities, and how to tell nothing but the truth in a way that always allowed for telling more than the truth. From the short story he learned wonderfully precise lessons in the use of dialogue for the purposes of exposition. Even the simpler stories showed this power. In the struggle with his materials he learned to keep the poker face of the true artist. Or, if you changed the image to another game, he learned the art of relaying important hints to his partner the reader without revealing all at once the full content of his holdings. From the short story he gained a skill in the economical transfer of impressions—without special rhetoric or apparent trickery. His deepest trust was placed in the cumulative effect of ostensibly simple, carefully selective statement, with occasional reiteration of key phrases for thematic emphasis.

Like James, he has been rightly called an architect rather than a manipulator, and he himself has said that prose is architecture rather than interior decoration—an esthetic fact which the short story taught him.[3] The writing and rewriting of the stories gave him invaluable experience in the "hows" of fiction, and suggested almost endless possibilities for future development. When he was ready to launch out into the novel, he might have said, as Henry James did about *Roderick Hudson*: "I had but hugged the shore on sundry previous small occasions; bumping about, to acquire skill, in the shallow waters and sandy coves of the short story."[4] The difference was that on occasion, though not invariably, Hemingway's cove dropped off quickly into waters that were deep enough to float an iceberg.

Through the year 1939, he had published fifty-five short stories.[5] This count does not include all the sixteen short miniatures of *In Our Time* or several others which appear as interludes among the technical expositions of *Death in the Afternoon*. Most of the fifty-five were collected in 1938 in *The Fifth Column and the First Forty-nine Stories*. There omitted was "The Man with the Tyrolese Hat" from *Der Querschnitt* (1936). Also still unreprinted in 1951 were three stories, first printed in *Esquire Magazine*, about Chicote's Madrid bar during the Spanish Civil War, as well as two others first published in *Cosmopolitan* in 1939. The volume of 1938 contained four stories not previously brought together: "Old Man at the Bridge," cabled from Barcelona in April, 1938; "The Capital of the World," a fine story on the "athlete-dying-young" theme, with a setting in Madrid and, as leading character, a boy from Estremadura; and the two long stories which grew out of Hemingway's hunting-trip in Africa, "The Short Happy Life of Francis Macomber" and "The Snows of Kilimanjaro." But the first forty-five stories may be conveniently taken as a kind of unit, since they were all written within ten years, and since they represent what Hemingway thought worthy of including in his first three collections: *In Our Time* (1925), *Men Without Women* (1927), and *Winner Take Nothing* (1933). Taken together or separately, they are among the great short stories of modern literature.

Their range of symbolic effects is even greater than the variety of subjects and themes employed. The subjects and themes, in turn, are far more various than has been commonly supposed. Like any writer with a passion for craftsmanship, Hemingway not only accepts but also sets himself the most difficult experimental problems. Few writers of the past fifty years, and no American writers of the same period except James and Faulkner, have grappled so manfully with extremely difficult problems in communication. One cannot be aware of the real extent of this experimentation (much of it highly successful, though there are some lapses) until he has read through the first three collections attempting to watch both the surfaces and the real inward content. Even that task, though pleasurable as a voyage of discovery, is harder than it sounds. For it is much the same with the short stories as with *The Sun Also Rises* and *A Farewell to Arms*: they are so readable as straight narratives that one is prepared to accept them at face-value—to admire the sharp lines and clean curves of the eighth of the iceberg above the surface, and to ignore the real causes of the dignity or worth of the movement.

With perhaps half a dozen exceptions, each of the short stories doubly repays the closest reading. The point could be illustrated as many times as there are stories to serve as illustrations. As one example, there is the Chekhov-like "Alpine Idyll," an apparently simple tale in which two American sportsmen have gone skiing in Switzerland. On the way to a village inn in a Swiss valley, the Americans pass a cemetery where a burial has just taken place. When they reach the inn, they drink at one table; at another table, the village sexton splits a bottle of wine with a Swiss peasant from the lonely mountain-country up above. When the peasant leaves to go to another tavern down the street, the Americans hear the story behind the burial.

In the winter the peasant's wife died. Since he could not bury her, he placed the body in his woodshed. There it froze stiff in the intense mountain cold. Whenever the peasant went to get wood to keep himself warm, he found that the body was in his way. So he stood it up against the wall. Later, since he often went for wood at night, carrying a lantern, and since the open jaws of the corpse provided a convenient high place, he took to hanging his lantern in his dead wife's mouth. Evidently he thought nothing of it at the time. By spring, when he was able to bring the body to the valley for burial, the mouth had become noticeably ragged. This is the shocking anecdote under which the story is built.

Actually, however, the story is not "about" the peasant. Its subject, several times emphasized early in the narrative, is "not ever doing anything too long." The Americans have been trying some spring skiing high in the Silvretta. Much as they love the sport, they have found it a queerly unpleasant experience. May is too late in the season to be up there. "I was a little tired of skiing," says one. "We had stayed too long. . . . I was glad to be down, away from the unnatural high mountain spring, into this May morning in the valley." When the story of the peasant and his wife is told, the idea of the "unnatural" and the idea of "not ever doing anything too long" are both driven home with a special twist of the knife. For the peasant has lived too long in an unnatural situation; his sense of human dignity and decency has temporarily atrophied. When he gets down into the valley, where it is spring and people are living naturally and wholesomely, he sees how far he has strayed from the natural and the wholesome, and he is then deeply ashamed of himself. For spring in the valley has been established by the skier's internal monologue as the "natural" place. In the carefully wrought terms of the story, the valley stands in opposition to the unnatural high mountain spring. The arrival of this season in the area near his lonely hut has activated the peasant to bring his wife's body down to the valley for burial.

But for him the descent has been especially meaningful—nothing less, in short, than a coming to judgment before the priest and the sexton. Here again, the point is made possible by careful previous preparation. One of the skiers has commented on the oppressiveness of the spring sun in the high Silvretta. "You could not get away from the sun." It is a factual and true statement of the skier's feeling of acute discomfort when the open staring eye of the sun overheated him and spoiled the snow he wished to ski on. But it is also a crafty symbolic statement which can later be brought to bear on the unspoken shame of the peasant, who could not get away from the open staring eye of the "natural" people who in a sense brought him to judgment. Like "Alpine Idyll," many of the stories deserve to be read with as much awareness, and as closely, as one would read a good modern poem.

The consideration of "Alpine Idyll" makes another point relevant: the frequent implication that Hemingway is a sportswriter. In some of the hop-skip-and-jump critiques of Hemingway, the reader is likely to find "Alpine Idyll" classified as a skiing story. But to say that Hemingway sometimes deals with sports like horse-racing, boxing, bullfighting, fishing, and skiing really tells very little even about the "sports-stories." None of them is primarily "about" a sport; and only ten of the first forty-five make special or incidental use of any sport at all. The point of "Cross-Country Snow," which opens with a breathlessly described skiing episode, is something quite different from the statement that skiing is fun. The true function of the opening is to summarize, dramatize, and establish firmly a phase of masculine living (men-without-women) which is being justly challenged by another phase of living—and in such a way that a state of tension is set up between the two. When a choice is compelled, Nick Adams, one of the skiers, readily accepts the second phase. Similarly, although one might classify "Out of

Season" as a fishing story, the point of the story is that nothing (including fishing) is done. The strength of the story is the portrayal of the officious guide Peduzzi, a fine characterization. He serves to focus sharply the "out-of-season" theme, which relates both to the young man's relations with his wife Tiny, and to the proposal (by Peduzzi) that the young man fish out of season in evasion of the local game laws.

If one turns from these to the two long stories, "Fifty Grand" and "The Undefeated," both of which devote considerable space to the close descriptions of athletic events, it might be argued that here, anyhow, Hemingway's real interest is in the athletic events.[6] Not so. His interest is in the athletes, and not so much because they are athletes as because they are people. The two stories may be seen as complementary studies in superannuation. Jack Brennan, the aging welterweight fighting his last fight in Madison Square Garden, is a rough American equivalent to the veteran Manolo Garcia, meeting his last bull under the arclights of the bullring in Madrid.

Both men show, in crucial situations, the courage which has sustained them through their earlier careers. Both are finished. Jack earns his fifty thousand both by standing up under the intentional low blow of his opponent and by thinking fast enough under conditions of extreme pain to return the low blow, lose the fight, and win the money he has bet on his opponent. Manolo earns the right to keep his *coleta*, the badge of the professional matador, by a courage that is much greater than his aging skill, or, for that matter, his luck. The stories are as different in conception and execution as the Spanish temperament is from the Irish-American, or the bullfight from the prizefight. The sign at the center of the Brennan story is a certified check for fifty thousand dollars; a bullfighter's pigtail is the sign at the center of the other. One could almost believe that the stories were meant to point up some kind of international contrast.

Yet the atmosphere in which both stories transpire is one of admirable courage. The aging athletes Brennan and Garcia stand in marked opposition to another pair who are united by their too early acceptance of defeat. These are the half-symbolic Ole Andreson, the intended victim of Al and Max in "The Killers"—the only real classic to emerge from the American gang wars of the prohibition era except W. R. Burnett's *Little Caesar*—and the half-symbolic figure of William Campbell, the man under the half-symbolic sheet in the story half-symbolically called "A Pursuit Race."

"Half-symbolic" is an awkward term. What makes it necessary in talking about stories like "A Pursuit Race" and "The Killers" is that both Andreson and Campbell are real enough to be accepted in non-symbolic terms. They are dressed in the sharp vocabulary of the naturalistic writer. We are given (almost coldly) the place, the facts, the scene, out of which grows, however, an awful climate of hopelessness and despair. It is impossible to escape the conviction that the function of these two is to stand for something much larger than themselves—a whole, widespread human predicament, deep in the grain of human affairs—with Andreson and Campbell as the indexes.

The Chesterfield-coated killers, Al and Max, are likewise the indexes of a wider horror than their cheap and ugly hoodlumism could ever be in itself. Nowadays the generic term for that horror is fascism, and it may not be stretching a point to suggest that, with "The Killers," Hemingway solidly dramatized the point of view towards human life which makes fascism possible. If that is so, then the figures of Andreson and even Campbell take on a meaning wide as all the modern world. They are the victims, the men who have given up the fight for life and liberty. Nothing can rouse them any more.

Whatever it is that William Campbell seeks to escape by remaining in bed, the ultimate horror gets its most searching treatment in "A Clean Well-Lighted Place," a superb story and quite properly one of Hemingway's favorites. It shows once again that remarkable union of the naturalistic and the symbolic which is possibly his central triumph in the realm of practical esthetics. The "place" of the title is a Spanish café. Before the story is over; this place has come to stand as an image of light, cleanness, and order against the dark chaos of its counter-symbol in the story: the idea of *nada*, or nothingness. The *nada*-concept is located and pinned to the map by a kind of triangulation-process. The three elements consist in the respective relationships of an old waiter and a young waiter to an elderly man who sits drinking brandy every night in their clean, well-lighted café.

The old waiter and the young waiter are in opposition. They stand (by knowledge, temperament, experience, and insight) on either side of one of the great fences which exist in the world for the purpose of dividing sheep from goats. The young waiter would like to go home to bed, and is impatient with the old drinker of brandy. The old waiter, on the other hand, knows very well why the old patron comes often, gets drunk, stays late, and leaves only when he must. For the old waiter, like the old patron, belongs to the great brotherhood: all those "who like to stay late at the café . . . all those who do not want to go to bed . . . all those who need a light for the night." He is reluctant to see his own café close—both because he can sympathize with all the benighted brethren, and for the very personal reason that he, too, needs the cleanness, the light, and the order of the place as an insulation against the dark.

The unspoken brotherly relationship between the old waiter and the old patron is dramatized in the opening dialogue, where the two waiters discuss the drinker of brandy as he sits quietly at one of the tables. The key notion here is that the young and rather stupid waiter has not the slightest conception of the special significance which the old waiter attaches to his young confrere's careless and unspecialized use of the word *nothing*.

Young Waiter:	Last week he tried to commit suicide.
Old Waiter:	Why?
Young Waiter:	He was in despair.
Old Waiter:	What about?
Young Waiter:	Nothing.
Old Waiter:	How do you know it was nothing?
Young Waiter:	He has plenty of money.

They are speaking in Spanish. For the old waiter, the word *nothing* (or *nada*) contains huge actuality. The great skill displayed in the story is the development, through the most carefully controlled understatement, of the young waiter's mere *nothing* into the old waiter's Something—a Something called Nothing which is so huge, terrible, overbearing, inevitable, and omnipresent that, once experienced, it can never be forgotten. Sometimes in the day, or for a time at night in a clean, well-lighted place, it can be held temporarily at bay. What links the old waiter and the old patron most profoundly is their brotherhood in arms against this beast in the jungle.

Several other stories among the first forty-five—perhaps most notably the one called "A Way You'll Never Be"—engage the *nada*-concept. And whoever tries the experiment of reading "Big Two-Hearted River" immediately after "A Clean Well-Lighted Place" may discover, perhaps to his astonishment, that the *nada*-concept really serves as a frame for what is ostensibly one of Hemingway's happiest stories.

If we read the river-story singly, looking merely at what it says, there is probably no more effective account of euphoria in the language, even when one takes comparative account of *The Compleat Angler*, Hazlitt on the pleasures of hiking, Keats on the autumn harvest, Thoreau on the Merrimack, Belloc on "The Mowing of a Field," or Frost on "Hyla Brook." It tells with great simplicity of a lone fisherman's expedition after trout. He gets a sandwich and coffee in the railway station at St. Ignace, Michigan, and then rides the train northwest to the town of Seney, which has been destroyed by fire. From there he hikes under a heavy pack over the burned ground until he reaches a rolling pine plain. After a nap in a grove of trees, he moves on to his campsite near the Two-Hearted River. There he makes camp, eats, and sleeps. Finally, as sum and crown of the expedition, there is the detailed story of a morning's fishing downstream from the camp. At the surface of the story one finds an absolute and very satisfying reportorial accuracy. The journey can even be followed on a survey-map.

During one of the colloquies of Dean Gauss, Fitzgerald, and Hemingway in the summer of 1925, "Big Two-Hearted River" came up for consideration. Both of Hemingway's friends had read it in the spring number of Ernest Walsh's little magazine, *This Quarter.* Half in fun, half in seriousness, they now accused him of "having written a story in which nothing happened," with the result that it was "lacking in human interest." Hemingway, Dean Gauss continues, "countered by insisting that we were just ordinary book reviewers and hadn't even taken the trouble to find out what he had been trying to do." This anecdote is a typical instance of the unfortunately widespread assumption that Hemingway's hand can be read at a glance. Dean Gauss remarks that his own return to the story was profitable. There was much more there than had first met his eye.[7]

For here, as elsewhere in Hemingway, something is going on down under. One might echo Hamlet's words to the ghost of his father: "Well said, old mole, canst work i' the earth so fast?"—and with just Hamlet's mixture of admiration and excitement. Malcolm Cowley, one of the few genuinely sympathetic critics of Hemingway, has suggested that "the whole fishing expedition . . . might be regarded as an incantation, a spell to banish evil spirits."[8] The story is full of rituals. There is, for example, the long hike across the country—a ritual of endurance, for Nick does not stop to eat until he has made camp and can feel that he has earned the right to supper. There is the ritual of home-making, the raising-up of a wall against the dark; the ritual of food-preparation and thoughtful, grateful eating; of bedmaking and deep untroubled sleep. Next morning comes the ritual of bait-catching, intelligently done and timed rightly before the sun has warmed and dried the grasshoppers. When Nick threads one on his hook, the grasshopper holds the hook with his front feet and spits tobacco-juice on it—as if for fisherman's luck. "The grasshopper," as Cowley says, "is playing its own part in a ritual." The whole of the fishing is conducted according to the ritualistic codes of fair play. When Nick catches a trout too small to keep, he carefully wets his hands before touching the fish so as not to disturb the mucous coating on the scales and thus destroy the fish he is trying to save. Down under, in short, the close reader finds a carefully determined order of virtue and simplicity which goes far towards explaining from below the oddly satisfying effect of the surface story.

Still, there is more to the symbolism of the story than a ritual of self-disciplined moral conduct. Two very carefully prepared atmospheric symbols begin and end the account. One is the burned ground near the town of Seney. The other is the swamp which lies farther down the Big Two-Hearted River than Nick yet wishes to go. Both are somehow sinister. One probably legitimate guess on the background of the first is that Nick, who is said to have been away for a long time, is in fact a returned war veteran, going fishing both for fun and for therapeutic purposes. In some special way, the destroyed town of Seney and the scorched earth around it carry the hint of war—the area of destruction Nick must pass through in order to reach the high rolling pine plain where the exorcism is to take place. In much the same way, the swamp symbolizes an area of the sinister which Nick wishes to avoid, at least for the time being.

The pine plain, the quiet grove where he naps, the security of the camp, the pleasures of the open river are, all together, Nick's "clean, well-lighted place." In the afternoon grove, carefully described as an "island" of pine trees, Nick does not have to turn on any light or exert any vigilance while he peacefully slumbers. The same kind of feeling returns that night at the camp after he has rigged his shelter-half and crawled inside. "It smelled pleasantly of canvas. Already there was something mysterious and home-like. . . . He was settled: Nothing could touch him. . . . He was there, in the good place. He was in his home where he had made it." Back in the low country around Seney, even the grasshoppers had turned dark from living in the burned-over ground. Up ahead in the swamp "the big cedars came together overhead, the sun did not come through, except in patches; in the fast deep water, in the half light, the fishing would be tragic. . . . Nick did not want it." For now, on his island between sinister and sinister, Nick wants to keep his fishing tender and if possible comic.

II. The Education of Nicholas Adams

"Big Two-Hearted River" was based on an expedition which Hemingway once made to Michigan's northern peninsula. His determination to write only those aspects of experience with which he was personally acquainted gave a number of the first forty-five stories the flavor of fictionalized personal history. He was always prepared to invent people and circumstances, to choose backgrounds which would throw his people into three-dimensional relief, and to employ as symbols those elements of the physical setting which could be psychologically justified by the time and place he was writing about. But during the decade when the first forty-five stories were written, he was unwilling to stray very far from the life he knew by direct personal contact, or to do any more guessing than was absolutely necessary.

The recurrent figure of Nicholas Adams is not of course Hemingway, though the places Nick goes and the events he watches are ordinarily places Hemingway had visited or events about which he had heard on good authority and could assimilate to his own experience of comparable ones. Future biographers will have to proceed warily to separate autobiographical elements from the nexus of invented circumstances in which they may be lodged. For present purposes it is enough to notice that well over half of the first forty-five stories center on Nick Adams, or other young men who could easily be mistaken for him.

They might be arranged under some such title as "The Education of Nicholas Adams." It could even be said that when placed end to end they do for the twentieth century roughly what Henry Adams did for the nineteenth, though with obvious differences in formality of approach. The education of Henry Adams in Boston, Quincy, Berlin, London, and Washington presented an informative contrast with the education of Nicholas Adams in Chicago, northern Michigan, Italy, and Switzerland. Nick's life in the twentieth century was on the whole considerably more spectacular than Henry's in the nineteenth; it was franker, less polite, less diplomatic. Chicago, where Nick was born just before the turn of the century, was a rougher climate than Henry's mid-Victorian Boston, just as Nick's Ojibway Indians were far more primitive than Henry's Boston Irish. Partly because of the times he lived in and partly, no doubt, because he was of a more adventurous temperament, Nick came more easily on examples of barbarism than Henry was to know until his visit to the South Seas. In place of the Great Exposition of 1900 which so stimulated Henry's imagination, Nick was involved in the World's Fair of 1914-1918. But in retrospect one parallelism stood out momentously: both Henry and Nicholas had occasion to marvel bitterly at how badly their respective worlds were governed.

Nick's father, Dr. Henry Adams, played a notable part in Nick's early education. He was a busy and kindly physician whose chief avocations were hunting and fishing. There was opportunity for both in the Michigan wood and lake country where the Adams family regularly summered. Mrs. Adams was a Christian Scientist; her temperament was as artistic as that of her husband was scientific. After the death of Nick's grandfather she designed a new house for the family. But Nick was his father's son, loving his father "very much and for a long time." From the son's fictional reminiscences a memorable portrait of Dr. Henry Adams is made to emerge. He was a large-framed man with a full dark beard, a hawklike nose, striking deepset eyes, and an almost telescopic power of far-sightedness. Though they gradually grew apart, they were the best of companions during Nick's boyhood. In middle life Dr. Adams died by his own hand for reasons that Nick sorrowfully hints at but does not reveal.

Ten of the stories record Nick's growing-up. He recalls the move from one house to another and the accidental burning of Dr. Adams's collection of Indian arrowheads and preserved snakes. One Fourth of July, he remembers (and it is one of the century's best stories of the growing-up of puppy love) there was a ride in a neighbor's wagon back from town past nine drunken Indians, while bad news of his girl, Indian number ten in the story called "Ten Indians," was relayed to him by his father on his return home. Nick had already had his adolescent sex-initiation with the same girl, a half-breed named Trudy. He watched a very humiliating argument between his father and a crew of sawyers, and a terrifying Caesarean birth and suicide (addition and subtraction simultaneously achieved) at the Indian settlement. Nick's best friend in Michigan was a boy named Bill who could talk baseball, fishing, and reading with equal ease. Both in Michigan and in Illinois Nick encountered the underworld. It was part of his informal education to be manhandled by two gangsters in a Chicago lunchroom, and to share supper with two tramps, one of them a dangerously punch-drunk ex-prizefighter, in the woods near Mancelona, Michigan.

Like Hemingway, Nick Adams went to war. The earliest glimpses of his career as soldier come in the sixth and seventh miniatures of *In Our Time*. One shows Nick fiercely praying while Austrian artillery pounds the Italian trenches near Fossalta di Piave. In the other, he has been hit in the spine by an Austrian bullet and is leaning back with paralyzed legs against the wall of an Italian church. "Now I Lay Me," one of the longer stories, shows Nick as twice-wounded Tenente Adams, troubled by insomnia and talking out the night with his Italian orderly, a fellow-Chicagoan. "In Another Country" does not name its narrator, but it could well be the same young Tenente in conversation with an Italian major, a fellow-patient in the base hospital at Milan. In "A Way You'll Never Be," Nick is reporting back to battalion headquarters in American uniform. Though he is still recuperating from a severe wound and battle-shock, he is supposed to help build morale among Italian troops by means of the uniform. It is meant as a sign that the A. E. F. will shortly come to their support.

There are no Nick Adams stories of the homecoming, the process which Henry Adams found so instructive after his service abroad. The fate of the male character in "A Very Short Story" might, however, be thought of as one episode in the postwar adventures of Nick Adams. In a base-hospital at Padua, he falls in love with a nurse named Luz—an idea much expanded and altered in *A Farewell to Arms*. But when the young man returns to Chicago to get a good job so that he can marry

Luz, he soon receives a letter saying that she has fallen in love with a major in the Arditi. The protagonist in "Soldier's Home" is called Harold Krebs, and he is a native of Oklahoma rather than Illinois. But once again the story might have had Nick Adams as its central character. Like Nick's mother, Mrs. Krebs is a sentimental woman who shows an indisposition to face reality and is unable to understand what has happened to her boy in the war.

Nick Adams returned to Europe not long after the armistice. "Cross-Country Snow" reveals that he is married to a girl named Helen who is expecting a baby. "Out of Season" and "Alpine Idyll" could easily be associated with Nick's life on the continent, while the very moving "Fathers and Sons," which stands as the concluding story in Hemingway's collected short fiction, shows Nick on one of his return trips to the United States, driving his own son through familiar country and thinking back to the life and the too early death of the boy's grandfather, Dr. Henry Adams.

The story of Nick's education, so far as we have it, differs in no essential way from that of almost any middle-class American male who started life at the beginning of the present century or even with the generation of 1920. After the comparatively happy boyhood and the experimental adolescence, the young males went off to war; and after the war, in a time of parlous peace, they set out to marry and build themselves families and get their work done. The story of Adams is a presented vision of our time. There is every reason why it should arouse in us, to use the phrase of Conrad, "that feeling of unavoidable solidarity" which "binds men to each other and all mankind to the visible world."

Future biographers, able to examine the Nick Adams stories against the full and detailed background of Hemingway's life from his birth on July 21, 1899, until, say, his thirty-first birthday in 1930, should uncover some valuable data on the methods by which he refashioned reality into the shape of a short story. What they may fail to see—and what a contemporary evaluator is justified in pointing out—is that Hemingway's aim in the Nick Adams stories is always the aim of an artist. He is deeply interested in the communication of an effect, or several effects together, in such a way as to evoke the deep response of shared human experience. To record for posterity another chapter in his own fictional autobiography does not interest him at all.

III. Many Circles

"Really, universally, relations stop nowhere," said Henry James in one of his prefaces, "and the exquisite problem of the artist is externally but to draw, by a geometry of his own, the circle within which they shall happily *appear* to do so."[9] The first forty-five stories of Hemingway draw many such circles—concentric, tangential, or overlapping—in which to contain the great variety of human relations which interest him. Two of the circles, and they might be seen as tangential, are those called Home and Not-Home. Nick Adams is perfectly at home in his tent in the Michigan wilderness, but the institution that is supposed to be home for the returned veteran Krebs merely causes him acute discomfort. Bed is home to William Campbell. The sheet drawn up over his face is a protection against the Not-Home of the active world, though it is also, in movies and in morgues, the accepted ritualistic sign that the person underneath is dead. The clean, well-lighted café is much more home than his actual home to the old Spaniard who comes there nightly to stay until the place closes.

The Not-Home is another of the names of *nada*, which Carlyle once rhetorically defined as the vast circumambient realm of nothingness and night. It was perhaps never more sharply drawn than by Goya in the horrific etching which he calls "Nada." An arc of the *nada*-circle runs all the way through Hemingway's work from the night-fears of Jake Barnes to the "horrorous" of Philip Rawlings and the ingrowing remorse of Richard Cantwell. Malcolm Cowley has well described him as one of "the haunted and nocturnal writers," akin, in his deeper reaches, to Melville and Hawthorne.[10] Another way of defining *nada* might be to say, indeed, that it falls about midway between the "Black

Man" of Hawthorne and the "White Whale" of Melville. In the first forty-five stories, this besieging horror of the limitless, the hallucinatory, the heartland of darkness, bulks like a Jungian Shadow behind the lives of many of the protagonists. Outside the circle which Hemingway has drawn by the special magic of his geometry, man's relations to the shadow stop nowhere.

But the Home-circle has another alternate than that of *nada*. This is the idea of male companionship, rough and friendly camaraderie, an informal brotherhood with by-laws which are not written down but are perfectly understood and rigidly adhered to by the contracting parties. Hemingway summed up the matter in his title *Men Without Women*. For woman, closely associated with the Home-symbol, stands in opposition, perhaps even in a kind of enmity, to that wholly happy and normal condition which two men, hiking or drinking or talking together, can build like a world of their own. One sees this world in the Burguete of Jake Barnes and Bill Gorton, in the Gorizia of Lieutenant Henry and Doctor Rinaldi, in the Guadarrama hide-out of Robert Jordan and Anselmo, and in the Gritti Palace Hotel dining-room where Colonel Cantwell and the Gran Maestro (with their unspoken loyalties, their completely shared ethical code, and their rough and friendly badinage) discuss together the latest affairs of *El Ordine Militar, Nobile y Espirituoso de los Caballeros de Brusadelli*.

"Dramatize it, dramatize it," cried Henry James. "Then, and not sooner, would one see."[11] The most direct dramatization of the men-without-women theme occurs in "Cross-Country Snow." Here Nick Adams and his friend George, between whom there is something of a father-and-son relationship, are skiing near Montreux. When they stop for wine at the inn, the obvious pregnancy of their waitress reminds George that Nick's wife Helen is expecting a child. Both men know that the birth of the child will certainly interrupt and probably destroy their comradeship. "Maybe we'll never go skiing again," says George. "We've got to," Nick answers. "It isn't worth while if you can't." George wishes, boy-like, that they could make some kind of promise about it. "There isn't any good in promising," says young Nick Adams. "It's hell, isn't it?" says George. "No, not exactly," says Nick.

Nick and George are as free and happy as Jake and Bill at Burguete. On the other side, for Nick, is all that involvement with woman, all the approaching domestication, all that half-ruefully, uncomplainingly accepted responsibility which will arrive at the moment Nick's fatherhood begins. It is not exactly hell. That is the province of *nada*. Nick recognizes, without complaint, that domestic responsibility presents a powerful case. It could, conceivably, cancel out those things in his life that are symbolized by the skiing with a good companion. And really, universally, the opposed relations of Men-without-women and Men-with-women stop nowhere. The conversational episode in the inn near Montreux is simply the little circle in which they *appear* to do so.

Closely related to the Men-without-women theme is that of fathers and sons. In the early Nick Adams stories Nick is seen as the son of a father; in the latest, he is the father of a son. Some half-dozen of the first forty-five stories draw circles around the father-son relationship. It is movingly dramatized, for example, through Nick's sympathy with his father's shame and anger after the encounter with the sawyers, in which Dr. Adams has been insultingly bested. The following conversation closes "The Doctor and the Doctor's Wife":

> "Your mother wants you to come and see her," the doctor said.
> "I want to go with you," Nick said.
> "All right. Come on, then," his father said. . . .
> "I know where there's black squirrels, Daddy," Nick said.
> "All right," said his father. "Let's go there."

At the other end of the line there is Nick's unspoken sympathy for his own son "Schatz" in the little story called "A Day's Wait." Not knowing the difference between Fahrenheit and centigrade thermometers, the boy (who had gone to school in France) naturally supposes that with a temperature of 102 degrees he will certainly die. It was common talk among his French schoolmates that you could not live with a temperature of 44 degrees, normal being 37 degrees. During the day's wait, he manages to keep a firm and stoical grip on himself. When he learns the truth, which is also the time when Nick first understands what is troubling the boy, the hold gradually relaxes. "The next day," says Nick, with a laconic quality that nearly conceals his own emotion, the boy's hold on himself "was very slack and he cried very easily at little things that were of no importance."

A third aspect of the father-and-son theme is the inevitable and paradoxical gulf between generations. It shows very clearly in the early story, "My Old Man," with its contrast between Joe's adoring innocence and his father's vicious world of thrown horse-races. But the paradox of togetherness and separateness is nowhere more poignantly dramatized than in the Nick Adams story called "Fathers and Sons." One great skill of the story is its compression of the generations of men, until the whole Adams clan of grandfather, father, son, and son's son are seen in a line, each visible over his son's shoulder. Each father is near his son, each son near his father. Yet between each generation comes the wall which neither side can fully cross—or would want to if it were possible.

IV. Many Marriages

Paradox is also at work in what may be called Hemingway's "marriage-group," that very considerable number of the first forty-five stories where the subject is some form of male-female relationship. Like Chaucer or Shakespeare or Keats or Browning, he watches with fascination the odd wave-like operation of attraction and repulsion between the two sexes. In his poems "Meeting at Night" and "Parting at Morning," Browning dramatizes the magnetic attraction of a tryst, and the "need for a world of men" which afterwards draws the lover away as rapidly as he came. Hemingway's stories often engage this paradox.

The women in Hemingway nearly always fail to understand fully the strength and extent of the attraction-repulsion phenomenon. Often, however, they are compelled—and it is on the whole an unhappy experience for them—to recognize its existence. One example will serve. "Up in Michigan," the earliest story in the collection, written in Paris in December, 1921, is one of the very few which Hemingway chooses to tell from the woman's point of view. Here a fine, neat country girl named Liz Coates worships a fine handsome blacksmith named Jim Gilmore from a respectful distance. One foggy evening, after a hunting trip, a good dinner, some whiskey, and exposure to the heat of an open fire, Jim rudely, painfully, and crudely seduces Liz, on a cold boat-dock. Afterwards, being unable to talk to or even to wake her importunate lover, Liz covers him with her coat and walks home. This story is the first in a long line of similar instances where male virility, though often rough and wayward in its manifestations, seems to be the axis on which the world of womankind revolves.

"Cat in the Rain," another story taken in part from the woman's point of view, presents a corner of the female world in which the male is only tangentially involved. It was written at Rapallo in May, 1923. From the window of a hotel room where her husband is reading and she is fidgeting, a young wife sees a cat outside in the rain. When she goes to get it, the animal (which somehow stands in her mind for comfortable bourgeois domesticity) has disappeared. This fact is very close to tragic because of the cat's association in her mind with many other things she longs for: long hair that she can do in a knot at the back of her neck; a candle-lighted dining-table where her own silver gleams; the season of spring and nice weather; and, of course, some new clothes. But when she puts these wishes into words, her husband mildly advises her to shut up and find something to read. "Anyway," says the young wife, "I want a cat. I want a cat. I want a cat now. If I can't have long hair or any fun, I can have a cat." The poor girl is the referee in a face-off between the actual and the possible. The actual is made of rain, boredom, a preoccupied husband, and irrational yearnings. The possible is made of silver, spring, fun, a new coiffure, and new dresses. Between actual and possible stands the cat. It is finally sent up to her by the kindly old inn-keeper, whose sympathetic deference is greater than that of the young husband.

In "The Kreutzer Sonata," Tolstoi presents an extreme example of the mild schizophrenia where a desired involvement and a desired freedom co-exist in the mind of the male. Two of Hemingway's stories approach the same problem in a comic spirit. In "The End of Something," Nick bluntly concludes his serious love affair with Marjorie, evidently by previous agreement with his friend Bill. In "The Three-Day Blow," while the wind of autumn rises in background accompaniment, Nick and Bill converse on the mature wisdom they showed in having stopped the love affair before it went too far. Despite this wisdom, Nick cannot help feeling uncomfortable about the finality of the termination. Thus when Bill rather cynically guesses that it might not be so final after all, Nick is wonderfully relieved. He can always go into town where Marjorie lives on the coming Saturday night. It is "a good thing to have in reserve."

Despite the need for detachment after involvement, Hemingway's work always stresses the essential normality and rightness of the male-female relationship.[12] Anything which distorts it, anything which brings it to an unhappy conclusion, is basically a kind of tragedy. In 1918, for example, there was a major in a Milan hospital whose wounded right hand had shrunk until it was no bigger than a baby's. Before the war he had been the best fencer in Italy. He was now using an exercise machine which was supposed to strengthen and enlarge the withered hand. Beside him at these sessions was a young American, taking similar treatments for a wounded leg, but more hopeful of its restoration. One day the major asked the American if he were married, and the American replied that he would like to be.

"The more of a fool you are," the major said. He seemed very angry. "A man must not marry."

"Why, Signor Maggiore?"

"Don't call me 'Signor Maggiore.'"

"Why must not a man marry?"

"He cannot marry. He cannot marry," he said angrily. "If he is to lose everything, he should not place himself in a position to lose that. He should not place himself in a position to lose. He should find things he cannot lose."

The major's wife had just died of pneumonia. Death is the absolute distortion, the unequivocal conclusion. The story, and there is much more to it, is called "In Another Country." The country is Italy; but it is also another country still, a country (it is just possible) where a man can find things he cannot lose.

Divorce or separation is a form of death in Hemingway's marriage-group. In the ironic story called "A Canary for One," the narrative turns upon a point of information not revealed until the final sentence: "We were returning to Paris to set up separate residences." Hemingway's strategy here is to establish through dialogue a parallel between the about-to-separate husband and wife and an enforced separation about which they hear on the train-ride between Cannes and the Gare de Lyon in Paris. They share a compartment with a deaf American lady who is taking home to her daughter a canary which she has picked up during a Cook's Tour. The lady's conviction that "American men make the best husbands" embroils the reader in a double irony. Two years before, she has broken up a match between her daughter and a Swiss engineering student on the grounds that "I couldn't have her marrying a foreigner." The daughter's reaction has not been favorable. "She doesn't seem to take an interest in anything. She doesn't care about things." The canary is a consolation prize, a substitute interest which will obviously fail. But the lady will not give up her belief that Americans make the best husbands, even though she is in the same compartment with an American couple whose marriage has failed.

The canary (if the lady would face it) and the couple (if the lady knew about them) might together penetrate the lady's rock-ribbed assurance that she is in the right. Both the married people must henceforth content themselves with those forlorn substitutes for each other of which, in another domestic situation, the canary is the epitome. But the lady's deafness is itself a symbol of her impenetrability to suggestion; and she will never know how much the canary will mean to the about-to-separate American couple as a symbol of distortion.

Other stories explore the predicament of divorce. Mr. Johnson, a writer waiting for his train in the station café at Vevey, desperately supposes that he can blunt the edge of the shame he feels by talking over his imminent divorce with three dignified Swiss porters. Though he buys them wine, and curiously raises what for him is the central question, he is met by that sympathetic but somewhat enigmatic politeness which was to be expected.

"You say you have never been divorced?"

"No," says one porter. "It would be too expensive. Besides, I have never married."

"Ah," says Johnson. "And these other gentlemen?"

"They are married."

"You like the married state?" says Johnson to one of them.

"Oui. C'est normal."

"Exactly," says Johnson. "Et vous, monsieur?"

"Ça va," says the third porter.

"Pour moi," says Johnson, "ça ne va pas."

Seeing then, after a futile attempt to change the subject, that his bull-blundering investigation has come to nothing, Johnson excuses himself and goes outside. "It had only made him feel nasty"—because he has possibly embarrassed the porters while certainly embarrassing himself, but mainly because he has recognized, with more shame and discomfort than ever, the normality of the married state, the "abnormality" of his own, and, finally and acutely, that whole nexus of half-humorous shrugging acceptance which is summed up in the second porter's "Ça va." Pour Monsieur Johnson, ça ne va pas.

If the healthy, married state, or its approximate equivalent, is strongly recommended in these stories as the normal situation for men and women, one finds also the occasional recognition of other forms of abnormality than divorce. There is, for example, the extreme travesty of the relationship between "Mr. and Mrs. Elliot," who at last settle into an old-maid marriage, all calm and acceptable superficially, all in jagged remnants underneath. Another story, "The Sea Change," examines at its crux the problem of an otherwise satisfactory liaison. The girl faces the pull of an unnatural attraction, and the lover sees that he has no choice but to let her go. Except for one pronoun, and a noun which the girl rejects as too ugly to apply to her own situation, the story might be that of an ordinary lovers' triangle, with the girl leaving one man for another. The pronoun appears in the man's fierce threat towards the third corner of the triangle: "I'll kill her," he cries.

V. Many Must Have It

To say that Hemingway is preoccupied with such subjects would be wrong. His preoccupation is rather with the healthy norm of ordinary sexual behavior. He merely sees that the normality of the norm is sometimes most effectively measured in terms of departures from it. Furthermore, a writer dedicated, like Hemingway, to the rendering of things as they are soon recognizes that departures from the usual are numerous enough to make ignoring them a fault of seeing. His personal views, which can be determined inductively, seem to range from the artist's simple acceptance of the fact that abnormality exists up to an outright scorn full of moral echoes of disgust and disapproval, or over into an amused raillery at the expense of the afflicted. Somewhere near the area of simple acceptance would be the story called "A Simple Enquiry," in which an Italian major asks his youthful orderly certain guarded but leading questions. These are familiar enough in an amusing way to all who have ever been through the stock interview with the army psychiatrist at an induction center. Before this particular interview is over, the reader is aware that the major's interests are not, on the whole, scientific.

Among the humorous stories is one called "The Light of the World." Hemingway included it among the six or seven which he liked best, though he said that "nobody else ever liked" it.[13] One need not like the substance of the story, or the people, or the language. But even with these reservations, one can still enjoy the story's triumph, which is that it adds up to a very complicated defense of the normal against the abnormal. The scene is a provincial railroad depot in northern Michigan at an autumn nightfall. Two tough youngsters, coming in, find themselves in the midst of ten men and five women. The group conversation, conducted in roaring comic terms, establishes the homosexuality of one of the men to serve as contrast to the loudmouthed lying sentimentality of one of the five prostitutes. She says that she was once the true love of Steve Ketchel, a prizefighter. Her forthright contradictor, an even fatter professional tart named Alice, stands (at least in context) for the normal, the honest, and the sound. The raucous play of human emotion, bald as a turkey-egg, loud as a brawl, sets up an effective contrast to the furtive yearnings of the homosexual cook. In an odd way, and not without some strain on the moral judgment, the huge Alice in her iridescent silk dress comes to be the true heroine of the comedy. Love may be, as the sentimental blonde asserts, the light of the world. But an even stronger light may be cast by the honest common sense of people like Alice, the Michigan Wife of Bath.

Hemingway's skills as a comic writer are probably not enough appreciated. "The Gambler, the Nun, and the Radio," for example, is a fine and subtle study, depending to a great degree on the humor of character, and setting up a memorable contrast among three levels of the apprehension of reality.[14] So is the portrait of the old French couple in "Wine of Wyoming." Here as elsewhere in the first forty-five stories, it is his championship of the normal and the natural which runs like a backbone down through the substance of the tales he elects to tell.[15]

His devotion to the honest and the actual is a moral decision which also happens to coincide with his esthetic views.

The record, if it is examined justly and with detachment, simply does not bear out the frequent critical implication that he invokes the spectacular or leans on the unusual to carry the burden of his stories. If "Hills Like White Elephants" throws light into the nether regions of selfish human abnormality—which is one way of looking at the matter of abortion—one can balance it with such insights into the normal married state as "Cat in the Rain." The raving sentimentality of the peroxide blonde in "The Light of the World" is neatly deflated by the solid honesty of Alice, who has long since left (if she was ever inside) her friend's cheap and banal wonderland. Even the nightly excursions of the old Spanish waiter into that vast *nada* which lies outside the normal world of everyday affairs are wrenched back by a final twist into the realm of the recognizable. "After all," he says to himself, "it is probably only insomnia. Many must have it." The world of Hemingway's short stories is above all the world we know. Many of us have it—or at least enough of it so that we easily recognize its outlines in his pages.

His oddly continuing reputation as an "archpriest of violence" really finds little support in the first forty-five stories. The overwhelming majority are extremely non-athletic. Their points are carried by talk far more often than by action. Outwardly, at least, nothing much happens, even though several kinds of burning emotion are implied and at intervals may erupt into the briefest violence of language. Otherwise there is seldom more movement than such as is necessary to raise a glass to the lips, row a boat across an inlet, cast a fly into a troutstream, or ski down a snowy slope into the true center of a story.

At café tables, in quiet rooms, or in the compartments of trains, men and women talk together with a concentrated diffidence which almost conceals the intensity of their feelings. Upon examination, it turns out to be this very intensity, this intensity very close to the intensity of poetry, which has deceived some of his critics into supposing that Hemingway is an exponent of violence for its own sake. Even in the relatively rare athletic stories, this is never so. He is after intensity, and his brand of intensity is to be achieved not by physical exercise but only through the exercise of the utmost restraint.[16]

From *Hemingway: The Writer as Artist* (Princeton, NJ: Princeton University Press, 1980): 117-142. Copyright ©1980 Princeton University Press. Reprinted by permission of Princeton University Press.

Notes

1. *The Fifth Column and the First Forty-nine Stories*, New York, 1938, p. 369.
2. *A Farewell to Arms*, New York, 1948, p. 77.
3. *Death in the Afternoon*, New York, 1932, p. 191.
4. Henry James, *Works*, New York edition, Vol. 1, preface, p. vi.
5. For titles and publication dates of these short stories, see bibliography. "The Man with the Tyrolese Hat" is actually an extract from *Green Hills of Africa* about the Austrian trader Kandisky.
6. Hemingway grouped these two stories with "My Old Man" as belonging to another category than stories like "Out of Season." These three were "the kind that are easy for me to write." His own preferences among the early stories were for "Big Two-Hearted River," "Indian Camp," "Soldier's Home," and the first and last paragraphs of "Out of Season." Ernest Hemingway to F. Scott Fitzgerald, from the Vorarlberg, *ca.* 12/20/25.
7. Christian Gauss to Carlos Baker, 12/26/50.
8. Malcolm Cowley, introd., *The Portable Hemingway*, New York, 1944, p. xix.
9. James, *Works*, New York edition, Vol. 1, p. vii.
10. Cowley, *The Portable Hemingway*, introd., p. vii.
11. James, *Works*, New York edition, Vol. 17, p. xxvii.
12. A passage of dialogue between Hemingway and the Old Lady (*Death in the Afternoon*, 179-180) bears on this point. "Do you know any true stories about those unfortunate people?" says the Old Lady, meaning by unfortunate the sexually abnormal. "A few," answers Hemingway, "but in general they lack drama, as do all tales of abnormality, since no one can predict what will happen in the normal while all tales of the abnormal end much the same."

It might be added that Hemingway everywhere celebrates the normal values of sexual intercourse between a man and a woman who are in love. It is probable that he agrees with the opinion of Remy de Gourmont: "Il y aurait peut-être une certaine corrélation entre la copulation complète et profonde et le développement cérébral." See Ezra Pound's postscript to his translation of de Gourmont's *Natural Philosophy of Love*, published by Boni and Liveright, New York, 1922.

13. One of Hemingway's letters to Perkins suggests that this story has some points

in common with Maupassant's *La Maison Tellier.* Ernest Hemingway to Maxwell Perkins, 7/31/33.

14. This story evidently grew out of Hemingway's hospitalization in Billings, Montana, following an automobile accident in November 1930. The story was finished early in February 1933.

15. "Wine of Wyoming" is apparently related to Hemingway's sojourn in the Sheridan area during the summer of 1928. The story contains topical allusions to the presidential candidacy of Governor Alfred E. Smith.

16. The origin of the titles *Men Without Women* and *Winner Take Nothing* may be noted for the record. The first was evidently a twist on the title of a novel by Ford, *Women and Men.* Hemingway's title was given in turn a twist by Wyndham Lewis for his critical book, *Men Without Art.* Hemingway's jocular explanation of his choice of the title was that he hoped the book would have a big sale among graduates of Vassar and homosexuals. Ernest Hemingway to F. Scott Fitzgerald, *ca.* late September 1927. But he had already given Perkins a serious explanation: "In all of these [stories], almost, the softening feminine influence [is] absent," whether as a result of "training, discipline, death, or other causes." Ernest Hemingway to Maxwell Perkins, 2/14/27. Hemingway had decided on the *Winner Take Nothing* title by 6/11/33. The title derives from the epigraph of the book. This epigraph, ostensibly drawn from an antique book of rules for gaming, was actually written by Hemingway himself. Ernest Hemingway to Carlos Baker, 11/22/51.

The Personal Stories:
Paris and Provence, 1926-1927 _____

Hilary K. Justice

> . . . but when you come to be successful, when you commence to earn
> money, when you are really successful, then your family and everybody no
> longer treats you like a genius, they treat you like a man who has become
> successful.
>
> —Gertrude Stein, *Picasso*

> . . . for ye are like unto whited sepulchers, which indeed appear beautiful
> outward, but are within full of dead men's bones . . .
>
> —Matthew 23:27

Between April of 1924 and September of 1926, when Hemingway began work on the next pair of marriage tale-Nick Adams stories, he had finished the stories for the 1925 collection *In Our Time*, met F. Scott Fitzgerald, written *The Torrents of Spring* (the satire that would allow him to switch publishers from Boni & Liveright to Scribner's), and written and finished authorial emendation to *The Sun Also Rises*, his roman à clef about Pamplona and the "dangerous summer" of 1925. He had also met Pauline Pfeiffer, the woman who would become his second wife, and whose relationship with him (and with his first and last wives, Hadley and Mary) would provide the basis for one of *The Garden of Eden*'s interwoven plots. Between the early period and this later dark period, Hemingway's relationship to his writing changed. He began to embed subtle layers in his writing, layers that affected the stories' meanings but would be legible only to his circle of intimates.[1] The differences between writer and author, and the respective relationships of these roles to the texts, thus began to grow.

The Dark Period Stories (Fall 1926)

The fall of 1926 was Hemingway's darkest period to date. That August, Hadley and Ernest separated; she insisted that he and Pauline spend one hundred days apart before she would give Ernest the divorce he sought. During this dark period, Hemingway wrote another pair of stories in the marriage tale-Nick Adams sequence, "Now I Lay Me," which contains the infamous burning of Dr. Adams's collections, and "A Canary for One," in which a marital separation brings the earlier marriage tales to "the conclusion they had predicted" (Smith, *Guide* 161). These paired stories, like the earlier ones, seem unrelated. But in their composition, Hemingway began to clarify and compress the connections he perceived among intergenerational homosocial betrayal (father/son; son/father), honeymoons, pregnancy, and the destruction of homes by literal and metaphorical fire. This semiotic web would inform his next stories and, much later, combine with them to form the climax of *The Garden of Eden*: the scene in which Catherine burns the suitcase containing the manuscript of David's Nick Adams-like elephant story.

The writing of three sections of "A Canary for One" deserves close attention, as their genetic evolution contributes directly to the then-developing skeins of images, motifs, and anxieties that Hemingway rearticulated in his later related works. Two of these sections contribute literally to the recurring images: the view from the train of the burning farmhouse and the women's conversation about Vevey, where the separating couple spent their honeymoon. The third section, the discussion between the unnamed American woman (their *lit salon* companion) and the wife about the relative merits of marrying foreigners and American men, resonates biographically to an extent thus far unaddressed by critics and touches on the problems of being both private writer and public author, problems that were beginning to come to the fore for Hemingway.

The first of the three relevant compositional moments occurs near the beginning of "A Canary for One." The story begins with the characters on a train heading for Paris. From the train, the American husband sees the first of two houses that evoke, respectively, intact and then broken domesticity: "The train passed very quickly a long, red stone house with a garden and four thick palm-trees with tables under them in the shade" (258). The image of the peaceful, restful red stone house gives way to another view from the train: "As it was getting dark the train passed a farmhouse burning in a field. Motor-cars were stopped along the road and bedding and things from inside the farmhouse were spread in the field. Many people were watching the house burn" (258-59). In the first draft of this story, this section read as follows: "As it was getting dark the train passed a burning farmhouse in a field. Many people were watching it burn and motor cars were stopped along the road /.and/ and /b/ Bedding and furniture were /piled/ spread in the field" (KL/EH 307, 5; /deletions/).

Hemingway's changes during this section's genetic evolution result in a slight lessening of the impact of the image (to the extent that one can soften the impact of a burning house). In this first draft, these sentences comprised their own paragraph, set apart on the page from the rest of the text. Had this distinction remained in the published version, the structure would have immediately underscored the image's importance to the story. In the next draft, however, Hemingway merged this paragraph with the previous and subsequent ones (KL/EH 308, 2), thus granting the image an impressionist aspect it would not otherwise have standing alone. As published, the image is but one of many glimpsed from the *train rapide*. Embedded within a larger paragraph in the published version, this section does not lose any of its ultimate significance; rather, the extent of its significance is harder to detect in a first reading.

A second reading, which the text structurally requires (as I will discuss in a moment), heightens the affective impact of the burning farmhouse and clarifies its function within the story as a visual projection of the internal reality of the characters' disintegrated marriage. Further, in this section, the narrator's selective reporting of what he sees portrays, in fiction, Hemingway's own practice of "[displacing] emotional content onto the terrain" (Kennedy 109, 111).[2] As modified in the second draft (KL/EH 309, 2), the scene is subtly altered to emphasize the scene as spectacle. Hemingway emphasized the voyeuristic spectators by splitting the original sentence, "Many people were watching it burn [and] motor cars were stopped along the road" (KL/EH 308, 5) into two: "Motor-cars were stopped along the road and bedding and things were spread in the field. Many people were watching the house burn" (KL/EH 309, 2). The "motor-cars" and "many people" of this latter version linguistically surround the "bedding and things." The house's most intimate contents are thus "spread" for public consumption in what was, and still could be, a fertile field. The noun "bedding" connotes the related verb and invokes the iconographic marriage bed and the manner in which it was defiled (for Hemingway, if not overtly for his narrator).

The fire despoils this marriage bed, rendering it vulnerable to visual exploitation by the "many"; by publishing this story, Hemingway similarly courted the exposure of his private guilt and Hadley's private pain. His guilt over his adulterous relationship with Pauline, the biographical source for the burning house, is never overtly addressed in the story, although it appears encoded as the catastrophic flames. Although he may have been compelled to write the story for therapeutic reasons, by spreading the Hemingways' dirty linen in public, he courted exposure. Indeed, he almost begged for it, for although his readers in 1927 obviously did not have access to the biographical details that are now generally available, Hadley and Pauline did, as would his son John when he grew old enough to understand why his father left his mother. The greater a reader's familiarity with the particulars of Hemingway's life in August and September of 1926, the greater the significance of the flames that destroy the house in the story. Two readers in particular, Hadley and Pauline, would read these details in very specific ways.

In September of 1926, the month Hemingway wrote this story, Pauline left Paris for her parents' home in Piggott, Arkansas, to endure the period of separation imposed on the lovers by Hadley. While writing "A Canary for One," Hemingway did not know if Pauline would return from her exile. His impulse to write the story stemmed at least partially from guilt over the destruction of his marriage to Hadley, but also from the fear that his relationship with Pauline might be destroyed as well.[3] Pauline and her family were actively Catholic, and the balance between her own guilt over adultery and her love for Ernest was a delicate one. During the writing of "Canary," Hemingway thus not only felt guilty but also feared that he might have risked everything for nothing.

When he decided to publish the story with unseemly haste, he may have been hedging his bets; he later, in *A Moveable Feast*, said that he had had the misfortune to love both women (and he would immortalize this misfortune in *The Garden of Eden*, which would be set in this period). *Scribner's Magazine* accepted "A Canary for One" for publication on November 11, 1926, at most two months after it was written. Hemingway thus must have submitted it almost immediately upon completion (transatlantic mail was at that time shipped by boat). When *Scribner's* accepted the story, only his immediate social circle could have broken the story's private codes (his family in the States did not know yet what was happening in Paris, although they would when the story appeared in *Men Without Women* later in 1927 [Reynolds, *Chronology* 47 and 49]).[4] His decision to publish "A Canary for One" has been judged insensitive and cruel to Hadley and John, but only because modern readers know the end of his private story—that Pauline did marry him. At the time, not even Hemingway knew how the private story—the real story—would turn out.

His haste in publishing "A Canary for One" was, though, more cunning than insensitive (although insensitive in its cunning). Had events unfolded differently, if Pauline had chosen to end their relationship, the publication of the story would have served two purposes: to sting Pauline's conscience and to publicly tender Ernest's abjection before Hadley. The story appeared in *Scribner's* in April of 1927 (Hanneman 145). Had Pauline chosen not to marry him, she would thus have read, no doubt painfully, the published story when she otherwise would have been planning their May wedding. The private message it contained for Pauline was hidden—poorly, perhaps, but hidden—from all but a few. The private message it contained for Hadley, although quite different, was equally well hidden. Had his personal life resolved otherwise, what Pauline would have read with guilt for having condemned Ernest to a "wrecked" life would have been read by Hadley as a public testimonial of his regret for and sorrow at having ruined their marriage.

His fear of having possibly destroyed three adult lives manifests in a later image in the story, the three train cars "that had been in a wreck," "splintered open and the roofs sagged in" (261). Like the bedding and nonspecific "things" in the burning farmhouse image, much of the affective impact of the three wrecked cars stems from the opening up of what was once a closed system.[5] In the original draft, Hemingway described the three cars (it is tempting to name them Ernest, Hadley, and Pauline) as follows: "The train stopped at a switch. Outside ^the window^ were three cars that had been in a wreck. They were ^splintered and^ opened up as boats are /opened up/ cross-sectioned in a/n/ ^steamship^ advertisement /in a folder/ showing the different decks or as houses are opened up by a bombardment" (KL/EH 307, 13; /deletions/; ^insertions^).

Although this section was changed in subsequent drafts, Hemingway's fixation on the "opening up" and "advertisement" aspects of the wreck combines with the subtly increased emphasis on the public spectacle of the burning farmhouse to pinpoint a central anxiety in his domestic situation—the literal publication (the making public) of his intimate life. Indeed, when he wrote the story, he was living in a studio borrowed from Gerald Murphy, a central figure in American expatriate society.[6] He had also moved some of his and Hadley's belongings through the streets of the Left Bank in a borrowed wheelbarrow. The Hemingway scandal was, like the "bedding and things" from the burning house, strewn about in public, advertising his situation in a way inimical to his Victorian Oak Park upbringing.[7]

The third section of the story that bears closer analysis here is the conversation between the American lady and the narrator's wife concerning Vevey, Switzerland, as the site for romance and early love. This honeymoon reference places "A Canary for One" at the pivot point between the earlier marriage tales (1923-1924) and the honeymoon stories proper (1927). The American lady's daughter, to whom she is taking the canary of the title, fell in love in Vevey; the American lady, not wanting her daughter to marry a foreigner (despite his being from "a very good family" [261]), "took her away, of course" (260).

Vevey is probably the fictional representation of Schruns, Austria, where the newly married Ernest and Hadley spent a skiing holiday shortly after moving to Europe (although their honeymoon, strictly speaking, was spent at his family's cabin in Michigan), and where Pauline had vacationed with both of them at the beginning of that year (1926). The American lady says of her daughter and the Swiss man in the story's first draft, "They met skiing there in Vevey. They used to go skiing together and go on long walks together" (KL/EH 307, 12). These lines describe not only his first time in Schruns with Hadley but also the later trip with Hadley and Pauline.[8] Hemingway removed the skiing reference in the second draft (KL/EH 308, 5), possibly because Hadley would associate it too strongly with Pauline, and vice versa; reminding each of the other would have undercut his private objectives in publishing the story.

The first appearance of this honeymoon reference during the composition of "A Canary for One" occurs in an unusual place for a Hemingway draft: the verso of a page (page 12) in the handwritten first draft of the story. The use of the verso in Hemingway's early writings is exceedingly rare; he generally wrote his insertions, even long ones, between existing lines and would continue, if necessary, vertically into the margins. The insertion, which was to be included after the "skiing" line (also an insertion) on page 13, reads as follows:

"I know Vevey," said my wife. "We were there on our honeymoon."

"/How romantic that must have been,/ ^Were you really? That must have been lovely." said the American lady.

"It /is/ ^was a^ lovely ^place^," said my wife.

"Yes," said the American lady "Isn't it lovely." (KL/EH 307, 12v; /deletions/; ^insertions^)

The use of the verso for this insertion may indicate that the honeymoon idea occurred to Hemingway while rereading the first draft (as opposed to while rewriting it; he almost always made in-progress revisions, as I have said, on the recto sides). As such, the honeymoon reference in "Canary" stands as a strange kind of afterthought in Hemingway's compositional process. Although we cannot know for sure, it seems that Hemingway broke his usual composition habits and chose to re-read this story in between drafts, rather than while redrafting it (the absence of verso marks in the manuscripts of other stories may support this interpretation). The unusual lack of chronological and emotional distance between the story's related biographical event and the composition of its quasi-autobiographical text may account for Hemingway's unusual attention to it. A later draft was to receive even more unusual attention (as I will discuss momentarily).

Although in the published version, the honeymoon reference survives to underscore on all levels the emotional distance the couple has traveled since their honeymoon, the first draft of this story shifts abruptly from the painful memory of the honeymoon to the view of the wrecked train cars with the line "The train stopped at a switch." This switch is the fictionalized encoding of the switching of women, resulting in the three "wrecked" lives represented visually by the wrecked train cars, with their guts exposed to the most casual observer.

Hemingway toned down this psychologically obvious passage in the published version; however, the no less psychologically suggestive prattle of the American lady regarding her successful interposition between her daughter and the suitor survived excision. When he wrote the story, Hemingway doubtless already feared what would, in fact, happen: that Pauline's mother would put pressure on her daughter to extricate herself from the situation in order to save Hemingway's marriage and family (*SL* 220). His knowledge that the Pfeiffer family was socially prominent and reasonably affluent probably combined with Pauline's job with *Vogue* in Paris to produce the women's seemingly inane conversation in "Canary" about Paris fashion houses, *vendeuses*, and the adult daughter's measurements (of which "there was not much chance of their changing now" [260], ostensibly because she had stopped growing, but also because the sterility of her thwarted love affair would not, now, result in pregnancy). Hemingway's writing of this fictional conversation thus allowed him to imagine himself the thwarted lover in a conversation between Hadley and Mrs. Pfeiffer, replete with its ironic insistence that "American men make the best husbands" (stated twice, 260).

The biographical back story of "Canary," considered carefully, suggests the emergence of a new awareness of the problems of occupying multiple roles as writer and author. (This awareness was to become an overt preoccupation in *Death in the Afternoon*, a few years later; see chapter 4.) Although the American lady objects to her daughter's lover because he is a "foreigner," two factors indicate that, biographically, writer or author might be substituted without completely giving way to speculation and fantasy.

The first of these factors is Hemingway's knowledge of the circumstances surrounding the courtship of F. Scott and Zelda Fitzgerald, whom he had met in 1925. Zelda, the daughter of a wealthy and locally important Southern family, had refused to marry Scott until he could support her in style. *This Side of Paradise* launched him to the fore of American letters, and its popularity provided him the income, or at least the promise thereof, with which to marry Zelda.[9] Hemingway's disdain for Zelda and what he saw as her interference with Scott's writing must have unsettled him, as he was living in relative penury and planning to make a socially similar match.[10]

The second factor is less easy to pinpoint biographically but is of far broader scope. Hemingway may have felt that his voluntary expatriation rendered him "foreign" to his friends from the United States; certainly, his experiences with (or at least witnessing of) the wild side of Paris, the Montparnasse of the Jazz Age, alienated him in his own mind from Oak Park.[11] Later stories, most notably "The Sea Change" (which takes as one of its subjects the uncomfortable distance of the writer from normal lives), contribute to Hemingway's understanding of himself as a writerly other. This otherness may appear encoded as "foreign" in "A Canary for One."

The American lady's problems with continental "foreigners" stems from their lack of reticence (she initially thinks the narrator and his wife are English because they lack the openness she ascribes to continental Europeans; she intends her mistake as a compliment). The problems of the writer, which figure prominently in "A Sea Change" but also, more subtly, in "Canary," involve the compulsion to make public (literally through publication) even the most painful and intimate of private experiences. Additionally, *The Sun Also Rises*, Hemingway's first novel and roman à clef, was due to be published within a month (October 22 [Hanneman 14]). While writing "A Canary for One," Hemingway may have been worried (rightly, and too late) about the reactions of the people upon whom the characters in *The Sun Also Rises* were based. Yet "A Canary for One" was another similarly exploitative project, especially considering that less than two months had passed since Ernest and Hadley had returned to Paris to set up separate residences. Guilt over his writerly compulsion to expose his own personal life (however excruciating) and to capitalize on the vulnerabilities of those closest to him, however authentic his observations, may explain why he tore the entire third draft (KL/EH 309) into several pieces, most of which he later preserved (part of the first page is missing).

This artifactual violence is nearly unique in Hemingway's extensive archive; he preserved nearly every draft of everything he wrote. The violence to which he subjected this second typescript (KL/EH 309) betrays his anger and his guilt; it informs the writing of the story but also reveals which role will prevail. Although the man tore the pages seven times, the writer preserved them and the changes made on them, preparing very shortly thereafter a clean typescript for submission to *Scribner's*. After all, as the narrator insists in the first drafts, "My wife and I are not characters in this story" (KL/EH 307, 9; 308, 3). This excised line provides a textual analog to the flames and the train wreck in that it breaks open the story, exposing and advertising the writerly text behind the authorial one.

In the last line of "A Canary for One," the reader learns that the married American couple is, like Ernest and Hadley before them, "returning to Paris to set up separate residences" (261), and that the story has chronicled their last moments together. This last line requires that one reread the story in order to appreciate the irony of their conversation with the American woman, and pertinence of the narration of various scenes that the husband has seen from the train.[12] Hemingway thus forces his readers to relive the experience with excruciating awareness, just as he did while writing.

In this 1926 story, Hemingway came as close as he had yet to acknowledging the deep discomfort he felt at making the private public (which happens in any divorce, and in all his Personal writing).[13] (He would pathologize this discomfort much later.) He also began, metaphorically, to play with fire as his symbol of choice for the deliberate betrayal and destruction of the emotional bonds within a marriage. In the earliest fragment of what became "Now I Lay Me" (KL/EH 618), young Nicky (Hemingway originally wrote "Ernie," the only place in his manuscripts where he makes this error) assists his mother with the burning of his father's prized personal possessions (including the nicely Freudian snakes that his naturalist father had preserved in jars), only to realize later that by helping his mother he has betrayed his father. Both the marriage tale theme and the theme of intergenerational, father-son betrayal will reemerge, newly fashioned, in the stories Hemingway wrote while on his honeymoon with Pauline in May 1927.

The Early Honeymoon Fiction (May 1927)

During the writing of the early honeymoon fiction ("Hills Like White Elephants" and "Ten Indians"), the schism between writer and author grew even wider and had increasingly serious repercussions in the texts. In these stories, especially "Hills Like White Elephants," the writer-author split reached its most profound distance to date. In addition, the concurrent composition of "Hills" and "Ten Indians" illuminates a highly personal linkage between honeymoons and fatherhood, between romantic commitment and homosocial betrayal. When considered in light of the story of Hadley, the lost valise of manuscripts, and her subsequent pregnancy, these two stories, taken together, mark an early milestone in Hemingway's developing personal semiotic of love and fatherhood, signified by suitcases and elephants (both of which connect directly to romantic and paternal commitment in "Hills Like White Elephants") and food (which serves as inadequate nourishment in counterpoint to romantic and paternal betrayal in the final version of "Ten Indians"). A much older Hemingway would return to this honeymoon, these stories, and these specific images in *The Garden of Eden*. Just as writing Nick Adams into the Michigan woods allowed Hemingway access to the Edenic memories of his adolescent freedom, dramatizing his Provençal honeymoon in *The Garden of Eden* would return an aging Hemingway to the time when he most enjoyed writing.

During the 1927 honeymoon, Hemingway was able finally to finish "Ten Indians," the ending of which had eluded him for over a year and a half. In this final version, Nick's father literally stumbles upon Nick's girlfriend, Prudie (the tenth Indian of the title), with another male while Nick is in town for the Fourth of July with friends. Nick returns home after seeing the other nine passed out drunk on the side of the road, whereupon his father tells him about Prudie's infidelity. Two earlier drafts of the ending exist, both of which were written during the long deterioration of his first marriage (Smith, *Guide* 197). The first draft, the 1925 Chartres version, was written in a French school notebook, or *cahier* (KL/EH 202c; David Bourne, in *The Garden of Eden*, writes his own Nick Adams-like story in a similar *cahier* whilst on his own Provençal honeymoon). In this draft, Nick Adams functions as a witness to his girlfriend Prudie's central but unidentified trauma (Smith, *Guide* 197). In the 1926 Madrid version, Prudie loses her sympathetic role and takes on that of Nick's sexual and romantic betrayer, the role she would play in each subsequent version. In this version, the affective focus shifts briefly to Nick but is complicated by an additional shift, at the end, to his father, who has revealed Prudie's unfaithfulness. After Nick goes to bed, Dr. Adams confronts feelings of inadequacy as a father (he prays, "Dear God, for Christ's sake keep me from ever telling things to a kid" [KL/EH 728 and 729; Smith, *Guide* 197-98]) and, perhaps, as a husband (he lies "crossways in the big double bed to take up as much room as he could. He was a very lonely man" [KL/EH 728 and 729; Smith, *Guide* 198]). The story takes place in the Michigan cabin where Ernest and Hadley had, like Hemingway's parents before them, spent their honeymoon,[14] which strongly suggests the possibility that, for Dr. Adams, this empty bed was his honeymoon bed.

The honeymoon, or Provence, version of "Ten Indians" (KL/EH 727 and 730) places Nick, and Nick alone, squarely in the story's affective foreground and reduces Dr. Adams's role to one of witness, messenger, and inadequate nurturer. This final version clarifies Dr. Adams's relationship to the concept of betrayal in this story: he is no longer even suggested as the object of betrayal. He has become, exclusively, its agent. Not only is he the messenger of bad news, but his inadequacy as a parent compounds his implication: he can offer his emotionally injured son nothing but an extra piece of pie by way of comfort. In contrast to the kinship Nick sees in the Gardner family at the beginning of the story, the Adams family members exist in emotionally sterile cocoons, alone even when physically together.

Hemingway's honeymoon version of "Ten Indians" reorients the intergenerational betrayal evident in the burning episode of "Now I Lay Me" from the betrayal of father by son to the betrayal of son by father, in both cases because of a woman. In "Now I Lay Me," the son

Nicky/Ernie is cast by his mother as an unwitting accomplice in a betrayal; in "Ten Indians," the father, Dr. Adams, is cast by Hemingway as a conflicted accomplice in a similar betrayal. Both betrayals hint strongly at emasculation (Mrs. Adams burns, among other things, Dr. Adams's collection of flint arrowheads as well as the snakes; Prudie "threshes around" in the woods with another male), and both betrayals are homosocial. In the honeymoon writing, however, the direction is reversed: in the honeymoon, father betrays son. Hemingway's reinscription of guilt away from the son and onto the father during these months is biographically fitting. During this dark period, he neglected to inform his parents of his separation from Hadley; during the honeymoon, he had yet to inform them of the wedding. This minor betrayal pales in comparison to the larger one that Hemingway, as a father, had perpetrated on his own son because of a woman: by leaving Hadley for Pauline in 1926, Hemingway had betrayed not only his wife but three-year-old John as well. Young Nick, in these stories, thus figures not only as Hemingway's avatar but implies Hemingway's strong identification with his own young son. In the 1924 "Cross-Country Snow," Hemingway had reluctantly implicated Nick Adams in marriage and fatherhood; in these later Nick Adams stories, Nick became even less of an escape for him. Perhaps because of this, Hemingway would soon abandon the Nick stories and not return to them for twenty years, in the writing of *The Garden of Eden* and "The Last Good Country."[15]

"Hills Like White Elephants," the marriage tale in the honeymoon pair, seems to connect with "Ten Indians" in that the theme of father-child betrayal reappears in the characters' debate whether or not to abort an unexpected pregnancy. "Hills" also introduces, biographically, the last of the four early psychological issues that will reemerge, transformed, in *The Garden of Eden*: gender switching, or cross-gendered experimentation.[16]

In order to identify the deeply hidden gender switching in the writerly text of "Hills," I must explicate the story, as it was published, in some detail. The unnamed man advocates the abortion; Jig, his girlfriend, is open to imagining a future that includes their child. Critics have nearly universally read the ending of this story as indicating that the man wins the struggle and that Jig and the unborn child lose. But "Hills" can be read, with equal accuracy, in two ways. The traditional critical reading has the story ending either with the abortion or a breakup; another viewpoint can see the couple choosing to stay together and not to have the abortion. The traditional reading is supported, almost perfectly, by the published text (what I term the authorial version); the second is supported equally well by the writerly text represented in the story's only extant manuscript and its compositional context.

"Hills Like White Elephants" stands as perhaps the earliest textual evidence of Hemingway's own cross-gendering experiments, in which his own metaphorically biographical role in the story is played not by the man, but by the woman, Jig. Because *The Garden of Eden* relies so heavily on this text and the writing of it, and because my reading of this story as cross-gendered autobiography diametrically opposes that of nearly every other critic since the story's publication, I will provide an extensive close reading of both the published (authorial) version and its single extant manuscript (the writer's text) in this chapter before considering its contributions to the later novel in the next.

As a starting point, consider the following passage from *The Garden of Eden*: "David wished that he had brought a casting rod and spoons so that he might cast out across the flow of water" (7). The term "spoons" provides a nearly invisible link to one of the earlier stories, "Hills Like White Elephants." A spoon in fishing refers to a bright, concave metal disk around which fish hooks are attached. Another term for such a device, which functions as both lure and hook, is a "jig."

In "Hills Like White Elephants," Hemingway names the young woman who is considering an abortion—Jig. From the perspective of her lover, who initially desires neither commitment nor complications (who, rather, has an immature wish to undo the pregnancy so that they will be as they were before), the fishing connotation of her name is particularly apt. To him, Jig really is a bright lure with potentially dangerous hooks. The American man in "Hills" would agree, at least initially, with Bill's warning (in "The Three-Day Blow") that "Once a man's married, he's absolutely bitched" (90).

"Hills Like White Elephants" shares with *The Garden of Eden* not only its "jig" reference but, more importantly, its intimate connection to a Grau du Roi honeymoon, having been written during that of Ernest and Pauline Hemingway in 1927. Furthermore, it shares *The Garden of Eden*'s most heavily charged (if somewhat unlikely) images: suitcases and elephants. Finally, it marks a complete schism between the authorial text and that of the writer. Despite the fact that the words are the same in the authorial and writerly texts, the two end differently—and their equally well-supported endings are mutually exclusive.

Stanley Renner's essay, "Moving to the Girl's Side of 'Hills Like White Elephants,'" offers a revolutionary reading of the published story's conclusion: "[Jig] decides not to have an abortion, and her companion, though not without strong misgivings, acquiesces in her decision" (27). This conclusion becomes clear for Renner through "a study of Hemingway's characterization of the pregnant girl" (27), which he traces through five stages, or "movements," in the text. Although Renner's conclusion differs strikingly from that of every other critic in the story's seventy-plus-year history (who argue either that Jig concedes and undergoes the abortion despite her own desires or that she leaves her intractable lover), Renner is strongly supported by a biographical detail that critical responses to the story neglect: the dedication of the manuscript to Pauline Pfeiffer, "Mss for Pauline—Well, well, well" (KL/EH 473, 12). Paul Smith wonders at the apparent paradox between this dedication and the story's ending, as traditionally read, especially given Pauline's Catholic faith (*Guide* 206). Michael Reynolds notes the "disturbing fact that Hemingway completed the story while on his honeymoon with Pauline" in May 1927 (*Chronology* 7-8).

Yet neither Smith nor Reynolds develops this evocative thread, and beyond their statement of fact and expression of puzzlement,[17] biographical information is absent in critical responses to the story, an absence most likely due to the lack of evidence that Pauline (or, for that matter, Hadley) ever had an abortion. That this story lacks the evident autobiographical basis of the earlier marriage tales is apparently so obvious that it does not warrant mention.

But questions remain. Why would Hemingway give to the Catholic Pauline, his new bride, a story in which either a relationship is destroyed or a pregnancy terminated? This is especially troubling given that the date of composition indicates that this manuscript may have been a wedding present, from husband to wife.[18] What to make of the fact that Hemingway himself referred to this story as one of his "hard" stories, implying in a letter to his editor Maxwell Perkins that "hard" meant "better"?[19]

Renner's aggressive reading of the story's physiospatial rhetoric partially answers these questions. If the story does not end tragically, then it is indeed hard—much harder than can be accounted for by the mere omission of the word "abortion." Further, if the man does "capitulate," as Renner argues (28), then the matter of the manuscript as wedding present loses some of (but not all) its shock value. If one keeps the circumstances of the story's production firmly in mind while reading the story, Renner's persuasive argument for resolution is strengthened. Yet why have generations of readers, from Dorothy Parker to Allen Josephs,[20] responded so emphatically with exactly the opposite interpretation—that the story is a tragedy? In order to resolve questions arising from the story's ambiguity, e.g., why the published story seems to support at least two equal and opposite readings of its ending, I propose first to examine the textual elements that create that ambiguity, and then to marshal archival and biographical information to support and extend Renner's general claims.

Both sides of the critical debate (Renner, opposing literally all other critics) have textual support—perhaps because of the near balance

Hemingway ascribes to the rhetorical sides in the story. Nearly everything in the story, even the white elephants of the title, supports two equally likely but opposite meanings. A first denotation of white elephants is unwanted junk. But not just any unwanted junk; this is the junk you bring to a white elephant sale because although you find it worthless, someone else might not. Sure enough, at the second mention of white elephants in the narrative, Jig finds the hills "lovely" (212). An additional, historical exegesis of a white elephant embraces the term's positive and negative connotations: a white elephant is a gift bringing both honor and ruin to its recipient.[21] At first glance, it means one thing. At second, it means two—not one of two, but one and two. Honor and ruin.

The story's valley setting is bisected, "this" side (the infertile side, "brown and dry," with "no trees"), and "the other" side (the fertile side, with fields of grain, the river, and trees), by not one but "two lines of rails," between which the couple sits "at a table in the shade" (211). The setting is introduced in two stages, first within the opening paragraph, where we are given the bleak view; the second describes the "lovely" view (213). At first glance, the valley is one way: barren. Later, we learn that it is two: both barren and fertile, simultaneously. So which hills are like white elephants? The narrative states that "the hills across the valley . . . were long and white," and that "on this side there [were] . . . no trees" (211). When Jig defends her choice of simile, however, she states that she "meant the coloring of their skin through the trees" (212). There are no trees on "this" side; she therefore must mean the trees she remembers seeing before sitting down, which have yet to appear in the text. Her companion does not look, but if he did, he, "close against the side of the station" (211), would only see the barren side. Valleys are valleys by virtue of lying between two lines of hills; by definition and by textual determination the "hills like white elephants" must be on both sides, but only after a careful reading and wrestling with the word "across" does this become clear.[22] Of course the hills lie across the valley—the station is between them; whichever way you look, they are "across" (211, 212). The hills on both sides, then, are "like white elephants."

Just as the valley lies between the two lines of hills, the station sits between two lines of rails, presumably representing two directions of travel ("to Madrid" and "to Barcelona"). One line is on the fertile side; one on the barren side. When the man moves the suitcases across, to the "other tracks" (214), we first assume that he moves them in order to put them onto the train to Madrid (which at that point is "coming in five minutes" [214]). But those tracks are on the "other" side, the "fertile" side, which we know from the fact that Jig moves to the end of the station to look at it, where she sees the "river," across the valley, "through the trees" (213). Why, in a story in which every detail of setting is so carefully determined—even overdetermined—would the train headed toward the abortion come on the "fertile" side of the valley? This leads, of course, to two additional questions. Why, at the end of the story, is Jig smiling? And why does the American man need an *anis* in the bar when his beer awaits at the table?

The first time one reads the story, one assumes that Jig's smile is forced, that she is being submissive and conciliatory; conversely, one might also assume that she smiles because she has decided to leave her lover and have the baby on her own (Hannum 47; Renner 27). But once one remembers which side is which (by remembering Jig's movement to look toward the distance "through the trees"), Renner's argument that she smiles because the man has capitulated (34) also makes sense—even more so when one remembers that her first smile, to the Spanish waitress, is "to thank her" (214) nonverbally, in the only language they share. Jig and the man also appear to share only one language, that same nonverbal language (which comes as no surprise given the probable basis of their relationship). If the first smile means "I don't speak your language, but thank you," the second, which follows so hard upon the first, may mean exactly the same thing, in which case the third and final smile could easily follow suit: "Thank you for telling me with your actions what you could not communicate in words." At first her smile means one thing; later, perhaps another. Unlike the inclusive meanings of "across" and "white elephants," however, the two possible meanings of the man's moving the suitcases and of Jig's smiles are mutually exclusive. Either they are taking the train to have the abortion or they are not. Either Jig smiles to thank him honestly or to mask her true emotions. How are we to discern the difference? Hemingway has not, for all his overdetermination of setting, clearly designated either set of rails "to Madrid."

Hemingway provides a possible clue with the timing. We know that the train is due "in five minutes" (214) and that it will stop for two (211). The man, therefore, has seven minutes to announce that he will move the suitcases, move them, look "up the tracks" and "not see the train," go into the bar, order an *anis*, drink it, look at the people "waiting reasonably" while drinking, come out through the curtain, and rejoin Jig at the table (to "finish the beer," as she states earlier [214]). There is absolutely no way to know for sure whether this takes more or less than seven minutes, and Hemingway, again, does not say. This information may or may not be valuable—another potential white elephant.

What do we know for sure? The story is almost perfectly symmetrical. In its first section, the setting is established in the narration, introducing "this" barren half of the valley. The couple sits together in a "shadow" (211) at a table and is interrupted briefly by the waitress. After looking at the bamboo curtain and holding two of its strands in her hand, Jig announces her concession to the man's wishes that she terminate her pregnancy, rises, and moves alone to the end of the station. The second section of the story, like the first, begins with a description of setting (now, of the other, fertile side of the valley). Many of the elements present in the first section are repeated in the second, but with the active roles reversed: Jig sees a second shadow (213), the couple again sits at the table, the waitress interrupts, and the man looks at nearby objects (the two bags). He then moves, alone, to the other side, carrying the bags; pauses to look and ruminate; and then rejoins Jig at the table. The two then, presumably, board the train to Madrid for the abortion. The story's physical action is "perfectly simple" (213). Or is it?

Two actions are missing from the narration and thus from the description. Although Hemingway does not tell us when Jig drops the strands of beads, he does not need to. Their release must occur before she leaves the table; the most likely moment is at her climactic line "Then I'll do it. Because I don't care about me" (213). If she underscores these words with such an action, however unconsciously, her action-oriented companion may be more likely to notice that something is amiss.

What Hemingway does need to tell us, and what has gone unremarked since the story's publication in 1927, is that at the narrative fulcrum, the man joins Jig at the end of the station. When Jig laments, "we could have all this," the man responds, "What did you say?" Smith notes at this point that "many have wondered why she does not stalk off" and leave him (*Guide* 211). Why indeed? Because the man's question suggests, as does so much else in the story, two mutually exclusive interpretations: either he has not been paying attention and is therefore a selfish cad (which he has certainly proved to this point), or else he quite legitimately does not hear her. The next several lines of dialogue evince such tight stichomythia that he apparently must hear her lament, but the text later reveals that this is a false assumption, the result of narrative misdirection. After the man says, "You mustn't feel that way," "*they* sat down at the table" (214; emphasis added). For both to sit, both must have been standing. The man therefore must have moved during the dialogue. But when? And why?

The reader must work backward through the text. The only plausible moment for him to move is as he asks that difficult question, "What did you say?" Prior to this line, Jig is alone; subsequent to it the dialogue is so tight that motion is not only improbable but illogical. The pronoun "they" reveals that the man's movement is, like Poe's purloined letter, hidden in plain sight. The man's movement changes his "Come on back" from an imperative to a plea. If the question "What did you say?"

is not damnably insensitive, as Smith has suggested, but rather a mere request for repetition (and he does want to know what she said; he moves to hear her), what else may we, disgusted like Jig by the man's apparent callousness, have missed?

We have missed the beginning of understanding that the man's words have begun to evince, and which his motion to join her underscores. Reading backward yet again, we can scan no farther for this beginning than the exchange at which Jig drops the beads: "I'll do it. Because I don't care about me," prompting the man's question "What do you mean?" (213). Prior to this question, he has expressed interest only in a short-term (but permanent) solution to what he perceives as an "unhappy" problem (212). As Renner argues (31), when confronted with "I don't care about me," he may begin, however dimly, to perceive that what he sees as expedient, Jig sees as a sacrifice. If "I don't care about me" jolts his complacency, and if his retort, "Well, I care about you," is honest, then the remainder of the story should reveal his attempts to reopen communication and to convey a willingness to listen to her side. As Pamela Smiley notes, he can speak only his own limited language, relying on "the repetition of key words and phrases" (9), and he cannot understand Jig's. He can, however, read her actions. He will discover that his earlier insincerity has contaminated the very words he must now employ to elicit an opposite response. His efforts will be frustrated even further by Jig's reasonable (given his stance thus far) resistance to his words. He must transform himself from antagonist to hero in slightly less than two pages of narrative and slightly less than thirty minutes of dramatic time.

Returning to the stichomythic dialogue (from "What did you say?" to "We'll wait and see" [213]), the evidence for a shift in the man's rhetorical position appears almost immediately. The dialogue begins in the indicative mood ("We can/can't have everything"). After Jig's statement that "once they take it away you can never get it back," the man breaks the indicative can-can't pattern with "They haven't taken it away" (213). He is thus attempting to reopen the discussion. This is so subtle that Jig (and many readers) miss this verbal "action." His tactic fails; he continues to try to convince her that the debate is still open with two statements, "I don't want you to do anything that you don't want to do—" and "But you've got to realize—." These lines unfortunately echo, nearly verbatim, his earlier, insincere words: "But I don't want you to do it if you really don't want to" (213). Jig interrupts both later statements, having already heard too many variations on these words to trust them now.

From this moment, the story develops in an intricate calculus of the repetition of and variations on existing elements. The characters resume their original positions at the table, and much of the action from the story's opening section is repeated: one character looks at things, one does not; one character tries to communicate, the other refuses to listen; the waitress interrupts a tense moment by bringing beer; the man translates for Jig; one character moves to the other side, and the narrative voice speaks from that character's perspective. Now, though, the couple's respective positions in the spatial and communication dynamics are reversed.

Jig has spent the entire story looking at her surroundings (hills, ground, curtain, fields, and shadow); the man has yet to look directly at anything. He does so now: first at her, then at the table, the bags, the tracks, and, finally, the people in the bar (214). Jig, in this second section, does not appear to look at anything. Just as the man is the one who looks, he is the one who now confronts the urgency of their situation and who must attempt to communicate this urgency to her, just as she tried (and failed) to do initially. Her orientation has been spatial (imaginative) throughout; his must be temporal (goal directed): whereas she perceived the possibility of "the whole world" (213), he can only perceive the ticking of the clock, the train's timetable, and the rising odds against resolution.

Unfortunately, at this point in the story, we and Jig are confronted with a veritable plethora of indefinite pronouns, nine of which are obviously indefinite ("it") and one of which in its first instance appears to be definite ("we") but by its second, at least in the manuscript, is quite the opposite:

> "You've got to realize . . . that I don't want you to do it if you don't want to. I'm perfectly willing to go through with it if it means anything to you."
> "Doesn't it mean anything to you? We could get along."
> "Of course it does. But I don't want anybody but you. I don't want any one else. And I know it's perfectly simple:"
> "Yes, you know it's perfectly simple."
> "It's all right for you to say that but I do know it." (214)

Two lines from this section of dialogue proved the most elusive to Hemingway as he reworked them through no fewer than four complete versions between the first draft and publication (KL/EH 473, 10). The published version reads:

> "Doesn't it mean anything to you? We could get along."
> "Of course it does. But I don't want anybody but you. I don't want any-one else. And I know it's perfectly simple." (214)

In the first draft, this section of dialogue reads two ways:

> 1. "It doesn't mean anything to you?"
> "Of course it does. But it's just a question of expediency. And I know it's perfectly simple."
> 2. "Doesn't it mean anything to you?"
> "Of course it does. But I don't want anybody but you. I don't want any-one else. I know how the other thing is. And I know it's perfectly simple."

By the end of the first draft, Jig's initially strong accusation "It doesn't mean anything to you?" has been weakened slightly, but the man's attitude remains essentially unchanged. Both first draft versions indicate that his position never wavers.

Critical Insights

The second-sitting revisions, the final ones made on the manuscript, also contain two versions of this section (the latter of which matches the published text).[23] The first raises the abortion debate to a new level, one that recognizes the baby as a real third person:

> 3. "Doesn't it mean anything to you? Three of us could get along." "Of course it does. And I know we could."

Hemingway rejected this version in favor of the more ambiguous published text, rightly excising Jig's reference to the "three of us" as a flaw—not necessarily of content, but of effect. The phrase is too direct, too obvious, and represents too efficient a form of communication to be consistent with these characters. "To explain is to destroy," as Nakjavani notes in his investigation into Hemingway's style (43). Even so, Hemingway tried these same three words again during the second sitting at a later point in the story, but this time in the man's lines:

> He did not say anything but looked at /her/ the bags against the wall of the station. There were /stickers/ labels on them from all the hotels where they had /spent nights/ stopped.
>
> "But I don't want you to," he said, "I don't care anything about it. /*Three of us could get/*" (KL/EH 473, 10-11; emphasis added; /deletions/)

Thus after "He did not say anything," he does say something—too much and too directly, judging from the fact that Hemingway did not even complete the sentence before crossing it out. Although Hemingway's oft-quoted assertion regarding the lingering affective resonance, of "things left out" must be invoked with caution, the rhetorical shift from "expediency" to "three of us" is diametric and total. Of all the things "left out," or at least crossed out, of all Hemingway's stories, these three words may be the most startling, as they support without question the existence of an interpretive possibility that Renner alone has articulated.

The man has been misunderstood in his first foray toward the language of commitment. His reply to Jig's sarcasm, "but I do know it," indicates both that he does know what he is trying to say, and that he knows with equal certainty that he is failing miserably. When she asks that they "please please please please please please please stop talking," the man is forced to comply to prove the sincerity of his claim that he would "do anything for you" (214). He is dutifully silent "but looked at the bags" (214). This sentence could as easily have read "*and* looked at the bags"; the conjunction "but" serves to link his consideration of the bags to what he would say had he not bound himself unwittingly to silence.

The labels remind him of their nights together and spur him to attempt communication once more: "But I don't want you to . . . I don't care anything about it" (214). Although in the published text, the man certainly does not continue by asserting that the three of them could get along, the repetition of "but" in this passage indicates that he knows the matter is too important for him to keep silent. Once again, though, the effect of his words is the opposite of what he intends. "I don't care anything about it" is a terrible rhetorical fumble. Neither Jig, who threatens to scream, nor the reader, who might want to, can locate an antecedent for that crucial "it"—which in the manuscript refers to neither abortion nor baby, but to his earlier stance in the debate. Frustrated and overwhelmed, he is capitulating—reluctantly, to be sure, but he is finally conceding.

The story's ultimate ambiguity resides in the nearly perfect balance Hemingway crafted in the manuscript between the representative sides, both spatial and rhetorical. A collation of the manuscript (KL/EH 473) with the text of the first edition (the 1927 edition of *Men Without Women*) reveals that the nearly overwhelming ambiguity in the story was the result of emendations made during a second writing session, which included the man's surprising "three of us." This set of emendations reveals a striking difference between the narrative in its first draft and that which became the published version.

In the first draft, the story reads as many have read the published text: the man's character and attitude remain static throughout, and Jig must either defer to his judgment regarding the abortion or end the relationship. During the second sitting, however, Hemingway made the following subtle changes, which, taken together, allow for the interpretation Renner proposes. To Jig's apology, "I just meant the coloring of their skin," he added "through the trees" (KL/EH 473, 5). After "It's the only thing that's made us unhappy," he added "The girl looked / away/ at the bead curtain, /and/ put her hand out and took hold of two of the strings of beads" (KL/EH 473, 6). He added "The shadow of a cloud moved across the field of grain and she saw the river through the trees" (KL/EH 473, 8). He changed the imperative, paternalistic "But you must realize" to the more pleading "you've got to realize" (KL/EH 473, 9). He reworked the difficult dialogue, added a "please," and nearly let the cat out of the bag with "three of us" (KL/EH 473, 10-11). He also added Jig's second smile, her response to "I'd better take the bags over to the other side of the station" (KL/EH 473, 11). By adding a few phrases and sentences, a please, and a smile, Hemingway made an alternative ending possible.

As a set, these second-sitting emendations heighten the story's ambiguity. Why do we care about the trees? They orient us within the setting and cement both characters' perceptions spatially. The beads? Because we and the man can see Jig considering her options and deciding. The addition of the line containing the cloud's shadow provides not only an evocative image (potentially ominous, from Jig's perception, but potentially bringing the cool relief of rain to a parched valley) but, more importantly, reminds us about the trees, in case we missed them the first time (and we need to know where the trees are, so we know that both lines of hills are "like white elephants"). Why a second smile? Because it links her first and her third, and because it provides us with her immediate response to the man's decision to move the bags. Is she saying thank you again, and for much more than just carrying the heavy bags? The bags are "heavy" indeed if they contain not only their literal contents but also their possible metaphorical meaning. Prior to the man's movement, they suggest the superficiality of the relationship: they bear only the surface symbols of a peripatetic existence. As the man carries them, however, they are two, they are full, and they are heavy. They now have internal content and heft and bear a closer affinity to the weighty commitment of parenthood.

As the man moves the bags to the other side (and, not incidentally, into the light), the narrative voice shifts to his perspective and indicates his distance from the train (which he does not see). This underscores his distance from the people who will, unlike himself, "reasonably" board the train for which they have been waiting, rather than some later train that will take them into an uncertain future. From his perspective, abortion would have been the "reasonable" course of action. The recent debate must have felt anything but "reasonable" to him. But he has learned that his perspective is just that: his. As he sits in the interior space, which Kozikowski obliquely associates with the womb (108), one wonders why he is there, if not to steady his nerves and to let the idea of impending fatherhood start to sink in.

Smith notes that the first draft of this section reads quite differently from the published text: "There must be some actual world. There must be some place you could touch where people were calm and reasonable. Once it had all been as simple as this bar" (Smith, *Guide* 205; KL/ EH 473, 2). Smith asserts that "They were all waiting reasonably for the train," with which Hemingway replaced these deleted lines during the second sitting, functions as a "[reduction of] the whole perception to the inserted sentence with its metaphoric adverb" (205). This interpretation is consistent with the reading that proposes that the man's "benighted vision" remains unaltered, yet by making this second-sitting change, Hemingway lends "reasonably" more rhetorical weight than Smith suggests. It may function not as a "reducing" metaphor, but rather as a metaphor for the distance traveled by the man, who literally turns his back on reason when he rejoins Jig outside. From his perspective, he has been hooked and landed by Jig, in keeping with her name.

Although several critics have discussed the relevance of "Jig" most extensively (O'Brien 20; Abdoo 240), one definition is consistently and surprisingly left out. According to the 1913 edition of *Webster's Revised Unabridged Dictionary*, a jig is not only a dance, a mechanical sheath, etc. (as critics have noted); it is also "a trolling bait, consisting of a bright spoon and a hook attached" (800). That Hemingway would be unaware of the connotational possibilities of "bright lure" and "hook" to Jig's name is highly unlikely, especially in light of David Bourne's wish for such a device in *The Garden of Eden* (7).

In response to the white elephant aspect of their situation, the man may have done the honorable thing, but the lingering negative affect derives from his focus on their previous life as having been ruined. When the man emerges from the bar, the "three of them" have barely survived the struggle in this isolated valley arena. His movements and her smiles are actions, in the language of the arena, the language that does not require words, and the only language in which the two communicate fluently. This is not to say that the story presents the reader with a blissful vision of the union or its future. It does not. Physiospatial communication may avert the unnecessary termination of an unplanned but not entirely unwelcome pregnancy, yet gendered miscommunication will extend beyond the closing of the arena into real life. The two will have to learn to communicate verbally; the prognosis can be only guarded at best.

A partial answer, then, to the disturbing question of why Hemingway gave Pauline this story within three weeks of their Catholic wedding is that Pauline, reading the manuscript, could see instantly what has taken so long to reconstruct here: that not only does the American man change his mind halfway through the story, but that Ernest Hemingway did too, halfway through the writing. He initially wrote the story as most people interpret it and then laid over it a nearly transparent layer consisting of a few minute changes that transform the initially simple story entirely. The subtlety of this transformation nearly disappears from the story as it was published, among others in the already-titled *Men Without Women*. But Pauline, on her honeymoon in 1927, had access to the writerly text, and as such to two sources of information that a reader holding just the published text does not. The first, of course, was the twelve-page manuscript, visual evidence of the transformation that Hemingway had wrought on the story. What had been a "perfectly simple" story in the first draft had become a narrative palimpsest, an almost perfectly symmetrical and diabolically ambiguous story, one that can end with nearly equal certainty in tragic disunity or Aristotelian comic unity. Pauline's second advantage was her intimate knowledge of what the word "abortion" meant to Hemingway within the context of their relationship—in other words, in the mind of the writer.

During the writing of "Hills Like White Elephants," he deviated from his then-usual composition method, which was to prepare his own typescripts and to make emendations as he prepared various typed drafts. By December 6, 1926, he had broken his typewriter (Bruccoli, *The Only Thing That Counts* 53), and he presumably did not bring the one he borrowed to Grau du Roi. His own had been damaged, perhaps by heavy key pounding as he wrote desperate, forbidden letters to Pauline during the bleak hundred-day separation initially prescribed by Hadley as a condition for divorce.

These letters and cables, several of which are unfinished (KL/EH Correspondence), reveal Hemingway's despair as communications from Pauline grew sporadic and finally stopped altogether. He knew from her sister Virginia (Jinny) that their mother, with whom Pauline was staying in Piggott, Arkansas, was preying on Pauline's guilt at destroying Hemingway's marriage and family.[24] Unable to control Piggott from Paris, Hemingway waited, in a "black depression" (*SL* 234), for Pauline's decision either to return to marry him in Paris or to accept a job in New York. He would not know her decision, for sure, until she sailed.

Hemingway waged a long-distance written campaign against and for Pauline's conscience. In his letters, one can trace the evolution of one of his most elusive metaphors—the metaphor that was to be left out of "Hills Like White Elephants." The metaphor originated in his encoding of their relationship as a nascent body. In his letter of November 12, 1926, he attempts to persuade her that the stakes of her decision outweigh the obvious sins of adultery and divorce; he implies that their reunion is a matter of life and death: "It was certain that your mother would feel badly about your marrying some one [*sic*] who was divorced, about breaking up a home, about getting into a mess—and it is certain too that silent disapproval is the most *deadly*" (*SL* 220; emphasis added).

Hemingway rhetorically alleviates adultery and divorce by renaming them "mess" and then by juxtaposing that relatively benign noun with the weighty descriptive "deadly." This charged adverb marks the conception of what was initially a relatively simple metaphor: for their relationship to be in "deadly" peril, it must be somehow "alive." It is mortally threatened by Pauline's apparent decision to break off the relationship: "evidently we are to be smashed by choice—our own free choice—in a grievous matter, with deliberate and full consent" (*SL* 222).

Hemingway next elaborates this metaphor by giving the relationship a body. Under the conditions of this evolving metaphor, love can potentially realize embodiment (metaphysical birth) through the motion of bodies (in this case, Pauline) across space (the Atlantic) toward union (marriage/intercourse). The strange alchemy of Hemingway's creative mind will resolve this traditional erotic vision into one of his most subtle works by capitalizing on his having placed the burden of the metaphorical tenor, relationship as body, on the improbable vehicle, surgery: "But I won't and I won't think about it and maybe you'll come back and maybe there will be something left of you and maybe we'll have a little guts and not try self sacrifices in the middle of surgical operations and maybe we'll come through and maybe and maybe and maybe and maybe" (*SL* 222).

The "surgical operations" in question here seem to refer both to the divorce from Hadley and the separation from Pauline, "self sacrifices" indicating Pauline's possible inclination to listen to her mother (*SL* 220) and perhaps (as Hemingway feared) to end their relationship.

Hemingway combines the "surgical operation" motif with the idea of "sacrifice" in a later letter, dated December 3, as he recasts Pauline's apparent decision to stay in the United States as a decision to "abort" their embryonic relationship: "You see Pfife I think that when two people love each other [going away from each other] works almost as bad as an *abortion*. . . . But the deliberate keeping apart when all you have is each other does something bad to you and lately it has me all shot to hell inside" (*SL* 234; emphasis added).

Hemingway here implies that their relationship is (and thus the two of them are) metaphorically pregnant; he asserts that his pain, his fear that Pauline will reject him, is akin to that of a pregnant mother who is shot in the womb. Although this is certainly melodramatic, Hemingway's self-representation as somehow pregnant underscores the possibility that as a writer he considered the couple in "Hills Like White Elephants" a very heavily fictionalized, cross-gendered representation of his and Pauline's relationship during the fall of 1926. Two people in love, his vision asserts, create between them a metaphorical pregnancy; to sacrifice it is to abort the union. Pauline finally decided against sacrifice in favor of union. On December 30, 1926, she sailed for France (Kert 198), moving her suitcases to the other side of the Atlantic. The wedding took place in Paris on May 10, 1927.

Furthermore, biographer Carlos Baker asserts (fortuitously, but problematically) that Hemingway "began the story in the first person," identifying the author's March 31, 1927, letter to Fitzgerald as the source for one of the story's images: "We sat at a table in the shade of the station" (595n). Although the line was typed onto the page before Hemingway reused the paper for the letter and thus is disconnected from the actual text of the letter,[25] Smith notes that the same letter also contains the "Well, well, well" phrase from the dedication (*Guide* 206; *SL* 249). Further, the text of the letter itself contains the lines, "Pauline is *fine* and back from America. I've been in love with her so damned long that certainly is *fine* to see a little something of her" (*SL* 249; emphasis added). The "black depression" is over and, although he sounds a little bitter about it, there's nothing wrong with him. He, like Jig at the end of the story, feels fine.

Well, well, well, indeed.

Most readers do not, of course, have Pauline's advantages of having read Hemingway's letters to her and of reading the holograph manuscript. Only scholars familiar with Smith's work have any knowledge of the dedication, which has never appeared with the published story. "Hills Like White Elephants" is the only story manuscript so dedicated, and perhaps Hemingway intended the dedication for Pauline's eyes only. Much about the abortion is left out of this deceptively simple "abortion story" (Baker 595)—not only the word itself, but also its metaphorical status in the context of the newlyweds' intimate history, and the dedication that provides the sign marked "To Biography." In its stead, Hemingway presents us with a narrative palimpsest, a structural and interpretive theme and variation.

The palimpsest of the published text, like much in the story itself— the white elephants, "Jig," the shadow of a cloud, "across," the smiles, the act of moving the suitcases, nearly every spoken pronoun (Josephs 55), and almost all the dialogue—can almost impossibly support two equal and opposite meanings. But no matter how we choose, each by each, to approach the story, to resolve these oppositions, the story is about much more than the end of a shallow relationship or the expedient operation necessary to keep it that way.

The reemergence of the themes and images of "Hills Like White Elephants" in *The Garden of Eden* (specifically, the gender-switching experiments in which David and Catherine indulge), and the manner with which Hemingway treated them in that later novel, supports and affirms the reading of "Hills" as based on cross-gendered autobiography. The highly charged images of suitcases, elephants, food, and fire from these early, paired stories all resurface in *Eden*, the story of a honeymoon set, at least initially, at Grau du Roi, where Hemingway wrote "Hills." In *The Garden of Eden*, begun approximately twenty years after Hemingway's own honeymoon, questions of betrayal and commitment reemerge in conjunction with these same symbols, but in the service of even the larger issue only hinted at in these early stories: writing, and its dangerous transformation of the private to create the public, as I will discuss in the next chapter. Although critics have long noted the autobiographical sources for the stories, and biographers have implied that Hemingway seemed to have a singularly undeveloped conscience when confronted with the choice between maintaining privacy and transforming his intimate life (and those of his acquaintances) into public property in his writing, none has explicitly addressed the act of writing as the site of this transformation and, consequently, as an act and site that would become, for Hemingway, "the Last Good Country" to which he ever strove to return. In other words, the act of transforming memory into text became, in itself, a place and a time for Hemingway.

Returning to this place and time became ever more difficult, because his increasing public acclaim as author and, later, icon interfered materially with the collection of fresh experiences to remember and transform into text. By the end of his life it was not his children who encumbered him, but the baggage of his multiple and conflicting identities, roles, and responsibilities, all of which he had eagerly courted. In other words, and at the risk of sounding tautological, his writing, once it became public, interfered with his writing. Being Hemingway, he would naturally address this experience in writing.

In 1927, however, domestic matters still dominated much of his thoughts and his writing. He had just left his first wife, Hadley, having publicly chronicled in his Personal fiction his unhappiness with the marriage and the intimate secrets of his betrayal of her with another woman, and having flirted with exposing his delight with his new bride with the publication of "Hills Like White Elephants." Despite this delight, and the heights of complexity to which it brought his writing, he would later claim to have loved Hadley "first and best" (quoted in Burwell 30). Between 1923 and 1929, Hemingway became the writer he would similarly claim to love the same way. This period was the last during which Hemingway the writer would own his own writing, and the next-to-last time he would own his own life. His hard-won freedom was, paradoxically, about to end.

From *The Bones of the Others: The Hemingway Text from the Lost Manuscripts to the Posthumous Novels* (Kent, OH: Kent State University Press, 2006). Copyright © 2006 by Kent State University Press. Reprinted by permission of Kent State University Press.

Abbreviations

KL/EH: Items in the Hemingway Collection, John F. Kennedy Library, Boston. Numbers given in the text, e.g., 422.1/2, 15, indicate the file number (e.g., 422.1), folder number (e.g., 2), and page number (e.g., 15).
SL: Selected Letters 1917-1961 (Ed. Carlos Baker).

Notes

1. These subtleties are now discernible to general readers in part because of the opening of archival materials, which in 1926 were, of course, still private.

2. Kennedy's discussion of the "displacement of emotional content onto fictive terrain" in *Imagining Paris* refers specifically to Hemingway's writing of *The Sun Also Rises*. This displacement, however, figures centrally in much, if not all, of Hemingway's fiction writing. Kennedy refers here to Hemingway's own practice, but Hemingway's first-person narrators often perform the same displacement that Hemingway does (especially in the early fiction, as here, in "A Canary for One"). This is but one of many reasons why it is often difficult to separate Hemingway's characters (especially his narrators) from Hemingway himself. As Jackson Benson notes in an early assessment of Hemingway criticism, "many of us in Hemingway studies have trod very close to the line of biographical fallacy. It is a temptation that comes out of the nature of the material itself: if a writer chooses to use his own name as the name of the central character in the early drafts of his fiction [NB: Hemingway did this once], if he models his characters very closely after his own family and friends, and if he appears to be using his writing, often in very direct ways, as a tool to expiate the ghosts and goblins of his own psyche, then the critic is almost inevitably involved in some very sticky critical problems" (32-33). Benson illustrates his point by citing Bertram Sarason, who "met some resistance" from some of the "characters" (not people) he attempted to interview for his work on *The Sun Also Rises* (33).

3. Readers familiar with Hemingway's biography know that Pauline did, in fact, return to marry Ernest; it is thus easy to forget that Hemingway himself did not yet know this and as such to read the story as concerned exclusively with Ernest and Hadley and not as a representation of his fear of losing both women. In the fall of 1926, double loss was still a possible outcome.

4. The "story of the story" is not without its own irony: six days after Scribner's accepted the story, Hadley agreed to divorce and Hemingway immediately cabled Pauline to join him in Paris.

5. Unlike the "burning house" section, as it was finally published, the "wrecked cars" passage, which occurs near the end of the story, appears in its own two-sentence paragraph for greater impact.

6. Gerald and his wife Sara, upon whom Fitzgerald would loosely base the Divers in *Tender Is the Night*, were friendly with Fitzgerald and Picasso; Picasso was an intimate of Gertrude Stein's; and all were connected with Sylvia Beach, who was Joyce's publisher and well known throughout literary Paris. Secrets among the tightly knit group of literary expatriates in Paris must have been very difficult, if not impossible, to keep. (See Vaill.)

7. Although he never set a story there, Oak Park figures centrally in much of what he wrote. In his Christmas letter to his parents that year, he carefully avoided mentioning the separation from Hadley, although he knew by that time that the marriage was over—Hadley would soon initiate divorce proceedings on the grounds of desertion—and that Pauline was coming back to France to marry him.

8. The lines also prefigure the Switzerland idyll, during which Frederic and Catherine await the birth of their child in *A Farewell to Arms*.

9. For the complete narrative of Scott and Zelda's difficult courtship, see Milford (24-62) and especially Bryer and Barks.

10. At this time, Gerald Murphy had deposited a loan into Hemingway's account; Hemingway had promised *The Sun Also Rises* royalties to Hadley (Reynolds, *Homecoming* 58, 91; Reynolds, *Chronology* 47).

11. See Kennedy (chap. 3) for an excellent summary and critical assessment of this alienation and how it manifested in Hemingway's psyche and writing.

12. In his consideration of the drafts of this story, Donaldson ("Preparing") argues convincingly that the ending is not a surprise, as previous critics had argued, but rather is carefully foreshadowed by the various images in the story.

13. Hemingway would overtly identify this anxiety in a later story, "The Sea Change" (published in 1933), although in that story the character's anxiety is not about the effect of publication on himself (for Hemingway, that would come much later) but about the effect of his writing on his romantic relationships. Hemingway seems to have consciously realized this sometime between "A Canary for One" and "The Sea Change," probably after his friends' reactions to their appearing as recognizable characters (in fictional situations) in *The Sun Also Rises* made the obvious dangers of his personal writing clear to him.

14. This information is from oral tradition (Hemingway Birthplace Tour, Ernest Hemingway Foundation of Oak Park).

15. In *The Garden of Eden*, protagonist David Bourne writes his own Nick Adams-

like story, a boyhood story of hunting in Africa with his father. The unpublished half of the *Eden* manuscript introduces yet another Nick, in this case a character who is central to the novel's second plot. (Neither this Nick nor this subplot appears in the published version.) Although this Nick is not named Adams, the name was simply too important to Hemingway for there not to be a deliberate resonance. See chapter 3.

16. In *The Garden of Eden*, Catherine experiments with becoming a "boy" and asks that David, likewise, try to be her "girl." David and Catherine do in bed what Hemingway did in the writing of "Hills."

17. Spilka ("Barbershop" 367), Smith (*Guide*), and Reynolds (*Chronology*) note the honeymoon composition of the story but do not address its possible critical ramifications.

18. The first and only holograph lists Hemingway's return address as "c/o Guaranty Trust" (KL/EH 473, 1), indicating that he was away from Paris. The absence of an emended typescript suggests professional preparation and that it was mailed to Perkins from the honeymoon, along with a letter dated May 27, 1927, stating, "Here are two more stories for the book [*Men Without Women*]" (*SL* 251).

19. Hemingway informed Perkins that "Stories like Fifty Grand, My Old Man and that sort are no where near as good stories, in the end, as a story like Hills Like White Elephants or Sea Change. But a book needs them because people understand them easily and it gives them the necessary confidence in the stories that are hard for them" (Bruccoli, *The Only Thing That Counts* 188).

20. Parker characterizes "Hills" as "delicate and tragic" (94); Josephs implies that the story illustrates "the end of love" (58). Pamela Smiley's response differs in that she argues that both characters are simultaneously victims and perpetrators of "gender-linked miscommunication." She relocates responsibility for the "tragedy" but agrees with the majority that the outcome looks bleak.

21. Smith summarizes critical discussion of the various meanings of white elephant: "the realization of a mistake" (Sheldon Grebstein), "an annoyingly useless gift; . . . also . . . a possession of great value" (Joseph DeFalco), the unborn child and "a fully pregnant woman" (Lewis Weeks), and "a present" causing "ruin" (John Hollander) (*Guide* 208).

22. The extent to which the story's ending depends on which hills are like white elephants is evident from a mistranslation of "across" in the story's current French translation by Robillard and Duhamel, which begins "*A l'autre côté de la vallée*" (9). The story's title in this translation is, thus, "Paradis perdu [Paradise Lost]."

23. Collation reveals that the story was composed in three sittings: first draft, second sitting (revisions made on the same pages but at a later time), and final editing. The first draft appears to have been written rather quickly, in large, generously spaced letters, with very few same-draft changes. Second-sitting emendations are characterized by smaller handwriting, heavier pencil, and a different angle on the page, all of which are consistent throughout this set of emendations. No substantive material was added or deleted after this sitting.

24. Reynolds notes that Hemingway was in contact with Jinny, who had remained in Paris when her sister returned to Arkansas, and that Jinny "provided a shrewd analysis of what Pauline was facing in Piggott" (*Homecoming* 75). Information regarding

Hemingway's feelings and actions during this period in what follows is drawn directly or inferred from his 1926 correspondence with Pauline (Baker and KL/EH Correspondence).

25. The line appears upside down, in between lines of the letter to Fitzgerald, which suggests that Hemingway typed the line and then reused the paper, explaining the line's strange appearance on the page to Fitzgerald, in the body of the letter, as "the start of something" (KL/EH Correspondence).

Works Cited

Abdoo, Sherlyn. "Hemingway's 'Hills Like White Elephants.'" *Explicator* 49.4 (Summer 1991): 238-40.

Baker, Carlos. *Ernest Hemingway: A Life Story*. New York: Collier, 1969.

Benson, Jackson J. "Hemingway Criticism: Getting at the Hard Questions." *Hemingway: A Revaluation*. Ed. Donald R. Noble. Troy, N.Y.: Whitston, 1983. 7-47.

Bruccoli, Matthew J., with Robert W. Trogdon, eds. *The Only Thing That Counts: The Ernest Hemingway-Maxwell Perkins Correspondence*. New York: Scribner's, 1996.

Bryer, Jackson R., and Cathy W. Barks, eds. *Dear Scott, Dearest Zelda: The Love Letters of F. Scott and Zelda Fitzgerald*. New York: St. Martin's Press, 2002.

Burwell, Rose Marie. *Hemingway: The Postwar Years and the Posthumous Novels*. Cambridge Studies in American Literature and Culture, 96. Cambridge: Cambridge University Press, 1996.

Donaldson, Scott. "Preparing for the End: Hemingway's Revisions of 'A Canary for One.'" *Studies in American Fiction* 6 (Autumn 1978): 203-11.

Fitzgerald, F. Scott. *Tender Is the Night*. 1933. New York: Scribner's, 1995
_____. *This Side of Paradise*. New York: Scribner's, 1920.

Hanneman, Audre. *Ernest Hemingway: A Comprehensive Bibliography*. Princeton, N.J.: Princeton University Press, 1967.

Hannum, Howard L. "'Jig Jig to Dirty Ears': White Elephants to Let." *Hemingway Review* 11.1 (Spring 1991): 46-59.

Hemingway, Ernest. "A Canary for One." 1927. Hemingway, *Complete Short Stories* 258-61.
_____. "A Canary for One." Drafts. Files 307, 308, 309. Hemingway Collection. John F. Kennedy Library, Boston.
_____. *The Complete Short Stories of Ernest Hemingway*. Finca Vigía Edition. New York: Scribner's, 1987.
_____. Correspondence. Hemingway Collection. John F. Kennedy Library, Boston.
_____. "Cross-Country Snow." 1925. Hemingway, *Complete Short Stories* 143-47.
_____. "Cross-Country Snow." Drafts. Files 344, 345, 346, 696. Hemingway Collection. John F. Kennedy Library, Boston.

_____. *Death in the Afternoon*. New York: Scribner's, 1932.

_____. *A Farewell to Arms*. New York: Scribner's, 1929.

_____. *The Garden of Eden*. New York: Scribner's, 1986.

_____. *The Garden of Eden*. Drafts. Files 422.1, 422.2, 422.9. Hemingway Collection. John F. Kennedy Library, Boston.

_____. "Hills Like White Elephants." 1927. Hemingway, *Complete Short Stories* 211-14.

_____. "Hills Like White Elephants." Drafts. Files 472, 473. Hemingway Collection. John F. Kennedy Library, Boston.

_____. *In Our Time*. New York: Boni & Liveright, 1925.

_____. "The Last Good Country." 1972. Hemingway, *Complete Short Stories* 504-44.

_____. *Men Without Women*. New York: Scribner's, 1927.

_____. *A Moveable Feast*. New York: Scribner's, 1964.

_____. *The Nick Adams Stories*. New York: Scribner's, 1972.

_____. "Now I Lay Me." 1927. Hemingway, *Complete Short Stories* 276-82.

_____. "Now I Lay Me." Drafts. Files 618, 619, 620, 622. Hemingway Collection. John F. Kennedy Library, Boston.

_____. "Now I Lay Me." Hemingway, *Men Without Women* 218-32.

_____. *Paradis perdu suivi de la cinquième colonne*. 1949. Trans. Henri Robillard and Marcel Duhamel. France: Gallimard/Folio, 1995.

_____. "The Sea Change." 1933. Hemingway, *Complete Short Stories* 302-5.

_____. "The Sea Change." Drafts. Files 222, 678, 679, 680, 681, 681a, 734, 735. Hemingway Collection. John F. Kennedy Library, Boston.

_____. *Selected Letters 1917-1961*. Ed. Carlos Baker. New York: Charles Scribner's Sons, 1981.

_____. *The Sun Also Rises*. New York: Scribner's, 1926.

_____. "Ten Indians." 1927. Hemingway, *Complete Short Stories* 253-57.

_____. "Ten Indians." Drafts. Files 202C, 727, 728, 729, 730. Hemingway Collection. John F. Kennedy Library, Boston.

_____. "The Three-Day Blow." 1924. Hemingway, *Complete Short Stories* 85-93.

_____. *The Torrents of Spring*. New York: Scribner's, 1926.

"Jig." *Webster's Revised Unabridged Dictionary*. Ed. Noah Porter. New York: G. & C. Merriam Co., 1913. 800.

Josephs, Allen. "How Did Hemingway Write?" *North Dakota Quarterly* 63.3 (Summer 1996): 50-64.

Kennedy, J. Gerald. *Imagining Paris: Exile, Writing, and American Identity*. New Haven, Conn.: Yale University Press, 1993.

Kert, Bernice. *The Hemingway Women*. New York: W. W. Norton, 1998.

Kozikowski, Stanley. "Hemingway's 'Hills Like White Elephants.'" *Explicator* 52 (Winter 1994): 107-9.

Milford, Nancy. *Zelda: A Biography*. New York: Harper & Row, 1970.

Nakjavani, Erik. "The Aesthetics of Silence: Hemingway's Art of the Short Story." *Hemingway Review* 3.2 (Spring 1984): 38-45.

O'Brien, Timothy D. "Allusion, Word-Play, and the Central Conflict in 'Hills Like White Elephants.'" *Hemingway Review* 12.1 (Fall 1992): 19-26.

Parker, Dorothy. "Review of *Men Without Women*." *New Yorker* Oct. 29, 1927: 92-94.

Renner, Stanley. "Moving to the Girl's Side of 'Hills Like White Elephants.'" *Hemingway Review* 15.1 (Fall 1995): 27-41.

Reynolds, Michael S. *Hemingway: An Annotated Chronology*. Detroit, Mich.: Omnigraphics, 1991.

_____. *Hemingway: The American Homecoming*. Oxford: Basil Blackwell, 1992.

Smiley, Pamela. "Gender-Linked Miscommunication in 'Hills Like White Elephants.'" *Hemingway Review* 8.1 (Fall 1988): 2-12.

Smith, Paul. *A Reader's Guide to the Short Stories of Ernest Hemingway*. Boston: McGraw-Hill, 1989.

Spilka, Mark. "Hemingway's Barbershop Quintet: *The Garden of Eden* Manuscript." Wagner-Martin 349-72.

Vaill, Amanda. *Everybody Was So Young: Gerald and Sara Murphy—A Lost Generation Love Story*. Boston: Houghton Mifflin, 1998.

Recurrence in Hemingway and Cézanne_____

Ron Berman

Words and also forms in Hemingway have second lives; especially those motifs (trees, rocks, roadways) deriving from visual art. Hemingway himself identified Paul Cézanne as an influence on his work. For Hemingway, the main issue was Cézanne's ability to interpret landscape. Neither was concerned with documentary accuracy—although recent scholarship comparing photographs of Cézanne's scenes to his painted versions of them makes useful inferences about the way that depiction changes as well as represents facts (Machotka 1-7). Meyer Schapiro wrote that "the visible world is not simply represented on Cézanne's canvas. It is recreated through strokes of color, among which are many that we cannot identify with an object and yet are necessary for the harmony of the whole" (quoted in Kelder 386). But that phrase "recreated" needs to be examined with respect to Hemingway's work. It means seeing things in a particular way; and also making more than one interpretation of the same thing.

A number of critics have tried to deal with Hemingway's ideas about visual and verbal art. One attempt concludes that "Indian Camp" is constructed around "cyclical events" and repeated motifs (Hagemann 108). Another, that the reiteration of natural forms in "Big Two-Hearted River" can be traced to specific work like Cézanne's "The Poplars" and "Farmyard at Auvers" (Johnston 29-30).[1] A basic book on Hemingway and the arts has a chapter on landscape and writing. It too notes the quality of reiteration. Certain landscapes "remain a constant" in the fiction (Watts 44).

Hemingway acknowledged connections between his own work and visual art, especially the painting of Cézanne. The Lillian Ross interview at the Metropolitan Museum of Art in 1949 is often adduced:

After we reached the Cézannes and Degas and the other Impressionists, Hemingway became more and more excited, and discoursed on what each artist could do and how and what he had learned from each. . . . Hemingway spent several minutes looking at Cézanne's "Rocks—Forest of Fontaine- bleau." "This is what we try to do in writing, this and this, and the woods, and the rocks we have to climb over," he said. "Cézanne is my painter, after the early painters. . . . I can make a landscape like Mr. Paul Cézanne. I learned how to make a landscape from Mr. Paul Cézanne by walking through the Luxembourg Museum a thousand times." (Ross 36)

Reiteration and sequence dominate the statement. Hemingway ad- dresses a painter and also painters before him. He implies familiarity with the way that a particular school of painting turns and returns to its subjects. There is even reiteration in his language, although Ross does not pursue a definition of "this . . . this and this." When Hemingway says he walked through the museum "a thousand times" the repeti- tion—which is fairly startling—draws no blood. She treats the state- ment as an exaggeration, but it is meant to be evidence that he saw the same thing in necessarily different ways.

Cézanne often reiterated or recast the subjects of his paintings. The rocks of Fontainebleau were part of an immense body of work redone in order to capture as many aspects of the landscape as possible. Here are some titles keyed to the catalogue of John Rewald: *Rochers à L'Estaque, Dans le Parc du Château Noir, Rochers et Branches à Bibémus, Sous Bois Devant Les Grottes Au-dessus du Château Noir, Rochers et Arbres, Intérieur de Forêt, Pins et Rochers, Arbres et Rochers dans le Parc du Château Noir, Rochers Près des Grottes Au- dessus du Château Noir.* This list does not include related subjects like the rock formations of the Mont Sainte-Victoire paintings. The forms of "the woods, and the rocks" were constantly reworked by Cézanne. These forms and certain others were continuously reinvented by Hem- ingway (Watts 146-149). Cézanne redrew and repainted an unending series of versions of landscapes in pencil, oils, and watercolors. Land- scape scenes are variations on a central subject—and even titles are re- iterations. This could not have been unknown to Hemingway.

Hemingway did not specify the immense number of versions of Cézanne's most essential element of landscape, the trees that provide vertical forms for the Fontainebleau painting. There are, for example: *L'Estaque, L'Estaque—Rochers, Pins et Mer, Marroniers et Ferme du Jas de Bouffan*, the many versions of *Sous-Bois*; *Les Grandes-Arbres, Le Grand Pin, L'Allée à Chantilly, Dans la Forèt de Fontainebleau*. However, one reiterated subject in Cézanne—curves in the road—can be traced because Hemingway invoked it a number of times and made it recognizably part of his own *language* as well as landscape.

The Cézannes that I have in mind among many others are *Maisons Au Bord d'une Route, La Route Tournante* (1881), *Le Tournant de Route Près de Valhermeil, La Route Tournante à La Roche-Guyon, La Montagne Sainte-Victoire au Grand-Pin, La Route en Provence, La Route Tournante en Sous-Bois, La Route Tournante* (1904), *Matinée de Printemps à Saint-Antonin*, and *La Route Tournante en Haut du Chemin des Lauves*. To these must be added numerous views of farms and towns, and, always, the series of paintings of Mont Sainte-Victoire. Cézanne's late landscapes—his "curves in the road"—have been called new visions of nature (Novotny 110-111). Perhaps the issue left unpursued by the Ross interview—what, after all, was Hemingway referring to when he said that he had "learned" something of immense importance?—can be clarified. Evidently, one thing learned was the art of reiteration: "In the . . . *Mont Sainte-Victoire* series . . . variations, studied like successive geological strata, grew out of Cézanne's ceaseless experimentation with the theme. They stem also from the different centering of the subject, which Cézanne insisted upon considering from every possible angle (left, right, forward, backward, high, low), according to the position in which he placed himself. The theme became a pretext for variations whose multiplicity distanced him from the concrete object" (Monnier 116).

The central location for these ideas is in Hemingway's work of the 1920s. Here is the opening of "The Three-Day Blow":

The rain stopped as Nick turned into the road that went up through the orchard. The fruit had been picked and the fall wind blew through the bare trees. . . . The road came out of the orchard on to the top of the hill. There was the cottage, the porch bare, smoke coming from the chimney. In back was the garage, the chicken coop and the second-growth timber like a hedge against the woods behind. The big trees swayed far over in the wind as he watched. It was the first of the autumn storms. (*SS* 115)

The passage has embedded in it a number of allusions to the landscape of Cézanne. The phrase "on top of the road" translates part of the title of *Le Mont Sainte-Victoire Au-dessus de la Route du Tholonet* and also of *Maison Près d'un Tournant en Haut du Chemin des Lauves* (Rubin 400, 414). The phrase "the road came out of the orchard on to the top of the hill" not only contains the language of many titled paintings but is seen from their perspective. The phrase "the big trees" that "swayed far over in the wind" is literal Cézanne as in the pencil and watercolor *Les Grands Arbres*, the oil *Les Grandes Arbres au Jas du Bouffon*, and a number of drawings. As for the second part of Hemingway's line, Lionello Venturi gave his own title to *Les Grandes Arbres: "Bare Trees in the Fury of the Wind"* (qtd. in Rubin 412). That may be because Cézanne himself had in 1863 written a poem, "The Great Pine," in connection with this subject and containing the line "The tree shaken by the fury of the winds" (qtd. in Schapiro 108).

Hemingway's opening lines are about more than one subject. In 1957, he completed a group of chapters for the book that was to become *A Moveable Feast*. He gave them to his wife Mary for typing— one of them told "how it was to be writing 'The Three-Day Blow' at a table in a café on the Place St.-Michel." But she was "disappointed to discover that the sketches contained so little that was straightforwardly autobiographical" (Baker 352). There is also very little that is straightforwardly documentary. In the section of *A Moveable Feast* that Baker describes, Hemingway writes that "in Paris I could write about Michigan." He meant that literally: "I was writing about up in Michigan and since it was a wild, cold, blowing day it was that sort of day in the story." Scholars are aware that he links the writing of the stories of this period to Paris and especially to Impressionism, but it will be useful for all readers to get his own sense of connection: "I could walk through the gardens and then go to the Musée du Luxembourg where the great paintings were that have now mostly been transferred to the Louvre and the Jeu de Paume. I went there nearly every day for the Cézannes and to see the Manets and the Monets and the other Impressionists that I had first come to know about in the Art Institute of Chicago. I was learning something from the painting of Cézanne that made writing simple true sentences far from enough to make the stories have the dimensions that I was trying to put in them" (*MF* 7, 13).

Possibly more than technique was involved. Hemingway came to Cézanne at a time when his stock was very high. Roger Fry had in 1914 called him "the Christopher Columbus of a new continent of form" (qtd. in Osborne 215-216). By 1927, when Fry's book on Cézanne appeared, he was understood to be not only the leading post-Impressionist but also a world-historical figure. Fry himself was seen to be such a figure.[2] Fry wrote about Cézanne from 1906 on, organized exhibitions of his work in 1910, bought his paintings for J. P. Morgan and the Metropolitan Museum, and coined the term "post-Impressionism." Virginia Woolf's biography of Roger Fry makes a number of important observations: she believes that Fry's book on Cézanne was his most significant work, and that it was significant both for its author and its subject. Woolf states that the theme of this book is the definition of artistic identity opposed to received opinion. She cites Fry on "the double story" of Cézanne, i.e., his creating a technique and then becoming "the great protagonist of individual prowess against the herd" (Woolf 284-286). So, when we say that anyone might have been influenced by Cézanne or ideas about him in the first decades of the 20th century, we necessarily mean that viewers such as Hemingway came to the painter through ideas generated by his leading critic. What were some of those ideas? First, that the painter's intellectualism was an important part of his total effect. Second, that he provided a new kind of technical language for art. Third, that the artist was himself a model for independent thought. Here is Fry on the late work, those landscapes so much admired by Hemingway:

> A picture belonging to M. Vollard . . . represents a road plunging from the immediate foreground into a wood of poplars, through which we surmise the presence of a rock face, which rises up behind and dominates the tree tops. . . . the more one looks the more do these dispersed indications begin to play together, to compose rhythmic phrases which articulate the apparent confusion, till at last all seems to come together to the eye into an austere and impressive architectural construction, which is all the more moving in that it emerges from this apparent chaos. It is perhaps in works like these that Cézanne reveals the extraordinary profundity of his imagination. He seems in them to attain to heights of concentration and elimination of all that is not pure plastic idea, which still outrange our pictorial apprehension. . . . the completest revelation of his spirit may be found in these latest creations. (Fry 78-79)

There are certain essentials: the motif of the road, the organization of detail into harmony, the warning that there are elements in his work that outrange our "pictorial apprehension." Above all, there is the conception of landscape as a dominant idea.

Pavel Machotka has gone to archives and also, so far as they can be known, to Cézanne's locations. He has collected photographs of the sites, and taken new ones from approximate perspectives. His reconstruction tries to account for the season and time of day of the original; change, damage, and natural cycles in the sites; differing versions of the same scene. The reasons he gives for the project are helpful for Hemingway's own reiteration: chief among them that "more than one painting" is needed to produce coherence of idea or motif—and also to be faithful to the variations of nature (Machotka 1-2). A single motif requires many versions, an idea often restated in Cézanne's letters and interviews. Hemingway scholars have tried to examine his landscape in terms of fidelity to "place." R. W. B. Lewis sees "place" first of all as recognizable terrain. He concentrates on Hemingway's local knowledge and on the primacy of fact in any given description of city or country. But he acknowledges also that such description is not a matter of documentation. "Place" is always modified by idea (Lewis 119-121, 143).

That is a useful context for the opening of Hemingway's "The Three-Day Blow" in which the *route tournante* comes over a hill to a particular terrain. Getting there, we see the scene—but in a delimited way: "There was the cottage, the porch bare, smoke coming from the chimney. In back was the garage, the chicken coop and the second-growth timber like a hedge against the woods behind" (*SS* 115). The usual descriptives are not there. There are no colors in this most important part of the opening. There is form but no draftsmanship—a trait in Cézanne much criticized by those who came after Roger Fry. Two things become apparent, the first that this passage is about perception not place; the second that it is seen in black and white. This is a drawing, not a painting, pencil without the usual watercolor. There is another perspective: "They stood together, looking out across the country, down over the orchard, beyond the road, across the lower fields and the woods of the point to the lake. The wind was blowing straight down the lake. They could see the surf along Ten Mile point." Here too there is the total absence of color—and no attempt to differentiate, describe, or compare objects within the scene. The curving road has taken us to a familiar but at the same time an unexpected place, a Michigan landscape seen in Impressionist terms.[3]

The terrain in Hemingway's stories and novels of the 1920s is seen from the viewpoint of "curves in the road" arriving at (even, to borrow Fry's phrasing, plunging into) landscapes of the mind (Novotny 111). "Indian Camp" begins by following a road that winds through the woods, arriving, finally at a point in back of the hills. In order to get where they are going, which is both a real and a metaphorical place,

Nick and his father have to come "around a bend" towards an equivocal light (*SS* 92). In "The Battler" Nick starts along a smooth roadbed "going out of sight around the curve" (*SS* 129). In "Big Two-Hearted River," he walks along a road "climbing to cross the range of hills" that separates two realms (*SS* 211). "The Three-Day Blow" begins with a road that appears and disappears, going up through an orchard then "to the top of the hill" (*SS* 115). In "In Another Country" the roads wind across land and water, but recurve to meet and "always . . . you crossed a bridge across a canal to enter the hospital" (*SS* 267). The road in "An Alpine Idyll" stops at a cemetery, then climbs and twists into the hills where anything can happen. The motif is at its most dominant in the middle chapters of *The Sun Also Rises* where the *route tournante* takes us not only into the Spanish Pyrenees but into Cézanne's world of color and forms: "For a while the country was much as it had been; then, climbing all the time, we crossed the top of a Col, the road winding back and forth on itself, and then it was really Spain" (*SAR* 93).

There have been different kinds of histories of the *route tournante* in visual art and literature. Sometimes they coalesce. In art history, roads have a technical function of separating the planes of a landscape. One example—startling in its delineation of limits—is Armand Guillaumin's "The Outskirts of Paris," done about 1874. If ever one wants to see a road "winding back and forth on itself" while fragmenting nature into parcels, this is the oil painting to look at. Yet here technique and meaning shade into each other: about half the painting is taken up by the recurved road, which speaks either to a pleasing sense of geometry or to a baffled sense of the segregation of things natural behind barriers (Chatelain, 108-109). The sense of a division of realms is strong: between men and nature, between the artist and the object before him. In Hemingway, the winding road is by no means a still, formal part of a described scene. It is an entry into a divided realm. The point has been strongly made: in his analysis of "Rocks at Fontainebleau" Meyer Schapiro points out that "there is a similar landscape in the writing of Flaubert. . . . In his great novel, *The Sentimental Education*," he describes the same forest of Fontainebleau as the setting of two lovers who have left Paris for the peace of nature during the convulsions of 1848: "The path zigzags between the stunted pines under the rocks with angular profiles. . . . But the fury of their chaos makes one think rather of volcanoes, deluges and great forgotten cataclysms" (118).[4] Schapiro says that this scene from the novel is even more disturbing than Paris. It reminds us of natural disorder—which becomes coupled with our own sense of inevitable human disorder.

The openings of both "Indian Camp" and "The Battler" are illuminated by the following passage about the "limited access" into some of Cézanne's *routes tournantes*: "A clear visual path is frustrated, in the first composition, by the restless violence of the overlapping planes formed by the rocks; in the second, by the aggressive jutting of the rock at the framing edge and by the densely grouped, multi-colored foliage, which forms another barrier across the road and denies the eye a place to rest; in the third, by the ominously insistent intrusion of the trees and their branches into the line of sight" (Kelder 390-391). "Indian Camp" has this kind of topography, with its access going "through a meadow that was soaking wet with dew" along a trail that first "went into the woods" and then to a "road that ran back into the hills" (91). The words replicate Cézanne's titles, the terrain replicates his scenes. Hemingway uses the road—which, in order to arrive in the frame, even "came around a bend"—to repeat motifs of Impressionist perception. Boundaries are in fact barriers. Volumes are in sharp contrast, with the shapeless and organic completely unclarified.[5] The road, which is after all a figure of more than one kind of perspective, does not grant "access" to the meadow, woods, or hills. It would appear as if the geometry of culture does not have "access" to the irregularity of nature, so that the burden of the story has been prefigured.

In this story, Hemingway raises a large question about the separation of things knowable and those not knowable. He works with the conflict of visual components. His mountains and forest edges are not only volumes and planes but lines of limitation. Isaiah Berlin was later to use the concept of "access" in a related way. In a skeptical essay on the possibility of shaping reality, he concluded that there was no possibility of doing so. There would always be unreachable areas in the world, and also within the mind: "The belief that somewhere there exists a solution for every problem, though it may be concealed and difficult of access . . . is the major assumption that is presupposed in the whole of Western thought. Moral and political questions, in this respect, did not differ from others." Berlin thinks that while everything is open to inquiry, few things are permeable to it (170, 173-74). Wittgenstein set the rules about discovering meaning in experience. Here is his opinion—it is a memorable one—of Bertrand Russell's confusion of certainties: "Russell's works should be bound in two colours . . . those dealing with mathematical logic in red—and all students of philosophy should read them; those dealing with ethics and politics in blue—and no one should be allowed to read them" (qtd. in Glock, 207). Explanation has its limits, and they are quickly reached. That matters greatly as a context for a story full of questions without answers.

The idea of "access" denied applies to Hemingway. The premise of roads and also of inquiries is that they go somewhere. *Routes tournantes* invariably fail to reach certain symbolic objects on their horizon. They reach but cannot penetrate the barriers of rocks, woods, mountains. In "Indian Camp" Nick asks the question "Where are we going?" and the answer is necessarily qualified. Perhaps it can be provided from "The Battler," in which we are "a long way off from anywhere." There is always "the curve" and, as usual, it goes "out of sight" from foreground to background (*SS* 129). Once again there are the undefined volumes of woods and swamp. These make their own demands on interpretation. (A recent history of the novel makes the point that "the place between water and land functions . . . as a threshold. Its presence signifies the necessity of passing from one state to another").[6] In "The Battler," the roadway devolves from track to trail to a path "at the edge of the trees" (*SS* 130). We move from perspective to a point beyond viewing, and from technique to meaning—we now know the tendency of the story, from known to unknown. It is characteristic in Hemingway to begin on a straight road or roadway, then to experience an entirely different kind of locus of movement—and also of the mind.

"The Battler" begins with Nick being thrown off a freight train, and walking, tired, cold and hungry, along the railroad tracks. We begin with straight lines, which is to say within the Western mind. But Nick is surrounded by dark woods and impenetrable swamps, the psychic meanings of which are sufficiently clear. When Nick gets to the campfire that he has seen from the railroad tracks he finds a man called Ad who has been wrecked by life. Ad has been in the ring, and he took a good punch. The trouble is, he took too many of them. But it may not have been the ring that broke him. The meeting is something so different from Nick's orderly middle-class past that it makes such a past itself unreal. He expects logic in experience; Ad Francis is there to show that chaos is as likely as order. He has been a heroic figure—"I could take it" he says, "Don't you think I could take it, kid?"—but the ring has deformed him, made him, as he says, "crazy" (*SS* 131). He has been married, or pretended to be married, to a woman who may—or may not—have been his sister. He welcomes Nick to the fire, then transparently tries to take Nick's knife in order to stab him. So, we have Ad being crazy, incompatible reasons for it, and Ad wanting to kill Nick. It's often been remarked that in these stories Nick always learns something, but what he learns here is that there may not be any answers.

In the middle of it all, Bugs heats a skillet, and ham, eggs, and bread materialize: "As the skillet grew hot the grease sputtered and Bugs . . . turned the ham and broke eggs into the skillet, tipping it from side to side to baste the eggs with the hot fat" (*SS* 133). One kind of detail belongs to the constancy of nature: there is precise description of things—fire heats, ham slices are held on bread by gravity, bread picks up gravy by osmosis, eggs run because liquids seek their own level. The laws of mechanics are working, but a second kind of detail seems less Newtonian: Bugs tells a wonderful story-within-the-story about how Ad

Francis went mad, gives Nick more food and coffee, then calmly hits Ad with an antique blackjack that has seen a lot of use. He is precise, just putting Ad to sleep with a well-placed tap. Nick leaves the camp, looks backward, sees Bugs waking his friend up and giving him some more coffee. The story moves relativistically from one set of boundaries to another. They have no intersection.

The most sustained of Hemingway's landscapes of the 1920s are those in *The Sun Also Rises*. All are approached from railroad tracks, roads, trails, and paths that circle and rise and then disappear:

> There were wide fire-gaps cut through the pines, and you could look up them like avenues and see wooded hills way off. . . . then we were out in the country, green and rolling, and the road climbing all the time. . . . then the road turned off and commenced to climb and we were going way up close along a hillside, with a valley below and hills stretched off back toward the sea. . . . then, climbing all the time, we crossed the top of a Col, the road winding back and forth on itself . . . and the road ran down to the right, and we saw a whole new range of mountains . . . and the road went on, very white and straight ahead, and then lifted to a little rise. . . . away off you could see the plateau of Pamplona rising out of the plain, and the walls of the city, and the great brown cathedral and the broken skyline of the other churches . . . the road slanting up steeply and dustily with shade-trees on both sides, and then leveling out. . . . And as we went out along the road with the dust powdering the trees and down the hill, we had a fine view, back through the trees, of the town rising up from the bluff above the river. . . . The road climbed up into the hills and left the rich grain-fields below . . . and the hills were rocky and hard-baked clay furrowed by the rain. We came around a curve into a town, and on both sides opened out a sudden green valley. . . . Far back the fields were squares of green and brown on the hillsides. Making the horizon were the brown mountains. They were strangely shaped. As we climbed higher the horizon kept changing. As the bus ground slowly up the road we could see other mountains coming up in the south. Then the road came over the crest, flattened out, and went into a

forest. It was a forest of cork oaks, and the sun came through the trees in patches . . . and ahead of us was a rolling green plain, with dark mountains behind it. (*SAR* 88-108)

Hemingway's *routes tournantes* are more allusive than we may think. I have by no means covered all of his versions of the road winding through Spain—while it simultaneously traverses the landscapes of Cézanne. It goes through a particular part of Cézanne—I think that the best way to get at Hemingway's reiterations of the *route tournante* is through the Mont Sainte-Victoire paintings.

Arguing from technique, Pavel Machotka calls the ten canvases on this subject done between 1902 and 1906 Cézanne's culminating work. They provide the volumes and also the green and brown (ocher) in Hemingway's own version. They provide the translations from planes of entry and of view. They have, as Cézanne himself noted, the property of never having colors "join at the edges." They alternate "meadows" and "full sun." Above all, they create a succession of views with new understanding of a landscape reached at different points. But the consideration of technique inevitably reaches a point of meaning, and Machotka concludes that just as his own photographs of the scene are inadequate so is the argument from technique. This is a culminating series of works because nothing else has managed in this way to translate space onto canvas (119).

The "space" in question is the distant view of the mountain made accessible, *but only to a limited extent,* by roads that rise and curve and disappear. Towards the end of his life, in 1901, Cézanne bought a modest property halfway up the hill of Les Lauves north of Aix. Here is where he spent the days making the last paintings of Mont Sainte-Victoire. He rarely changed his perspective of the mountain, but kept on painting it from different angles, at different times, and in different colors. No single image represents a final view of the subject. None of these paintings is ever able to resolve—and none of them care to provide—any final interpretation of the scene. The components of these views are invariably earth and sky: The entry into these components is invariably through *routes tournantes* like those "countless gently climbing, descending, and curving roads with hills in the background" around Les Lauves.[7] The roads are everywhere, yet there are in all these canvases areas that cannot be fully explained. On this, the painter was adamant, even stating that a blank space would be preferable to inserting something that would fake comprehension. Landscape was by no means open to visual understanding—we recall Fry's statement that it might "outrange our pictorial apprehension."

In a letter to his son in 1906 Cézanne remarked "that as a painter I am becoming more clear-sighted before nature, but with me the realization of my sensations is always painful. I cannot attain the intensity that is unfolded before my senses. I do not have the magnificent richness of coloring that animates nature" (qtd. in Rewald, "Last Motifs," 104). The solution is to keep repainting certain motifs at different times and from different angles. The same subject needs to be repeated in the hope that at some point its meaning will reveal itself. During an interview in the same year, 1906, Cézanne took out a number of paintings from all over his house and "followed the limits of the various planes on his canvases. He showed exactly how far he had succeeded in suggesting the depth and where the solution had not yet been found" (Rewald, *Paintings* I, 539-540). Implicit is the idea that a painting is not simply exposition. It concerns information withheld. Another interview conducted by Joachim Gasquet (printed in Paris in 1926) finds Cézanne discoursing at some length about the point at which description may—or may not—be adequate to the subject:

> You see, a motif is this. . . . (He put his hands together . . . drew them apart, ten fingers open, then slowly, very slowly brought them together again, clasped them, squeezed them tightly, meshing them.) That's what one should try to achieve. . . . If one hand is held too high or too low, it won't work. Not a single link should be too slack, leaving a hole through which the emotion, the light, the truth can escape. You must understand that I

work on the whole canvas, on everything at once. With one impulse, with undivided faith, I approach all the scattered bits and pieces. . . . Everything we see falls apart, vanishes, doesn't it? Nature is always the same, but nothing in her that appears to us lasts. . . . What is there underneath? Maybe nothing. Maybe everything. Everything, you understand! So I bring together her wandering hands. . . . I take something at right, something at left, here, there, everywhere, her tones, her colors, her nuances, I set them down, I bring them together. . . . They form lines. They become objects, rocks, trees, without my planning. They take on volume, value. . . . But if there is the slightest distraction, if I fail just a little bit, above all if I interpret too much one day, if today I am carried away by a theory which runs counter to that of yesterday, if I think while I paint, if I meddle, whoosh! Everything goes to pieces. (qtd. in Rewald, *Paintings* I, 546)[8]

To be aware of this interview is to put the Ross interview into perspective. There is the relentless empiricism that marks both Cézanne's work and Hemingway's. Iteration means the discovery of an identity more complex than any single given statement about it. As expected, Cézanne is concerned with two main issues: constant reinterpretation, and the extraction of meaning from technique. We are prepared to think of the rocks and trees in their landscapes as real and also as symbolic entities. There is the conclusion that one may find either "everything" or "nothing" in a scene. The remark, like Hemingway's observation to Ross about "what we try to do" is elliptical: writing and painting can succeed and also fail in depiction. And even when they do succeed in their statement there are barriers for cognition.

Gasquet took down Cézanne's opinion that the issue of painting a landscape finally becomes one of adequate "language." Painting, according to Cézanne, was the "deciphering" of a "text." The process, in fact, is that of establishing "two parallel texts" of visualization and the statement of meaning. In the Ross interview Hemingway talks about paintings and motifs, here Cézanne talks about language and texts. Both imply that the study of terrain and composition exceeds the mastery of topography. I have not cited everything stated or claimed by Cézanne, but the more one looks at this interview (published in 1926), the better Hemingway looks at the Met.

In summarizing the last landscapes, Meyer Schapiro begins with technique, emphasizing the importance of changing colors from point to point, and making sense out of separated details. Then he adds that "the distant landscape resolves to some degree the strains of the foreground world . . . . dualities that remain divided, tense, and unstable in the observer's space" (74). This conclusion makes sense when applied to *The Sun Also Rises*. As Schapiro points out, there is a kind of double drama in process, that of the eye's movement through terrain, and that of building a kind of intellectual "harmony." The scene has "externalized" something not easily articulated. Momentarily there has been control achieved over experience (Schapiro 74). Both Machotka and Schapiro—and the many art historians cited by Rewald in his definitive study—find the Mont Sainte-Victoire iterations to have considerable spiritual depth; even unstated religious feeling. When Jake and Bill finally reach water in the mountains they make an embarrassed but effective iteration of their own, retelling Genesis within a landscape by the banks of a stream. In the scene, a road rises into the woods, then turns in its curving way across the fields. Schapiro states of "Road at Chantilly" that the path through the trees seems to be "a modest, unlikely theme" (80). But it is everywhere in Cézanne and Hemingway.

Notes

1. Beginning with this article, I have cited many titles of Cézanne. These titles, whether in English or French, exist in variant forms. Whenever a title is cited it is in the form used by the source. Different publications are cited because of variations in the reproduction (color, size, detail, quality) of paintings or drawings.

2. See Pavel Machotka (xiii, 1-7). Jakob Rosenberg states that Fry's critical under-

standing of Cézanne has not been surpassed (101). For a full treatment of Fry's stand-ing see Alfred Werner's introduction to Fry's *Cézanne: A Study of His Development* (i-xiii).

3. The Hemingway scene should be compared to Cézanne's *Route tournante en Haut du Chemin des Lauves*, which is reproduced in Machotka (114). I have used the term "Impressionism" as Hemingway used it, as a kind of shorthand including post-Impressionism.

4. See Hemingway's letter "To Henry Strater, Nordquist Ranch, 14 October 1932": "A man can be a hell of a serious artist and not have to make his living by it—see Flaubert, Cézanne and Co" (*SL* 369). The remark is enigmatic without knowing the conclusion of Roger Fry's *Cézanne: A Study of His Development*. According to Fry, Flaubert and Cézanne were connected by romanticism, technique, "infinitely labori-ous" reconstruction of their work—and by their financial independence which allowed them to do their work without kowtowing to critics. (87-88).

5. See Meyer Schapiro's discussion of "Turning Road at Montgeroult" (112).

6. A number of modern novels begin "on a shore, strand, bank, or marsh," including those of Conrad, Flaubert, Joyce, and Woolf (Doody 321).

7. Rewald points out that these roads, which were "all over the region of Aix," be-came part of the paintings of Mont Sainte-Victoire (*Paintings* 1, 545).

8. Rewald alludes in his elaborate notes to E. H. Gombrich, Max Raphael, Lionello Venturi, and other historians of art. My discussion of the Mont Sainte-Victoire paint-ings relies on these citations. See *Paintings* I: 539, 545-547. Note especially Rewald's judgment of the reliability of the Gasquet interview.

Works Cited

Baker, Carlos. *Hemingway: The Writer as Artist*. Princeton: Princeton UP, 1973.

Berlin, Isaiah. *The Sense of Reality*. New York: Farrar, Straus and Giroux, 1996.

Chatelain, Jean, et al. *Impressionism: A Centenary Exhibition*. Paris: Metropolitan Museum of Art, 1974.

Doody, Margaret Anne. *The True Story of the Novel*. New Brunswick: Rutgers UP, 1997.

Fry, Roger. *Cézanne: A Study of His Development*. New York: Farrar, Straus and Giroux, 1970.

Glock, Hans-Johann. "Wittgenstein and Reason." In *Wittgenstein: Biography and Philosophy*. Ed. James C. Klagge. Cambridge: Cambridge UP, 2001. 195-220.

Hagemann, Meyly Chin. "Hemingway's Secret: Visual to Verbal Art." *Journal of Modern Literature* 7.1 (February 1979): 87-112.

Hemingway, Ernest. *Ernest Hemingway: Selected Letters, 1917- 1961*. Ed. Carlos Baker. New York: Scribner's, 1981.

——————. *A Moveable Feast*. New York: Scribner's, 1964.

——————. *The Short Stories of Ernest Hemingway*. New York: Simon & Schuster, 1995.

_____. *The Sun Also Rises*. New York: Scribner's, 1970.

Johnston, Kenneth G. "Hemingway and Cézanne: Doing the Country." *American Literature* 56.1 (March 1984): 28-37.

Kelder, Diane. *The Great Book of French Impressionism*. New York: Cross River, 1980.

Lewis, R. W. B. "Hemingway's Sense of Place." In *Hemingway In Our Time*. Ed. Richard Astro and Jackson R. Benson. Corvallis: Oregon State UP, 1974. 113-43.

Machotka, Pavel. *Cézanne: Landscape into Art*. New Haven: Yale UP, 1996.

Monnier, Geneviève. "The Late Watercolors." In Rubin, 113-18.

Novotny, F. "The Late Landscape Paintings." In Rubin, 107-11.

Osborne, Harold. Ed. *The Oxford Companion to Art*. Oxford: Clarendon Press, 1970.

Rewald, John. "The Last Motifs at Aix." In Rubin. 83-106.

_____. *The Paintings of Paul Cézanne: A Catalogue Raisonné*. 2 vols. New York: Harry N. Abrams, 1996.

Rubin, William. Ed. *Cézanne: The Late Work*. New York: Museum of Modern Art, 1977.

Rosenberg, Jakob. *On Quality in Art*. Princeton: Princeton UP, 1967.

Ross, Lillian. "How Do You Like It Now, Gentlemen?" In *Hemingway: A Collection of Critical Essays*. Ed. Robert P. Weeks. Englewood Cliffs: Prentice-Hall, 1962. 17-39.

Schapiro, Meyer. *Cézanne*. New York: Abrams, 1952.

Watts, Emily Stipes. *Ernest Hemingway and the Arts*. Urbana: U of Illinois P, 1971.

Woolf, Virginia. *Roger Fry: A Biography*. London: Hogarth, 1940.

The Scapegoat, the Bankrupt, and the Bullfighter:
Shadows of a Lost Man in *The Sun Also Rises*_____

Neil Heims

"To reveal a great unsatisfied desire is to reveal one's inferiority."

—Stendhal, *On Love*

I

It may seem odd to think of *The Sun Also Rises* as an allegorical novel,[1] but Hemingway's characters, although vivid individuals, are also types. Jake represents a hard-boiled, hard-drinking, cynical, and sentimental stoic of a newspaperman, a man locked in a struggle with his own defeat; Mike, a wastrel, a blustering drunk, a bankrupt, the scion of a wealthy Scots family living on an allowance, an impotent man who bluffs his way through. Pedro Romero is the embodiment of a young, handsome, exquisitely macho, virtuoso matador, an emblem of natural power and indomitable bravery; Montoya, the hotel keeper, of a bullfight aficionado, secret in his passion until he recognizes a kindred spirit; Brett, of a promiscuous, dissolute femme fatale, the incarnation of Duke Ellington's lonely "Sophisticated Lady"; Cohn, of an anti-Semite's idea of a Jew, pushy and passive, sexually and socially untrustworthy, superior and suffering, the consummate unwanted outsider. Homosexuals are fey and fluttering cardboard pansies; Spanish peasants come from a Hollywood back lot, friendly, wine-soaked, and childlike. Jake's concierge is a typical Parisian concierge.

Hemingway's settings, exact and faithfully detailed mappings of cities and vibrant renditions of countrysides, also carry symbolic weight. Paris is civilized; social intercourse there is governed by monetary transactions. Spain is primitive and real, earthy; social intercourse there depends on unspoken affinities that arise from an uncorrupted human depth. Uncorrupted nature, whether in the form of a mountain road, a trout stream, or the sea, is true, cleansing, and restorative. Hemingway's prose, plain, vivid, stripped-down, and bare, driven much more by polysyndeton than by metaphor, nevertheless reconstructs and lays out the psychology of experience and perception peculiar to his narrator, Jake Barnes.[2] Look at the first paragraph of chapter 3. Jake perceives experience as a series of images passing by, frame after single frame. It is the equivalent in prose of taking one day at a time.

> It was a warm spring night and I sat at a table on the terrace of the Napolitain after Robert had gone, watching it get dark and the electric signs come on, and the red and green stop-and-go traffic-signal, and the crowd going by, and the horse-cabs clippety-clopping along at the edge of the solid taxi traffic, and the *poules* going by, singly and in pairs, looking for the evening meal. I watched a good-looking girl walk past the table and watched her go up the street and lost sight of her, and watched another, and then saw the first one coming back again. She went by once more and I caught her eye, and she came over and sat down at the table.

The Sun Also Rises, despite the sprawl of its story and the size of its cast, is fundamentally an anatomy of Jake Barnes's melancholy, a diagram of his spirit, the drama of his conflicts, the plan of his survival after suffering a traumatic wound in the Great War. It presents the impulses of his inner characteristics as the actions of some of the novel's other characters. Having been sexually injured in the war and being, consequently, incapable of the sexual expression of love or the orgastic release of passion, Jake Barnes is a man haunted by a shadow life. Robert Cohn, Mike Campbell, and Pedro Romero can each be read as his emanations, the shadows he casts. Each presents and represents one of his aspects. Aside from being real figures themselves, they can be read as allegorical representations of characteristic aspects of Jake.

Robert Cohn is Jake's dark shadow and his unwanted double, the secret self he has disciplined himself not to reveal. He is Jake as a failure, as an outcast, and stripped of the grace and irony that protect the integrity of his sensibility despite his sexual incapacity. Cohn is the man Jake does not want to be who does what Jake wishes to do and cannot do. Cohn does what Jake is too disciplined to do and would not. From the opening sentence, Cohn haunts the book. Like a foul specter he disturbs everyone else's experience. Everyone wishes he would just go away. Bill Gorton, Jake's buddy rather than one of his shadows, the man who accepts Jake as a man despite his injury and who attributes anything objectionable about Cohn to the fact that he is a Jew, repeatedly wishes Cohn in hell. But Cohn does not go away until he has played his part in the allegorical representation of the drama of Jake's impossible desire for Brett and his ambivalence toward Romero. Jake's admiration for Romero is open, but the very attribute that elicits that admiration, the natural power that Romero has that Jake has lost, must also call forth Jake's resentment, not easily admitted or acknowledged, but expressed in Cohn's behavior by displacement.

"Robert Cohn was once middleweight boxing champion of Princeton," the narrative begins, giving Cohn pride of place and suggesting the possibility that he is the focus of the novel. But his privilege is immediately usurped. "Do not think that I," the narrator interrupts one sentence into the narrative, his "I" taking the pride of place away from Robert Cohn and at the same time making the reader his confidant, "am very much impressed by that as a boxing title." He does not say why he is not. Instead, he gives his knife one more twist. The sentence ends "but it meant a lot to Cohn." With just that coda, Robert Cohn is entirely discredited, diminished, made something of a fool. Cohn takes pride in what has little value for the narrator. The reason for Cohn's pride, which is also at the root of Jake's contempt, is that Cohn is a Jew. He boxed in order "to counteract the feeling of inferiority and shyness he had felt on being treated as a Jew at Princeton." Jake does not argue that his sense of inferiority was mistaken.

Hemingway's strength as a writer shows in his ability to draw two portraits simultaneously and to manipulate the reader's attitude regarding each. As Jake frames Cohn as a misfit and an outsider, he also defines himself. He is cynical but essentially good-hearted. His dislike for Cohn is moderated by pity for him. He seems to understand that Cohn is at an existential disadvantage, inevitably, just because he is a Jew. Jake has a similar closet pity for himself as he lives with the irreversible consequences of his castration in the war. Both Jake and Cohn must endure a diminution of their value as persons. Being a Jew, regarded as a taint at Princeton, Jake reports, taints Cohn in Jake's mind, too, perhaps somewhat mitigating the taint of his own sexual incapacity and reducing his ability to see his brotherhood with Cohn, and it taints Cohn in the minds of others like Bill, Mike, and Brett. If there was any doubt about Jake's attitude toward Jews, that Cohn's Jewishness gives Jake an opportunity to feel superior to him and different from him, it is resolved when Jake reports that when Cohn's nose was broken in the ring, "it certainly improved his nose." Comments disparaging Cohn because he is Jewish and disparaging Jews as a group proceed as a matter of course throughout the book.

Whether this routine anti-Semitism reflects the intrusion of an unworthy prejudice of Hemingway's or is a characteristic of the temperament of his characters is of particular importance in determining the artistic and psychological depth of *The Sun Also Rises* and how it is to be read. If the novel merely includes undigested bits of anti-Semitism, then it is weakened, as is Hemingway's command of his material. But if the anti-Semitism is included as a deliberate and defining attribute of Hemingway's characters, then it provides the reader with an important way of understanding Jake's own personal anguish and the collective psychology of his friends. Then, anti-Semitism is not something that defines Jews; it suggests something about those who denigrate Jews. As he presents it, rather than seeming a blot on him, Jake attempts to mask his anti-Semitism as a form of tolerance. The seductive tone of confidentiality and intimacy that Jake establishes with the reader in the opening sentences tends to make the reader his accomplice rather than his judge: Jake appears to mitigate Robert Cohn's faults even as he broadcasts them. Jake accepts that being Jewish must diminish Cohn, but despite that, he says, "I rather liked him." Similarly, talking of the novel Cohn wrote, Jake says, "It was really not such a bad novel as the critics later called it, although it was a very poor novel." Jake manages to belittle Cohn's work and still appears magnanimous. Implicit is his pride that he, Jake, the apparent author of the book we are reading, is the superior writer. Implicit, too, is the sense, once more, that Cohn is Jake's feared and unwanted self, the man he might be were he not graced by being himself, the loser he must not let himself be, an inferior writer, a two-bit newspaper stringer rather than a first-rate novelist, the butt of jokes and disdain because of his ghastly wound. For just these reasons, Jake condescends to Cohn.

In the last chapter, Hemingway gives a clear indication that he is using anti-Semitism to define something about his characters, that it is not an accidental prejudice of his own marring the book but a deliberate component of his work reflecting a psychic mechanism that needs to be taken into account for understanding his characters and Jake especially. Speaking of Brett's financial state, Mike Campbell says, "She never has any money. She gets five hundred quid a year and pays three hundred and fifty of it in interest to Jews." Bill, casually, consistently, and unthinkingly anti-Semitic, says, "I suppose they get it at the source." "Quite," Mike says, but then adds, correcting his assumption, "They're not really Jews. We just call them Jews. They're Scotsmen, I believe." Although he *calls* them Jews, the usurers are not Jews! They are not the alien Other whose demeaned presence ensures "our" superiority. They are of Mike's own tribe. In this way, using Mike's aside, Hemingway explodes the anti-Semitism of the novel, showing it to belong to the narrator and his friends, not to the author. Jews, once again, in *The Sun Also Rises*, as they have been throughout history, are used as a type, as scapegoats, as those upon whom the faults of others are projected. The idea "Jews" is a fictional construct, created by the anti-Semitism of Jake and his crowd, attached to actual Jews; "Jews" are made into the people to whom the lost characters of *The Sun Also Rises* can feel superior. And Robert Cohn is their embodiment and representative in the book. Cohn, like "the Jews," is blamed for—and, as a character in Jake's lost world, created to embody—the sins, unacceptable desires and attitudes, or misdeeds of others.

Mike Campbell's troubles, for example, have nothing to do with Jews. He is bankrupt not because of Jews but because, in the muddle caused by his drinking, he was not alert to the fact that his business partner was cheating him until it was too late. His difficult relationship with Brett results only from the way she is and the way he is. Like Jake, he is an impotent man. He is economically impotent and infantilized, relying on the allowance he gets from his mother. In addition, despite being sexually whole, he is, although about to be married to Brett, hardly her lover. She seems to be marrying him because of the impossibility of a sexual relationship with Jake, and he accepts her rampant, apparently built-in promiscuity, seeking oblivion in alcohol and drowning his anger in drink until it erupts in drunken explosions. As a lost man, he mirrors Jake. As an angry man, he has Robert Cohn to vilify, to taunt, to blame, and to damn, not because Cohn has slept with Brett but because *as a Jew* he has slept with Brett. Mike can express his jealous anger at Brett's promiscuity, which his position as a scapegrace and a bankrupt makes it difficult for him to express in other instances of her sexual betrayal, because his unworthiness with regard to her other, non-Jewish, lovers, when the lover is Cohn, dissolves. Cohn, being Jewish, is prima facie, in Mike's world, inferior to him.

In the drama of Jake's thwarted passion, Robert Cohn plays the scapegoat. Cohn performs the acts Jake wishes to but cannot, not only sleeping with Brett but also expressing jealousy of Romero and, perhaps worst, openly showing the pain of not being able to have Brett as a lover. Consequently, Cohn is vilified, shamed, and pathetic. Jake is only peripherally embarrassed when he leaves Pamplona. After Brett sleeps with Romero and Cohn beats him up, Montoya will neither look at Jake nor talk to him. But Cohn is a pariah; he must disappear, not just from Pamplona but from the pages of the novel.

II

Being a strong narrator, Jake exerts a powerful influence on the way the reader receives the story he tells. It is easy to accept his point of view and his understanding of the material. Yet Hemingway does give, inside Jake's account, enough information for the reader to get free of Jake's influence. This demands, however, that the reader examine the events of Jake's narrative and his motives scrupulously. Motives are by nature difficult to determine. An omniscient, godlike, third-person narrator can state them, and a reader must accept them as givens. But in a subjective, first-person narrative like *The Sun Also Rises* givens are not absolutes, and truths or even facts must be established by the process of juxtaposition, through the comparison and contrasting of events. How Jake and his crowd regard particular actions may not be the way a reader ought to judge them.

Robert Cohn's attitude toward Brett is really not very different, after all, from Brett's attitude toward Romero—and this is something the reader must construct by reading the accounts of both free of Jake's influence. Brett, for Cohn, and Romero, for Brett, represent unattainable objects that become possibilities. Both Brett and Romero are physically striking, universally admired and desired, and embodiments of a dazzling hauteur. Nor is Cohn's insatiable longing for Brett very different from Jake's. Jake suffers like Cohn. He endures tormented nights and cries in his bed. But he bears his suffering without showing it to the world. He is a withdrawn man, not an outcast. Cohn lacks Jake's capacity not to show his wounds publicly. His display of vulnerability and pain is defined as Jewish and condemned by Jake and his crowd because it violates the code of maintaining an ironic surface demeanor in spite of profound inner misery.

Once Cohn has been wounded by Brett, after she has lived with him for a week in San Sebastian and then abandoned him—their affair having had no meaning for her—Cohn goes to pieces. He cannot let Brett out of his sight, or shake off his desire for her, or believe she really does not care for him. He suffers openly, without Jake's ironic stoicism, and he will go to any lengths, even of self-abasement, to possess her, unable to accept that she has rejected him. His anguish, his transparency, and his openly evident need disgust the others, and they call his suffering Jewish. "I hate him," Brett tells Jake with a shiver. "I hate his damned suffering." But after Brett sees Romero and falls for him, she is equally obsessed and equally desperate, and equally she suffers. "I'm a goner," she tells Jake repeatedly. "I'm a goner. I can't help it. It's tearing me all up inside. . . . I've got to do something I really want to do. I've lost my self-respect." Jake shows compassion and takes her to the bar where Romero is, brings them together and then leaves them alone, forging a tacit understanding by a glance with Romero. Brett suffers the same attack of desire as Cohn and pursues her desire with the same intensity, but she is among the elect and Cohn among the damned. She is desired by everyone and calls the shots. To the other characters, Cohn is undesirable, not just because he exposes the depth of pain the others take pride in concealing, and not just because of the existential blight that comes with being a Jew, but because *as a Jew*, Cohn *cannot* possess the powerful masculine qualities that sanctify a man, the qualities that Jake sees embodied in the bullfighter. Because Romero is a supreme embodiment of masculinity, Jake can identify with Romero as Brett's lover and allow Romero to be his proxy. The idea of Cohn, on the other hand, being his stand-in is unpardonable.

Until he goes to San Sebastian with Brett, Cohn is simply a man of the wrong sensibility, which is largely assumed to be the consequence of his being a Jew. He lacks an essential manliness that Jake possesses, despite Jake's sexual powerlessness. Male potency, as Hemingway constructs it for Jake, is not a genital attribute but a function of an embodied sensibility, a sensibility Jake and his friends not only possess but also define by the way they act, even when they act disgracefully, as Mike is prone to do. They are all of the same tribe. Cohn is outside the tribe because he is Jewish. He lacks the capacity to appreciate the right things; he is missing a passion that fires the other men in the book.

He does not connect with them in the unspoken way they do with each other. The first direct indication that Cohn is a deficient man, after Jake has told about Cohn's days at Princeton, his novel, and his failed marriage, comes in a snatch of dialogue with Jake. "I can't stand it to think my life is going so fast and I'm not really living it," Cohn complains. To comfort him, Jake responds, "Nobody ever lives their life all the way up except bullfighters." "I'm not interested in bullfighters," Cohn says, revealing a shattering unworthiness. "That's an abnormal life." Additionally, Cohn has what Jake considers are the wrong dreams, generated by what he judges are the wrong stimuli:

> He had been reading W. H. Hudson. That sounds like an innocent occupation, but Cohn had read and reread "The Purple Land." "The Purple Land" is a very sinister book if read too late in life. It recounts splendid imaginary amorous adventures of a perfect English gentleman in an intensely romantic land, the scenery of which is very well described. For a man to take it at thirty-four as a guide-book to what life holds is about as safe as it would be for a man of the same age to enter Wall Street direct from a French convent, equipped with a complete set of the more practical [Horatio] Alger books. Cohn, I believe, took every word of "The Purple Land" as literally as though it had been an R. G. Dun [financial] report.

There is something ironically revealing in Jake's assessment, for it reflects his own condition as well as Cohn's and, consequently, a resemblance that would not please him to recognize. At the heart of *The Purple Land*, beyond the "splendid . . . adventures" of its English hero, adventures that include the hero's involvement in revolutionary movements as well as "amorous" encounters, adventures that transform him from "a perfect English gentleman" into an egalitarian democrat and admirer of tribal folkways—as Jake is an admirer of the simple Spanish country folk—there is a vision of a society free of the constraints of civilization, class, and hierarchy. Hudson presents the vision of a republican society of men in touch with nature and with their own natural power, wild but sociable. Cohn's is really not a very different vision of escape from European alienation as the one Jake cherishes of Spain, with its peasants and bullfighters.

Once Cohn has returned from San Sebastian, after he has been Brett's lover, the other men's attitudes toward him change. He is not simply disdained because he is a Jew. He is despised—not just because he shows that he is tormented by jealous love but because *as a Jew* he was presumptuous and did not know his place. When Cohn first sees Brett and looks at her, it bothers Jake. "He looked a great deal as his compatriot must have looked when he saw the promised land," Jake writes with cutting derision, comparing Cohn to the biblical Moses and Brett to the land of Canaan.[3] "He had that look of eager, deserving expectation." Jake resents Cohn's desire less than he resents Cohn's sense of being entitled to his desire. In the creation of the story, Hemingway is complicit with Jake, for Hemingway constructs Cohn's liaison with Brett as a glimpse not of what he can achieve but of what must slip from his grasp. Cohn bears the pain of the symbolic expulsion from Eden that the others in *The Sun Also Rises* also experience in their own lives, but without their fabled "grace under pressure."

III

In chapter 3, while Jake is with his friends and a prostitute he has taken to dinner at a bar where people go to dance, "a crowd of young men, some in jerseys and some in their shirt sleeves, got out" of two taxis. "I could see their hands and newly washed wavy hair in the light from the door," Jake writes. "The policeman standing by the door looked at me and smiled." The smile signified the amused condescension that two heterosexual men can share at the sight of homosexuals. Jake describes the homosexuals stereotypically and concludes by noting that "with them was Brett. She looked very lovely and she was very much with them." He is enraged at the homosexuals without clearly knowing why. "They are supposed to be amusing. And you should be tolerant," Jake writes, "but I wanted to swing on one, any one, to shatter that superior, simpering composure."

"Superior, simpering composure"! "Superior" is the word Jake uses to describe what most grates on him about Robert Cohn. He takes it to be attributable to Cohn's Jewishness, and he takes it to be an unearned attribute. But just because Jake attributes an air of superiority to Cohn or to the homosexuals does not mean that it really belongs to them. His use of the word more likely indicates that Jake feels inferior to them, but rather than recognizing that shameful feeling, he attributes a feeling of superiority to them. At the same time, Jake actually does feel superior to Cohn and to the homosexuals because he is not them. Their presumed superiority is not what he defines as real superiority—Pedro Romero embodies that for him—but it is a denigration of manliness, a matter of "simpering." Jake resents their composure when *he* is not at all composed. He is distraught. In fact, Jake is jealous of the men with Brett because they are capable of sexual expression as he is not and enraged because, in his mind, they, unlike his friends, who are also sexually whole, denigrate that sexual capability by their homosexuality. What Jake sees is that they hold cheap the power they have, the lack of which so terribly afflicts him. He is envious, a particularly dangerous sensation for a man to feel who is set on maintaining the image of his equanimity and maintaining his inner balance at all cost. He disdains the homosexuals because he derives his identity by defining himself as their superior, and he resents them because, in biological fact, he is not. It is characteristic of Jake to establish his identity and his authenticity at the expense of others. Even Jake's friendship with Bill is defined by what it is not.

It is not the sort of friendship that Robert Cohn could have with either of them. Although Cohn is set to go on a fishing trip in Spain with them before the bullfights in Pamplona, at the last moment he backs out. Bill's response when he hears that Cohn is staying behind: "As for this Robert Cohn, he makes me sick, and he can go to hell, and I'm damned glad he's staying here so we won't have him fishing with us."

The excitement of their friendship involves "trout fishing in the Irati River . . . get[ting] tight now at lunch on the wine of the country, and then tak[ing] a swell bus ride." They take the bus ride, get drunk, check into an inn, eat, drink, sleep, and in the morning set out for the stream. They fool around, do some serious fishing, drink rusty-tasting wine, spar verbally, kidding each other, and bond. "Listen," Bill says to Jake, "You're a hell of a good guy, and I'm fonder of you than anybody on earth. I couldn't tell you that in New York. It'd mean I was a faggot." Bill continues, but changes the key and spins a drunken riff about Abraham Lincoln being in love with General Grant. When it ends, Jake says, "Old Bill." Bill responds with gruff affection: "You bum." They have understood each other on a level deeper than words. And they countercheck their affection, affirming it by denial and contrasting it to homosexual affection and, consequently, in their minds authenticate it by the contrast.

During the climactic bullfight in chapter 18, at a critical moment, Jake shifts attention away from the bullring and his account of Romero's masterful way of working with a nearly blind bull to the reaction of a group of English tourists from Biarritz sitting behind him. Jake has just explained to the reader that Romero "had to get so close that the bull saw his body, and would start for it, and then shift the bull's charge to the flannel and finish out the pass in the classic manner." "'What's he afraid of the bull for?'" he then reports overhearing one of the Biarritz tourists sitting behind him say. "'The bull's so dumb he only goes after the cloth.' 'He's just a young bullfighter. He hasn't learned it yet. . . . Probably he's nervous now.'" By introducing the comments of the gauche tourists from Biarritz, who can appreciate neither bull nor bullfighter, Hemingway does not add to the drama of the bullring, nor is there really much reason that readers should care about the opinions of these fleetingly present spectators. But they rile Jake. He even refers to them sarcastically, a few sentences later, when he mentions Romero's "imperceptible jerk that so offended the critical judgment of the Biarritz bullfight experts." Hemingway includes them because they play a role in the drama of Jake's construction of himself. Their presence gives Jake the opportunity to show once again his own superior status as an aficionado by highlighting the vapidity and vulgarity of their response. He is once more reaffirmed in his own mind as the better man and in the reader's as a man worried about, and needing to prove, his worth.

Jake continually contrasts his sensitivity to someone else's lack of sensitivity for the purpose of self-promotion. On the first venture into Spain, when he, Bill, and Cohn plan to go fishing, while Cohn is still with them, Jake describes the bus ride through the mountains in rhapsodic and loving detail. He is like a kid in his excitement, sitting "up in the front with the driver." "I turned around," he notes. "Robert Cohn was asleep." The magic is lost on him. In the previous paragraph, Jake noted that "the driver had to honk and slow down to avoid running into two donkeys that were sleeping in the road." Cohn is implicitly compared to a donkey. Bill, who is made of the same mettle as Jake, on the other hand, "looked and nodded his head."

The continuous degradation of Robert Cohn, a degradation that, in the minds of the characters in the book, results from the taint upon his personality inevitably caused by his identity as a Jew, serves the purpose of making him an ideal scapegoat, someone upon whom to project all one's faults and to whom one can feel superior. Indeed, he performs the supreme sacrilege against the culture of bullfighting that Jake reveres when he injures Romero.

IV

If Robert Cohn is the marplot and devil of *The Sun Also Rises*, Pedro Romero is its champion angel and, like Cohn, one of Jake's emanations. Cohn is the image of Jake's diminished self, crippled in his sensibility even if whole in his body; Romero is the realization of Jake's ideal self, sound in spirit, sound sexually, achieving what Jake can only desire. Cohn is the man whom Jake struggles not to be; Romero embodies the perfection Jake cannot attain but which Jake approaches by the grace of his appreciation for Romero. Describing Romero, Jake says:

> Pedro Romero had the greatness. He loved bullfighting, and I think he loved the bulls, and I think he loved Brett. Everything of which he could control the locality he did in front of her all that afternoon. Never once did he look up. He made it stronger that way, and did it for himself, too, as well as for her. Because he did not look up to ask if it pleased he did it all for himself inside, and it strengthened him, and yet he did it for her, too. But he did not do it for her at any loss to himself. He gained by it all through the afternoon.

Romero is perfect and perfectly contained within his perfection. He is potent, a master of the bulls he fights and of himself. He is not a suitor standing outside wracked by desire like Cohn and like Jake but sufficient unto himself and consequently attractive to Brett. Unlike his response to Cohn's attraction to Brett, Jake does not openly resent Romero's attraction to Brett or wonder about hers for him. He accepts the inevitability, even the aesthetic rightness, of their liaison, and he facilitates it. But he knows it is not a good thing for Romero's purity as a bullfighter. Jake is not only betraying Romero by bringing Brett to him but also betraying an ideal; he is betraying Montoya, the guardian of that ideal; and he is betraying himself, as a man with an ideal—the culture of bullfighting—and as a man with desires—his love of Brett. That Jake can perpetrate these betrayals allows the reader to surmise that resentment of Romero must unconsciously accompany Jake's esteem for him.

The climactic event of *The Sun Also Rises* is not Brett's liaison with Romero but the confrontation between Robert Cohn and Romero during which Cohn badly hurts Romero, repeatedly punching him as Romero repeatedly, unsuccessfully, rises to respond, never knocked unconscious. Although it works as realism, the narrative clearly functions as the account of conflicting attitudes within Jake, attitudes represented by the figures of Cohn and Romero. Both are Jake's surrogates. Through Romero, Jake finally is able to make love with Brett. Through Cohn, Jake releases his suppressed jealousy and resentment of Romero, jealousy and resentment that must result from Romero's ability to be the man Jake cannot be. Thus Jake's desire for Brett is fulfilled vicariously through Romero, and his repressed desire to punish Romero for his powers, the powers Jake lacks, is effected through Cohn. By constructing a fiction in which he makes Romero Jake's proxy as a lover and Cohn Jake's proxy as an injured and avenging man—making Cohn to blame for the retributive harm that comes to Romero, not Jake—Hemingway has created in Jake a character who realizes his own desires without personally achieving them. In Jake, Hemingway has constructed the drama of a man who does not enact his drama himself but who watches it enacted by others.

Notes

1. Allegory is a literary technique used to make concrete representations of abstract things (ideas, states of mind, conditions of the spirit, sensations, and the like) by turning characteristics into characters. It is most recognizable and familiar in the form of medieval and early Renaissance romances and plays populated by characters that represent the vices and the virtues. When the concept of chastity, for example, appears on the page or the stage in the form of a modest maiden impervious to any assault on her virtue, we are in the literary territory of allegory. In *The Sun Also Rises*, cast within the conventions of realism, allegory is a way of presenting the submerged and internal psychological drama that Jake Barnes must endure because of an injury that affects both his body and his soul.

2. Polysyndeton is a literary device in which ideas, events, images, and so on are narrated through the repetition of conjunctions, most often by the word "and," as in the passage cited here.

3. Because of his sins against God, Moses was allowed to see, but not to enter, the land of Canaan.

"Sign the Wire with Love":
The Morality of Surplus in *The Sun Also Rises*_____

George Cheatham

Bill Gorton's mocking words as Jake Barnes returns from digging worms for trout fishing offer an interesting point of entry into *The Sun Also Rises*:

> "I saw you out the window," [Bill] said. "Didn't want to interrupt you. What were you doing? Burying your money?"
>
> "You lazy bum!"
>
> "Been working for the common good? Splendid. I want you to do that every morning." (113)

For Bill's joke foregrounds Jake's middle-class obsession with money—with working to make it and with spending it efficiently for his own pleasure. The ironically Marxist joke figures a distinction between surplus and exactitude, subtly undercutting Jake's repeatedly professed desire for the latter, and so calls into question the orthodoxy, I suppose it is, of what Scott Donaldson has called a "morality of compensation" in the novel.

Donaldson explains this morality of compensation as the "code" of the whole novel, which Jake explicitly states:

> Just exchange of values. You gave up something and got something else. Or you worked for something. You paid some way for everything that was any good. I paid my way into enough things that I liked, so that I had a good time. Either you paid by learning about them, or by experience, or by taking chances, or by money. Enjoying living was learning to get your money's worth and knowing when you had it. You could get your money's worth. The world was a good place to buy in. (148)

This code, Donaldson explains, pervades the novel through the metaphor of finance which illustrates the moral strength or weakness of the novel's various characters:

> Though physically impotent and mentally tortured, Jake Barnes remains morally sound, while Mike Campbell, Robert Cohn, and Brett Ashley, who are physically whole, have become morally decadent. . . . money and its uses form the metaphor by which the moral responsibility of Jake, Bill, and Pedro is measured against the carelessness of Brett, Mike, and Robert. Financial soundness mirrors moral strength. (77)

Well, certainly, to an extent. But Donaldson's thesis raises at least two basic questions which I wish to explore. First, isn't such an analysis rather too pat, rather too much like an equation which can be rather too easily problematized. And, second, isn't such an explicit exposition as that in Jake's meditations rather uncharacteristic of Hemingway, whose usual technique is to explore central concerns indirectly, through apparent trifles?

First, Donaldson's thesis is clear: Jake, Bill, and Pedro = financial and thus moral responsibility; Brett, Mike, and Robert = financial and thus moral carelessness; financial soundness = moral strength. But the entire pattern is undercut by Bill's joke, for example, which briefly foregrounds the miserly ("Burying your money?") and selfish (Bill, finally, doesn't use the worms) tinge to what Donaldson approvingly calls Jake's "meticulousness about money" and so, however subtly, aligns Jake with Robert Cohn, the stereotyped "Jew," and against Bill Gorton.

Certainly, as Donaldson says, Cohn is apparently "tightfisted with his money" (80).

But isn't Jake somewhat tightfisted as well? What else can one infer from this exchange with Cohn about the bus trip to Burguette:

> "I'm not going up to-day." [Cohn said]. "You and Bill go on ahead."
>
> "I've got your ticket."
>
> "Give it to me. I'll get the money back.
>
> "It's five pesetas."
>
> Robert Cohn took out a silver five-peseta piece and gave it to me. (100)

By this time in the story, of course, Jake, "blind, unforgivingly jealous" (99) of the affair with Brett, hates Cohn and probably demands his five pesetas out of spite. Even so Jake's understated insistence is notable. That his hatred manifests itself financially, even if only to cover his emotions, is telling. Cohn's "wonderful quality of bringing out the worst in everybody" (98) brings out of Jake a sense of rigid exactitude in financial matters. It brings out an undertone of miserliness to Jake's desire, his obsession, to "get his money's worth" which connects him, ironically, with Cohn and so clouds Donaldson's equation.

Jake's quibbling with the hostess in Burguette, although Donaldson cites it approvingly as part of Jake's trying "very hard always to get his money's worth" (76), is similar. Jake first balks at the high price of the lodging, twelve pesetas, but he accepts it when his and Bill's wine is included in that price:

> The girl brought in a big bowl of hot vegetable soup and the wine. We had fried trout afterward and some sort of a stew and a big bowl full of wild strawberries. We did not lose money on the wine, and the girl was shy but nice about bringing it. The old woman looked in once and counted the empty bottles. After supper we went up-stairs and smoked and read in bed to keep warm. Once in the night I woke and heard the wind blowing. It felt good to be warm and in bed. (110-111)

I quote this passage at some length to show the jarring note of Jake's concern about money. The bounty of the meal and comfort of the bed anticipate the understated spiritual goodness of the entire Burguette episode, typified by Bill's mock sermon of the next day:

We should not question. Our stay on earth is not for long. Let us rejoice and believe and give thanks. . . . Let us rejoice in our blessings. Let us utilize the fowls of the air. Let us utilize the product of the vine. (122)

Framed in such a context, Jake's thought, however fleeting, that he is drinking enough wine to get his money's worth, and thereby financially besting the old woman, seems at best petty, at worst blasphemous, depending on how seriously one takes Bill's preaching. At least to a degree Jake is drinking for the wrong reason, not joyfully but commercially. The unpleasant undertone of miserliness here and elsewhere, subtle though it is, is enough to call into question Donaldson's thesis, according to which even such minor tremors in the metaphor of finance would threaten the whole moral structure of the novel.

Many of Bill Gorton's expenditures, on the other hand, are marked by a certain lavishness which disturbs Jake but aligns Bill with the financial carelessness of Brett and Mike rather than the meticulousness of Jake, further vexing Donaldson's division. The redundant shoe-shines Bill buys Mike, for example, make Jake "a little uncomfortable" (173). And Bill's stuffed animals, which are similar to the shoe-shines, bring up the second question I started with: Isn't such an explicit morality of compensation as that in Jake's meditations rather uncharacteristic of Hemingway, whose usual technique is to explore central concerns indirectly, through apparent trifles? The central concern in this case seems more properly called the morality of surplus than the morality of compensation, and it's explored indirectly through the apparent trifle of Bill's stuffed dogs rather than directly in Jake's meditations.

Bill, in fact, not Jake, first introduces what Donaldson calls the "code" of the novel—the concept of "exchange of values":

"Here's a taxidermist's," Bill said. "Want to buy anything? Nice stuffed dog?"

"Come on," I said. "You're pie-eyed."

"Pretty nice stuffed dogs." Bill said. "Certainly brighten up your flat."

"Come on."

"Just one stuffed dog. I can take 'em or leave 'em alone. But listen, Jake. Just one stuffed dog."

"Come on."

"Mean everything in the world to you after you bought it. Simple exchange of values. You give them money. They give you a stuffed dog."

"We'll get one on the way back."

"All right. Have it your own way. Road to hell paved with unbought stuffed dogs. Not my fault." (72-3)

Bill introduces the concept in such a context, though, that Jake's unqualified echoing of it seems at least a little odd. A stuffed dog is so superfluous, so gratuitously non-utilitarian, as to mock in advance Jake's notion of exchange as equivalence.

The two continue their conversation:

"How'd you feel that way about dogs so sudden?" [Jake asked.]

"Always felt that way about dogs. Always been a great lover of stuffed animals."

We stopped and had a drink.

"Certainly like to drink," Bill said. "You ought to try it sometimes, Jake."

"You're about a hundred and forty-four ahead of me."

"Ought not to daunt you. Never be daunted. Secret of my success. Never been daunted. Never been daunted in public." (73)

Jake, though, seems to be daunted. That is, he seems to draw back from, even to fear, both here and throughout the novel, the sort of loss of control, the sort of risk, the sort of financial and moral inexactitude, exemplified by Bill's drunken excess. Such superfluity as Jake fears, however, such inexactitude of exchange, is essentially human. It is natural for humans to transcend their own limits. What we call culture or history is, after all, an open-ended transformation of fixed boundaries, a transcendence of mere appetite, a rich surplus over precise measure. It is this capacity for a certain lavish infringement of exact limit which distinguishes humankind (Eagleton).

Surplus, however, is radically ambivalent. And this creative tendency to exceed oneself is also the source of destructiveness. Hence Jake's fear. He's literally and figuratively gun shy. For the war, on a large scale, pervasively figures the destructive use of surplus throughout *The Sun Also Rises*. A colossal cultural over-reaching into too much—too much wealth, power, greed, rhetoric, patriotism—that "dirty war" has in some way wrecked the lives of a generation. The war has stripped away its excess in self-destruction leaving a kind of nothingness at its center, a lack—figured most clearly in Jake's wound. And as a defensive response to both the war's excess and the threat of that nothingness, Jake embraces exactitude. A world stripped clean of excess is an exact one—one in which a person can precisely balance both his financial and moral checkbook, as it were, one in which a person can precisely know the values, one in which, as Jake asserts, "You could get your money's worth."

The talkative waiter probably knows how to get his money's worth. He's probably daunted too. He certainly shares if not Jake's fear of destructive excess at least Jake's sense of the waste of it. Following the death of the peasant gored during the encierro, the waiter, himself not an aficionado, denounces bull-fighting:

> "Badly cogido through the back," he said. He put the pots down at the table and sat down in the chair at the table. "A big horn wound. All for fun. Just for fun. What do you think of that? . . . Muerto. Dead. He's dead. With a horn through him. All for morning fun. Es muy flamenco." (197-98)

This waiter, of course, will never run the bulls. But, for that matter, Jake doesn't run them either. He only watches, and he barely manages to do that. Jake describes two encierros, both of which he almost misses by oversleeping. One he watches—significantly, I think—from the balcony of Cohn's room, where he's slept, wearing Cohn's coat; the other he almost misses, hung over and groggy from the previous night's drunken fight with Cohn.

But although he doesn't face the bulls himself, Jake, unlike the waiter, at least recognizes the value deriving from such confrontations. And he recognizes further, with some trepidation, that it's not just bull-fighters who must work either in or out of the terrain of the bull. "In bull-fighting." says Jake, "they speak of the terrain of the bull and the terrain of the bull-fighter. As long as a bull-fighter stays in his own terrain he is comparatively safe. Each time he enters into the terrain of the bull he is in great danger" (213). The terrain of the bull specifically and the whole fiesta generally figure that tenuous ground between too much and nothing where creative excess resides. Jake, however, after the destruction of the war, alternately fears and desires this excess, and the novel maps his alternate advances into and retreats from this tenuous ground, into and from the terrain of the bull.

The road to hell doesn't traverse this tenuous ground, of course, and it is, as Bill Gorton says, paved with unbought stuffed dogs. That is, crass, utilitarian quantifying of experience, of life, of whatever is damning. And whatever sort of salvation or redemption there is lies in surplus, in the exceeding of exact equivalence. Experiences, for example, exceed the sort of valuation that Jake, in his night-time meditations, would like to give them:

> We walked on and circled the island. The river was dark and a bateau mouche went by. all bright with lights, going fast and quiet up and out of sight under the bridge. Down the river was Notre Dame squatting against the night sky. We crossed to the left bank of the Seine by the wooden foot-bridge from the Quai de Bethune, and stopped on the bridge and looked down the river at Notre Dame. Standing on the bridge the island looked dark, the houses were high against the sky, and the trees were shadows.
>
> "It's pretty grand," Bill said. "God, I love to get back." (77)

Notions of equivalence, of exact valuation, are radically vexed by such moments as this one on the bridge—like stuffed dogs which, mysteriously, mean "everything in the world" to you after you buy them (72). Or like Brett, who by any equitable standard of valuation clearly isn't worth what Jake pays to indulge her selfish desire for Romero. As Michael Reynolds says,

> By pimping for Brett, [Jake] has cancelled his membership in the select club of aficionados. Montoya may have once forgiven him his drunken friends, but he will never forgive him for assisting in Pedro Romero's corruption. The novel's most understated passage occurs when Jake pays his hotel bill. He tells us: "Montoya did not come near us." This, the cruelest line in the book, goes without comment. . . . Jake, who started with so few assets, now has even fewer to get him through the night. If the novel "is such a hell of a sad story," as Hemingway said it was, the sadness resides in Jake's loss. (132)

Yet somehow Jake's morality is mirrored in this very loss, not, as Donaldson says, in his financial soundness. For by returning to Brett, Jake re-enters—decisively, I think—the terrain of the bull, that tenuous ground between too much and nothing:

> That was it. Send a girl off with one man. Introduce her to another to go off with him. Now go and bring her back. And sign the wire with love. That was it all right. (239)

Such forgiveness simply doesn't add up, to use Donaldson's metaphor. Has Jake paid for Brett with Montoya? Is she then his? Must he now pay again? Is he getting his money's worth? Unlike Jake's checkbook, the relationship just doesn't balance. Nor should it, for the relationship involves a simple exchange of values. When introducing the concept of exchange of values, we remember, Bill Gorton says,

Mean everything in the world to you after you bought it. Simple exchange of values. You give them money. They give you a stuffed dog. (73)

When echoing this concept, however, Jake makes a subtle but deeply significant revision:

Just exchange of values. You gave up something and got something else. (148)

Both phrases—simple exchange of values and just exchange of values—are radically ambiguous. Just exchanges are mere exchanges, sure, but they are also equitable exchanges, legal, correct, proper, exact, accurate, uniform exchanges. Simple exchanges, on the other hand, are mere exchanges as well, but they are also artless, open, guileless, innocent, humble, wretched, pitiful, silly, foolish exchanges. This understated trifle, the distinction between *just* and *simple*, is perhaps the moral center of the novel.

No, Jake's rescue of Brett doesn't add up. For Jake, having lost his penis in the war, will not be, as it were, stuffing Brett. Hemingway probably intended such a sexual implication, since the stuffed and probably mounted dogs are part of a series of such images, most obviously the final mounted policeman with his raised baton. Were Jake able to have intercourse, he and Brett would fit, match, balance, in the conventional sexual equation $1 + 1 = 1$. Without a penis, however, with this nothing in the middle caused by the destructive excess of the war, Jake no longer fits. Hence his fear and its attendant risk, nothingness. And hence his obsession with balance, with exactitude. But only in such a wretched, pitiful, and foolish imbalance as that of his relationship with Brett does Jake's humanity, his morality, reside. His simple forgiveness of Brett exceeds exact equivalence. It is a gratuitous excess of the strict requirements of justice, a kind of nothing, a refusal to calculate debt, out of which something may come.

Works Cited

Donaldson, Scott. "Hemingway's Morality of Compensation." *Ernest Hemingway's The Sun Also Rises*. Ed. Harold Bloom. New York: Chelsea House, 1987. 71-90.

Eagleton, Terry. *William Shakespeare*. Oxford: Blackwell, 1986.

Hemingway, Ernest. *The Sun Also Rises*. New York: Scribner's, 1970.

Reynolds, Michael. "False Dawn: *The Sun Also Rises* Manuscript." *Ernest Hemingway's The Sun Also Rises*. Ed. Harold Bloom. New York: Chelsea House, 1987. 117-32.

Frederic Henry's Escape and the Pose of Passivity

Scott Donaldson

I

Sheridan Baker distinguishes between the early Hemingway hero, a passive young man somewhat given to self-pity, and the later, far more active and courageous hero.[1] Nick Adams is a boy things happen to, Robert Jordan a man who makes them happen. This neat classification breaks down, however, when applied to the complicated narrator protagonist of *A Farewell to Arms*. Frederic Henry consistently depicts himself as a passive victim inundated by the flow of events. "The world" was against him and Catherine. "They" caught the lovers off base—and killed Catherine as one of "the very good and the very gentle and the very brave" who die young. But Frederic, who survives, belongs to another category, and his determinism is hardly convincing. Assign blame though he will to anonymous scapegoats, he is still deeply implicated in the death of his lover.[2]

It is the same in war as in love. At the beginning, Frederic tells us, he simply goes along. An American in Rome when World War I breaks out, he joins the Italian ambulance corps for no particular reason: "There isn't always an explanation for everything." He falls into the drinking and whoring routine of the other officers at Gorizia largely out of inertia. He follows and gives orders as required, but hardly as a consequence of patriotism or dedication to any cause. He suffers a series of disillusionments—his wound, the "war disgust" of his comrades, the overt pacifism of his men, the theatricality and incompetence of the Italian military generally, the final moral chaos of the retreat from Caporetto—which reach a climax with his plunge into the Tagliamento to avoid summary execution.

When he emerges from the river, Frederic is presumably reborn.[3] But is he? Now he is on his own, and he must act to escape. Yet he has not sloughed off his old skin, and before completing his flight he will cover himself with that same cloak of passivity he donned when describing his relationship with Catherine—and for much the same reason. Rinaldi was right about Frederic Henry. He is the quintessential "Anglo-Saxon remorse boy," so driven by guilt that he is unwilling—even when telling his story years later—to accept responsibility for his actions.[4] This view, implicit in the text of the novel, gains added authority in those fragments which Hemingway chose to delete before publishing.[5]

II

Consider Frederic's behavior after he escapes the murderous carabinieri—a part of the novel that has received little critical attention. While still being swept along by the swollen waters of the river, he begins to map out a course of action. He considers taking off his boots and clothes but decides against it, since he would be "in a bad position" should he land barefoot. He will need his boots, for he already knows where he is going—to Mestre—and that to get there he will have to hike to the main rail line between Venice and Trieste. Why must he reach Mestre? He does not tell us at once, but it comes out later in conversation with Catherine: because he has an old order of movement authorizing travel from Mestre to Milan, and he needs only alter the date. In Milan, of course, he expects to find Catherine at the hospital.

When he reaches shore safely, Tenente Henry begins "to think out" what he should do next. He wrings out his clothes, and before putting his coat back on cuts off the cloth stars that identify him as an officer. The battle police (who were shooting officers indiscriminately) have taken his pistol, so he conceals his empty holster underneath the coat. Encountering a machine-gun detachment, he limps to masquerade as one of the wounded and is not challenged. He crosses the flat Venetian plain to the rail line and jumps aboard a canvas-covered gondola car, avoiding one guard's notice and "contemptuously" staring down another, who concludes he must have something to do with the train. He clambers inside the car, bumping his head on the guns within. He washes the blood away with rainwater since he will have to get off before the train reaches Mestre and he does "not want to look conspicuous." He is on his way back to his lover, and tries to think of nothing but their reunion and escape: "Probably have to go damned quickly. She would go. I knew she would go. When would we go? That was something to think about. It was getting dark. I lay and thought where we would go. There were many places."

The next day in Milan, Frederic engages in three different conversations that confirm Switzerland as their destination. The first of these occurs when he goes to the wine shop in Milan for early morning coffee and bread. The owner of the wine shop realizes at once that Frederic has deserted: he has seen the lieutenant come "down the wall" from the train and notices the bare spots on the sleeves where the stars have been cut away. But he is sympathetic and offers to put Frederic up, to arrange for false leave papers, and to help him leave the country. Nothing comes of this proposal, for the understandably cautious fugitive keeps insisting that he is in no trouble and needs no assistance.

In an earlier draft, Frederic actually did contract for forged papers.[6] This is the deleted passage, which originally followed the wine shop owner's offer of leave papers midway on p. 239 of the text:

"I have no need for papers. I have papers. As for the stars, they never wear them at the front."

I thought a minute.

"I will be back."

"Only you must tell me now."

"A Tessera [identity card]," I said, "and leave papers."

"Write the name."

"Give me a pencil." I wrote a name[7] on the edge of a newspaper. "Some one will call for them."

"Who?"

"I don't know. He will bring the photograph for the Tessera. You will know me by that."

"All right. That will be one hundred and fifty lire."

"Here is fifty."

"Do not worry Tenente."

"What do you say?"

"I say do not worry."

"I do not worry. I am not in trouble."

"You are not in trouble if you stay with me."

"I must go."

"Come back. Come again."

"I will see you."

"Come at any time."

"Don't forget I am your friend," he said when I went out. He was a strange enough man.

"Good," I said.

Sheldon Norman Grebstein and Michael S. Reynolds have both observed that when Hemingway cut this passage he tightened the plot of the novel.[8] With an identity card and leave papers, Frederic might have remained in Italy and avoided arrest for some time. Without them, he must leave the country very soon. But the deletion also functions in two other ways: to avoid a lapse in credibility and to flesh out the character of the protagonist. A man on the run, Frederic would be unlikely to repose trust in the first stranger who accosts him after his desertion. Furthermore, to go through the spy-story machinations outlined here—giving "a name" apparently not his own, sending an intermediary to pick up the counterfeit papers, paying but one-third down to encourage delivery, and maintaining despite this damning evidence that he has nothing to worry about—would war against the lieutenant's nature. He already feels guilty, as we shall see. Active participation in illegal intrigue would only exacerbate that guilt.

Leaving the wine shop, Frederic skirts the train station, where there were sure to be military police, and goes to see the porter of the hospital and his wife. They tell him that Miss Barkley has gone to Stresa, on Lake Maggiore, with "the other lady English." After extracting a promise ("It is very important") that they tell no one he has been there, he immediately takes a cab to see Simmons, an American singer trying to break into Italian opera he'd met while recuperating from his wounds. Lieutenant Henry's plan is now taking shape. He has visited Lake Maggiore before—earlier, he and Catherine had planned to vacation at Pallanza, as preferable to Stresa because further from Milan— and surely knows that the lake extends into Switzerland. So upon awakening Simmons, he wastes no time in coming to the point. He's in a jam, he tells the singer; and asks about "the procedure in going to Switzerland." He knows that the Swiss will intern him, but wonders what that means. "Nothing," Simmons reassures him. "It's very simple. You can go anywhere. I think you just have to report or something."

Even with Simmons Frederic is somewhat evasive. It's not yet "definite" that he's fleeing the police. He "think(s)" he's through with the war. But Simmons does not insist on the details, and like the wine shop owner he's more than willing to help. When Frederic asks him to go out and buy civilian clothes for his use, Simmons won't hear of it; take anything of mine, he commands (Frederic probably decided to call on Simmons rather than some other acquaintance because they were of a size). Thus the lieutenant is relieved of the danger of traveling around Italy in an officer's uniform with his stars cut off and his holster empty, without leave papers or proper orders. The way is clear for escape, and before leaving Frederic ascertains the means. Yes, he tells Simmons, he still has his passport.

"Then get dressed, my dear fellow, and off to old Helvetia."
"It's not that simple. I have to go to Stresa first."
"Ideal, my dear fellow. You just row a boat across."

Once in Stresa, Frederic continues to lay the groundwork for his flight. He takes a carriage to the hotel, since it "was better"—less attention-provoking—"to arrive in a carriage" than on foot. He looks up Emilio the barman he used to fish with, lies to him about his civilian clothes ("I'm on leave. Convalescing-leave"), discovers where Catherine and Miss Ferguson are staying, and—most important of all—chats with him about fishing. The next morning, he persuades Emilio to leave the bar and take him out into the lake to troll. They catch no fish, but after two vermouths at the Isola dei Pescatori—the fisherman's island, which was not a tourist attraction like the Isola Bella they row past, and hence a safer stopping place[9]—he learns of Emilio's disaffection with the war (if called, the barman says, he won't go) and admits that he himself had been a fool to enlist. Little else of consequence passes between them, but they have reached a tacit understanding. "Any time you want it," Emilio remarks after padlocking his boat, "I'll give you the key."

Up to this point, Frederic has moved purposefully toward his goal. As a fugitive from military justice, he has repeatedly been forced to act, in both senses of the verb. He has calculated his chances, and calculated well. Finally he has located Catherine and found where he can get a boat to take them to the neutral country down the lake. Yet with his lover he is all wide-eyed innocence and passivity; now he will "act" only in the theatrical sense. He understands precisely what must be done, but waits for her—and then for Emilio—to tell him what that is. By adopting this pose, he appears far less calculating in her eyes. By involving her and the barman, he tries to parcel out shares of his guilt.

After a long night of love-making, Catherine queries Frederic about his status.

> "But won't they arrest you if they catch you out of uniform?"
> "They'll probably shoot me."
> "Then we'll not stay here. We'll get out of the country."

He has, he confesses, "thought something of that," but continues his charade, waiting for her to drag the scheme out of him.

> "What would you do if they came to arrest you?"
> "Shoot them."
> "You see how silly you are. I won't let you go out of the hotel until we leave here."
> "Where are we going to go?"

But Catherine will not cooperate: "Please don't be that way, darling. We'll go wherever you say. But please find some place to go right away." So Frederic reluctantly reveals his plan: "Switzerland is down the lake, we can go there."

That midnight, as a rainstorm sweeps across Lake Maggiore, Emilio comes to announce that the military police will arrest Frederic in the morning, and the lieutenant once again plays the game of "tell me what to do." When the barman knocks, Frederic takes him into the bathroom (so as not to waken Catherine, or alert her to his deviousness), and disingenuously asks, "What's the matter Emilio? Are you in trouble?" No, it is the Tenente who is in trouble, and this incredible dialogue ensues:

> "Why are they going to arrest me?"
> "For something about the war."
> "Do you know what?"
> "No. But I know that they know you were here before as an officer and now you are here out of uniform. After this retreat they arrest everybody."
> *I thought a minute.*
> "What time do they come to arrest me?"
> "In the morning. I don't know the time."
> *"What do you say to do?"*
> He put his hat in the washbowl. It was very wet and had been dripping on the floor.

"If you have nothing to fear an arrest is nothing. But it is always bad to be arrested—especially now."

"I don't want to be arrested."

"Then go to Switzerland."

"*How?*"

"In my boat."

"There is a storm," I said.

"The storm is over. It is rough but you will be all right."

"*When should we go?*"

"Right away. They might come to arrest you early in the morning.

"I thought a minute" is an exact repetition of a phrase used before, when Frederic—in the deleted passage—determined to purchase false leave papers. In both places, it is a sign that he is about to embark on a course of deception. In this case, the deception consists of suggesting to Emilio—in the questions italicized—that the notion of crossing to Switzerland in his boat has never occurred to Lieutenant Henry. This is patently untrue, as the barman, like Hemingway's readers, must realize. But Frederic's purpose is not simply to fool Emilio. He is after bigger game: the raging tooth of conscience within.

III

Lieutenant Henry, in the version of the tale he presents, is provided with every possible reason to bid a farewell to arms. As an officer with a foreign accent separated from his men, he faces almost certain death from the carabinieri unless he runs. But long before that climactic moment, Frederic has brought up example after example of soldiers trying to opt out of the war. Rinaldi, we learn, has few real wounds to treat early in the war, except for self-inflicted wounds. Frederic meets an Italian soldier with a hernia who has slipped his truss, and advises him to bloody his head as well to avoid being sent back to the front lines. The soldier does so, but the ruse does not work. When the lieutenant himself is wounded, the doctor dictates as he works: ". . . with possible fracture of the skull. Incurred in the line of duty. That's what keeps you from being court-martialed for self-inflicted wounds." Later, Miss Van Campen accuses him of contracting jaundice to avoid return to active duty; in denying the charge Frederic admits that both he and Miss Van Campen have seen plenty of self-inflicted wounds. When he eventually rejoins his unit, things have gone so badly that even the Major talks of desertion: "If I was away I do not believe I would come back."

During the retreat Frederic serves as a kind of moral policeman. He not only prevents his men from looting, but goes so far as to shoot one of the two sergeants who hitch a ride with the ambulances but refuse to help when the vehicles mire down in mud. Bonello, who finishes off the wounded man (he's always wanted to kill a sergeant, he says), slips away himself the next day to surrender to the Austrians. In the confusion, Aymo is gunned down by "friendly fire" from Italian bullets. Frederic and the faithful Piani are left to plod along with the rest of the retreating soldiers, who chant "Andiamo a casa" and cast aside their weapons. "They think if they throw away their rifles they can't make them fight," Piani explains, but his lieutenant disapproves. Despite all the precedents he's cited, then, Frederic sticks to his mission and his men up to the moment when he must either escape or be executed.

Furthermore, once he has escaped nearly every civilian he meets either assists him in his flight or reinforces his conviction that the war is senseless and badly managed. The wine shop owner's offer of forged papers is only partly attributable to the profit motive. "Don't forget that I am your friend," he tells Frederic, in the text as well as in the deleted passage. Is he through with the war? Simmons inquires. "Good boy. I always knew you had sense." Emilio the barman has served in Abyssinia and hates war. The wise Count Greffi thinks the war is, really, "stupid." And Catherine, especially, reassures Frederic that he has done the right thing. Yet no amount of reassurance can shake him free of his nagging sense of guilt. Hemingway conveys the persistence of this debilitating emotion in two ways: through Lieutenant Henry's unsuccessful attempts to rationalize his desertion, and through his equally unsuccessful attempts to shut the war out of his consciousness.

On the train to Mestre, Frederic calls up an analogy to justify his flight:

> You were out of it now. You had no more obligation. If they shot floor-walkers after a fire in a department store because they spoke with an accent they had always had, then certainly the floorwalkers would not be expected to return when the store opened again for business. They might seek other employment; if there was any other employment and the police did not get them.

The analogy seems curious until one reflects that Frederic had functioned during the retreat much as a floorwalker functions—to prevent thievery.[10] Then he goes on, in internal monologue, to discuss "the outward forms" of soldiery. He would like to take the uniform off, and he has removed the stars "for convenience," but it was "no point of honor." The abstract word "honor," rising to Frederic's mind at this moment, comes from the conscience which will not let him stop "thinking"—a code word, in this novel, for the functioning of the superego. He wished the Italians "all the luck": some good and brave and calm and sensible men were fighting for their cause. "But it was not my show any more and I wished this bloody train would get to Mestre and I would eat and stop thinking. I would have to stop."

That he cannot stop is shown on the next train ride Hemingway describes, when Frederic is en route from Milan to Stresa in Simmons's civilian clothes. Presumably he should be happy: he is on his way to Catherine. But he misses the feeling of "being held" by his clothes that a uniform has provided, and feels "as sad as the wet Lombard country" outside the window. He shares the compartment with some aviators:

They avoided looking at me and were very scornful of a civilian my age. I did not feel insulted. In the old days I would have insulted them and picked a fight. They got off at Gallarte and I was glad to be alone. . . . I was damned lonely and was glad when the train got to Stresa.

"In the old days"—two days before—Frederic would not have stood for the scornful attitude of the aviators. Now he accepts their view of him as a slacker, a point emphasized in a sentence Hemingway cut from the novel as, undoubtedly, belaboring the obvious. "I did not feel indignant [vs. insulted]," he originally wrote. "I felt they were right."[11]

Ensconced at the bar of the Grand Hôtel & des Isles Borromées, his nerves and stomach soothed by three cool, clean martinis, the same number of sandwiches, and olives, salted almonds, and potato chips, Frederic begins to feel "civilized," by which he means that he "did not think at all." But the barman asks some question that starts the thought processes going again:

"Don't talk about the war," I said. The war was a long way away. Maybe there wasn't any war. There was no war here. Then I realized it was over for me. But I did not have the feeling that it was really over. I had the feeling of a boy who thinks of what is happening at a certain hour at the schoolhouse from which he has played truant.

The pattern is the same in the bar as on the train to Mestre. The fugitive insists to himself that he is through, that the war is over for him, that it isn't his show any longer, but then he cannot help touching the wound, striking a note of self-recrimination. Even when pleasantly fuzzy on gin, he is reminded of childhood truancies. Thus he tells Count Greffi like Emilio that he does want to talk about the war ("About anything else"), but soon brings up the subject himself. "What do you think of the war really?" he asks the ancient nobleman.

Nurse Catherine Barkley provides the best medication—sex—to enable Frederic to forget.[12] That she is later to perform this function is foreshadowed on their second meeting, when Lieutenant Henry initiates this exchange:

> "Let's drop the war."
> "It's very hard. There's no place to drop it."
> "Let's drop it anyway."
> "All right."

He then kisses her, is slapped, and the kiss and the slap succeed: at least "we have gotten away from the war," he observes. But they haven't, nor will they ever, despite the oblivion-inducing therapy she administers. Immediately after telling her that they will go to Switzerland, Frederic seeks and gets her reassurance:

> "I feel like a criminal. I've deserted from the army."
> "Darling, *please* be sensible. It's not deserting from the army. It's only the Italian army."
> I laughed. "You're a fine girl. Let's get back into bed. I feel fine in bed."
> A little while later Catherine said, "You don't feel like a criminal do you?"
> "No," I said. "Not when I'm with you."

But they cannot make love all the time, and when Frederic returns from fishing and finds Catherine gone, he "lay down on the bed and tried to keep from thinking" without success until Catherine came back and "it was all right again." His life, he tells her, used to be full of everything. His job in the army had given purpose to his existence. "Now if you aren't with me I haven't a thing in the world."

Safe in Switzerland, the two lovers ride a carriage to their hotel, where Hemingway introduces an ironic commentary on Frederic's problem. He is still groggy from the long night of rowing, and neglects to tip the soldier who has brought them and their bags to Locarno. "You've forgotten the army," Catherine remarks, and for the moment she's right. But very soon, during the idyllic first days at Montreux, the narcotic begins to wear off: "We slept well and if I woke in the night I knew it was from only one cause," Frederic observes. What was the cause? "The war seemed as far away as the football games of some one else's college. But I knew from the papers that they were still fighting in the mountains because the snow would not come."[13] Later, when Catherine urges him to fall asleep simultaneously with her, he is unable to do so and lies "awake for quite a long time thinking about things." What things? "About Rinaldi and the priest and lots of people I know," he tells Catherine, adding, "But I don't think about them much. I don't want to think about the war. I'm through with it." This is wishful thinking, for Frederic's declaration, "I don't think about them much" is undercut by his next sentence, "I don't want to think about the war."

Hemingway emphasizes Frederic's continuing absorption in the war through repeated references to his newspaper reading.[14] While convalescing in Milan after his operation, the wounded Tenente read all the papers he could get his hands on, including even the Boston papers with their stale news of stateside training camps. After he deserts, however, he tries to repudiate the habit. Riding the train to Stresa, "I had the paper but I did not read it because I did not want to read about the war. I was going to forget the war." Catherine is surprised, the morning after their reunion, to find that Frederic does not want to read the news. He'd always wanted the paper in the hospital. With characteristic understanding, she asks, "Was it so bad you don't want even to read about it?" Not for the moment, but he promises that he'll tell her about what happened if he "ever get(s) it straight" in his head. He never does tell her, yet that very afternoon when she is away he sits in a lounge chair at the bar and reads the bad news in the paper. "The army had not stood at the Tagliamento. They were falling back to the Piave." At the Guttingens' cottage in the mountains, no papers are available, so he catches up on the news when they come down to Montreux. While Catherine is at the hairdresser, he drinks beer and eats pretzels and reads "about disaster"—the war was going badly everywhere—in "the

Corriere della Sera and the English and American papers from Paris." The night they move to the hotel in Lausanne, he lies in bed drinking a whiskey and soda (liquor like sex makes him feel better temporarily) and reads the papers he has bought at the station. "It was March, 1918, and the German offensive had started in France." During the three weeks they spend at the hotel, his days fall into a routine. In the morning he boxes at the gym, takes a shower, walks along the streets "smelling the spring in the air," stops at a café "to sit and watch the people and read the paper and drink a vermouth," and then meets Catherine at the hotel for lunch. During the afternoon of her protracted labor, Frederic kills time reading the paper. Sent out to eat supper, he takes a seat across from an elderly man with an evening paper and, "not thinking at all," reads about "the break through on the British front." When the man, annoyed that Frederic is reading the back of his paper, folds it over, he considers asking the waiter for one of his own but decides against it: "I could not concentrate." He has been unable to forget the war; now Catherine's Caesarean has given him something else to shut his mind to. "It was the only thing to do," the doctor assures him when she has hemorrhaged and died. "The operation proved—." But Frederic cuts him short: "I do not want to talk about it."

IV

Eventually Frederic Henry does bring himself to talk about his tragic love affair and about the horror of the war: ergo, *A Farewell to Arms*. But it is important to remember that we have the story *as he tells it to us*. Maxwell Perkins, Hemingway's editor at Scribners, thought like some others that the novel was insufficiently integrated. "The serious flaw in the book," he wrote Owen Wister on May 17, 1929, "is that the two great elements you named—one of which would make it a picture of war, and the other of which would make it a duo of love and passion—do not fully combine. It begins as one thing wholly, and ends up wholly as the other thing."[15] But Perkins and Wister missed the point. The subject of the novel is not love and war, in whatever combination, but Frederic Henry.

Hemingway was careful, in commenting on the novel, to refer to his protagonist as "the invented character," thus distinguishing between author and narrator. And he issued a further warning: that he was not to be held accountable for "the opinions" of his narrators.[16]

Both Frederic Henry and Ernest Hemingway were Americans wounded on the Italian front and both fell in love with nurses. Otherwise, they have not much in common. Frederic is certainly older than his creator, for one thing. Hemingway was only 18 when he came to Italy—not as an officer in any army but as a Red Cross ambulance driver—in the last summer of the war. Frederic, on the other hand, had enlisted in the Italian army three years earlier, and even before that he had been studying architecture in Rome. Unlike the raw youth only a year out of Oak Park high school, he has been around enough to acquire a good deal of knowledge. He knows the geography of Italy very well indeed, as his movements after deserting testify. He even knows how the war should be fought: as Napoleon would have fought it, by waiting until the Austrians came down from the mountains and then whipping them.

Despite his background of experience, however, the lieutenant does not conduct himself bravely or intelligently as a warrior. He is no Othello, nor even a Hemingway. After Frederic is wounded, Rinaldi tries to get him the Medaglia d'Argento. Hadn't he done anything heroic? Rinaldi wants to know. Didn't he carry anyone on his back? No, Frederic replies, he was "blown up while eating cheese." It hardly matters. He has been wounded, he is an American, the offensive has been successful, and Rinaldi thinks they can get him the silver. Hemingway was in fact awarded the silver, but for better reasons. Unlike his narrator, young Hemingway *did* carry another soldier on his back while wounded himself. During the retreat Lieutenant Henry is given his one chance to command, and makes a botch of it. He orders his three ambulances onto side roads where they bog down permanently. He shoots the uncooperative sergeant to no particular effect for when the others proceed on foot, the lieutenant leads good soldier Aymo to a senseless death and Bonello surrenders to save his skin knowing Frederic will not turn him in. In sum, the Tenente loses his ambulances and all his men but one, and it is—as he reflects—largely his own fault.

By showing Frederic's lack of courage and competence, Hemingway aimed to achieve a certain distance from his narrator. That he was determined to maintain this separation is illustrated by his decision to delete reflective passages in which the narrator's thoughts too closely resemble his own. In one of these, Frederic in conversation with the priest asserts that he loves lots of things: "The night. The Day. Food. Drink. Girls. Italy. Pictures. Places. Swimming. Portofino. Paris. Spring. Summer. Summer. Fall. Winter. Heat. Cold. Smells. Sleep. Newspapers. Reading." All this, Frederic remarks, "sounds better in Italian." It also sounds very much like the vigorously alive Hemingway, in love with all that life had to offer.[17] So does an excised digression on the subject of fear:

> (When I had first gone to the war it had all been like a picture or a story or a dream in which you know you can wake up when it gets too bad. . . . I had the believe [sic] in physical immortality which is given fortunate young men in order that they may think about other things and that is withdrawn without notice when they need it most. After its withdrawal I was not greatly worried because the spells of fear were always physical, always caused by an imminent danger, and always transitory. . . . I suppose the third stage, of being afraid at night, started about at this point. . . .)[18]

Fear and how to combat it was a topic that obsessed Hemingway, but did not much concern his narrator.

In two other eliminated passages, Frederic demonstrates a capacity for love that is missing from the novel. In the first, the protagonist says that he felt a sense of oneness with Catherine the moment she appeared at the hospital in Milan. "We had come together as though we were two

pieces of mercury that unite to make one. . . . We were one person."
Then, in an attempted revision, Hemingway wrote this dialogue:

> "You sweet," I [Frederic] said. "You were wonderful to get here."
>
> "It wasn't very hard. It may be hard to stay."
>
> "Feel our heart," I said.
>
> "It's the same."[19]

These sentiments are transferred in the novel to Catherine. When Frederic sees her, he says that he is in love with her, that he's crazy about her, that he wants her. But when *she* says, "Feel our hearts beating," he only replies, "I don't care about our hearts. I want you. I'm just mad about you." It is she who insists on their being "one person" throughout. The effect of the change is to transfer sympathy from Frederic to Catherine, since he emphasizes physical satisfaction, while she alone is so romantically smitten as to lose herself in their love. The other excision shows Frederic thinking long and bitter thoughts about loss and the inadequacy of conventional religious consolation. What follows is but part of an extended interior monologue:

> . . . They say the only way you can keep a thing is to lose it and this may be true but I do not admire it. The only thing I know is that if you love anything enough they take it away from you. This may all be done in infinite wisdom but whoever does it is not my friend. I am afraid of god at night but I would have admired him more if he would have stopped the war or never have let it start. Maybe he did stop it but whoever stopped it did not do it prettily. And if it is the Lord that giveth and the Lord that taketh away I do not admire him for taking Catherine away. . . ."[20]

Here was the kind of stitchery, linking love and war, that Perkins might have applauded. But Hemingway left it out, probably because its inclusion might have aroused undue empathy with his narrator.

On yet another discarded page of manuscript Hemingway typed a sentence that might stand as a motto for his novel: "The position of the survivor of a great calamity is seldom admirable."[21] Indeed it is not, since no special glamour—rather the reverse—attaches to simply having survived, and when one's friends and lover are not so fortunate, one is liable like Frederic Henry to suffer from excessive guilt.

"There is generally nothing to which we are so sensitive," Karl Jaspers observed in his study of collective guilt in Germany during and after World War II, "as to any hint that we are considered guilty." Such sensitivity finds expression in more than one way, however. Most Germans, Jaspers discovered, reacted aggressively by accusing their accusers. When wall posters went up in German towns during the summer of 1945, with pictures from Belsen and "the crucial statement, You are the guilty! consciences grew uneasy . . . and something rebelled: Who indicts me there? . . . It is only human that the accused, whether justly or unjustly charged, tries to defend himself."[22] But when the accusation is not public but comes from within, the tendency may be, as with Frederic, to internalize the guilt, hug it to one's bosom, and retreat into inactivity.

Actually, Frederic does twice face accusations after his desertion. The first takes the form of the aviator's silent scorn, and he mutely accepts their judgment. The other, more overt accuser is Catherine's friend Miss Ferguson, who lashes out at Frederic in Stresa. What is he doing in mufti? she asks. He's "sneaky," she tells him, "like a snake" for getting Catherine with child and then turning up unexpectedly to take her away. Though Catherine makes a joke of it ("We'll both sneak off"), Frederic is not amused, probably because he is reminded of the dissimulation he has just gone through to avoid capture. So he remains quiet, and since no one else points a finger, he has no one to lash out against. Yet it *is* "only human" to defend oneself, even against one's own accusations. All of *A Farewell to Arms*, from this point of view, may be considered the narrator's *apologia pro vita sua*.

Throughout the book Frederic paints himself as a man more sinned against than sinning, as a passive victim of circumstances. Yet the por-

---

Frederic Henry's Escape

trait is not, finally, to the life, as Hemingway shows by daubing in occasional brush strokes of his own. One of these is the analogy between Frederic and (not the guileful snake but) the crafty fox. Walking one evening in the brisk mid-January cold of the mountains above Montreux, Frederic and Catherine twice see foxes in the woods. This is unusual, for foxes rarely show themselves. And when a fox sleeps, Frederic points out, he wraps his tail around him to keep warm. Then he adds:

"I always wanted to have a tail like that. Wouldn't it be fun if we had brushes like a fox?"

"It might be very difficult dressing."

"We'd have clothes made, or live in a country where it wouldn't make any difference."

"We live in a country where nothing makes any difference."

This peculiar exchange suggests a good deal about Hemingway's protagonist. Catherine has done all anyone could to protect him: she pulls his cloak around the two of them, makes a tent of her hair, administers the soporific of sex and humor ("It's only the Italian army") to his hyperactive superego, urges him off to "old Helvetia," a neutral country where to her, at least, "nothing makes any difference." But it has not been enough, and Frederic still thinks conspiratorially of disguises and how to keep himself safe and warm. Like the wily fox in the woods, he pretends to an innocence he does not possess; the comparison itself constitutes a *caveat* against accepting as gospel Frederic Henry's presentation of himself. In the end, his pose of passivity cannot hide the guilt underneath, nor can he dissipate the guilt by play-acting or by writing about it. Hemingway's untrustworthy narrator remains a principal agent of both his farewells—to war as to love.

From *Hemingway: A Revaluation* (Albany, NY: Whitston Publishing Company, 1983): 165-185.

Notes

1. Sheridan Baker, *Ernest Hemingway: An Introduction and Interpretation* (New York: Holt, Rinehart and Winston, 1967), p. 2.

2. This was the subject of "Frederic Henry, Selfish Lover," the paper I presented at the Alabama conference. In slightly amended form that paper constitutes a portion of the chapter on love in *By Force of Will: The Life and Art of Ernest Hemingway* (New York: Viking, 1977).

3. Malcolm Cowley first proposed the idea of Frederic's rebirth in his introduction to *The Portable Hemingway* (New York: Viking, 1944).

4. Delbert E. Wylder discusses Frederic Henry's guilt at length, but does not elaborate on the narrator's strategy of passivity nor his behavior during his flight. See Wylder, *Hemingway's Heroes* (Albuquerque: University of New Mexico Press, 1969), pp. 66-95.

5. These deletions were made from the pencil manuscript, Ms-64, now among the Hemingway papers at the Kennedy library. I am indebted to Mary Hemingway for permission to examine the manuscript, and to Jo August and William Johnson of the library for their generous assistance. Michael S. Reynolds's *Hemingway's First War: The Making of "A Farewell to Arms"* (Princeton: Princeton University Press, 1976) contains a definitive discussion of Hemingway's alterations. Sheldon Norman Grebstein's *Hemingway's Craft* (Carbondale: Southern Illinois University Press, 1973) comments on several of the deletions. Both books reproduce some of the deleted passages.

6. Ms-64, pp. 470-471.

7. Reynolds incorrectly renders "a name" as "the name." Reynolds, p. 291.

8. Grebstein, pp. 211-212; Reynolds, pp. 35-36.

9. Reynolds, p. 233, calls attention to this point.

10. Hemingway may have been thinking of a 1921 fire in a Paris department store that took the lives of 150 people. See "142 French Youths Killed in Fire at Dance Hall," *International Herald Tribune* (2 November 1970), p. 2.

11. Ms-64, p. 477.

12. Stanley Cooperman, in "Death and *Cojones*: Hemingway's *A Farewell to Arms*," *South Atlantic Quarterly*, 63 (Winter 1964), pp. 85-92, sees Frederic as requiring of Catherine not love "but medication and in this respect he is less the Byronic lover than patient." Cooperman also writes: "The hyena of passivity—always a nightmare for Hemingway—reduces Frederic Henry to a spiritual *castrado*."

13. While rowing across Lake Maggiore in the rain, Frederic thinks that it must be snowing in the mountains, but he is apparently mistaken.

14. See Reynolds, pp. 101-103, for observations on the "motif of newspaper reading."

15. The letter from Perkins is quoted in Reynolds, p. 76.

16. Quoted in Arthur L. Scott, "In Defense of Robert Cohn," *College English*, 18 (March 1957), p. 309.

17. Ms-64, pp. 168-170.

18. Ms-64, pp. 235-236.

19. Ms-64, pp. 201-209.
20. Ms-64, pp. 586-588.
21. This motto is noted by Reynolds, p. 60.
22. Karl Jaspers, *The Question of German Guilt* (New York: Dial, 1947), pp. 47-107.

Three Wounded Warriors_____

Mark Spilka

In late September 1929, when Ernest Hemingway first met Allen Tate in Sylvia Beach's Paris bookshop, there was more on his mind than Tate's indirect discovery, through Defoe, of Marryat's strong influence on his work; he was, in fact, far more deeply troubled by Tate's discovery, in his review of *The Sun Also Rises*, of his penchant for sentimentalizing his own weaknesses through fictional personas like Jake Barnes. Thus, in a letter to Carlos Baker dated April 2, 1963, Tate recalls not only how Hemingway had accosted him "without preliminary" about wrongly attributed influences, but had also accosted him about the Barnes-like impotence of their mutual friend, Ford Madox Ford:

> We walked up the street to the Place de l'Odeon and had an aperitif at the old Café Voltaire. . . . The next subject he introduced I can repeat almost in his words; "Ford's a friend of yours. You know he's impotent, don't you?" . . . I listened, but finally said that his impotence didn't concern me, even if it were true that he was impotent, since I was not a woman. I learned soon in the local gossip of the *petit cercle Americain* that Ford had been one of the first persons to help Ernest, and as you know Ernest couldn't bear being grateful to anybody.[1]

Tate may be making another indirect discovery here, for not only had Ford befriended Ernest and made him subeditor of his literary journal, the *transatlantic review*; he had also written a "tale of passion," *The Good Soldier* (1915), which like *The Sun Also Rises* is narrated by an "impotent" man and may well have served as another hidden source of influence! At any rate, Tate's response to Ernest—that he was not a woman, and so untroubled by Ford's presumed impotence—was exactly right, and seems to have scaled the fast friendship which from then on held between them. It was the assurance Ernest needed of a common toughness of outlook, a common stake in that hard-boiled modern sensibility that each of them—as novelist and critic—was now serving, and (not least among these assurances) a common witty maleness.

Actually Tate had challenged such assurances in his harsh review of *The Sun Also Rises*. As we have seen, in his two previous reviews of Hemingway's work for *The Nation*, he had welcomed him for the seriousness and integrity of his prose in *In Our Time*—"the most completely realized naturalistic fiction of the age"—and had praised his "indirect irony" and satiric bent in *The Torrents of Spring*, deeming the book itself "a small masterpiece of American fiction."[2] But in reviewing *The Sun Also Rises* he had sharply registered his disappointment at Hemingway's lapse from the achievement of *In Our Time*:

> The present novel by the author of "In Our Time" supports the recent prophecy that he will be the "big man in American letters." At the time the prophecy was delivered it was meaningless because it was equivocal. Many of the possible interpretations now being eliminated, we fear it has turned out to mean something which we shall all regret. Mr. Hemingway has written a book that will be talked about, praised, perhaps imitated. . . . [He] has produced a successful novel, but not without returning some violence upon the integrity achieved in his first book. He decided for reasons of his own to write a popular novel, or he wrote the only novel which he could write. . . . One infers moreover that although sentimentality appears explicitly for the first time in his prose, it must have always been there.[3]

There we have it. Hemingway, betraying his artistic integrity, pandering to the public, had revealed the hidden sentimental basis of his early prose:

> The method used in "In Our Time" was *pointilliste*, and the sentimentality was submerged. With great skill he reversed the usual and most general formula of prose fiction: instead of selecting the details of physical back-

ground and of human behavior for the intensification of a dramatic situation, he employed the minimum of drama for the greatest possible intensification of the observed object. . . . The exception, important as such, in Mr. Hemingway's work is the story of Mr. and Mrs. Elliott. Here the definite dramatic conflict inherent in a sexual relation emerged as fantasy, and significantly; presumably he could not handle it otherwise without giving himself away. (43)

Here Tate all but accuses the author of projecting his own impotence upon one of his characters, the poet Elliott, whose marriage to an older Southern woman is barren and whose penchant for long poems becomes an obvious substitution for his failed relations with his wife, now happily sharing her bed with an old girlfriend. Thus, when Hemingway turns his attention from intensified objects to intensified dramatic situations, home truths will out. In *The Sun Also Rises*, a full-length novel, his characters are not only puppets and caricatures, unable to stand by themselves; they are also products of a sentimental failure founded in impotence:

It is not that Hemingway is, in the term which he uses in the contempt for the big word, hard-boiled; it is that he is not hard-boiled enough, in the artistic sense. . . . And he actually betrays the interior machinery of his hard-boiled attitude: "It is awfully easy to be hard-boiled about everything in the daytime, but at might it is another thing," says Jake, the sexually impotent, musing on the futile accessibility of Brett. The history of his sentimentality is thus complete. (43)

Understandably enough, Hemingway was stung by this treatment from a previously strong admirer. In a letter to Maxwell Perkins written on December 21, 1926, a week after the appearance of Tate's review in *The Nation*, he begins with news of Edmund Wilson's enthusiasm for the novel ("best . . . by any one of my generation"), then praises the editor of *Scribner's Magazine* for proposing to run together three complementary stories that "would make a fine group. And perhaps cheer up Dos, Allen Tate, and the other boys who fear I'm on the toboggan." Then, in a long postscript, he begins with his friend Dos Passos's criticism of the Pamplona scenes in the novel, and ends, significantly, with Tate's several criticisms of his characters and, above all, his toughness:

> Critics, this is still Mr. Tate—have a habit of hanging attributes on you themselves—and then when they find you're not that way accusing you of sailing under false colours—Mr. Tate feels so badly that I'm not as hard-boiled as he had publicly announced. As a matter of fact I have not been at all hard-boiled since July 8, 1918—on the night of which I discovered that that also was Vanity.[4]

The title of Tate's review for *The Nation* had been "Hard-Boiled." July 8, 1918, was, of course, the night on which Hemingway was wounded by shell fire and machine-gun fire while serving canteen supplies in the Italian trenches at Fossalta. It would not be the last time he would use the authority of being wounded as an answer to unwounded critics. But the interesting point, in view of the later public hardening of his personal attitudes, is his insistence on his own vulnerability, his own stake in his character's nightly fears. Indeed, he shares in the kind of self-pity to which Tate objects in his fiction, as to a sentimental indulgence unworthy of true art, a disclosure of personal impotence.

Jake and Brett

What are we to make, then, of Jake Barnes's sexual wound? Hemingway was certainly not an impotent man when he created that curious condition—a lost portion of the penis—for his first-person narrator. His own wounds had been to the legs and scrotum, the latter a mere infection suggesting perhaps that worse had been barely avoided. In a late letter (December 9, 1951) he explained to a Rinehart editor, as an example of the complications of a writer's involvement in his own fictions, "the whole genesis of The Sun Also Rises":

> It came from a personal experience in that when I had been wounded at one time there had been an infection from pieces of wool cloth being driven into the scrotum. Because of this I got to know other kids who had genitourinary wounds and I wondered what a man's life would have been like after that if his penis had been lost and his testicles and spermatic cord remained intact. I had known a boy that had happened to. So I took him and made him into a foreign correspondent in Paris, and, inventing, tried to find out what his problems would be when he was in love with someone who was in love with him and there was nothing that they could do about it. . . . But I was not Jake Barnes. My own wound had healed rapidly and well and I was quit for a short session with the catheter.[5]

The last point is interesting in that there is nothing in the novel to indicate if or when Jake was quit with the catheter, or how he urinates now. But more interesting still is the choice of war wounds for an unmarried foreign correspondent in Paris otherwise much like himself. We know that Hemingway's close relations with his friend Duff Twysden, the ostensible model for Jake's beloved Brett Ashley, had much to do with the choice. As Scott Fitzgerald (who knew something about that relation) opined, Jake seems more like a man trapped in a "moral chastity belt" than a sexually wounded warrior: and indeed, it was Hemingway's marital fidelity to Hadley that apparently kept him from having an affair with Duff; so too, Fitzgerald implies, Jake Barnes with Brett, though there is no Hadley in the novel.[6]

There may, however, be an Agnes von Kurowsky. Barnes and Lady Ashley had met each other in a British hospital where Brett worked as a nurse's aide, just as Ernest had met Agnes at a Milan hospital where she worked as an American Red Cross nurse. This prefiguring of the plot of A Farewell to Arms is no more than a background notation in The Sun Also Rises; but it does remind us of the emotional damage Ernest had sustained from his rejection after the war by Agnes von Kurowsky and his complicity in that rejection. If Jake's sexual wound can be read as an instance of the way in which war undermines the possibilities of "true love," then we begin to understand to some extent why Hemingway chose that curious condition as an index to the postwar malaise, the barrenness of wasteland relations among the expatriates he knew in Paris—and brought with him to Pamplona. It was in a way a self-inflicted wound he was dealing with which had the war's connivance.

Lawrence's Clifford Chatterley, paralyzed from the waist down by a war wound, is a good example of such projected impotence since he functions obviously enough as the bearer of Lawrence's condition while he was writing the novel, the victim by that point in his life of tubercular dysfunction. But Hemingway was there before him with Jake Barnes, as of course Joyce had been there before Hemingway with Leopold Bloom, his imagined Jewish alter ego in *Ulysses*, and Henry James with Strether in *The Ambassadors*, and Ford Madox Ford with Dowell in *The Good Soldier*; and much farther back, Laurence Sterne with *Tristram Shandy*. The tradition of impotent narration or of impotent heroes, whether comic, serious, or tragic, is an old and honorable one; and our only question is what went into Hemingway's decision to employ it.

Our most recent clue comes from the posthumously published edition of *The Garden of Eden* (1986), the hero of which engages in androgynous forms of lovemaking with his adventurous young wife in the south of postwar France, and at one point in the original manuscript imagines himself as one of the lesbian lovers in a mysterious statue by Rodin, called variously *Ovid's Metamorphoses*, *Daphnis and Chloe*, and *Volupté*, and deriving from a group called *The Damned Women* from *The Gates of Hell*.[7] Since the hero also changes sex roles at night with his beloved, we have one interesting explanation for Hemingway's postwar choice of a symbol for his own unmanning by war wounds and the American nurses who tend them: for if Jake remains "capable of all normal feelings as a *man* but incapable of consummating them," as Hemingway told George Plimpton in a famous interview, his physical wound suggests also the female genitals as men erroneously imagine them, at least according to Freud.[8] The exact nature of the wound, moreover, is literally nowhere spelled out or explained in the novel; we have only Hemingway's word for the intended condition. It becomes clear nonetheless from the type of mannish heroine he imagines, after Lady Duff Twysden's British example, that an exchange of sexual roles has indeed occurred, prefiguring that of *The Garden of Eden*, and that it is Jake and not Brett who wears that traditionally female protection, the chastity belt.

What are we to make, then, of Brett Ashley's British mannishness? Her Britishness, as we have seen, goes back to that quasi-British establishment, the Hemingway household in Oak Park presided over by Abba Ernest Hall, a British emigrant in mid-nineteenth century, and his talented daughter Grace, with his wife's brother Tyley Hancock, another mid-century emigrant, as a frequent visitor. These American Fauntleroys, tourers of the British Isles, one of whom almost sang before the queen, others of whom wore muttonchop whiskers and walked tiny dogs, set the at times bantering, smoking, and tippling, at times religiously serious, tones of the household; and the talented Grace's music lessons and concerts helped to further differentiate that home from those of surrounding neighbors like the Hemingways, from whom Grace's husband Clarence, the young doctor whom she met when he tended her dying mother, had gravitated. In Grace and Clarence's favorite Victorian novel, *John Halifax, Gentleman*, one of Dinah Mulock Craik's most striking figures was the Catholic Lady Caroline Brithwood, who came to no good end, and whom we may take as the first fictional harbinger of Lady Ashley in young Ernest's boyhood reading.

Lady Caroline's appeal, in this staunchly moral novel, stems from the mixture in her portraiture of Catholic leniency with European license. In *The Sun Also Rises*, of course, it is Jake Barnes who is the lenient Catholic, Brett Ashley the licensed European; but the combination is striking, especially if we consider Jake for a moment as an aspect of his beloved British lady, or her lesbian lover:

> Brett was damned good-looking. She wore a slipover jersey sweater and a tweed skirt, and her hair was brushed back like a boy's. She started all that. She was built with curves like the hull of a racing yacht, and you missed none of it with that wool jersey. . . .
>
> I told the driver to go to the Parc Monsouris, and got in, and slammed the door. Brett was leaning back in the corner, her eyes closed. I got in and sat beside her. The cab started with a jerk.
>
> "Oh darling, I've been so miserable," Brett said. . . .
>
> The taxi went up the hill. . . . We were sitting apart and we jolted close together going down the old street. Brett's hat was off. Her head was back. I saw her face in the lights from the open shops, then it was dark . . . and I kissed her. Our lips were tight together and then she turned away. . . .
>
> "Don't touch me" she said, "please don't touch me." . . .
>
> "Don't you love me?"
>
> "Love you? I simply turn all to jelly when you touch me."
>
> "Isn't there anything we can do about it? . . .
>
> "I don't know," she said. "I don't want to go through that hell again." . . .
>
> On the Boulevard Raspail . . . Brett said: "Would you mind very much if I asked you to do something?
>
> "Don't be silly."
>
> "Kiss me just once more before we get there."
>
> When the taxi stopped I got out and paid. Brett came out putting on her hat. She gave me her hand as she stepped down. Her hand was shaky. "I say, do I look too much of a mess?" She pulled her man's felt hat down and started in for the bar. . . .
>
> "Hello, you chaps," Brett said. "I'm going to have a drink."[9]

The cab ride is a setup for the ending, when Jake and Brett are in another such cab in Madrid, pressed together as the cab slows down, with

Brett saying, "Oh, Jake. . . . We could have had such a damned good time together," and Jake replying: "Yes. Isn't it pretty to think so." A hard-boiled ending, but those early kisses tell us otherwise. For through them Jake's vulnerability to pain through the essential feminization of his power to love has been established; like a woman, he cannot penetrate his beloved but can only rouse and be roused by her through fervent kisses; nor is he ready, at this early stage of the sexual revolution, for those oral-genital solutions which recent critics have been willing to impose upon him. His maleness then is like Brett's, who with her boy's haircut and man's felt hat may be said to remind us of the more active lesbian lover in the Rodin statue, named playfully Daphnis in one version to an obvious Chloe. Which again makes us wonder if Jake is not in some sense an aspect of his beloved—not really her chivalric admirer, like Robert Cohn, but rather her masculine girlfriend, her admiring Catherine from the novel years ahead who similarly stops her car on the return from Nice to kiss her lesbian lover, then tells her androgynous husband about it and makes him kiss her too—or, in Jake's more abject moments, her selfless Catherine from the novel next in line.

True enough, we see Jake enduring a form of love about which nothing can be done, working out what could be called a peculiarly male predicament, a sad form of a common wartime joke, in accord with Hemingway's stated plan; and in his struggles against his own self-pity we see a standard of male conduct against which we are asked to measure Robert Cohn's more abject slavishness to his beloved lady, and Mike Campbell's, and even (more to its favor) young Pedro Romero's manly devotion. And truer still, we are asked to judge Brett's liberation as a displacement of male privilege and power in matters of the heart and loins, a sterile wasteland consequence of postwar change. But what if the secret agenda is to admire and emulate Brett Ashley? What if Brett is the woman Jake would in some sense like to be?

"She started all that," he tells us admiringly, and perhaps even predictively. Brett's style-setting creativity becomes, in *The Garden of*

Eden, the leading characteristic of Catherine Bourne, whose smart boyish haircuts, blond hair dyes and matching fisherman's shirts and pants—all shared with her androgynous husband David—are plainly expressions of the new postwar mannishness, the new rivalry with men for attention and power, for a larger stake in the sociosexual pie: new sexual freedoms and privileges, then, new license. They are also forms of artistry, like Catherine's unexpected talent for talk; and if Brett's talent is less for talk than for putting chaps through hell, she is oddly also the same risk-taking character, the same sexual adventurer we ultimately meet in Catherine Bourne, though strictly heterosexual in her conquests—except perhaps with Jacob Barnes. "I suppose she only wanted what she couldn't have," muses the latter, not seeing as yet how well those words describe himself (31).

I do not mean to imply here that Jacob, a soulful wrestler with his own physical condition, would also like to make it with bullfighters and other males—that seems to me misleading—but rather that—in accord with the oddly common attraction for men of lesbian lovemaking, the imagining into it that exercises suppressed femininity, and indeed the need for such imagining, such identification with the original nurturing sources of love—he wants Brett in a womanly way. Hemingway's childhood twinning with his older sister Marcelline may have made him more sensitive to such desires and more strongly liable first to suppress and then ultimately to express them; but he was in fact expressing something common, difficult, and quite possibly crucial to coming of age as a man in this century's white bourgeois circles. His admiration for the liberated ladies of the 1920s was widely shared, and his ultimate enslavement by their androgynous powers may tell us more about ourselves and our times than we care to know.

Certainly Jake is enslaved by Brett as are Robert Cohn and Mike Campbell and even Pedro Romero, who escapes her only through her charitable withdrawal of her devastating love. That is the Ulyssean predicament, the Circean circle. But there are worshipful precedents for it in childhood that make it seem less ironic and pitiful (in a novel struggling to get beyond those judgments) than inevitable and rather touching. One thinks of Guy Halifax's boyhood crush on Lady Caroline, in *John Halifax, Gentleman*, as a possible source in this regard of Circe's awful power. Lady Caroline, whom I earlier described as "a handsome charming hedonist hellbent on adultery," was also "the magic centre of any society wherein she chose to move," an irresistible charmer, like Brett, floating easily "upon and among the pleasantnesses of life," above the ravages of pain. Ultimately, like Brett, she is ravaged by pain, and has done her share of ravaging; but when we first meet her at Longfield, the Halifax estate after which Grace Hemingway would name her farm and music sanctuary across the lake in northern Michigan, the wicked lady receives a curious certification as the preferred romantic mother of little Guy Halifax. This "little gentleman from his cradle" is the first to announce her arrival; he boldly asks her, "Isn't this a pretty view?" as they approach the house, and having touched her green gown (as opposed to his mother's gray), he proceeds to install himself as "her admiring knight attendant everywhere."[10] Later, as a young adult in Paris, he will even strike her seducer and abandoner, Sir Gerard Vermilye, just as Robert Cohn will strike Lady Ashley's rival admirers in Pamplona. Meanwhile in childhood he gathers for her that magnificent arum lily which would eventually appear on the Hemingway family shield, and at bedtime lifts up his face to her to be kissed as by a new and more romantic mother. The kiss is thwarted since Lady Caroline, as we earlier saw, is unable to return it because of sudden distress at her own sinful condition—an earlier version, perhaps, of Lady Ashley's "Don't touch me." At any rate, this confessed adulteress, who resembles Brett in that she defends her sin vigorously on the grounds of her husband's brutality and her lover's kindness and devotion, but who is nonetheless so far gone that she finds the pastoral domestic love of the Halifaxes impossible for herself, even as Brett can't live "quietly in the country . . . with [her] own true love" (55)—this wicked woman is Guy Halifax's "pretty lady," and quite possibly Ernest Hemingway's earliest source of attraction to

Brett's prototype, Duff Twysden, his first preferred alternative to real and fictional mothers like Ursula Halifax and Grace Hemingway—the romantic lady, then, of his boyhood reading dreams.

Still another "romantic lady" would figure in the making of Brett Ashley. Critics have long noted the influence of Michael Arlen's heroine Iris March, in *The Green Hat*, possibly because of the fetish made of Brett's man's hat but also because of the modern twist on an old tradition. As Allen Tate observed in criticizing Hemingway for sparing certain characters in *The Sun Also Rises* from equitable judgment, Brett "becomes the attractive wayward lady of Sir Arthur Pinero and Michael Arlen"; whereas "Petronius's Circe, the archetype of all the Bretts, was neither appealing nor deformed" (44). Such observations are useful in that Brett is indeed given special treatment, early on, as "one of us"—that is to say, "one of us" stoical and perhaps Conradian survivors—and is granted a certain nobility at the end for her refusal to destroy the worthy Pedro, to say nothing of her repeated returns to Jake Barnes for support and reassurance, as to the novel's touchstone for stoic endurance. Similarly Arlen's attractively wayward heroine in *The Green Hat* is given more than the usual share of male honor as she protects her suicidal first husband's good name at the expense of her own, assuming to herself the "impurity" (i.e., syphilis) that killed him, and then, in another grand gesture of self-denial, sending her true love back to his wife before roaring off in her yellow Hispano-Suiza to a fiery and quite melodramatic death; and Iris too is characterized as "one of us" and is said to "meet men on their own ground always."[11] Even so, Brett is probably based on still another Arlen heroine in more important ways. Thus, as Carlos Baker reports, Scott Fitzgerald had passed the time on a motor trip with Hemingway in May 1925 "by providing detailed summaries of the plots of the novels of Michael Arlen," one of which—a tale called "The Romantic Lady"—seems to have moved him (though he denied it) to go and do likewise.[12]

"The Romantic Lady" is a Men's Club story told to the narrator by his good friend Noel Anson, whom the narrator has not seen for six years and who has been divorced just six months before, he at once explains, by "a perfect woman." Much later in the evening Anson reserves for his friend the title story, proceeding in a manner our narrator likens to Marlow's as he leads his transfixed hearer "inexorably through the labyrinth of Lord Jim's career, and through many another such intricacy of Conradian imagination."[13] Anson calls it an "ageless tale of the inevitable lady sitting alone in an inevitable [theatre] box" (4)—a story, that is, of a genteel pickup, the twist being that the picker here is in fact himself picked by the lady though he proceeds at first otherwise. Thus, while sitting alone in a stall one night at the old Imperial, Anson suddenly sees in the upper boxes "a marvellous lady in white, amazing and alone and unashamed" (4-5). He at once works out a note inviting this instance of "real, exquisite life" to dinner, receives a reply to call at her box after the revue—and is taken home by her to a table already set for dinner. In other words, he is her guest; she, not he, is the host for dinner, and she actually laughs at him for imagining he has "picked [her] up":

> "'Don't you know that it was decided this morning that you should come to supper with me, decided quite, quite early? Or some one like you, perhaps not so charming—but then I have been so lucky—. . . . Are you very angry with me?'"
>
> "She was very close to me, smiling, intimate. Pure coquetry of course,—but what perfect *technique*! You knew that she was playing, but that did not prevent the blood rushing to your head; and she was so clean, so much 'one of us'! . . .
>
> "'Anger isn't exactly one of my emotions at the moment,' I said, stupidly enough. 'But will you please be very gentle with me, because never, never have I met any one like you?'" (12-13)

The Conradian phrase is out; the lady is the right sort, she is "one of us": she is calling the shots, moreover, in what must be candidly recognized as a 1920s Mayfair version of "the zipless fuck," as Erica Jong would later call it—indeed, an anticipation of the new female terms for it as Jong would work them out ("will you please be very gentle with me . . . ?") through her own sexually adventurous ladies.[14]

Our more immediate problem, however, is Hemingway's similar terms for Brett's conquest, and the curious way they bear on modern marriage. For Arlen's lady is not only married; there is a portrait of her husband on the wall, "a very distinguished looking person . . . in the toy uniform of some foreign cavalry, gorgeously decorated," and with "a thin hawk-like face, which with its perfectly poised mixture of ferocity and courtesy would have carried its fortunate owner as easily into the heart of any schoolboy as into the boudoir of the most unattainable 'lady'" (15). One thinks of Count Mippipopolous, the Greek escort, replete with chauffeur, who drives Lady Brett around Paris in his limousine, brings Jake flowers, exhibits his arrow wounds, values food, wine, and love, and is also characterized by Brett as "one of us." Arlen's romantic lady's husband may have sat for that portrait too, since he turns up later in the story as the coachman who not only takes Anson home, but on being recognized by him, explains the lady's game. Thus he too had first met his wife at the theatre, had himself been picked by her for an evening's romance, and had been told by her upon parting—as Anson has just been told—to forget the address, to settle for one perfect night of love. Instead he had gone back the next day, she had been delighted by his return, had married him—and then tired of him, as she had grown tired of her previous husband to whom he too had then been introduced as his predecessor in the endless game of beautiful one-night stands. Indeed, marriage had been his punishment for insisting upon seeing her again:

". . . and I had to acquiesce in her mere affection for me—that affection with which all splendid women enshroud their dead loves. And how much in oneself dies with their dead love! Why, there dies the ritual of love, the sacrament of sex! For sex can be exalted to a sacrament only once in a lifetime, for the rest it's just a game, an indoor sport. . . ."

"You see, such women as she make their own laws. It is not her fault, nor her arrogance, it is ours, who are so consistently susceptible. Physically she belongs to the universe, not to one single man. She never belonged to me, I was just an expression of the world to her. She has never belonged to any one, she never will—for she is in quest of the ideal which even she will never find. And so she will go on, testing our—our quality and breaking our hearts." (34-35)

One thinks of Brett surrounded by wreathed dancers when the fiesta at Pamplona explodes (155); or "coming through the crowd in the square, walking, her head up, as though the fiesta were being staged in her honor" (206); or of the book's epigraph from Ecclesiastes—"the earth abideth forever"—and Hemingway's odd assertion that "the abiding earth" is the novel's hero.[15] If Arlen's romantic lady is any evidence, "abiding heroine" might be more to the point—"earthy" ladies who make their own laws, confine sex to adventurous one-night stands which, in Hemingway's more cynical world, do not mean anything, but which are in fact cynical enough in Arlen's formulation—his Marlovian narrator having been divorced six months before, he now reminds us, for having himself gone back for the punishment of marriage. "Be very gentle with me" indeed: those oddly passive, now androgynous remarks remind us all too tellingly that it was Pauline who pursued and won Ernest away from Hadley in 1926, the year in which *The Sun Also Rises* was first published.

Frederic and Catherine

In the same letter in which he recalls for Carlos Baker his first meeting with Hemingway, Allen Tate recalls also the hospital-like conditions under which he first read and—as it were—reviewed *A Farewell to Arms*:

I remember distinctly the time he brought me one of the first copies received from NY of *A Farewell to Arms*. I was in bed with flu at the Hotel de l'Odeon. He came to the door of our room, and asked Caroline to hand me the book so that he would not be exposed to the germs. He asked me how soon I could read it. I answered, at once. I began it as soon as he had left, and didn't put it aside until I had finished it. He came back the next morning to ask how I liked it; I said it was a masterpiece. (I still think it is.) He was very childlike: he wanted me to admire his latest book to counteract my rough handling of (I think) *The Torrents of Spring*.

It was of course *The Sun Also Rises* that Tate had roughly handled; *The Torrents of Spring* he had called "a small masterpiece"; but one can understand why, more than thirty years later, he would want to reverse that judgment, and he himself pleads in his opening statement: "What I remember goes back thirty years, and I may not remember it accurately; but some things stand out." At the moment what stands out, remarkably, is the association in Hemingway's mind of Tate's harsh judgment of Jake Barnes as a sentimental figure and Tate's reversal of that judgment where Frederic Henry was concerned. Yet Frederic is as much the passive victim of wounds and circumstances as Jake Barnes, and constitutes a kind of replay of Jake's wartime predicament, that which preceded the action of *The Sun Also Rises* now revisited, but this time with a female rather than a male victim of those damaging times, a woman who dies in childbirth rather than the Indian brave with the slashed foot in the bunk above her; indeed, the Indian brave survives to tell the tale.

What are we to make, then, of Frederic's suffering, which Tate from his convalescent's bed in 1929 (and still in 1962) finds unsentimental; whereas other critics have often thought quite otherwise about the degree of sentimentality in these two novels and in the portraits of their heroes? Perhaps a look at Robert Cohn, in *The Sun Also Rises*, will help us on our way.

I am referring now to the satire of Cohn's postwar role as the chivalric lover, the romantic fool who has not learned the war's painful lesson about the death of love, the dissolution of romance into one-night stands and brief affairs, the impossibility therefore of romantic marriage. When women like Brett become laws unto themselves, when men like Jake are unmanned—the knights devitalized even as the ladies acquire new knightly powers—there can be no chivalric romance, and only a fool like Cohn would continue to think so. One irony of the text, of course, is that Jake Barnes secretly continues to think so until the final revelation that Brett could not make a go of it with Pedro Romero, that she would destroy him by her liberated (or single standard) love, and that Jake's loss of a penis would in fact make no difference were it miraculously restored by some priestess of Isis, some Lawrencean goddess devoted to male ithyphallic powers—for as we see in the next novel, *A Farewell to Arms*, those types have also been victimized by the war, and only the Bretts and Irises and Daisies have survived it, and they can't be quiet in the country, not even with their own true Jakes, Napiers, and Gatsbys, their own unmanned or wounded or romantic postwar warriors.

Hemingway's direct confrontation, then, of Cohn's romantic folly, Cohn's sentimental view of the postwar possibilities of romantic love, and Hemingway's artful recognition of Jake's and his own complicity in that view, even as Jake serves as a stoic standard against it, had been missed by Tate, much to Ernest's disappointment and chagrin; he felt misunderstood by Tate's hard-boiled judgment of Jake himself as sentimental, for Hemingway too understood Jake's weakness. As for Cohn, whose Jewishness had troubled Tate in his review of *The Sun Also Rises* ("Robert Cohn is not only a bounder, he is a Jewish bounder. The other bounders, like Mike, Mr. Hemingway for some reason spares"), was not Hemingway himself also Hemingstein in his youth, a self-mocking (hence Jewish) outsider with intellectual pretensions, a would-be novelist and pugilist?[16] Such unarticulated feelings must have determined Hemingway's strong reaction to Tate's disapproval of his first real novel. What he missed in Tate's judgment, what we are now indeed able to see better for ourselves, was the connection Tate was making between Jake's self-pity as the "impotent" pursuer of an inaccessible woman, and the special treatment, the sparing, given to Brett as to Mike and other "tough" characters in the postwar waste-land. As the husband of a professional woman, Caroline Gordon, Tate may have known something about equity in the treatment of women characters that Hemingway did not and perhaps never would know: namely, that "Petronius's Circe, the archetype of all the Bretts, was nei-ther appealing nor deformed."[17]

But then why shouldn't Brett be appealing? As the free-floating he-donist of the postwar era, the style-setter, the mannish woman with whose sexual adventurousness shy or passive or frustrated men may identify, she may well be the woman we vulnerable males, we anti-heroes of the modern age, would all like to be, even as Catherine Barkley in the next novel is the healing woman whose ministrations we might all like to command. Hemingway's stake in creating new ver-sions of old archetypes has to be given its literary and perhaps cultural due. The war's devastations, and those of the culture that made the war, had indeed made it difficult for men and women alike to avoid the con-sequences of change: shifting power relations, new displacements of confidence and possibility, bewildering breakdowns of old values, old lines of support and reassurance. Elsewhere Tate would recall that "it was enormously difficult to live then, and not entirely pleasant"; the nineteenth century was at an end, a "vast change, the result of the first World War," had occurred; people were shocked out of their compla-cency; sensibility itself was altered; there were "external difficulties that everybody faced in that time," and at least "some of [Heming-way's] excellence was largely due" to them or to the way he faced them: with "a mind of great subtlety," with "enormous powers of selec-tive observation," and with "a first-rate intelligence." Indeed, "he's one of the most intelligent men I've ever known and one of the best-read," Tate had concluded, thus giving Hemingway, at last, the critic's finest kudos.[18]

What then was the well-read Hemingway doing with this amalgam-ation of Cohn and Barnes, this wounded wartime lover who learns the hard way that to be hard-boiled is also Vanity, who loves and loses arms romantic and military, and so undergoes firsthand the chivalric disillusionment of the First World War? We know that Hemingway was of two minds as to how to approach him: as a very foolish and excited young man like himself named Emmett Hancock, in his first attempt to write the novel; and as a somewhat jaded, somewhat older man named Frederic Henry in the novel at hand. "Emmett" obviously comes from Emmett County, Michigan, where Hemingway summered as a boy: and "Hancock" decidedly comes from the revolutionary Hancock side of Grace's family; it is her mother's maiden name. Frederic, on the other hand, comes from Frederic Moreau, the disillusioned hero of Flaubert's *L'Education Sentimentale* (one of the novel's possible titles), so that the choice of "Frederic" over "Emmett" reveals a shift from Hemingway's youthful enthusiasm for the war—still evident in the early Hancock fragment—to weary disaffection in the novel, even as the choice of "Henry" over "Hancock" suggests an ironic play on Patrick Henry, a patriot who, unlike Frederic, was willing to die nobly for his country. As for the addled nurse, Catherine Barkley, whom war-weary Lieutenant Henry meets on the Italian front, her most obvious literary prototype is Emily Brontë's addled heroine, Catherine Earnshaw Linton, who also identifies with a radically disaffected lover, dies in childbirth, and haunts him after death. She owes something more, however, to such live prototypes as Agnes von Kurowsky, Pauline Pfeiffer, and Hadley Richardson; and especially perhaps to the sheltered Hadley, who at twenty-nine was ready to break the world's jail with a younger Ernest, escape to the freer life in Paris, and so make amends for past confinements.[19]

Having lost a sweetheart in the war to whom she failed to yield herself, Catherine is ready to make similar breaks and amends with Frederic. Her compensatory love will prove selfless, nonetheless, and will involve a lesson in caring—or, as some critics call it, *caritas*—which might better be called a lesson in androgyny. Consideration for others—which Grace Hemingway expected of Ernest and taught him to show his sisters—is a Fauntleroy ideal endorsed by Christian gentlemen. For Ernest it was a feminine version of manly character, which helps to explain why Catherine is the exemplary "source of instruction" for Frederic in this novel. Their selfless love is formed in one hospital, moreover, and dissolved in another, in keeping with the author's childhood familiarity with his father's medical world, where male and female caring intermix, and with his own experience as a caring Red Cross corpsman who recovered from war wounds in a Milan hospital.

The first version of the novel begins, in fact, with Emmett Hancock's arrival at the Milan hospital; and in Book Two of the final version, Frederic Henry's love for Catherine Barkley begins there too. Until this point, Henry has taken Catherine as a windfall, a welcome change from the prostitutes he has known at the front and on leave. Unlike the younger Hancock, who had known no prostitutes and had never been naked before a woman outside his family but who had decidedly wanted a nurse "to fall in love with," the older Henry has "not wanted to fall in love with anyone."[20] But now, flat on his back in the hospital, he immediately falls in love with Catherine. Perhaps Hancock's eager expectation explains Henry's sudden reversal.

In the hospital, the wounded hero in both versions is in masterful command. Neither the porters nor the stretcher-bearers nor the elderly nurse they rouse know where to put him. He demands to be put in a room, dispenses tips to the porters and stretcher-bearers, tells the befuddled nurse she can leave him there to rest. As E. L. Doctorow observes of a similarly passive character, David Bourne in *The Garden of Eden*, he seems rather like an arriving American colonizer of foreign fields.[21] Indeed, he is nowhere more authoritative than when flat on his back and served by gentle attendants and adoring nurses; in previous chapters of the novel he has been relatively restrained with peers and subordinates. Plainly, his wounds, which certify his manliness and relieve him for a time from further heroism, are one source of his newfound authority. His position as the first and only male patient in a hospital overstaffed to serve him is another; and the author's early authority when surrounded by admiring sisters, both before and after his return from the war, is not irrelevant to it. In Henry's certified passivity, then, lies his greatest power; he has license to reign from his bed as Grace Hemingway had reigned when served breakfast there by her husband Clarence—or as Joyce's Molly had reigned when served by Leopold Bloom. In effect, he has finally arrived at something like a woman's passive power.

His feminization takes still other interesting forms. He is tenderized by love, made to care like the caring Catherine, in whom his selfhood is immediately invested. In a discarded passage, he feels that he goes out of the room whenever she leaves.[22] More crucially, he is like a woman in the lovemaking that takes place in his hospital room at night. As no one has yet puzzled out, he would have to lie on his back to perform properly, given the nature of his leg wounds, and Catherine would have to lie on top of him. This long-hidden and well-kept secret of the text is one Mary Welsh Hemingway implies about married love with Ernest and even quotes him on in *How It Was*, one Ernest seems to imply about himself and Hadley in *A Moveable Feast* and makes fictionally explicit, at the least, in his portrait of characters like himself and Hadley (the painters Nick and Barbara Sheldon) in *The Garden of Eden*.[23] That—James-like—Hemingway could not articulate that secret in *A Farewell to Arms* indicates the force not merely of censorship in the 1920s but of chauvinist taboos against it. The interesting thing is that Hemingway—for whom the idea of female dominance was so threatening—could so plainly imply the female dominant without being understood or held to his oblique confession. Of course, the straddling Catherine in the superior position was more than he was willing, much less able, then to specify; but for anyone interested in "how it was"—and we have long since become interested to excess—that iceberg conclusion was there for the drawing, or the thawing. Happily we now have books and movies that sanction female mountings of receptive males. But that Hemingway could overcome his own and everyone else's fear of female dominance—could give it tacit public expression—

seems to me remarkable. Compare explicit sexual writers of the day like Joyce, who could imagine an abjectly transvestite Bloom but not a masterfully supine one; or Lawrence, for whom supineness was an un-thinkable abandonment of ithyphallic powers! So perhaps Hemingway might also be supposed to have felt, but apparently did not; perhaps be-cause, like the supine Frederic, the wounded hero, he already felt mas-terful enough to enjoy it; perhaps because he saw good androgynous women like Catherine as unthreatening to his essential maleness, in the initial stages of love, and to that side of the male ego—male identity—the bitch woman seemed so immediately to jeopardize.

In *The Garden of Eden*, where the exchange of sex roles is an ex-plicit and troubling issue, his heroes would feel greater qualms. But in this novel the hero's power is never greater than in the hospital love scenes. Not only does he impregnate Catherine from his supine posi-tion; he is also delivered of his own shell fragments by the romantically named Dr. Valentini, who in turn offers to deliver Catherine's baby free. As the analogy between his operation and her Caesarean suggests, Catherine—lacking Valentini's assistance—cannot emulate Frederic's successful parturition. He undergoes and survives an ordeal by suffer-ing to which Catherine in her comparable situation will succumb.

Meanwhile, their hospital-based love enters a mystic phase. Before the operation she effaces herself, says she'll do, say, and want any-thing he wants. "There isn't any me any more," she concludes, "Just what you want" (106). Afterwards, in discussing why they needn't marry, she repeats her point: "There isn't any me any more. I'm you. Don't make up a separate me" (115). Her declaration, like Catherine Earnshaw's famous pronouncement—"I am Heathcliff"—is a time-honored Christian Romantic version of the union of two souls. The friendly priest at the front has predicted and blessed their union for the lesson in selfless caring it entails. But Catherine and (more ambiva-lently) Frederic are Romantics whose Christianity has lapsed: "You're my religion," she tells him now (116), and so invokes a Romantic her-esy, the religion of love, going back to the eleventh century (as the

Catholic Hemingway, then married to Pauline, well understood). Lacking any connection with God or immortality, this atheistic faith will eventually fail them, leaving the ambivalent Frederic alone and bereft with the memories here recalled. But for a time they are fused in mystic selflessness.

The androgynous nature of their fusion is further developed when they flee to Switzerland and Frederic's turn as the caring, selfless partner begins. This idyllic phase has been anticipated by Frederic's loving (indeed colonizing) description of the priest's home in Abruzzi, which he has failed to visit, but which he then imagines as a "place where . . . it was clear cold and dry and the snow was dry and powdery and hare-tracks in the snow and the peasants took off their hats and called you Lord and there was good hunting" (13). Switzerland is like that, except for the hunting, which Frederic selflessly eschews. He has abandoned sports and war for a world circumscribed by love, and now reads about them somewhat wistfully in newspapers. The escaped lovers reside, moreover, in the chalet near Montreux where Hemingway and Hadley once lived and which Ernest prized for its "ideal blend of wilderness and civilization."[24] In that idyllic region, the lovers read, play cards, stroll together in the powdered snow, stop at country inns, or visit the nearby village where Frederic watches with excitement while Catherine has her hair done at the hairdresser's—the kind of scene that becomes a leitmotif in *The Garden of Eden*, some twenty years ahead. Later the lovers decide that Frederic must grow a beard, or better still, let his hair grow long while she has hers cut short to match it: then they will be alike, one person, as they are now one person at night (298-300)—and this too will become a leitmotif in *Eden*. They settle now, however, for the beard, which grows splendidly through the winter, like a gradually reemerging form of male identity. In the spring the rains come, washing away the powdered snow; they move to Lausanne so Catherine can have her baby at the hospital; and Frederic takes up boxing at the local gym.

Their edenic love dissolves when Catherine dies from her Caesarean operation and their child is stillborn (a fate which Pauline and her first Caesarean child had just avoided).[25] Supposedly Catherine has been caught in that "biological trap" which, in its absurdity and futility, is the female equivalent for death on the modern battlefield; and certainly her death has been carefully foreshadowed in just these cosmic terms. You may enjoy edenic and androgynous bliss in this world, Hemingway surmises, but in the end "they" will take it from you. The punishment for stolen happiness is death. But since the same punishment is meted out to honest misery, and since death in childbirth has been unusual in white bourgeois circles since the end of the nineteenth century, the novel's tragic resolution seems arbitrary to many readers, and again suggests the displacement of an essentially Victorian dread onto alien grounds. It may be too that Catherine's small hips—that androgynous feature—have determined her fate in more ways than one. The love she offers so absorbs male identity that she is as threatening to it, finally, as any bitch heroine; and though she dies bravely, like a true Hemingway hero, it may be that she is sacrificed to male survival—so that this time the Indian in the upper bunk lives on!

Whatever the case, Hemingway bids farewell to androgynous love in this novel and turns for the next ten years to the problem of shoring up his own male identity. The legend of the hard-boiled "tough guy" writer, already predicted by Tate's asperities, may be said to have begun with the sentimental dodge of Catherine's death. It was not of course the world but those stronger women—Agnes, Grace, and Pauline— who brought to an end the androgynous idylls in Milan, Michigan, and Paris; and in Pauline's case especially we begin to see why this is so.

Ernest and Pauline

When Emmett Hancock first enters the Milan hospital, in the original beginning of *A Farewell to Arms*, he loses control of his urinary and sphincter muscles several times in succession, is cleaned up by nurses, has his sheets changed, and feels embarrassed at being "looked after like a baby."[26] We see no such embarrassing regression when his older counterpart, Frederic Henry, enters the same hospital; and yet at least two recent critics have remarked upon the "infantilism" of his ensuing love affair with Catherine Barkley. Thus, in approaching this novel as "Personal Metaphor," Millicent Bell finds the lovers' raptures "curiously suspect":

> Frederic has only delusively attached himself to an otherness. Far from the war's inordinate demand upon his responses, he has been converted to feeling in the isolation of his hospital bed, where, like a baby in its bassinet, he is totally passive, tended and comforted by female caretakers, the nurses, and particularly by this one. The image is regressive, and the ministering of Catherine, who looks after all his needs, including sexual, while he lies passive, is more maternal than connubial. The relation that now becomes the center of the novel is, indeed, peculiar enough to make us question it as a representation of adult love. More often noted than Frederic's passivity is the passivity of Catherine in this love affair, a passivity which has irritated readers (particularly female readers) because it seems to be a projection of male fantasies of the ideally submissive partner. It results from her desire to please. She is a sort of inflated rubber woman available at will to the onanistic dreamer. There is, in fact, a masturbatory quality to the love of each. The union of these two is a flight from outer reality and eventually from selfhood, which depends upon a recognition of the other; . . . of . . . the alien in the beloved and therefore the independent in itself. The otherness that Frederic and Catherine provide for one another is not enough to preserve their integral selves, and while the sounds of exteriority become more and more muffled in the novel, their personalities melt into one another.[27]

In her essay "Hemingway and the Secret Language of Hate," Faith Pullin similarly argues that Frederic and Catherine are ciphers rather than existing human beings and that Hemingway's talent is less for creating characters than for reporting the experience of extreme sensations and emotions; and she too raises the charge of infantilism:

War naturally simplifies the relationship between the sexes, by removing surfaces and revealing the basic power situation. Catherine confuses the Italians because they don't want nurses at the front, only whores; on the other hand, to be a nurse is in itself to be de-sexed, or rather, to be cast in the role of mother. Catherine's mistake is that she is to be a mother to a real child, thereby removing herself from a position of total subservience to the infantile demands of Frederic. To Catherine, sex seems to be something extraneous to herself, an abstract possession which can be used to please Frederic, but not, apparently, herself.[28]

Such well-taken charges are not, of course, new. In 1941 Edmund Wilson had noted Hemingway's increasing antagonism to women; he had also found Catherine and Frederic "not very convincing as personalities" and had called their love a "youthful erotic dream." In 1949 Gershon Legman had similarly remarked on Hemingway's extreme hatred of women; and Isaac Rosenfeld in 1951 and Richard Hovey in 1968 had made similar charges about mother love and narcissism.[29] But the new chorus of feminist critiques is nonetheless refreshing, and often newly perceptive, in taking over a protest that belongs to it. The only question I want to raise at this point is whether infantilism and self-repression altogether explain these relations, or whether feminization, or better still androgyny, might further explain them, especially if it serves now as the experiential "wound" against which Hemingway raises his artistic "bow." The kind of wound that Jake Barnes sustains in the previous novel; the fact (which Bell fails to note in this one) that Frederic is curiously masterful in his passivity; the interesting possibility, entertained by neither Bell nor Pullin, that Catherine is the active and superior partner in the hospital trysts (indeed, Judith Fetterley even speaks of her striking "aggressiveness . . . in the service of Frederic's passivity" and of the "inner space" created when she lets her hair fall over him "like a tent")[30]—all of this suggests a hidden agenda in these fictions, a secret and ambivalent language about androgynous impulses, a form of self-hatred and self-love of the female within the male

Critical Insights

that begins to define itself at this time as the secret wound in modern romantic relations as Hemingway saw them, against which he disciplined his masculine art.

If we suppose for a moment that Catherine is a vital part of Frederic, and not simply an inflatable rubber object of his fantasies, then we may well be witnessing a historic flight from tenderness, or from tender aspects of male humanity, with cultural as well as personal implications. Certainly the initial loss of Agnes von Kurowsky's love, the ensuing loss of Grace Hemingway's regard and approval, the frustrations with Duff Twysden, the loss of Hadley's love through separation and divorce, and the aggressive appropriations of Pauline, all point to a propensity in Hemingway for self-wounding which, while extremely painful for his life, yet proved to be extremely fruitful for his art; and if as Edmund Wilson surmises, his art was also then a gauge of public morale, then perhaps we are dealing also with a propensity of early modern times. Two observations by Millicent Bell may help to clarify these points.

In her insistence that Frederic and Catherine lack sufficient otherness, that selfhood itself "depends upon a recognition of the other," or of "the alien in the other and therefore the independent in itself," she is not simply complaining as others do that Hemingway fails to define characters, or that he defines emotions better than characters; she is tracing that phenomenon to a type of romantic love which the author here endorses: selfless fusion or interfusion by which these "personalities melt into each other." Hemingway's borrowed romantic ideal, the adolescent fusion so defiantly proclaimed in Brontë's *Wuthering Heights* (and so brilliantly presented there as a shared state of mind), is seen as a key to his creation of this "pitiful pair." More seriously, it is a variant of that "affective failure" Bell finds at work throughout the novel, that stylistic tension between realism and the seemingly irrelevant by which the war becomes "an objective correlative" of the narrator's state of mind, the lyrical projection of "an inner condition." And finally it is her attempt to define that condition which strikes me as most helpful:

In fact, an unvarying mood, established by the narrative voice, dominates everything it relates, bathes uniformly all the images and levels events which are seen always in one way only. That the principal descriptive elements— river, mountains, dust or mud, and above all, rain—are all present in the opening paragraphs suggests not so much that later scenes are being predicted as that the subsequent pages will disclose nothing that is not already evident in the consciousness that has begun its self-exhibition.[31]

Here and later, then, Bell suggests that it is not the events or the characters that make this novel compelling: it is the numbly elegiac style, the registration of loss and betrayal, the capturing of a state of mind that now becomes both public and personal as that "gauge of morale" that Wilson first defined: so that the failure to transcend that numbed impression which the tenderness between the hospital-based lovers should achieve becomes instead an unwitting sign of its pervasiveness. And here perhaps a few small objections should be registered, to the effect that Frederic's selfishness is not simply a revelation of the author's growing hatred of women, as these new critics hold, but in great part an intended exposure; and that the idyllic waiting time in Switzerland is not simply a failed attempt to show how Frederic overcomes his egotism, but in great part how he tries to, how he imagines himself into Catherine's states of mind in the clear cold mountain air (compare *Wuthering Heights*) which partakes of the selflessness of the priest's idyllic world, the Abruzzi, which Frederic has earlier failed to visit, though at least one critic (Judith Fetterley) reduces such strivings to securely selfish "inner space" in a work characterized by sexual nausea and murderous intent; and finally that Frederic's entry into Catherine's death struggles, as opposed to Hemingway's, is at least another stretching of male imagination (like that of the Indian in the upper bunk in "Indian Camp") into a woman's suffering—even if, as Fetterley justly holds, the only good woman in this novel is a dead one.[32] But let us stop a moment to sort things out.

Elsewhere I have remarked on how the love mode of *The Sun Also*

Rises differs markedly from that of *A Farewell to Arms*: how the stress is on male independence from the threat of absorption and destruction which the bitch heroine seems to represent; how the ideal of men without women becomes embodied through the survival of the young bullfighter, Pedro Romero, as a necessary option in postwar wasteland times.[33] Thus, whatever the sentimental hazards of Jake Barnes's self-pity, this novel seems in retrospect tougher and tauter than its successor, just as Brett Ashley seems tougher and tauter, or at least more carefully defined, than Catherine Barkley. The ideal not simply of stoic endurance, but of independent survival, whether for men or women, has been worked through with some effectiveness. To be a woman like Brett is finally more attractive, for men as well as women, than to be a woman like Catherine Barkley. But that may be precisely because with Catherine something in Frederic, and by the same token something in his creator Ernest, is lapsing or dying—namely, his capacity for nurturing tenderness, his sympathetic sameness, his identification with women in their selfless suffering rather than in their bitchy independence. As we shall see, that identification will return in other guises; but for the time being, the ideal of selfless romantic fusion, the *Wuthering Heights* mystique, seems to be lapsing out through that very aggressive passivity in Catherine on which feminist critics have in one way or another focused. The androgynous secret behind this kind of fusion, the androgynous threat to male identity, is finally more threateningly absorbing than abject service to the bitch goddess Brett Ashley, which at least drives men back upon themselves. So the extremely female Catherine dies that Frederic/Ernest may regain his maleness.

What, then, does it mean, at this point, if the "wound" is androgyny and not, as Philip Young so early established, the actual physical wounds that Hemingway himself sustained at Fossalta? For one thing, as we saw earlier, those physical wounds help to certify Frederic's manliness and so free him for a time from future heroism; for another, the obverse condition also obtains, in that Frederic can enjoy being weak, frail, "female," without being ashamed of his condition: the inevitable fear of being cowardly, unmanly, exposed to pain and death, is now transposed into a pleasurable condition since he has survived his wounds and can enjoy his obvious vulnerability. To be wounded, then, is both the badge of manhood and the secret entry into womanhood: it is not so much infantilism that now besets him as that vulnerability we attribute to both women and children but deny to men—hence his masterful response to being wounded and his immediate love for Catherine Barkley as for an aspect of himself, his extreme vulnerablity, that he is for a time free to accept.

Interestingly, it is Catherine rather than Frederic who will now face death bravely; and therein lies another meaningfully psychosocial implication. As we have seen, a number of recent critics have questioned the reality of Catherine's existence as a character, and some have presented her as a projection of male fantasies, with good cause. But there is a case to be made for her all-too-painful reality as an addled heroine, a woman so obsessed with culturally imposed guilt at her lover's virginal death as to want not simply to give herself sexually to some fantasized replacement for him—a game she half-knowingly plays with Frederic Henry—but also to die for him, to enter the biological trap so as to replace him with a child or join him in literal death. We can attribute all this, of course, to Hemingway's neurotic maneuverings of his heroine and to his chauvinistic emphasis on her madly "careless love"; but whatever her reckless ways, there is something bitterly true about her sacrificial selflessness as a cultural trap into which many women fall "in our time." Hemingway's case for Catherine, as for Frederic, is that she transcends her obsessions, is genuinely selfless and caring in her half-mad love, and therefore loves and dies well, even as Frederic loves better than he might otherwise have done. That seems to me a fairer statement of the book's or rather the author's intentions than we psychosocial critics generally grant him. What I am saying, then, is that Catherine is believable, as well as the object of male fantasies, since she is also the subject of female fantasies that we know to be "true," that do exist, however embarrassing we may find her enactment of them. Thus, if she annoys women readers today, it is precisely because she continues to deny herself in all-too-believable ways well lost and to protect Frederic thereby from confronting his own inveterate selfishness: a great many women do these terrible things for selfish men, all the time; and some men like Frederic try to respond in kind, and fail, since the kind is deadly for both, but deadlier for those like Catherine who try harder—which (as Pauline's letters to Ernest well attest) is also surely believable. Indeed, war openly, as well as peace insidiously, does place this premium on male primacy and survival—which is another reason why Catherine's supposedly analogous death seems so unconvincing: it is Frederic she dies for, if not for her previous lover, in what seems to be an interesting inversion of that genteel tradition, women and children first, but also a true inversion for fortunate male survivors.

Certainly these public meanings of the text are in keeping with its tired, elegiac tone, its war-weary rehearsal of inevitable loss and failure and of circumstantial betrayal. We know that Hemingway himself felt no such jaded emotions in World War I. Frederic Henry, the novel's hero, is older than Hemingway was then and considerably more experienced. He has been on the Italian front for a much longer time than Ernest, who spent only a few weeks there before being wounded; and he undergoes the disastrous retreat from Caparetto, which occurred a year before Hemingway even reached Italy.[34] His war-weariness, out of which the early chapters especially are narrated, and perhaps the entire book, was a state of mind Ernest never felt; and Frederic's decision to make a separate peace, to say farewell to arms military, was one Ernest never made. As we know from several sources, the wounded Ernest was an enthusiastic patriot, eager to return to the front—so eager that he returned too soon, came down with yellow jaundice, and had to be carted back to the hospital in Milan.[35] Thus, where Frederic Henry's disillusionment with the war occurs in the retreat from Caparetto, Ernest's was a postwar acquisition—much of it inspired by literary sources. He had absorbed his antiwar sentiments from postwar readings of poets like Owen and Sassoon and novelists and friends like Ford and Dos Passos. What he had read squared, however, with the military histories which then absorbed him and with what he had personally heard and seen at and behind the front; and it squared also with the disillusionment of his postwar return to Oak Park, where his own war stories had gradually palled and gone out of fashion, as he partly records in "Soldier's Home" (1924). In his long recuperation, during which he continued to wear his British cape and Red Cross uniform and his high military boots, he had even become a figure of fun to his neighbors.[36]

It was then, of course, that he also suffered the sequential blows of rejection by Agnes von Kurowsky and his mother and for a time had to bid farewell to arms romantic. But if Bell is right, it was his farewell to Hadley and his ensuing marriage to Pauline Pfeiffer that truly determined the novel's tone of loss and failure. His father's suicide came too late in the order of composition to affect the initial setting of narrative tone and consciousness by which Frederic may be identified as a "sufferer from blunted affect," or from "affective failure," as from "an emotional apparatus already in retreat from the responsibilities of response." Bell speaks further of his remarriage as creating "a keen sense of guilt . . . along with the recognition [of] compulsive forces he was powerless to restrain"; and also of stories related to the novel ("In Another Country" and "Now I Lay Me") which "suggest a fear associated with marriage—either one will somehow kill it oneself, as he had done with his own first marriage, or it will kill you, or at least emasculate you, as his mother had emasculated his father"; in either case "death and destruction arrive in the end."[37] His pessimistic feelings, then, about his own romantic sensibility and where it had led him had been crystallized by the marriage to Pauline, which in confirming one love had betrayed another. In this sense the dying Catherine is the dying love for Hadley, as for Agnes and Grace before her, whereas the brave Catherine who risks such a death might well be Pauline, as well as Hadley and Grace before her, by whom the guilt of sexuality itself, and its potentially tragic consequences, had severally been stirred. Certainly it was Pauline who had served him so aggressively, in his passivity, as to lead him to betray himself. Thus, with Pauline especially, the wounds of war and peace had crystallized as the wound of androgyny, the wound that is of identification with women and with the female within oneself, felt now as an almost intolerable vulnerability, a hidden emasculation, a secret loss of male identity, a self-betrayal—as that delayed time-bomb, *The Garden of Eden*, would eventually, in its own personally metaphoric ways, reveal.

From *Hemingway's Quarrel with Androgyny* (Lincoln: University of Nebraska Press, 1990): 197-222. Copyright © 1990 by University of Nebraska Press. Reprinted by permission of the University of Nebraska Press.

Notes

1. Allen Tate to Carlos Baker, 2 April 1963, Firestone Library, Princeton.
2. Tate, "Good Prose" and "The Spirituality of Roughnecks," as quoted in Stephens, *Ernest Hemingway*, 14, 26.
3. Tate, "Hard-Boiled," as quoted in Stephens, 42-43.
4. Hemingway, *Selected Letters*, 239-40.
5. Ibid., 745.
6. See Fitzgerald's long letter to Hemingway on cutting the early chapters, in Frederic Joseph Svoboda's *Hemingway and "The Sun Also Rises": The Crafting of a Style*, 140: "He isn't *like an impotent man. He's like a man in a sort of moral chastity belt*" (italics mine). See also Baker, *Ernest Hemingway*, 203: "The situation between Barnes and Brett Ashley, as Ernest imagined it, could very well be a projection of his own inhibitions about sleeping with Duff."
7. *The Garden of Eden* manuscript, bk. 1, chap. 1, pp. 17, 23-24, in Hemingway Collection, Kennedy Library, Boston, Mass. For reproductions of bronze and plaster versions of the statues in question, see especially *The Sculpture of Auguste Rodin*, ed. John L. Tancock.
8. Plimpton, "Ernest Hemingway," in *Writers at Work*.
9. Ernest Hemingway, *The Sun Also Rises*, 22, 24-28. Page references in the text are to this 1954 edition.
10. Craik, *John Halifax, Gentleman*, 175, 249-53.
11. Michael Arlen, *The Green Hat*, 95, 229, 231.
12. Baker, *Ernest Hemingway*, 189. See also *Selected Letters*, 238. For Fitzgerald's acute observation that the original opening chapters are indeed written in the effusive

style of Michael Arlen (to which Fitzgerald strongly objected), see Svoboda, *Hemingway*, 138: "You've done a lot of writing that honestly reminded me of Michael Arlen." See also chapter 14 of *The Torrents of Spring*, where Yogi Johnson tells a version of Arlen's "The Romantic Lady" in which a beautiful woman uses him for voyeuristic purposes (79-81). In *Along with Youth*, 65, Peter Griffin mistakes this obvious borrowing for autobiographical truth.

13. Michael Arlen, *The Romantic Lady*, 4. Page references in the text are to this 1921 New York edition.

14. See Erica Jong, *Fear of Flying*, and the novels that follow, especially *Fanny*, in which she more or less appropriates for her sex the previously male world of sexual adventure and conquest.

15. Hemingway to Maxwell Perkins, 19 November 1926, in *Selected Letters*, 229.

16. See Baker, *Ernest Hemingway*, 30, 41, for Hemingway's lifelong nickname "Hemingstein" and its high school origin in antisemitic games about pawnbrokers. His "Cohen and Stein" routine with his high school friend Ray Ohlsen is particularly relevant to Jake's affinities with Cohn in *The Sun Also Rises*.

17. Allen Tate, "Hard-Boiled," as quoted in Stephens, 44.

18. Tate, "Random Thoughts on the 1920s," *Minnesota Review* 1 (Fall 1970): 46-56.

19. For the Emmett Hancock chapters (Item 240, Hemingway Collection, Kennedy Library, Boston), see Bernard Oldsey, "The Original Beginning," in *Hemingway's Hidden Craft: The Writing of "A Farewell to Arms,"* 93-99. For Hadley's desire to break out of the world's jail with Ernest, see Sokoloff, *Hadley*, 1.

20. See Oldsey, "Original Beginning," 98, and Ernest Hemingway, *A Farewell to Arms*, 93. Page references in the text are to this 1957 edition.

21. Doctorow, "Braver Than We Thought," 45. Here Doctorow speaks of the hero's "consummate self-assurance in handling the waiters, maids and hoteliers of Europe who, in this book as in Hemingway's others, come forward to supply the food and drink, the corkscrews and ice-cubes and beds and fishing rods his young American colonists require."

22. *A Farewell to Arms* manuscript, variant p. 206, Hemingway Collection, Kennedy Library: "And now that she was gone down the corridor, I felt as though all of me was gone away with her." See also Michael S. Reynolds, *Hemingway's First War: The Making of "A Farewell to Arms,"* 289.

23. For the most explicit confirmation, see Mary Welsh Hemingway, *How It Was*, 467, where she quotes from a diary insert written by Ernest on 12 December 1953: "She has always wanted to be a boy and thinks as a boy without ever losing any femininity. . . . She loves me to be her girls, which I love to be, not being absolutely stupid. . . . In return she makes me awards and at night we do every sort of thing which pleases her and which pleases me. . . . Since I have never cared for any man . . . I loved feeling the embrace of Mary which came to me as something quite new and outside all tribal law." For more implicit references, see pp. 298-99 and 371. On p. 466 sodomy is also clownishly implied as part of their sexual repertoire, again by Ernest. For androgynous precedents with Hadley, see Hemingway, *A Moveable Feast*, 20-21, where, after a discussion of homosexuality versus lesbianism with Gertrude Stein, Ernest returns home to share his "newly acquired knowledge" with Hadley: "In the night we were

happy with our own knowledge we already had and other new knowledge we had acquired in the mountains." In *The Garden of Eden* manuscript at the Kennedy Library (where the phrase "outside all tribal law" frequently recurs), artists Nick and Barbara Sheldon make androgynous love as book 2, chapter 1, opens, with Barbara pressing down lightly but firmly on her supinely cooperative husband in a Paris flat like that which Ernest shared with Hadley, circa 1925. In book 3 Barbara's erotic attraction to Catherine Bourne (based largely on Pauline Pfeiffer) suggests also that the mountain knowledge referred to in *A Moveable Feast* may refer to androgynous activities inspired by Pauline Pfeiffer's visit to Schruns—at which time, according to reports on the Sokoloff tapes by Peter Griffin, she liked to crawl into bed with the Hemingways each morning.

24. Baker, *Ernest Hemingway*, 112.

25. Ibid., 250-51.

26. Oldsey, "Original Beginning," 98.

27. Millicent Bell, "*A Farewell to Arms*: Pseudoautobiography and Personal Metaphor," in *Ernest Hemingway: The Writer in Context*, ed. James Nagel, 114.

28. Faith Pullin, "Hemingway and the Secret Language of Hate," in *Ernest Hemingway: New Critical Essays*, ed. A. Robert Lee, 184-85.

29. See Wilson, "Hemingway: Gauge of Morale," in *Eight Essays*; Gershon Legman, *Love and Death*, 86-90; Isaac Rosenfeld, "A Farewell to Hemingway," *Kenyon Review* 13 (1951): 147-55; and Richard B. Hovey, *Hemingway: The Inward Terrain*, 75-76.

30. Judith Fetterley, "Hemingway's Resentful Cryptogram," in *The Resisting Reader:A Feminist Approach to American Fiction*, 59, 64.

31. Bell, "*A Farewell to Arms*," 111.

32. Fetterley, "Hemingway's Resentful Cryptogram," 52, 64, 71.

33. Spilka, "Hemingway and Fauntleroy," 350-52.

34. For an account of these differences and of the novel's genesis, Reynolds, *Hemingway's First War*, 3, 5.

35. See, for example, Henry Villard, "A Prize Specimen of Wounded Hero," *Yankee Magazine*, July 1979, 134-35; and Baker, *Ernest Hemingway*, 71-73.

36. Sanford, *At the Hemingways*, 190-92.

37. Bell, "*A Farewell to Arms*," 112-13, 115-16, 120, 123-24.

Works Cited

Arlen, Michael. *The Green Hat*. London: Cassell, 1968.

_____. *The Romantic Lady*. New York: Dodd, Mead, 1921.

Baker, Carlos. *Ernest Hemingway: A Life Story*. New York: Bantam, 1970.

Bell, Millicent. "*A Farewell to Arms*: Pseudoautobiography and Personal Metaphor." In *Ernest Hemingway: The Writer in Context*. Ed. James Nagel. Madison: University of Wisconsin Press, 1984.

Craik, Dinah Mulock. *John Halifax, Gentleman*. London: A. & C. Black, 1922; London: Dent, 1961.

Doctorow, E. L. "Braver Than We Thought." *New York Times Book Review*, 18 May 1986: 1, 44-45.

Fetterley, Judith. "Hemingway's Resentful Cryptogram." In *The Resisting Reader: A Feminist Approach to American Fiction*. Bloomington: Indiana University Press, 1981.

Griffin, Peter. *Along with Youth: Hemingway, the Early Years*. New York: Oxford University Press, 1985.

Hemingway, Ernest. *A Farewell to Arms*. New York: Scribner's, 1957.

_____. *A Farewell to Arms* Manuscript. Hemingway Collection, Kennedy Library, Boston, Mass.

_____. *The Garden of Eden*. New York: Scribner's 1986.

_____. *The Garden of Eden* Manuscripts. Hemingway Collection, Kennedy Library, Boston, Mass.

_____. *A Moveable Feast*. New York: Bantam, 1965.

_____. *Selected Letters, 1917-1961*. Ed. Carlos Baker. New York: Scribner's, 1981.

_____. *The Sun Also Rises*. New York: Scribner's, 1954.

_____. *The Torrents of Spring*. New York: Scribner's, 1972.

Hemingway, Mary Welsh. *How It Was*. New York: Ballantine Books, 1977.

Hovey, Richard B. *Hemingway: The Inward Terrain*. Seattle: University of Washington Press, 1968.

Jong, Erica. *Fanny: Being the True History of the Adventures of Fanny Hackabout-Jones*. New York: New American Library, 1980.

_____. *Fear of Flying*. New York: Holt, Rinehart and Winston, 1973.

Legman, Gershon. *Love and Death*. New York: Hacker Art Books, 1949.

Oldsey, Bernard. "The Original Beginning." In *Hemingway's Hidden Craft: The Writing of "A Farewell to Arms."* University Park: Pennsylvania State University Press, 1979.

Plimpton, George. "An Interview with Ernest Hemingway." *Paris Review* 18 (Spring 1958): 60-89. Reprinted in *Writers at Work: The "Paris Review" Interviews*. 2nd ser. New York: Viking Press, 1963.

Pullin, Faith. "Hemingway and the Secret Language of Hate." In *Ernest Hemingway: New Critical Essays*. Ed. A. Robert Lee. London and Toronto: Vision Press and Barnes and Noble, 1983.

Reynolds, Michael S. *Hemingway's First War: The Making of "A Farewell to Arms."* Princeton: Princeton University Press, 1975.

Rosenfeld, Isaac. "A Farewell to Hemingway." *Kenyon Review* 13 (1951): 147-55.

Sanford, Marcelline Hemingway. *At the Hemingways: A Family Portrait*. Boston: Little, Brown, 1962.

Sokoloff, Alice Hunt. *Hadley: The First Mrs. Hemingway*. New York: Dodd, Mead, 1971.

Spilka, Mark. "Hemingway and Fauntleroy: An Androgynous Pursuit." In *American Novelists Revisited: Essays in Feminist Criticism*. Ed. Fritz Fleischmann. Boston: G. K. Hall, 1982.

Stephens, Robert O., ed. *Ernest Hemingway: The Critical Reception.* New York: Burt Franklin, 1977.

Svoboda, Frederic Joseph. *Hemingway and "The Sun Also Rises": The Crafting of a Style.* Lawrence: University Press of Kansas, 1981.

Tancock, John L., ed. *The Sculpture of Auguste Rodin.* Philadelphia: Philadelphia Museum of Art, 1976.

Tate, Allen. "Good Prose." *The Nation* 122 (10 February 1926): 160-62.

_____. "Hard-Boiled." *The Nation* 123 (15 December 1926): 642-44.

_____. "Random Thoughts on the 1920s." *Minnesota Review* 1 (Fall 1970): 46-56.

_____. "The Spirituality of Roughnecks." *The Nation* 123 (28 July 1926): 89-90.

Villard, Henry. "A Prize Specimen of Wounded Hero." *Yankee Magazine*, July 1979: 134-35.

Wilson, Edmund. "Hemingway: Gauge of Morale." In *Eight Essays.* Garden City, N.Y.: Doubleday-Anchor Books, 1954.

Invalid Masculinity:
Silence, Hospitals, and Anesthesia in *A Farewell to Arms*_____

Diane Price Herndl

It's evening now, and everybody's scribbling away. . . . And not just letters, either. Diaries. Poems. At least two would-be poets in this hut alone.

Why? you have to ask yourself. I think it's a way of claiming immunity. First-person narrators can't die, so as long as we keep telling the story of our own lives we're safe. Ha bloody fucking ha.

(Barker, *Ghost Road* 115)

Between his own experience of being wounded in war and writing *A Farewell to Arms*, Ernest Hemingway wrote an essay called "How to Be Popular in Peace Though a Slacker in War" for the *Toronto Star Weekly* (Reynolds 136). This essay will take up the question of "slackers" in World War I, specifically those who were thought to be malingering in war hospitals. Many critics have commented on the passage in which nurse Van Campen accuses Frederic Henry of using alcoholism to avoid going back to the front, but such comments almost always focus on his misogynist response to her, rather than on her accusation itself. I do not intend to echo her charge here, to take Frederic Henry to task for staying in the hospital longer than he needs to, but to investigate questions about masculinity that arise from Hemingway's portrayal of the soldier as a suspect malingerer and a deserter. My investigation is going to look at Frederic Henry through the lens of Pat Barker's World War I trilogy—*Regeneration*, *Eye in the Door*, and *The Ghost Road*—not to offer a reading of Barker, but to use Barker's insights as a way of seeing Hemingway's.[1] I will be reading the wounded soldier as a performance of masculinity, to ask whether medicine in Hemingway's novel, as in Barker's, functions as a "technology of gender" that inscribes ideals of masculine behavior.

The Compulsion to Tell: Narration and Health

James Phelan describes the narrative paradox in *A Farewell to Arms* as one in which the narrator who is telling the story cannot be the same person who is experiencing the story. That is, the Frederic Henry who is the retrospective narrator already knows what the character Frederic Henry learns during the course of the story. I will articulate a different narrative paradox (but one that I think complements Phelan's): the narrator feels compelled to tell a story that the character cannot really articulate. The result is a novel focused on silence and stoicism. When Henry returns from the hospital, Rinaldi says to him, "Tell me all about everything." Henry responds, "There's nothing to tell" (*AFTA* 167). This interaction is representative of the narrative as a whole. Throughout, Frederic is torn between a compulsion to tell and his sense that he cannot, or should not, tell. Plenty of critics have diagnosed Catherine Barkley as insane, unbalanced, or crazy.[2] But critics almost always assume that Frederic Henry's malady is purely physical; he is the victim of shelling, in other words, but not shell shock.[3] To do so, I think, is to ignore one of the earliest commentaries on the war in the novel. Just before he is killed, the driver Passini comments: "Listen. There is nothing as bad as war. . . . When people realize how bad it is they cannot do anything to stop it because they go crazy" (50). I don't want to diagnose Frederic as insane, but I do want to cast some doubt on the precise nature of his malady, and raise the possibility that his *illness* is actually masculinity as it was presented to the World War I soldier.

In *A War Imagined*, Samuel Hynes, writing about the pioneering World War I psychiatrist W. H. R. Rivers (who is also one of Barker's main characters in her blend of fact and fiction), says of Rivers's method:

> He rejected the idea that men should suppress feelings, and helped his
> patients to accept and to express "unmanly" feelings; weeping, he told
> them, could be a help to grieving men, and there was no shame in breaking

down under stress. War was an inherently traumatic experience, and fear was a natural response to it—the problem was a medical, not a moral one. (185-186)

In a novel like *Regeneration*, a late 20th-century feminist writer like Pat Barker can focus on Rivers and his methods and overtly articulate the crisis of masculinity brought about by the experience of World War I. But an author like Ernest Hemingway, caught absolutely in the bind of early-20th-century models of masculinity himself, cannot. Using Barker and World War I historians as a lens, however, we can read the dilemma and paradox of Frederic Henry's narration. On the one hand, he feels acutely the need to tell about his horrific experiences of war— watching his comrades Passini and Aymo die, his own suffering and wounding, the shooting of the sergeant, his forced desertion, and Catherine's death. On the other hand, he feels the code of manliness that requires that he not be perceived as complaining or weeping.

In an essay about *Regeneration*, Greg Harris argues that what Barker dramatizes in the narrative is the conflict men feel between telling and not telling, between what they are feeling and what they believe they should feel:

> ... brutal experiences will be their reality, yet the most legitimate emotions that such anticipation might inspire—fear, angst, second thoughts—must be stifled. The men willingly suspend valid but invalidated emotions. . . . The gender codes, then, appear to the gendered subject as more legitimate than the private feelings they eclipse in the service of upholding a compulsory masculinity. (301)

Hemingway dramatizes this, too, but perhaps not in the self-conscious way that Barker does. Much of the narrative tension in the novel comes from Frederic Henry's simultaneous needs to tell and to keep quiet. This is exacerbated by Hemingway's style of narration, which Peter Schwenger identifies as explicitly masculine: "Plainly Hemingway's style is in one sense an extension of the masculine values he depicts: the restraint of emotion, the stiff upper lip, the *macho* hermeticism" (50). It is interesting that in employing a "masculine" style that resists the sentimentalism of a feminine style (one that would presumably focus on emotion) Frederic Henry may succumb to a different "female" problem—silence.

In her chapter on shell shock in *The Female Malady*, Elaine Showalter argues forcefully for reading shell shock as a kind of protest akin to the Victorian woman's use of hysteria as protest. "If the essence of manliness was not to complain," she argues, "then shell shock was the body language of masculine complaint, a disguised male protest not only against the war but against the concept of 'manliness' itself. . . . The heightened code of masculinity that dominated wartime was intolerable to surprisingly large numbers of men" (172). In *A Farewell to Arms*, Hemingway does not focus directly on the classic symptoms of shell shock—aphasia, memory loss, or paralysis. Instead, his focus is double—on a different form of silence (to which I will return), and on a form of self-medication, the very condition of which Nurse Van Patten accuses Frederic Henry, alcoholism. Drinking to excess, drinking to forget, drinking enough to be sick—these are repeated refrains. As he is convincing Henry to drink despite his recent jaundice, Rinaldi calls his own drinking "Self-destruction day by day. . . . It ruins the stomach and makes the hand shake. Just the thing for a surgeon" (172). Ultimately, as we shall see, drinking as self-medication assists in silence.

Before we get to that, perhaps it would be useful to look directly at that interaction between Van Campen and Henry:

"I suppose you can't be blamed for not wanting to go back to the front. But I should think you would try something more intelligent than producing jaundice with alcoholism. . . . I don't believe self-inflicted jaundice entitles you to a convalescent leave." . . .

"Have you ever had jaundice, Miss Van Campen?"

"No, but I have seen a great deal of it."

"You noticed how the patients enjoyed it?"

"I suppose it is better than the front."

"Miss Van Campen . . . did you ever know a man who tried to disable himself by kicking himself in the scrotum?" . . .

"I have known many men to escape the front through self-inflicted wounds." (*AFTA* 144)

We should read this conversation in light of the novel's repeated hints at the prevalence of self-inflicted wounds. One of the very first things we see Henry do in the course of his duty is assist a man with his self-inflicted wounds. The soldier has deliberately left off his truss to make his hernia worse, but knows that his own officers will recognize this as self-inflicted. Henry advises him to "fall down by the road and get a bump on your head" after thinking over the soldier's question: "You wouldn't want to go in the line all the time, would you?" (35). Even after Henry's legitimate wounding, the doctor needs to include "Incurred in the line of duty" in his report, telling Henry, "That's what keeps you from being court-martialled for self-inflicted wounds" (59). Hemingway repeatedly draws our attention to and then away from the question of self-inflicted wounds. Perhaps his point is to reassure us of Henry's masculinity—no "slacker" he—but we could also read it as a commentary on the whole self-destructiveness of wartime masculinity.[4] That is, masculinity itself becomes a self-inflicted wound.

We can read Frederic Henry against ideas of subjectivity and masculinity that would position him as destined to lose. Usually, these ideas are attributed to an unforgiving world: "If people bring so much courage to this world the world has to kill them to break them, so of course it kills them. The world breaks every one and afterward many are strong at the broken places. But those that will not break it kills" (*AFTA* 249). Such ideas often get posited in the novel not as "it" or "the world," but as "they": "You never had time to learn. They threw you in and told you the rules and the first time they caught you off base they killed you. Or they killed you gratuitously. . . . [But] they killed you in the end. You could count on that. Stay around and they would kill you" (327). Such sentiments are perhaps typical of a postwar modernist disillusionment, an alienation focused on the pointlessness of life and manifested later in existentialism.

It would be possible, though, to read these sentiments as figuring the condition of World War I masculinity, focused as it was on a particularly passive form of warfare.[5] Convinced by patriotic fervor to embrace military service as a path to masculine feats of heroism, most soldiers discovered that the war meant waiting in a trench to be shelled. That Frederic Henry doesn't engage in trench warfare doesn't obviate this point; most of his experience of war consists of waiting—waiting out bad weather, waiting for shelling to begin so that he can drive his ambulance, or waiting in the hospital to get well. He is wounded, in fact, while he is waiting. Sandra Gilbert has described World War I as "the apocalypse of masculinism": "paradoxically . . . the war to which so many men had gone in hope of becoming heroes ended up emasculating them . . . confining them as closely as any Victorian woman had been confined" (447-448). The novel depicts the war as anything but heroic; medals are awarded for nothing, wounds are sustained while eating spaghetti in a dugout, and death comes about randomly, without respect for one's manliness or bravery. Rinaldi explicitly wants Frederic to have been a hero:

> "Tell me exactly what happened. Did you do any heroic act?"
> "No . . . I was blown up while we were eating cheese."
> "Be serious. You must have done something heroic. . . ." (*AFTA* 63)

Under such circumstances of passivity, randomness, irrationality, and meaninglessness, maintaining a faith in old models of manhood proves impossible. Indeed, several critics have recently examined the novel in terms of the dilemmas of masculinity that it presents. Ira Elliott, for instance, argues that in the gap between the narrating "I" and the "I" who experienced the war, the novel stages "the instability of the culturally-fixed categories male/female and homo/heterosexual, an instability in large measure engendered by the collapse of the pre-war social order." Elliott contends that "Frederic's narrative . . . retreats from the 'truth' learned on the frontlines: gender, desire, and sex cannot be defined in oppositional binarisms" (292). Similarly, Charles Hatten argues that the novel represents a "crisis of masculinity," though he situates the crisis in "embattled sexual desire" and reads the misogyny in the novel as a failed attempt to resituate masculinity in physiology (77-78). Stephen Clifford reads Frederic as forced to choose between love for a woman and the homosocial world of masculinity. We can read Frederic Henry's narrative dilemmas, then, as a conflict between the very real need to tell about his experiences, and his finding that the story he has to tell does not tally with an early-20th-century masculinity. It should not be surprising then, if his experience of masculinity itself is threatened with invalidation.

The Compulsion to Stay Silent: Medicine as a Technology of Gender

Gerry Brenner argues that when we read the novel against the backdrop of the war's meaninglessness, "the thesis of *A Farewell to Arms* . . . is that no institution, belief system, value, or commitment can arm one against life's utter irrationality." Brenner sees the role of medicine in the novel as "symptomatic of the failure of any system that offers or allows the illusion that it can give humankind health, order, meaning, or significance" (131). Brenner, Clifford, Elliott, and Hatten all seem to me to be right in their readings of the crisis of masculinity and rationality that the novel stages. I want to refract their insights, though, to re-read the novel in terms of the way it stages a variety of "invalid masculinity"[6] and uses medicine as a technology of gender. Rather than reading the novel as a failure to reimagine gender roles, though, I will read it as a success of modern medicine, a success at constructing a modern, colonized masculinity that can perform in war.

I am borrowing the phrase "technologies of gender" from Teresa de Lauretis. She claims:

> (1) Gender is (a) representation—which is not to say that it does not have concrete or real implications, both social and subjective, for the material life of individuals. On the contrary,
> (2) The representation of gender is its construction—and in the simplest sense it can be said that all of Western Art and high culture is the engraving of the history of that construction.

It will not come as news that Hemingway is actively engaged in constructing masculinity. But I want to look at some of the specifics of how medicine is a part of that construction, especially when placed within a narrative that in some ways resists its own telling with strategic silences.

To look at silence in the novel is somewhat difficult, because, of course, silence simply *isn't there*. One has to look at moments when there *should* be something, when it makes the most sense that a narrator would want to describe an experience or a feeling, but doesn't. There are repeated instances of this. For example, after he is wounded, Frederic Henry never uses a metaphor or simile of any kind to describe his pain. He says "Good Christ" in response to questions about whether it hurts, and will comment that it "hurt badly" (*AFTA* 59-60), but there are no other descriptors. He once comments, "The pain had gone on and on with the legs bent and I could feel it going in and out of the bone" (83), but he does not comment on how he feels. In a conversation with Catherine, Frederic reinterprets the old adage that the brave man dies only once: "The brave dies perhaps two thousand deaths if he's intelligent. He simply doesn't mention them" (140). To this extent, Frederic maintains his image of the brave: he simply doesn't mention the pain. This accords with many other moments in the novel when we might expect some articulation of negative emotion or feelings—after he shoots the sergeant, after he is forced to desert the army, after

Catherine dies—Frederic is repeatedly silent when it would seem healthiest to voice some reaction.

Frederic's silence, then, becomes a technology of gender, a representation that enacts gender as it represents it. To follow this line of thought is to concur with Judith Butler's insights about the performance of gender. If we cannot read the words, the language, then we have to read the action, the performance. If we take seriously Butler's claim that "gender is . . . an identity tenuously constituted in time—an identity instituted through a *stylized repetition of acts*" rather than "a stable locus of agency" (402, author's emphasis), then we can see Frederic's repeated silences as constituting a notion of masculinity as numbness, as lack of feeling, as a kind of dissociation from self.

He learns this dissociation, I would argue, from medicine. The discourses of medicine and masculinity in this novel join forces to colonize male subjectivity, to remake men as fighting machines. Rinaldi jokingly tells Henry that he will "get [him] drunk and take out [his] liver and put [him] in a good Italian liver and make [him] a man again" after his bout of jaundice (*AFTA* 168). The novel very clearly challenges the question of what kind of "men" medicine makes. Military medicine is an interesting oxymoron, since the goal of such medicine is to make men well enough to go back to potentially much greater harm. This is a theme that Pat Barker makes explicit in her trilogy, as Greg Harris argues: "Barker examines how patriarchal constructions of masculinity colonize men's subjectivity in ways that, especially in wartime, prove oppressive, repressive, and wholly brutal in their effects on the male psyche" (303). Barker herself puts it this way, in the voice of Billy Prior's character in *The Ghost Road*:

We are [the hospital's] success stories. *Look at us*. We don't remember, we don't feel, we don't think—at least not beyond the confines of what's needed to do the job. By any proper civilized standard (but what does *that* mean *now*?) we are objects of horror. But our nerves are completely steady. And we are still alive. (200, author's emphasis)

In *A Farewell to Arms*, the patriarchal notions of masculinity are enforced through a medical narrative. Frederic Henry *tries* to tell his illness story, and tries to tell Catherine's illness story, but succeeds only in being told by that story. In his book on illness narratives, *The Wounded Storyteller*, Arthur Frank describes the shift into medical modernity as the moment when we are forced to surrender our "illness stories" to medicine itself:

> The *modern* experience of illness begins when popular experience is overtaken by technical expertise. . . . [A] core social expectation of being sick is surrendering oneself to the care of a physician. I understand this obligation of seeking medical care as a *narrative surrender* and mark it as the central moment in modernist illness experience. (5-6, author's emphasis)

Frank describes the modern experience of medicine as colonizing; one becomes a subject of medicine and is spoken of or for, but one doesn't actually speak one's own illness narrative. Reading *A Farewell to Arms* within this framework, we see that Frederic is not really able to find a voice to describe his suffering: the stoicism that he embraces as an ideal (and that Hemingway employs as a style) keeps him from really being able to give voice to what he's thinking or feeling. He surrenders his own story to the intertwined stories of medicine (recovery from wounds) and masculinity (keeping quiet about his suffering). Frederic Henry tries to narrate a story that is culturally untellable; that is why his narration seems that of a "dumb ox" at times (as Wyndham Lewis called him). But being a "dumb," that is, silent, sufferer is exactly what the military and modernist medicine promoted as an ideal. The resulting narrative becomes a story of looking for anesthesia, of looking for a way to stop feeling, to stay quiet, but to continue on despite pain.

The ideal that colonizes him also, I think, finally separates him from himself. Early in his experience of hospital life, Frederic begins to dissociate himself from the self that feels pain.[7] As the doctor probes his leg for bits of shrapnel, he can occasionally feel sharp pain where the anesthetic has not taken complete effect. He writes: "[The doctor] used a local anaesthetic called something or other 'snow,' which froze the tissue and avoided pain until the probe, the scalpel or the forceps got below the frozen portion. The anaesthetized area was clearly defined by the patient" (*AFTA* 94). Such a shift seems almost literally a surrender to the medical narrative, if not to the medical case study; Henry ceases telling his story and tells, instead, "the patient's" story. This narrative shift to the third person is extended later on in the novel, when Henry begins to disclaim parts of himself:

> My knee was stiff, but it had been very satisfactory. Valentini had done a fine job. I had done half the retreat on foot and swum part of the Tagliamento with his knee: It was his knee all right. The other knee was mine. Doctors did things to you and then it was not your body any more. The head was mine, and the inside of the belly. It was very hungry in there. I could feel it turn over on itself. The head was mine, but not to use, not to think with, only to remember and not too much remember. (230)

Despite referring to it as "my knee" at the beginning of this passage, Henry concludes that "it was not [his] body any more." It should be no surprise, then, that he doesn't recognize himself in the mirror while he is boxing (311). Within Frank's terms, Henry has become a medical, colonized, subject, no longer "his own man," but the man that medicine has made him. As Gayle Whittier explains, "If the wound disconnects the perceiving and feeling self from the body, the clinical agenda encourages such disconnection, altering the patient from someone who is his body to someone who '*has*' a body, the ownership of which is now under medical control" (8, author's emphasis). It is not his body anymore, and he can no longer use his head outside of the confines that have been dictated to him by an outside narrative, a narrative of medicalized, anaesthetized masculinity.

Anesthesia as Model

If anesthesia becomes the model for masculinity in *Farewell to Arms*, then we need re-read the conclusion of the novel and re-read Catherine's death. Readings of her death have varied tremendously, though we could represent their range as running from Judith Fetterley's famous dictum, that the end of the novel shows that for Hemingway "the only good woman is a dead one, and even then there are questions" (71), to Charles Hatten's conclusion that Catherine finally outdoes Frederic in a contest for masculine heroism: "dying stoically, she defeats Henry in the competition for status . . . she achieves exactly the sort of heroic stature that persistently eludes Henry. . . . Barkley achieves her powerful subversion of Henry's masculinity precisely by imitating masculinity" (96). Rather than read Catherine in the end as either of triumph of a fully passive femininity or a fully stoic masculinity, however, I would suggest that we read her in terms of the importance of an anesthetized unconsciousness.

The last chapter of the novel is full of references to unconsciousness, pain, and anesthesia, and is, like much of the novel, set in a hospital. It opens with Catherine beginning to feel labor pains, and with Frederic's returning to sleep even though she is clearly lying awake next to him in pain:

> "Are you all right, Cat?"
> "I've been having some pains, darling."
> "Regularly?"
> "No, not very."
> "If you have them at all regularly we'll go to the hospital."
> I was very sleepy and went back to sleep. (312)

He registers that she is in pain and rather than doing anything to help alleviate it, he sleeps. I do not mean here to indict him for callousness toward her (there is little he could do anyway), but to point out that going to sleep in the face of pain becomes a motif throughout the chapter.

When Catherine's labor pains do become regular and they go to the hospital, she is moved into a room where there is "gas" to help with the pain, where she is put all the way under when the pains become too bad. Like Frederic throughout the novel, Catherine never describes her pain, doesn't really complain, and never uses metaphors for the pain. She will call the pains "good ones" or "big ones" (*AFTA* 314, 317), and she repeatedly asks for the gas, at times quite insistently (316, 319, 322, 323, 324). She does comment, "I'm awfully tired. . . . And I hurt like hell. . . . I hurt dreadfully," but that is as far as she goes in complaining. And in my ellipses here she is asking after Frederic and complimenting his performance: "Are you all right, darling? . . . You were lovely to me" (326).

It isn't Catherine's noble suffering, though, that interests me. It is the counterpoint the chapter sets up between Catherine's anesthesia and Frederic's. The chapter is punctuated by his excursions out of the hospital to the little café for breakfast, lunch, and dinner. At each meal, he drinks alcohol, and as Catherine's pain grows worse, he drinks more. For instance, with breakfast, he has two glasses of wine (*AFTA* 325), but Catherine has not even started using anesthesia. In other words, he begins anesthesia before she does. When he returns from breakfast, she has been moved to a room where she can be given gas. At this point, Catherine has become giddy on the gas, and comments, "It wasn't much . . . I'm a fool about the gas. It's wonderful." To which Frederic replies, "We'll get some for the home" (317). He begins giving her the gas, time passes, and then he goes out for lunch and beer. When he comes back, she tells him that "when the pain came too badly [the doctor] put [her] all the way out" and Frederic tells her, "You're drunk" (319). The connections Hemingway draws here between alcohol and anesthesia seem pointed: Frederic drinks, Catherine becomes drunk, and perhaps they should get some gas for the home. As the labor wears on, Catherine comes to complain as much as she ever does: "Oh, it doesn't work any more. It doesn't work!" (322). Frederic's response is to give her more gas, turning the dial on the machine higher and higher.

After the caesarian (during which Catherine is unconscious) and the baby's death, once again Catherine sends Frederic out for a meal. This time, he drinks a considerable amount: "I ate the ham and eggs and drank the beer . . . I drank several glasses of beer. I was not thinking at all . . . I ordered another beer. I was not ready to leave yet . . . I drank another beer. There was quite a pile of saucers now on the table in front of me" (*AFTA* 329). The point here isn't that he's drunk, but that the alcohol accompanies a refusal to think, a refusal to feel, and precedes his stoic response to Catherine's death. Like her, he uses an anesthetic, and the structure of the chapter emphasizes the comparison.

The other comparison Hemingway emphasizes in this closing is the usefulness of medicine only for the purposes of death. The point of military medicine is to heal men to the extent that they can go and face death again; in Catherine's and the baby's case, medicine serves, again, only to precipitate death. Such a critique of medicine also calls into question the whole idea of "self-inflicted" wounds, of "malingering," or of "slackers." Catherine keeps insisting until almost the very end that she really will be all right, that she is making a fuss when she should be being brave. In being much worse than she seemed, or, more importantly, than the doctor has let on, Catherine may stand as a representative of other sufferers, who are really much worse than the doctors think. In suffering and dying from a "malady" as "self-inflicted" as pregnancy, she may also stand as a measure of the way that ideas of self-determination during war, or during the modernist era, even, no longer make sense.

Critics frequently read the novel as ending with Catherine's death, but it seems to me that the novel in fact ends with Frederic's surrender of narration, which is itself a kind of death—certainly he becomes as silent as she. If we return to the quotation from Pat Barker that I used as an epigraph, we see that her character, Billy Prior, maintains that narration is "a way of claiming immunity. First-person narrators can't die, so as long as we keep telling the story of our own lives we're safe" (*Ghost Road* 115). In stopping narrating, then, Frederic Henry ceases to claim immunity, ceases to try to keep safe. He not only stops feeling, but stops fighting against the "them" that would rule his life. The close of the novel therefore becomes emblematic for Frederic Henry's experience with medicine: he learns not to feel; he learns that it is not his body to do with as he pleases any more; he learns that he cannot really intervene or have any effect on outcomes. He can no more save Catherine than he could save his comrades. Colonized as a man, as a subject of military medicine, he has learned the lessons of World War I masculinity, and ceased to feel.

From *The Hemingway Review* 21, no. 1 (Fall 2001): 38-52. Copyright © 2001 by The Hemingway Society. Reprinted by permission of The Hemingway Society.

Notes

1. Though it is outside the scope of this essay, one could draw interesting parallels between Wilfred Owen, Siegfried Sassoon, Ernest Hemingway, and Pat Barker, especially as they represent pain and masculinity. Adrian Caesar looks at the English World War I poets and argues that for them suffering becomes not only a mode of masculinity, but that "in [their] work [there is] a celebration of war as a vehicle of pain and suffering, which is shared by the voyeuristic reader who peeps at the horror through parted fingers and is consciously or unconsciously thrilled and excited by it" (2). This is particularly significant for a reading of Hemingway's representation of suffering, war, and masculinity in light of Spilka's claim that Hemingway had developed much of his anti-war sentiments from reading Owen and Sassoon (among others) ("Hemingway and Fauntleroy" 352-353).

2. See Sandra Whipple Spanier's "Hemingway's Unknown Soldier" for the best survey of critical responses to Catherine (76-81).

3. Gerry Brenner and Stephen Clifford are exceptions. Brenner sees Henry as "disoriented" (138) and "a little out of his head" (139). Clifford points out that Frederic says to Catherine, "I'm crazy in love with you," and notes: "isn't it interesting that no critical readers have defined him as crazy. . . ." Clifford reads this as an indication of "narrative and gender bias in reading" (247).

4. Spilka reads Frederic Henry's wounding as less a testament to his masculinity than as a moment for Hemingway to experiment with androgyny. He points to Frederic's "manliness" in taking charge in the Milan hospital when they don't know what to do with him, but contrasts it to the "femininity" of his enforced passivity, and to gaining power through that passivity. He also points out that for Catherine and Frederic to have intercourse while he is wounded, Frederic would have to assume the "passive" position (*Hemingway's Quarrel* 212-213).

5. Spanier notes that both Catherine and Frederic are particularly passive and connects this to the effects of the war (89).

6. See Cohen, Elliott, and Hatten on the ways in which Hemingway seems to be using the novel as a kind of laboratory for exploring different modes of masculinity.

7. Though he never otherwise mentions anesthetic, Gerry Brenner comments that Frederic Henry holds off on mentioning Catherine Barkley until fairly late in the novel. "Sorely wounded, he avoids touching directly its most tender spot, Catherine. He keeps her offstage until his narrative is into its fourth chapter, enough time for its anesthetic, as it were, to take effect" (137).

Works Cited

Barker, Pat. *The Eye in the Door*. New York: Plume, 1993.

———. *The Ghost Road*. New York: Plume, 1995.

———. *Regeneration*. New York: Plume, 1991.

Brenner, Gerry. "A Hospitalized World." *Critical Essays on Ernest Hemingway's A Farewell to Arms*. Ed. George Monteiro. New York: G. K. Hall, 1994. 130-144.

Butler, Judith. "Performative Acts and Gender Construction: An Essay in Phenomenology and Feminist Theory." *Writing on the Body: Female Embodiment and Feminist Theory*. Eds. Katie Conboy, Nadice Medina, and Sarah Stanbury. New York: Columbia UP, 1997. 401-417.

Caesar, Adrian. *Taking it Like a Man: Suffering, Sexuality and the War Poets: Brooke, Sassoon, Owen, Graves*. Manchester: Manchester UP, 1993.

Clifford, Stephen. *Beyond the Heroic "I": Reading Lawrence, Hemingway, and "Masculinity."* Lewisburg, PA: Bucknell UP, 1998.

Cohen, Peter. "'I Won't Kiss You. I'll Send Your English Girl': Homoerotic Desire in *A Farewell to Arms*." *The Hemingway Review* 15.1 (Fall 1995): 42-53.

Comley, Nancy R., and Robert Scholes. *Hemingway's Genders: Rereading the Hemingway Text*. New Haven: Yale UP, 1994.

Donaldson, Scott, ed. *New Essays on A Farewell to Arms*. Cambridge: Cambridge UP, 1990.

Elliott, Ira. "*A Farewell to Arms* and Hemingway's Crisis of Masculine Values." *LIT* 4 (1993): 291-304.

Fetterley, Judith. *The Resisting Reader: A Feminist Approach to American Fiction*. Bloomington: Indiana UP, 1978.

Gilbert, Sandra. "Soldier's Heart: Literary Men, Literary Women, and the Great War." *Signs* 8.3 (1983): 422-50.

Harris, Greg. "Compulsory Masculinity, Britain, and the Great War: The Literary-Historical Work of Pat Barker." *Critique* 39.4 (1998): 290-304.

Hatten, Charles. "The Crisis of Masculinity, Reified Desire, and Catherine Barkley in *A Farewell to Arms*." *Journal of the History of Sexuality* 4.1 (1993): 76-98.

Hemingway, Ernest. *A Farewell to Arms*. New York: Scribner's, 1929.

Hynes, Samuel. *A War Imagined: The First World War and English Culture*. New York: Atheneum, 1991.

Lewis, Wyndham. "The 'Dumb Ox' in Love and War." *Twentieth-Century Interpretations of A Farewell to Arms*. Ed. Jay Gellens. Englewood Cliffs, NJ: Prentice-Hall, 1970. 72-90.

Phelan, James. "Distance, Voice, and Temporal Perspective in Frederic Henry's Narration: Successes, Problems, and Paradox." In Donaldson 53-74.

Reynolds, Michael S. *Hemingway's First War: The Making of A Farewell to Arms*. Princeton, NJ: Princeton UP, 1976.

Schwenger, Peter. *Phallic Critiques: Masculinity and Twentieth-Century Literature*. London: Routledge and Kegan Paul, 1984.

Spanier, Sandra Whipple. "Hemingway's Unknown Soldier: Catherine Barkley, the Critics, and the Great War." In Donaldson 75-108.

Spilka, Mark. *Hemingway's Quarrel with Androgyny*. Lincoln: U of Nebraska P, 1990.

_____. "Hemingway and Fauntleroy: An Androgynous Pursuit." *American Novelists Revisited: Essays in Feminist Criticism*. Ed. Fritz Fleischmann. Boston: G. K. Hall, 1982. 339-370.

Whittier, Gayle. "Clinical Gaze and the Erotic Body in *A Farewell to Arms*." *Studies in the Humanities* 23.1 (1996): 1-27.

"Everything Completely Knit Up":
Seeing *For Whom the Bell Tolls* Whole _____

A. Robert Lee

You see every damned word and action in this book depends upon every other word and action. You see he's laying there in the pine needles at the start and that is where he is at the end. He has his problem and all his life before him at the start and he has all his life in those days and, at the end there is only death for him and he truly isn't afraid of it at all because he has a chance to finish his mission.

But would all that be clear?

—Letter to Maxwell Perkins, 26 August 1940[1]

The most important thing in a work of art is that it should have a kind of focus—i.e. some place where all the rays meet or from which they issue. And this focus should not be capable of being completely explained in words. This, indeed, is the important thing about a good work of art, that its basic content can in its entirety be expressed only by itself.

—Tolstoy as reported by A. B. Goldenweiser[2]

1

In confiding to Maxwell Perkins, the shrewd Scribner's editor he shared with Scott Fitzgerald, Thomas Wolfe and others, the hope that *For Whom the Bell Tolls* would exhibit a 'clear' interdependence of all its essential detail—everything 'completely knit up and stowed away ship-shape' as he says earlier in his letter—Hemingway showed himself perfectly acute about what, and what not, ought to count in his novel. The issue he calls attention to, whether Robert Jordan embodies a sufficiently credible and inclusive viewpoint through whom to refract the drama of the Civil War and the Spanish soil itself, offers a most engaging critical point of departure. Does Jordan's three-day *partizan* mission at the bridge begun and ended 'there on the pine needles' serve convincingly as the book's fulcrum, the means through which its widening circle of other concerns is brought to overall imaginative order? More precisely, can we say that Jordan's consciousness and his undertaking behind enemy lines establish a sufficient centre for the novel's moral perspectives, or for its portraits of Pablo, El Sordo and the others as expressions of the human spirit under press of war and beleaguered by Fascism, or for Hemingway's long-standing preoccupation with Spain (begun in *The Sun Also Rises* and the shorter stories and carried forward through *Death in the Afternoon*, *The Spanish Earth* and *The Fifth Column*) as an essential arena for the conflict of good and bad faith? If, as he believed, and his letter is cast in characteristic telegraphese, 'every damned word and action' indeed depends upon 'every other word and action', then how well does *For Whom the Bell Tolls* meet Hemingway's own criteria?

Opinion has generally agreed that *For Whom the Bell Tolls* marks a more ambitious effort than both *The Sun Also Rises* and *A Farewell to Arms*, but that equally it falls down in several key aspects. Even among enthusiasts who greeted it on publication as a landmark achievement, the Spanish Civil War at last made over into epic and a work to be put alongside George Orwell's *Homage to Catalonia*, the cavils have been many and frequent. And though Hemingway's comments on the novel don't provide the only measure for its success or failure, they do direct us back to how *For Whom the Bell Tolls* operates as an imaginative whole. The issue has received a degree of attention, notably in their different ways by Philip Young and Carlos Baker,[3] but the full weight of Hemingway's own concern with whether, and in what manner, the novel achieves, in Tolstoy's terms, its 'focus', a 'place where all the rays meet or from which they issue', has not.

False trails were quick to emerge. Lesser sniping, for instance, to nobody's particular advantage, took after Hemingway's supposed politics in the novel. A number of unyielding Stalinists, with apparently untroubled conscience and in plain defiance of what Jordan says to be his own political outlook,[4] pronounced Hemingway soft on Fascism, or at least as having given tacit support to the Fascist cause by his conception of Jordan as the code hero acting only according to the dictates of his own will and by depicting the Loyalist side as dishevelled and both in need of and inevitably giving way to the unrelenting eventual smack of Franco's dictatorship. Conversely, many of more liberalish persuasion, including over time several ex-Party members, thought him duped by the efficiency of the Communist Party machine in the Spain of the 1930s. Hemingway, the argument runs, simply misunderstood long-term Soviet and Comintern operations in the Spanish struggle. Hence Robert Jordan as fellow-traveller, and Hemingway behind him, unwittingly abetted an ideology whose consequences for Europe were ultimately as pernicious as the ideology which produced Francoist authoritarianism. Such views grievously misread both Hemingway and his novel.

Other charges, also pertinent enough at first glance, have similarly hindered the business of seeing the novel whole. Hemingway is tasked with lacking an authentic historical consciousness, a comprehensive grasp of the full nuance of the Spanish past. Too perceptibly he writes selectively of Spain, the incorrigible Hispanophile whose insistence on Spanish peasant values as an exemplary moral way of being blinkered him to the country's infinitely subtler human complexity, not to mention the historic intricacy of its religion and politics. A Pablo, or Sordo, or Anselmo, even the glimpses of the Republican command-structure, simply fail to do full service as the carriers of Spanish identity. One needs a more representative human cast, a sharper sense of other political and regional groups–POUM, the Falangists, the Catholic Church hierarchy, the Catalans, the Gallegos or the Nationalists' Italian allies perhaps—seen across a time-span more appropriate to epic. Here again, however, criticism seems to ask of *For Whom the Bell Tolls* what insistently it is not, the historical *roman-fleuve*, a full-blown panorama of the Iberian past metamorphosing in all due complexity into the present.

In this connection, too, *For Whom the Bell Tolls* has regularly had to bear comparison with *War and Peace*, a standard which, as Hemingway several times ruefully observed, could hardly not appear rigged to make him come off the loser.[5] For despite apparent similarities of surface—a classic war and armies on the move, individual points of consciousness poised against the larger military operation—*For Whom the Bell Tolls* is not especially Tolstoyian, if by Tolstoyian one means the consciously philosophic depiction of 'war and peace' as recurring dialectical antimonies in the human make-up and set to a suitable scale of time and place. Hemingway's version of the Spanish Civil War in fact differs in almost every major aspect from Tolstoy's massive, Shakespearean conception of Napoleon's attempted invasion of imperial Russia. Simply as battle-terrain the Castilian hill and pine country behind Fascist lines north of Madrid hardly resembles the great set-pieces of Tolstoy's Austerlitz and his other principal battle-scenes. Nor can Robert Jordan, though the novel's central consciousness, be accurately thought the fictional equivalent of Tolstoy's Pierre or Prince Andrei. Unlike them, he is not there to give the longer, deliberated historical view. Which is not to say that Tolstoy isn't a relevant name to invoke. His general observation to A. B. Goldenweiser particularly applies. Though readers may disagree about the success with which Hemingway creates his 'focus', the point of centre from which the rest of the novel takes its imaginative departure, it can't be denied that in Robert Jordan and the bridge a centre does actually exist. No doubt, in part, this can be explained by the less comprehensive span of Hemingway's novel as against Tolstoy's. To invoke, say, Henry James's well-known unease about Tolstoy's 'loose, baggy monsters' in relation to *For Whom the Bell Tolls* would be to deny the kind of novel actually before us.

Then, there is the repeated, and vexed, question of Hemingway's women. Pilar as the incarnation of the earth madonna is routinely judged to lack all credibility, while Maria, adoring and healed of her rape by the Fascists through her too instantaneous love for Jordan, amounts to no more than a cipher, a figure out of barely disguised supremacist male fantasy. Although few readers would make any very emphatic case for either, especially Maria, when remembered within the context of the novel's detail—the local eventfulness of the preparations in the cave and Pilar's relationship with Pablo for instance—they hardly seem the *complete* disasters each has come to be designated almost by rote.

Hemingway's Spanglish has also been the occasion of great complaint.[6] His transliteration of the Spanish *tú* in a succession of thees and thous (though not something he in fact does all the time) irrecoverably mars the novel, giving it the look of near-parody, or at least of unacceptable stylistic clumsiness. This surely is to miss the point. Hemingway clearly wishes to signal something of the acute difference inherent in this Spanish peasant world, especially the argot in which events are understood and the residual habits of thought and speech passed down through generations. His thees and thous and consciously literal renderings of different blasphemies and curse-forms, it might fairly be argued, successfully imply an older ancestral community of usage, a romance or medieval chivalric world recalled precisely in the seeming stilted anachronisms of Anselmo and the other camp members.

The other repeated misgiving lies with Robert Jordan himself, allegedly yet one more of Hemingway's formulaic heroes in the line of Nick Adams (though Adams has rightly been recognized more for the tyro, the shocked initiate), Jake Barnes, Frederic Henry, and latterly, Thomas Hudson, a man who once again plays out the familiar Hemingway scenario of the tough-guy loser vindicated only by the separate peace he has made with what in *A Farewell to Arms* Frederic Henry laconically (and typically) invokes as the 'bitch' nature of History. Again this smacks of the superficial half-truth. Robert Jordan, in fact, is anything but the initiate which is Nick in the early Indian and war stories. Nor is he Jake Barnes, the sexual casualty of war and Jazz Age expatriation unable to achieve love with his ruined and ruinous Lady Brett. And nor is he Frederic Henry, the would-be healer cheated of Catherine and their child as a result of the flight from the Italian 'joke front' of

---

Caparetto. Unlike them, he consciously experiences at close focus the coming of his own death, an event the novel treats with scrupulous tact as a major ceremony of life and which both recalls the American Civil War times of his grandfather and binds him in shared, vulnerable mortality with Lieutenant Berrendo, his fellow combatant and symbolic and opposing *alter ego*, the Nationalist officer from Navarra on whom he has his gun trained while covering the retreat of Pablo and the women. There, as dramatically as anywhere in the novel, the touchstone of 'No man is an island', death as the common democratic human inevitability, is given vivid local force. To be sure, Jordan does share with Hemingway's other main protagonists the need to make his own separate peace against a collapsing international and moral order, but he does so on terms wholly specific to the psychology and situation given him by the novel. Too frequently, especially by adverse critics, Hemingway has been interpreted as though the novels and stories were episodes from a single ongoing serial, barely differentiated variations on the theme of the code.

Nor have these been the only worries to surface. Robert Jordan's interior monologues, for instance, represent an indulgence on Hemingway's part, occasions to re-invoke a partly autobiographical mid-Western American boyhood or engage in semi-documentary reminiscence of Gaylord's Hotel in Madrid and Republican notables like Karkov, Golz, Lister, Marty, Modesto and El Campesino. Even the action around the bridge has been thought a weakness, altogether too concentrated and archly symbolic in its echoes of Leonidas and Horatio and its use of the seventy-hour time-span as the measure of a single human life. The different flashbacks, too, from Pablo's taking of the Guardia Civil post and the flailing of the village's Fascists to the train blowing and Maria's rape, betray Hemingway into doing ostentatious set-pieces, easily detachable dramatic vignettes. El Sordo and Pablo, further, have been considered to balance off over-symmetrically as the good and bad *partizan* guerrilla leaders. Finally, the novel's general stylistic manner has about it too ritualized a quality, with the result that the whole reads as if the imaginative life had been rendered down to a point approaching woodenness.

Most of these recurring dissatisfactions, whatever their respective merits, have tended to divert attention from whether or not *For Whom the Bell Tolls* holds up as an imaginative whole, and if so, how that whole is achieved. Both in his letter to Perkins, and in the relevant correspondence of 1939-40 with his publisher Charles Scribner, Hemingway went out of his way to insist on this as the essential test. Furthermore, his standard can hardly be thought other than perfectly exacting in its own right: for how convincingly is *For Whom the Bell Tolls* 'knit up', the integrated and better sum of its contributing parts?

The point, at any rate, was not lost on Edmund Wilson. In one of the novel's earliest reviews, Wilson set the critical pace in handsome, intelligent style, alighting on precisely the same issue which had exercised Hemingway. For him, too, Jordan as consciousness and about his duties at the bridge serves as the novel's inescapable centre of gravity:

> [*For Whom the Bell Tolls*] is Hemingway's first attempt to compose a full-length novel, with real characters, and a built-up story. On the eve of a Loyalist attack in the Spanish Civil War, a young American who has enlisted on the Loyalist side goes out into the country held by the Fascists, under orders to blow up a bridge. He directs with considerable difficulty a band of peasant guerrillas, spends three nights in a cave in their company, blows up the bridge on schedule, and is finally shot by the Fascists. The method is the reverse of the ordinary method in novels of contemporary history, Franz Hoellering's or André Malraux's which undertake a general survey of a revolutionary crisis, shuttling back and forth among various groups of characters. There is little of this shuttling in 'For Whom the Bell Tolls', but it is all directly related to the main action: the blowing-up of the bridge. Through this episode the writer has aimed to reflect the whole course of the Spanish War, to show the tangle of elements that were engaged in it, and to exhibit the events in a larger perspective than that of the emergency of the moment.

So much, for Wilson, was positive, but he also had his reservations:

> The novel has certain weaknesses. A master of the concentrated short story, Hemingway is less sure of his grasp of the form of the elaborated novel. The shape of 'For Whom The Bell Tolls' is sometimes slack and sometimes bulging. It is certainly quite a little too long. You need space to make an epic of three days; but the story seems to slow up towards the end where the reader feels it ought to move faster; and the author has not found out how to mold or to cut the interior soliloquies of his hero. Nor are the excursions, outside the consciousness of the hero, whose point of view comprehends most of the book, conducted with consistent attention to the symmetry and point of the whole.[7]

Taken together, both Hemingway's own view of his novel, and Wilson's, usefully suggest how *For Whom the Bell Tolls* might most appropriately be understood and judged. Does it achieve the 'larger perspective', but at the expense of slackness? How true is it to say that the material which lies outside Robert Jordan's 'consciousness' insufficiently ties in with the central drama of the bridge-blowing and Robert's own immediate experience? We return, through Hemingway's first major critic, to the issue of the novel's 'attention to the symmetry and point of the whole', to whether *For Whom the Bell Tolls*, as Hemingway initially put matters, can indeed claim to be 'knit up'.

Before, however, turning to the novel's integration, a further point might be registered, and one not always given due emphasis. One doesn't have to think *For Whom the Bell Tolls* an unalloyed success to grant Hemingway the recognition of having taken on a subject of genuine consequence, the Spanish Civil War assuredly seen as a fiction with its own imagined cast and adventures, but also as depicting the profounder questions of personal allegiance, the moral drama of how to act under duress. The novel thus runs deeper than the oppositions of Republican as against Fascist, existentialist as against Christian values. In this, assuredly to his own design, Hemingway deserves his place alongside Orwell, Huxley, Koestler and Malraux, to number the better-known, in depicting perennial human vulnerability to authoritarian power. Hemingway, whatever else, really ought not to be denied the seriousness of his subject, nor the obvious care with which he has sought to give his story an appropriate form.

2

'*Un callejón sin salida*. A passageway with no exit'[8]: so Robert Jordan judges the predicament of El Sordo and his men trapped on the hilltop by the Nationalist troops and their supporting airpower. As much, however, might be said of his own situation, or at least the reader's emerging sense of his situation. In part, this has to do with the novel's thematic devices, the warning raids of the Fascist bombers, Pablo's well-taken peasant misgivings about the blowing of the bridge, Pilar's reading of Jordan's palm, and Golz's initial forebodings about the counter-offensive. Andrés's subsequent inability to get past military bureaucracy with Jordan's letter adds further credence to the operation's likely failure. But the novel's closing confirmation of a historic human tragedy being played through in small to its inescapable conclusion is also carried by the way Hemingway manages the structure of the novel. For the structure of *For Whom the Bell Tolls* reflects with extraordinary precision its theme, subject and means blended one into another, an achievement which, if not absolutely perfect in execution, merits considerable respect.

In some measure this match of subject and form might be thought to follow inevitably from a story so conceived as to honour almost to the letter the Aristotelian unities, the seventy-hour or three-day rite of passage made to do duty for the assumed norm of a human lifetime, the single locale of the hillside camp within range of the bridge, and the narrative unfolded as an integrated sequence of cause and effect. But it amounts to more than that: Hemingway goes further than simply to unify time, place and action. He keeps our attention as closely engaged as he does by making the bridge (and Jordan's consciousness of it and of his mission) not only the novel's thematic centre, but its structural centre. The different flashbacks and insets, Jordan's interior monologues and the transcription of daily life at the camp underline the bridge's importance as the place where the novel's action will reach its dramatic climax, but also its contribution to the novel's pattern as a species of lodestone, the essential hub of the narrative. It becomes, to use Tolstoy's image again, the place where the novel's 'rays' meet and find their 'focus'.

Whether we move through time-present, as in Jordan's arrival with Anselmo, his love-affair with Maria, Pablo's defection and life as given inside the camp, or through time-remembered, as in the account of Pablo's seizure of the Fascist command-post and the flailing of the village, or through a kind of parallel-time, as in Andrés's abortive endeavour to get the letter to Golz in time and El Sordo's doomed stand against the Nationalists, Hemingway works each of these sequences into the action at the bridge with meticulous timing and calculation. This is equally true of Jordan's monologues, the references back to his Montana upbringing and the memory of his father and grandfather and American Civil War figures like the Confederate grey ghost John Mosby, or the recall of his fellow-dynamiter and expatriate Kaskin, or the Gaylord's crowd, Golz, and others in the Republican command. In other words, despite obvious blemishes—Maria or Jordan's occasional too explicit political reflections—*For Whom the Bell Tolls* operates to genuine advantage on its strategy of centre and circumference, nearly every part working towards the whole, the whole securely reflective of each contributing part. I want to redirect attention first towards the novel's creation of its 'focus', then in turn at the flashbacks, the insets, and Jordan's interior monologues.

If analogues for the bridge in *For Whom the Bell Tolls* were to be advanced from other classic American texts, then Hawthorne's scaffold in *The Scarlet Letter* or Twain's raft in *Huckleberry Finn* would be among the most appropriate. For the bridge acts both as an emphatically literal point of reference, an actual thing in an actual war, but also as a larger touchstone for other local stands and battles, in the Spanish War and by implication all wars. It perhaps is not, to be sure, the deific Brooklyn Bridge of Hart Crane's poem—it does not lend of its curveship a myth to God—but it radiates, as the novel says early on, a 'solid flung metal grace' (35), an iconic power which grows in impact as Anselmo, Agustín, Pilar and Fernando (Pablo is the dissenter) come to see that it is here and finally that their stand must be made. They, in turn, speak of it in implicitly religious terms, the place of duty which if it is to cost them their lives must do so with all the dignity of an enterprise worthy of the sacrificial contract. In this, too, the bridge appropriately keeps us mindful of other bridges, other antecedent occasions on the Tiber and at the Concord where earlier legendary hero-warriors have found the final turn of their destiny. Both Jordan and Pilar sense this, Jordan in one of his soliloquies:

> My obligation is to the bridge, and to fulfill that, I must take no useless risk
> of myself until I complete that duty. (63)

and Pilar, slightly more euphorically, by identifying the bridge with the Republic:

> 'I am for the Republic,' the woman of Pablo said happily. 'And the Repub-
> lic is the bridge. Afterwards we will have time for other projects.' (53)

With a keen touch of irony, Hemingway shows, too, that as the bridge grows in importance for the band, and especially after Pablo's return from the 'loneliness' of his defection, so paradoxically at command headquarters, it recedes in tactical importance, a symptom of the impending larger collapse of the Loyalist forces. In this respect it becomes, also, an omen, of a kind with the triads of Fascist bombers which destroy El Sordo and penetrate into the hills and behind Republican lines. The appropriate general note is struck by Golz to his French subordinate Duval: '*Nous sommes foutus. Oui. Comme toujours*' (428). Though obviously unheard by Jordan, or the band, Golz's observation, by its confession of frailty, enhances, if anything, rather than diminishes, the human worth behind the action at the bridge.

Nowhere does the bridge loom more importantly than in the novel's closing sequence. To Jordan it becomes 'a dream bridge. A bloody dream bridge' (437), not only his designated target, the object planned against, spied upon, easy to dynamite, but the place where finally his boyhood dreams of heroic Civil War and Western frontier derring-do become for a moment utterly real, romance literally transformed into historic actuality. To an extent, thus, the novel aptly offers itself as slightly ritual in manner, for behind its surfaces lies the appeal to a discernibly larger, mythic paradigm of heroic action, the fugitive, shadowy memory of past and recollected other raids and counter-raids, whether the picture-book chivalry of childhood classics, or the epic moments from actual history. Hemingway hints a number of times, and adroitly, of the fascination most male childhoods display for heroic lore and deeds, often enough acted out in games and gang charades. For Jordan, he has the recall of a younger imagination nurtured both on the West and on his grandfather's stories of the Civil War, as well as his eager adolescent taste for the reading of adventure. In this sense the bridge joins personal memory to fact, an individual American past to the European and war-torn present. It also, as the considerable commentary on the novel has not failed to point out, serves as the place where life is brought up sharp against death, movement becomes stasis, and human connection undergoes split and severance. Without wanting unduly to add to this commentary, it ought to be stressed again how subtly conceived are the bridge's several purposes and resonances throughout *For Whom the Bell Tolls*.

But if the bridge functions as the novel's epicentre, around it Hemingway builds a busy composite human world, at each turn linking the bridge to life in the camp, especially the tangle of energies and tension among Pablo, Pilar, Anselmo, Maria, the gypsy Raphael, and the five others, the brothers Andrés and Eladio, and Agustín, Fernando and Primitivo. Hemingway's detailed evocation of this life—the edgy group loyalty, the stock of curses, superstitions, stories told, retold, and frequently embellished into legend, Jordan's wary relationship with both Pablo and Pilar, the ritual of meals and guard duties and the different spats—amounts to no small tour-de-force, *partizan* life under war vividly excerpted and caught on the page. Part of this life, too, is the monitoring consciousness of Robert Jordan, directing our attention both to the time-present as experienced at the camp, but also directing us backwards into past time and patterns of causation. Thus the bridge becomes dramatically more than some mere static point of reference, it offers a 'focus' in the larger Tolstoyian sense.

Take, at the start, Jordan's arrival at the camp with his dynamite under orders from Golz. In classic declarative style, Hemingway sets before us the essential terrain against which the novel's action will be enacted, 'the brown, pine-needled floor of the forest' (1), the knotty, tree-lined mountainside, the painterly mill and stream which lead on to the bridge. In Anselmo, he establishes the first of the *partizans*, the tough, grainy, companion mentor who guides both Jordan and the reader into the hidden world of Pablo. Anselmo's utterances nicely confirm the simple good faith he has in the Republic's cause, but also suggest a veteran who knows the terms on which he must live. 'I am an old man who will live until I die' (16) is his affecting answer to Pablo's taunts, for instance. He again conveys the human touch when he speaks to Jordan of God: 'Clearly I miss Him, having been brought up in religion. But now a man must be responsible for himself' (41). Anselmo also offers the perfect angle through which to encounter for the first time Pablo, a leader convincingly suspicious of Jordan's arrival, a drinker, and at once shrewd yet beset with contradiction, with a peasant's wary eye upon any disruption of what he knows as the best terms of safety. His general savvy in not being taken in by Jordan's blandishments works especially well:

'He is Pablo,' said the old man. . . .

'Good. I have heard much of you,' said Robert Jordan. . . .

'I have heard that you are an excellent guerrilla leader, that you are loyal to the republic and prove your loyalty through your acts, and that you are a man both serious and valiant. I bring you greetings from the General Staff.'

'Where did you hear all this?' asked Pablo. Robert Jordan registered that he was not taking any of the flattery. . . . 'What are you going to do with the dynamite?'

'Blow up a bridge.'

'What bridge?'

'That is my business.'

'If it is in this territory, it is my business. You cannot blow bridges close to where you live. You must live in one place and operate in another. I know my business. One who is alive, now, after a year, knows his business.' (10-11)

Hemingway then appropriately locates Pablo within an imagery of the hunter and the hunted, the knowing fox but also the vulnerable hare. As Pablo says, weariness in his tone:

I am tired of being hunted. Here we are all right. Now if you blow a bridge here, we will be hunted. If they know we are here and hunt for us with planes, they will find us. If they send Moors to hunt us out, they will find us and we must go. I am tired of all this. You hear? . . . What right have you, a foreigner, to come to me and tell me what I must do? . . .

To me, now, the most important is that we be not disturbed here. (15)

The accent convinces because it has about it the weary ring of experience, and because Pablo's scepticism acts as the right counter to the military planner's abstractions, tactics made at the desk and set down bloodlessly upon army maps, even by so disciplined and well-meaning a general as Golz. The hideaway mountain way of life which Pablo and his band have made for themselves, and into which Jordan has intruded, Hemingway then makes into a wholly credible imagined front-line arena, an uncertain provisional place which matches the justified uncertainty of men deeply at risk and with only few and precarious means of survival. That Jordan both sees this and tries to negotiate his way through to Pablo's trust adds further human depth to the novel's creation of a working centre.

The picture is then built up in accretions across the three days and nights Jordan spends in preparation for the attack on the bridge. The venial irresponsibility of Raphael, the gypsy, his mind always on the next meal or snaring a rabbit, is to have more serious consequences when he fails to guard the dynamite properly so allowing Pablo to attempt sabotage by destroying the plungers. Even the first glimpse of Maria, mute and temptingly pretty, suggests an appropriate element, the girl as Spain's vulnerability to the dark, vengeful angers of Fascism. But what most gives dynamic to the world of Pablo and the camp is Pilar and her strange, mesmeric hold over each aspect of daily life, the talk, the orders, the rituals of food and drink, and especially the bombast and cursing. Her first physical appearance confirms not exactly the gorgon conjured up by Raphael and the others, but a woman whose strength of will is expressed in her solid physical make-up:

> Robert Jordan saw a woman of about fifty almost as big as Pablo, almost as wide as she was tall, in black peasant skirt and waist, with heavy wool socks on heavy legs, black rope-soled shoes and a brown face like a model for a granite monument. She had big but nice looking hands and her thick curly black hair was twisted into a knot on her neck. (30)

She it is, too, who in her embrace of Jordan, her nursing of Maria, and above all, her fraught, complex 'marriage' with Pablo, expresses the standard for life and for the human meaning of the Loyalist cause. At the same time, she is not made by Hemingway into some easy emblem of matrilinear strength; she exhibits a gamut of feelings, motherly sentimentality as in the care of Maria, an inclination towards tough, in-the-grain emotion as in her stories of Pablo's role in the attack on the Fascist village and her affair with Finito, the energy of the vixen as in her cursing and direction of the camp's daily rhythm.

Hemingway manages the relationship with Pablo to especially fine effect. Even as she ponders the notion of killing Pablo, the leader gone slack on his past skills and bravery, so Pilar recalls with mixed sentiments a man for whom she has shown love, even though she has come to him from Finito and from other men. Hemingway also catches in their relationship the ambiguous Spanish construction of male and female roles, not to mention the awareness of a Castilian in relationship with a part-gypsy woman. The arguments and bids for authority can hardly be thought other than handsomely authentic. She it is, too, who presides over Maria like Juliet's nurse, over the love-affair with Jordan, and who, at the end, as Jordan is wounded, presides over the escape from Berrendo and his troops. She appropriately is also given the story of the flailing of the village to relate, told en route to the meeting with El Sordo, Pilar as witness and historian to the cruelties which any partisanship can inflict. Her presence touches every aspect of the camp's life, a portrait which allows Hemingway once more to underline the human dimension of his story and to give it a principle of continuity, and altogether a better, deeper creation than he has often been allowed.

The other feature of the camp life as centre has to be Jordan's love for Maria. Even though no convincing case has ever been established for Maria, the childlike submissive lover invented by a Hemingway hopelessly unable to imagine an adult woman according to his rebuking critics, the relationship as such hasn't always been given its due. Given the claustrophobic pressures of war (one recalls Stephen Crane's notion of the American Union army as a moving box in *The Red Badge of Courage*), and Jordan's odd ascetic life in the service of the Loyalist cause, the notion of sexual release through Maria isn't entirely without foundation. Hemingway, to be sure, errs badly in transforming the relationship into some version of a lifetime's love, again the trope of a life lived through in three representative days, but he suggests something deeply convincing in how men at war, their nerves kept sharp to the possibility of death or disabling injury, discover in themselves a more than customary drive towards sexual release. This does not deny that in *For Whom the Bell Tolls* the transaction goes all one way, towards fulfilling Jordan's needs not Maria's, his fantasy not hers. Maria can't honestly be thought other than a mistake, but the complex pressure of Jordan's needs, a man wound tight by his obligation to his mission, might be regarded more sympathetically than it usually has. For as Anselmo, Pablo and Pilar are given in distinctive terms, so Jordan—not only as *partizan*, volunteer Loyalist and Hispanophile, but a man possessed of complex emotional and sexual drives—is given a fuller personality than that merely of the behind-the-lines warrior.

Each of these four, and the picture draws further human detail from the band's other combatants, make up a gallery of types and voices. Their cumulative human weight of presence, and Hemingway's scrupulous observation of food, wine, camp and guard duties, and the constant working in of memory (not to say the ways in which a *partizan* group goes about its business of survival and hit-and-run harassment of the enemy) build into a substantive, credible whole. They provide the novel's continuity, its human time-present. As Jordan transforms them into a fighting unit, the instrument for Golz's policy, so the reader engages with both a representative world and one actively fleshed through by Hemingway. When, therefore, we encounter in turn the flashbacks, the insets and Jordan's soliloquies, we have, as it were, a secure touchstone, a sense of life persuasively imagined against which to set each in turn.

3

Just as Hemingway establishes in the bridge and camp life the novel's centre, so in almost all the dozen or so flashbacks he gives notice of the enclosing larger world of politics and Spanish history against which Jordan's action can be understood. Several deal with Jordan's own reminiscence, and perhaps belong more aptly with his interior soliloquies, but the others give *For Whom the Bell Tolls* its wider embrace of the Civil War and the historic clash of loyalties. The first we encounter, Jordan's meeting with Golz, blends with remarkable ease into the journey to Pablo's camp with Anselmo. The transition runs from carrying the dynamite, to Anselmo, to Golz's dialogue with Jordan:

> 'To blow the bridge is nothing,' Golz had said, the lamplight on his scarred, shaved head, pointing with a pencil on the big map. 'You understand?'
>
> 'Yes, I understand.'
>
> 'Absolutely nothing. Merely to blow the bridge is a failure.'
>
> 'Yes, Comrade General.'
>
> 'To blow the bridge at a stated hour based on the time set for the attack is how it should be done. You see that naturally. That is your right and how it should be done.' (4-5)

Where Golz, however, a portrait done with considerable sympathy, is all discipline and command, the depiction of Anselmo guiding Jordan to the camp translates the abstraction of orders into literal action. Hemingway also shrewdly shows Golz as a man with his own becoming traits—the jokes about his and Jordan's names and about their respective haircuts, the drink he offers—and as precisely the *Général Sovietique*, in touch with the larger campaign against the Fascists. The implication is just about right, Jordan as but one figure of many, his mission part of a more inclusive strategy.

The major other flashbacks, especially those I now want to call attention to—Pablo's attack on the Fascist village, Pilar's relationship with Finito and Maria's rape—similarly blend into the novel's creation of its time-present. Not only are they managed with great imaginative authority in themselves, but they contribute to the novel's overall scheme as essential forms of the past through which to understand the present impasse of Spanish history. They take their place, too, alongside other smaller points of recall, each located at appropriate intervals, reminding us of what was and what now is, past cause and present effect. These include the memory of Kaskin, killed by Jordan to prevent capture yet his own secret sharer in doing the dynamite work, or Joaquin's remembrance of the killing of his parents in Valladolid for having voted socialist, an event to set against Pablo's flailing of the Fascists, or the slightly indulgent remembrance of Karkov and Gaylord's, a reminder among other things of Jordan's own aspirations to write.

Jordan's harping back to his earlier American life also matches events in his Spanish experience. For instance, when he packs with meticulous care the dynamite it recalls for him the care he showed as a boy for his collection of bird eggs (48). His vivid memory of a black lynching in Ohio carries real implications for the barbarisms committed by both sides of the Spanish Civil War (116). Even the memory of the young Belgian soldier from the Eleventh Brigade whose emotional balance has been so disturbed that he cries all the time (136) suggests an analogy with Pablo and his lachrymose, relentless drinking. Similarly, the invocation of Jordan's journeyings, from Billings, Montana, to college, to France and Spain, ties in with the pasts given by the novel of Pilar, Pablo and Maria. The sum effect of both the larger and smaller flashbacks is one of thickening the narrative, so that the central thread within the camp and at the bridge indeed works outward and across time to a larger frame of allusion.

'I will tell it as it truly was' (99): in these terms Pilar begins the account of Pablo's attack on the Guardia barracks and his brute, systematic execution of the village's Fascists. The story is told, we need to be mindful, as Pilar, Jordan and Maria are on their way to El Sordo's camp, for whom history has reserved an equally sombre fate. Hemingway renders the account with great energetic flair, avenging humanity turned bestial by the sick, self-mutilating nature of civil war. Pablo's fear of what the event has transformed him into, Pilar's comforts to him, and the sad final lament of a crying woman, underline to a fine point the despoiling touch of the war, whether waged from Loyalist or Nationalist assumptions. The episode amounts to drama in its own terms, but also once more as a way of pulling into the novel's present the pressing reality of the immediate Spanish past. Pablo, the others, are the necessary veterans of this event, hunters as well as the hunted, at once killers and yet still vulnerable.

Pilar's recollection of Finito the novel tells in two sequences (Chapters 8 and 14), a story which calls up the Spain of the *corridas*, violence ritually controlled and defeated, and which Hemingway's *Death in the Afternoon* takes such impressive pains to document. Pilar's initial reminiscence refers us to the Spain of good food and wine (85), customs like the *Feria*, Spanish music and festivity at large. Her account of Finito's eventual death, a haunted, tubercular matador haemorrhaging from deep within towards collapse, Hemingway offers both as literal biography and, if not exactly as allegory, then as an implied metaphor of Spanish history. The story possesses its own slightly surreal, Goyaesque sadness, and the bull and *corrida* materials recall, to good effect, the world of Jake and Romero in *The Sun Also Rises*. That Pablo, a handler of picador horses for Finito, should become his successor with Pilar suggests also how the Civil War has likewise transformed irregulars into regulars, the handlers into the warriors: Once more, and in touching particularity, the novel builds before the reader an appropriate biographical past, the sense of literal prior circumstance, to Jordan's encounter with Pablo and Pilar at the camp.

Maria's rape (Chapter 31) is recalled as she and Jordan talk after their lovemaking, a past hurt healed and redeemed through their present intimacy. Or at least so one presumes Hemingway would have the relationship understood. The detail of the Falangist assault on the village, and the hair-cropping and rape itself, Hemingway relates with the same dramatic flair shown in the accounts of Pablo's exploits at the train and in the Fascist village. The lovemaking itself flatly does not carry imaginative conviction, any more than the implication of Maria as yet another instance of Spain's martyrdom, its vulnerability to the self-inflicted trauma of civil war. Maria's story, however, does refer us again to the broader historical context of the Spanish past, and of major importance, of the relationship of that past to the present mission at the bridge. Jordan's reflections point in the appropriate direction:

> What a people they have been. What sons of bitches from Cortez, Pizarro, Menéndez de Avila all down through Enrique Lister to Pablo. And what wonderful people. There is no finer and no worse people in the world. No kinder and no crueler. And who understands them? Not me, because if I did I would forgive it all. . . .
>
> Well, it was something to think about. Something to keep your mind from worrying about your work. It was sounder than pretending. God, he had done a lot of pretending tonight. And Pilar had been pretending all day. Sure. What if they were killed tomorrow? What did it matter as long as they did the bridge properly? That was all they had to do tomorrow. (354-55)

The past links to the present, and from Maria's story, as from Pablo's and Pilar's we pass forward to Jordan's obligations at the bridge. Hemingway's way of keeping his novel 'knit up' is again there to be seen.

4

The two principal insets in *For Whom the Bell Tolls*—the death of El Sordo and his men and Andrés's endeavour to get Jordan's message through to Golz—work, as I have suggested earlier, in a kind of parallel-time. They set the main line of action at the camp and bridge within a context of simultaneous action, the one vintage Hemingway military drama, the other a quite major insight into the petty bureaucratic vagaries of war. The first, as it were, points towards the best of American war fiction, the tradition embracing Stephen Crane, John Dos Passos,

Norman Mailer and latterly the realism of a work like *Soldier Blue*. The other hints of a more absurdist dimension, especially the crazed figure of Marty, the domain explored in novels like *Catch-22* and *Slaughterhouse-Five*. There are, to be sure, other insets in Hemingway's novel, the conversation of the Gallego guards at the post near the bridge and the several allusions to the journalist Karkov, but those of El Sordo and Andrés offer the best matching episodes to the three-day drama at the camp.

The story of El Sordo's death begins irresistibly:

> El Sordo was making his fight on a hilltop. He did not like this hill and when he saw it he thought it had the shape of a chancre. But he had no choice except this hill and he had picked it as far away as he could see it and galloped for it, the automatic rifle heavy on his back, the horse laboring, barrel heaving between his thighs, the sack of grenades swinging against one side, the sack of automatic rifle pans banging against the other, and Joaquin and Ignacio halting and firing to give him time to get the gun in place. (307)

The careful, declarative release of detail, and the vivid implicit drama of men cornered but turning to make their stand, carries the same authority as the opening description of soldiers on march through the dust in *A Farewell to Arms*. Their attempt to make their fortification against the superior force of Berrendo's Nationalist troops, and the references to La Pasionaria, the oaths and even the jokes, add reinforcing layers of credibility to the action. The hill, however, despite El Sordo's attempted ruse, indeed becomes a chancre, a lost, infected place once the bombers arrive. The stink of that kind of death—arbitrary and unfair—Hemingway catches in the physicality of his descriptions:

> Keeping a heavy fire on the hilltop, Lieutenant Berrendo pushed a patrol up to one of the bomb craters from where they could throw grenades onto the crest. He was taking no chances of any one being alive and waiting for

them in the mess that was up there and he threw four grenades into the confusion of dead horses, broken and split rocks, and torn yellow-stained ex-
plosive-stinking earth before he climbed out of the bomb crater and walked
over to have a look. (322)

The language works at one with the moral detritus of the action. The
hill is chancred, the earth 'stinking', the horses as dead and broken as
the baroque beasts in Picasso's Guernica. All of this is picked up at distant earshot, and guiltily, by Jordan and Anselmo and the others, evidence of their limited ability to act, and a reminder that their duty can
be directed only at the bridge. The El Sordo episode both parallels, and
acts as a commentary on, Jordan's own endeavour with Pablo to strike
back at the Fascist assault. Not only does Berrendo's final scrupulosity
in turning away from the act of decapitating El Sordo match Hemingway's willingness to grant him his dignity as he approaches Jordan at
the end, the whole pattern of strike and counter-strike helps locate the
novel's overall movement between hunters and hunted, winners and
vanquished.

The portrait of Andrés's attempt to deliver Jordan's letter turns on
another tack: the sheer infuriating way bureaucracy works in a war, especially a war fought with volunteer, improvisational military forces
against Spain's Fascist *putsch*. Andrés's initial guilt at having left his
comrades, the repeated challenges to his identity, and his eventual ride
on a motor-bike with Captain Gomez, the ex-barber, to H.Q. and to the
crazed, untender mercies of Comrade Marty, might well suggest a species of Catch-22 nightmare, war as a hallucinatory regime of orders,
paper, unacknowledged safe-conducts and arbitrary acts of command.
The release of Andrés and Gomez, through Karkov's intervention with
Marty, however, does no more than confirm that Golz's notion of 'Rien
à faire' (428) is indeed the right gloss on events. The whole sequence
works wonderfully well: it shows bureaucracy gone awry and contrasts
with the *partizan* action in the field. It also underlines how even the attack on the bridge, so carefully prepared for by Jordan, signifies the

merest small part in the pending overall collapse in the Loyalist resistance to Fascism. In this respect, it heightens our consciousness still more acutely of what is finally about to occur in 'the thing of the bridge'.

5

Jordan's interior monologues recur at intervals throughout the novel, glossing in precisely the same way as the flashbacks and the insets the general pulse of the action. They build up, in turn, the portrait of the historic, individual figure who is the novel's central consciousness. One line of retrospective contemplation helps us to see Pablo and Pilar and the camp, especially Jordan's wary sense of where and where not he can take command, when best to speak and when not. Another guides us back to his American origins, in Montana, with his father and grandfather, and into the education which eventually brought him across the Atlantic to France and Spain and into an awareness of how his life's necessary commitments to the Spanish Republic have come to be. Then there are his frequent contemplations of Spain itself, a history and for him a destiny, to which everything else would seem to have tended. At least that with justice can be said to be the import of his final soliloquy when, wounded, he attempts his *compte rendu*:

> I have fought for what I believed in for a year now. If we win here we will win everywhere. The world is a fine place and worth the fighting for and I hate very much to leave it. And you had a lot of luck, he told himself, to have had such a good life, You've had just as good a life as grandfather's though not as long. You've had as good a life as any one because of these last days. You do not want to complain when you have been so lucky. I wish there was some way to pass on what I've learned, though. Christ, I was learning fast there at the end. I'd like to talk to Karkov. That is in Madrid. Just over the hills there, and down across the plain. . . . There's no *one* thing that's true. It's all true. The way the planes are beautiful whether they are ours or theirs. The hell they are, he thought. (467)

The notion of a life contracted into the brief stay at the camp operates persuasively here because Jordan has demonstrably earned the right to his views. Whether we see his action in remaining behind as his last chivalric hurrah, or as the appropriate act of a seasoned *partizan*, his thoughts bring back into focus the whole contour of the novel: the arrival with Anselmo, Pablo's flight, the love of Maria, his warmth towards Pilar, the wider embrace of the war's planning and command in Madrid, and above all the motifs of earth and pine which begin the novel and to which Hemingway alludes in his letter to Maxwell Perkins. As the novel rounds to its last moment, Jordan and Berrendo, *partizan* and Nationalist officer, become a mutual nemesis, men whose shared destiny is to be, in John Donne's words, 'diminished' by each other's death. Through this last of Jordan's soliloquies, *For Whom the Bell Tolls* thus rightly closes on the allusion with which it began:

> He was waiting until the officer reached the sunlit place where the first trees of the pine forest joined the green slope of the meadow. He could feel his heart beating against the pine needle floor of the forest. (471)

It does not have to be argued yet again that *For Whom the Bell Tolls* displays flaws in plenty. Hemingway has been duly indicted on a variety of counts: most especially for Maria, his code material and supposed infantilist intoxication with death, the Spanglish and the monotonal flavour in stretches of the style. But if my argument has been at all apt, he deserves to be granted the success of the overall design behind his novel. Parts do fit the whole, and the whole, I believe, to a degree far greater than has generally been acknowledged, acts to carry and unify the energy of those parts. Hemingway has by no means won his due as the conscious pattern-maker in his longer fiction. *For Whom the Bell Tolls*, 'knit up' as it is, suggests he deserves better.

From *Ernest Hemingway: New Critical Essays* (London: Vision Press, 1983): 79-102. Copyright © 1983 by Rowman and Littlefield. Reprinted by permission of Rowman and Littlefield.

Notes

1. Carlos Baker (ed.), *Hemingway: Selected Letters, 1917-61*, (New York: Charles Scribner's Sons, 1981), p. 514.

2. Quoted in R. F. Christian, *Tolstoy's 'War and Peace'* (Oxford: Oxford University Press, 1962), pp. 104-8, 124-50, and reprinted in George Gibian (ed.), The Norton Critical Edition of *War and Peace* (New York: Norton, 1966), p. 1456. The original appeared as A. B. Goldenweiser, *Vblizi Tolstogo* (Moscow-Leningrad, 1959).

3. See Philip Young, *Ernest Hemingway* (New York: Rinehart & Company, Inc., 1952), pp. 75-82 and Carlos Baker, *Hemingway: The Writer as Artist* (Princeton University Press, 1952). See the Third Edition, pp. 246-59.

4. Jordan muses as following in one of his interior monologues: 'You're not a real Marxist and you know it. And you never could have. You believe in Liberty, Equality and Fraternity. You believe in Life, Liberty and the Pursuit of Happiness. Don't ever kid yourself with too much dialectics. They are for some but not for you. You have to put many things in abeyance to win a war. If this war is lost all of those things are lost' (p. 305).

5. For an indication of Hemingway's regard for Tolstoy, see his letter to Charles Scribner, 6 and 7 September 1949 (*Letters*, p. 673).

6. Most notably by Arturo Barea, in *Horizon*, May 1941.

7. Edmund Wilson, 'Return of Ernest Hemingway', *New Republic*, 103, 28 October 1940, pp. 591-92.

8. *For Whom the Bell Tolls* (New York: Charles Scribner's Sons, 1940), p. 305. All page references are to this edition.

Cultural Imperialism, Afro-Cuban Religion, and Santiago's Failure in Hemingway's *The Old Man and the Sea*_____

Philip Melling

At a critical moment in his battle with the sharks in *The Old Man and the Sea*, Santiago reaches under the stern for an oar handle "sawed off to about two and a half feet in length" and "from as high up as he could raise the club" he hits a *galano* across "the base of the brain" (*OMATS* 105). The shark slides down the fish, but other sharks appear and Santiago is left to wonder how much damage he could have inflicted if he had "used a bat with two hands" (106). His desire for a baseball bat is of crucial importance. Instead of wanting to dramatize an indigenous style with sacred tools (the symbolic, wooden axe of the Afro-Cuban god Chango comes to mind) Santiago wishes to replicate the actions of an American hero whose baseball exploits were the stuff of adventure in the local tabloids—Joe DiMaggio. Santiago's actions in the boat bring DiMaggio's personal history to mind. A fisherman's son from San Francisco, DiMaggio as a boy sneaked away from home to practice his batting technique with "a broken oar as a bat on the sandlots nearby" (Talese 246). Santiago lacks DiMaggio's genius with the bat but his actions are those of a baseball scholar and a dutiful fan. During World War II, DiMaggio "was the most talked-about man in America" and in one of the popular hits of the day, Les Brown's band reminded the fans how important the baseball star was to the war effort. As the song cried out: "Joe . . . Joe . . . DiMaggio . . . we want you on our side" (Talese 251).

Santiago's fixation with Joe DiMaggio is not a casual one. Carefully nurtured, it is a creation of the movies, radio programs, newsreels, and mass circulation newsprint which, during the post-war period, became an integral feature of the new diplomatic landscape of the United States. Nearly "all the techniques later employed for influencing cultures" outside the U.S., says Reinhold Wagnleitner, "were tested in

Latin America" during the 1930s and 1940s. "The Latin American strategy," initially designed to counter fascist influence, became the "central basis" for "later American cultural policies" in the fight against Communism. "The obvious appeal of popular culture" he argues, was based on "a Madison Avenue approach" and under the Department of State popular culture became "one of America's potent weapons" in the battle to win the hearts and minds of Latin America (Wagnleitner 62, 63).

One result, agrees Julio Garcia, director of the Havana Film and Television School, was the "colonial decimation" of the Latin American film industry:

> The American studios claimed it was due to market forces, but of course it wasn't. . . . In the 1930s and 1940s there were lots of great films being shown in our cinemas, then it dropped right off. . . . If we wanted some of their hits they would force us to take nine other films of lower quality. The glossy-produced films with big budgets were always put in the best cinemas, so Latin films screened in the less well-kept theatres. The public therefore assumed their own films were inherently inferior. (quoted in Payne 10)

Cultural imperialism buttressed economic imperialism during these years and cultural diplomacy, often conducted through the work of multinationals, lay at the heart of American foreign policy (Payne 10).

Jeremy Tunstall has shown that 75% of films watched by Cubans in 1948 were Hollywood productions (289). The newspaper industry also operated in a similar way. Between 1949 and 1963, America's export of books and printed material to Latin America multiplied ten-fold. Under the Media Guaranty Program (1948-1967), mass circulation newsprint became a daily feature of Latin American life (Wagnleitner 74). During these years, ordinary Cubans like Santiago were weaned away from their traditional faiths and, as Emily S. Rosenberg has written, "gravitated to the simplified messages of popular culture" (215): the language of American sport, music, film, and entertainment, all potent weapons in the fight against Communism. Latin American audiences were pandered to by a celebrity culture which did nothing to "combat injustice, poverty and ignorance," but "offered ethnocentric solutions disguised as internationalist ones . . . dignified by the name of rationality" (Rosenberg 86). Mass culture may have been democratic "in the sense that it appealed to a cross section of the social classes," but, as Rosenberg notes, it was oligarchic and "carefully contrived and narrowly controlled" as an instrument of economic and cultural influence (36). Furthermore, even though Cuban society at this time included a substantial black population, the role models presented to Latin American audiences were uniformly white. Few if any discussed the morality of such intervention, let alone the moral, economic, and political stagnation of Cuba in the 1950s that America's support for Batista helped create.

These were the issues at the back of Hemingway's mind when he told the people of San Francisco de Paula who met him at Havana airport in 1959 that his sympathies were with the Revolution and that he did not want to be "considered a Yankee" (Fuentes 274). We must set his comment against Santiago's advising young Manolin to "have faith in the Yankees" (*OMATS* 14), a remark made at a time when the Yankees in question, the New York Yankees baseball club, had a reputation for racial profiling. Under its manager, Casey Stengel, the Yankees club in the 1950s was well-known for its opposition to players of color and notorious for its refusal to field a multi-ethnic squad. Stories in the media about the "racism" of the "Yankee organization" were commonplace, writes Jules Tygiel, citing Jackie Robinson's description of "the Yankees management" as "prejudiced" (294, 295). Despite the fact that *The Old Man and the Sea* was written at a "high point" in a cultural movement that stressed the importance of *barroquismo* (an expression that incorporated a diversity of styles) and a philosophy of resistance to North American culture and art, Santiago's advice disqualifies him as an agent of *lo cubano* or Afro-Cuban cultural perspectives resisting the hegemonic influence of the United States (Martinez 289, 281).

Transmitted on Cuban television in the weeks following Hemingway's receipt of the Nobel Prize, a rarely seen interview reveals his desire to preserve the integrity of Cuban life.[1] In carefully considered, colloquial Spanish Hemingway tells how he has always tried to engage with the local community and "understand the sea" and its "influence" on the daily life of those who use it. The presence of the sea, he stresses, is what he has "tried to put into [his] writing . . . especially the sea on the north coast of Cuba" and its interactions, over the years, with settlement and culture. Hemingway also talks about the fishing village of Cojimar and the importance he attaches to its survival: "a very serious thing" he says, in a rapidly changing world. Cojimar's situation may be "serious" because of the decline in the local fishing industry, together with the effects of increased competition and the rising costs of both inshore and deep-sea fishing methods.

However, there are also issues of history to consider and cultural practices not in decline. For example, Hemingway had an extensive interest in anthropology dating back to his reading of James Frazer's *The Golden Bough* in the 1920s. In the library at the Finca Vigía, he also kept a copy of *Cultural Anthropology* by Melville Herskovitz and may have been influenced by the views of Herskovitz on family life and religious faith (Brasch and Sigman Item 3079). Herskovitz argued that the coastal settlers of the Caribbean islands had evolved through a practice of "transculturation" (Duany 22), an historical process incorporating the characteristics of African and European culture. This type of collaboration, claims Herskovitz, grew out of the relationship between faiths and religions of African origin—Santería, Payo Malombo, Payo Monte, Abakuá—and the Catholic Church. These diverse beliefs harmonized around the practice of saint worship. Santería, one such hybrid form of religion, says Diana H. Gonzalez-Kirby, "flourished rapidly" in the "minor" communities of northern and western Cuba. Villages like San Francisco de Paula and Cojimar were a living example of "the syncretisation of African belief" (Gonzalez-Kirby 42).

In 1949 Hemingway asked Malcolm Cowley to send him a copy of

Margaret A. Murray's *Witch-Cult in Western Europe*, noting what he called the "considerable witch-craft practised in the neighbourhood especially in Guanabacoa" (*SL* 681). What Hemingway probably meant by "witch-craft" were contemporary vestiges of the religion originally practiced by Yoruba slaves brought to Cuba from southwestern Nigeria in large numbers between 1820 and 1860. During the 19th century, Santería emerged as a compromise faith bringing together Yoruba beliefs and various facsimiles in the Catholic Church. According to Rafael Martinez and Charles Wetli, in Santería each god or goddess—Yemaya, goddess of the sea; Eshu, the trickster deity; Eleggua, the orisha who controls the laws of chance; Ochosi, the god of the hunt; Babalu-aye, patron of the sick and elderly—was twinned with a Catholic saint and given control of "a specific domain" and the "unique powers" peculiar to it (33). In Santería, the most significant African deities are the Seven African Powers, many of whom are represented as protectors of those who rely on the sea or live in close proximity to it (Martinez and Wetli 33).

Although there is little evidence to suggest that he was a formal practitioner, Hemingway was intrigued by Santería. It suited his superstitious nature—the dressing-up, the out-of-body experiences and precognition, the rabbits' feet and occasional fondness for earrings, the need to touch wood three times, the use of numbers, and the prayers for help (Fuentes 84). At the Finca, Hemingway showed a fondness for the "divine mascots" and figurative statues that, according to Migene Gonzalez-Wippler, are often suggestive of primordial life in Santería. He was also fond of different types of stones, especially the *chinas pelonas* and *otanes* used to attract the attention of the orishas and thought to contain magnetic properties. In apparent emulation of a common practice in Santería, Hemingway carried his favorite stones around with him as if he was seeking the approval of a "spiritual guide" and acknowledging the orisha with a "good-luck charm" (Gonzalez-Wippler 1982, 18).

Stones and shells are important to an understanding of Santería.

"The power of the orishas," say Rafael Martinez and Charles Wetli, resides in stones and Santería's ceremonial structures recognize the need to propitiate the gods through ritual acts such as the bathing and feeding of stones or the placing of stones close to the body (33). In Santería, ritual power is "seated" in stones, agrees Joseph Murphy, and transferred to the "head of the devotee" at the moment of initiation. "The juxtaposition of head and stones" lies at "the heart of the santería mysteries," particularly in the ceremony of "*asiento*." Here, the transfer of power from orisha to initiate is dramatized when stones are placed over the head of a novice (*iyawo*). The act of "seating" the stone fixes "knowledge" inside the head, enlightening those who require the benefit of its "spiritual power" (Murphy 87). Hemingway scholar Larry Grimes says that stones were allegedly placed above the entrance to the Finca during the time Hemingway lived there. If true, this may suggest that Hemingway sought power through ritual practice, "seating" the stone at the head of his house in order to signify spiritual favor (Grimes).

Hemingway's desire to acquaint himself with the history of witchcraft contrasts sharply with Santiago's interest in baseball scores in the local newspapers. The contrast between Santiago's needs and Hemingway's intensifies the further we go beyond sight of land (where the protection offered by Joe DiMaggio has no power). As the journey progresses, DiMaggio's influence is in inverse proportion to the spiritual potency of the African Powers. In Santería, each orisha requires a ritual of propitiation in the form of a sacrificial offering (blood, corn, coffee, or water), before the "devotee's problems" can be addressed in the material world. Interestingly, Santiago's world contains all the "magical properties" on which the orishas spiritually depend, including herbs, blood, wood, and stone (Murphy 134). Santiago is given what Joseph Murphy calls "unique" opportunities to honor the gods, but even though their demands are modest, he turns them down (116). Santiago avoids all contact with the *ebos* of Santería and those sacrificial moments when "gifts" are made available—a broken oar, deep water, yellow weed—as a route to propitiation (Murphy 15).

On his return to his village at the novella's end, even though he is physically exhausted and possibly dying, Santiago still plans to hunt again. He tells Manolin:

> "We must get a good killing lance and always have it on board. You can make the blade from a spring leaf from an old Ford. We can grind it in Guanabacoa. It should be sharp and not tempered so it will break. My knife broke." (*OMATS* 115)

This passage illustrates the distance that exists between Santiago as a commercial fisherman at a time of crisis and the Adamic solitary whom critics have invested with "mythic beliefs."[2] Rather than propitiate the orishas and invoke their power to subdue a rude and lawless world, Santiago seeks a weapon made from a cast-off American auto part for aid in vanquishing sharks. He has yet to learn that in Santería, only an orisha such as Oggun—father of sacrificial acts and an ironworker symbolized by a sacrificial knife and the spilling of blood—can change the sharks' behavior. And Oggun can only bestow his gifts through spiritual devotions and ritual acts of propitiation of the kind Santiago fails to perform.

Santiago also ignores Olokun, the great orisha of "sea depths who protected the ancestors on their terrible journey from Africa" (Murphy 1-2). In Santería, Olokun is honored with a song:

> Olokun, Owner of the Ocean
> Grandfather Olokun
> We bow before you father Olokun. (Murphy 1-2)

But Santiago does not "bow." He has "strange shoulders" (*OMATS* 15) which served him well in his early life as a child-adventurer to Africa and later as an arm wrestler when he fought the Negro from Cienfuegos. But Olokun is propitiated with simple things—shells, stones, cigars, rum, and acts of salutation—not feats of strength. Protection can be sought by utilizing basic commodities of everyday life such as coffee and paper. Santiago has an abundance of both—the paper he sleeps on, the coffee he drinks—but does not use either material to invoke the African Powers.

Santería is a "hybrid" religion, a "syncretism of black and white worlds" available to all people, irrespective of race and gender, and offering "opportunities" for propitiation through symbols, icons, objects, and dates (Murphy 116). Yet Santiago's life is a drama of missed opportunity and deliberate avoidance. On the one hand, he regards the eating of turtle meat as morally abhorrent. On the other, he eats turtle eggs "all through May" in preparation for "the truly big fish" that run "in September and October" (*OMATS* 34). The decision he makes is inconsistent as well as intriguing. Santiago relies on eating turtle eggs for strength rather than propitiating Yemaya with turtle meat (the *guemilere*), as he should do on her feast day (8 September). Nor does he sacrifice to Agallu and Oshun, the orishas that protect seas and rivers (Murphy 41). The avoidance seems wilful as Santiago goes to sea during hurricane season and needs all the help he can get. Santiago has "no mysticism about turtles"; instead, he relishes their voracious energy and wishes he could share their physical powers. Combative behavior and physical strength are important to him but spiritual appeasement isn't.

Santiago's Darwinism is moderated by a sentimental attitude toward marine life and the moral polarities that define natural adversaries and conflicts. He loves the loggerhead turtles who eat the poisonous Portuguese man o' war jellyfishes that foul his lines and sting "like a whiplash" (*OMATS* 33). The marlin who are his "friends" and "brothers" are enemies of the sharks that bring "*salao*" (7). The spiritualities that govern the sea are of secondary importance to the secular qualities of animals and the characteristics he ascribes to them. Physiological processes, moral innateness, blood lines, and transfusions of energy, not religious belief, are the reasons why Santiago eats turtle eggs to cure the "welts and sores on his arms and hands" (*OMATS* 32-3).

Strangely, he does not invoke Babalu-aye, the African orisha who heals "skin diseases," especially leprosy and the skin cancer from which Santiago suffers (Martinez 34). In Santería, Babalu-aye is represented as an impoverished old man who like Santiago lives alone in a wooden shack. The patron saint of those with arthritic problems, Babalu-aye can be propitiated with everyday things like pennies and water. Santiago could easily access this orisha, but does not even try.

If propitiation has any meaning for Santiago, it lies outside an Afro-Cuban community of saints. Instead, he seeks assistance from imperial faiths old and new as well as from celebrities in popular culture and popular Catholicism. His idea of partnership is non-egalitarian, based on a concept of self-help and private alliance with baseball stars and Catholic saints whose elite status inspires devotion. In Santiago's world, the "church" of baseball is not dissimilar to that of Rome (Chidester 219-238). The appeal of each relies on deference and the excitement generated by ritual events in metropolitan centers of power. African deities fall outside this particular theater. Faced with a choice between a Catholic icon or a facsimile of African or rural origin, Santiago prefers the Christian one. For this reason, he says "ten Our Fathers and ten Hail Mary's" (*OMATS* 60) to bring luck when he hooks the marlin, and then claims he will make a pilgrimage to the Virgen de Cobre should he bring the fish in. In Santería, the Virgen de Cobre corresponds with the orisha Oshun, patroness of love and sister of Yemaya, goddess of the sea. Santiago does not disclose the correspondence, but instead tells us that "he is not religious" (*OMATS* 60). It is difficult to explain the remark, bearing in mind that the man who makes it is a Cuban fisherman and that Havana Harbor, its fishermen and sailors, are protected by the Virgen de Regla and her twin, Yemaya. Santiago remains silent on the correspondence between saint and orisha, as if he is unable to embrace the "mental bridge" offered by Santería to those who "live," as Joseph Murphy puts it, "in two worlds" (121). Santiago has, it appears, no interest in the syncretism of a conquered race. Instead, he pledges an allegiance (of sorts) to the Catholic

Church and the inspiration he receives in the newspapers from saints of baseball such as Joe DiMaggio.

Resisting the influence of the African Powers—Yemaya, Eshu, Eleggua, and Ochosi—Santiago shows no interest in the talismanic properties of stones, beads, and cowry shells. On the contrary, he sees in baseball an antithesis to *Afro Cubanismo*. He venerates players of light skin, not just Joe DiMaggio, but Mike Gonzalez and Adolfo Luque, "white" Cubans who, because of their skin color, were given dispensation to play in the majors during and after World War I. Crucially, he ignores dark-skinned Cubans and black players excluded from the majors but welcomed in Cuba and the Caribbean. In Cuban baseball, says Donn Rogosin, "race mattered little" and blacks and whites "competed as equals" in the winter leagues (154). During this period, "the extensive, sustained interaction between Cuban and Negro league baseball . . . was of enormous significance" (Rogosin 155, 156). The Negro leagues hosted the Cuban Stars, comprised of both dark and light-skinned Cubans, some of whom, like Mike Gonzalez, also played in the major leagues. In Cuba, blacks and whites from the United States frequently played alongside each other. Cuba "became a traditional and important conduit of baseball information between white and black American players" (Rogosin 156). It created a racially-mixed community and gave black players such as John Henry Lloyd, Ray Dandridge, Willard Brown, and Willie Wells the opportunity to become full-time professionals and compete on equal terms with white players like Ty Cobb.

Santiago's racial attitudes come alive in his memory of arm-wrestling with a Negro in a tavern at Casablanca. The contest is remembered at a point in the story when Santiago is at a low ebb. It is his second day at sea without sleep. He has eaten little and is unable to haul the marlin back from the depths to which it has taken the line. Rather than invoke the orishas, he turns to his memory "to give himself more confidence." The decor of the tavern interior—the walls are "painted bright blue" and made of wood—contrasts with the "huge," menacing shadow cast by the Negro and the way the shadow moves on the wall as the hanging lamps shift in the breeze. This arm-wrestling match with "the strongest man on the docks" takes place over a day and a night and only concludes when the "negro" is beaten, his hand forced "down and down until it rested on the wood." The "negro" is a "great athlete" but he ends up ruined psychologically, his "confidence" "broken." Santiago, therefore, gains in "confidence" at the expense of the black community (*OMATS* 64-66).

If the breaking of a "fine" individual is necessary to ensure the triumph of Darwinism, the underlying need is to affirm the importance of protectorate power in the Caribbean. The belief that white individuals can invigorate themselves at the expense of people of color reminds us of how imperialism came of age in the United States. At the end of the 19th century, the United States developed an empire and acquired new lands through a process of pacification and physical control. Territory was acquired and traditional loyalties broken, says Walter L. Williams, as "religions and ceremonies" were "suppressed by government agents." This is true not only of American Indian lands but also of Africa and Asia, he argues, where swarms of "missionaries" promoted "new ways of thinking" thereby weakening "native confidence in their old ways of doing things" (237). According to Anders Stephanson, "empire as civilized domination showed the historical necessity of establishing order by means of force in the unruly sphere and thus allowing 'waste spaces' to be used in the 'interest of humanity'" (106).

Santiago mimics this procedure and puts an end to a putative *negrismo* by describing the contest with the "negro" as "finished" (*OMATS* 66). His opponent is no longer "the strongest man on the docks" and among the dockworkers, traditionally the best sports fans in Cuba (Rogosin 161); Santiago has become *El Campeón* (66). Santiago breaks the spirit of the black community by ruining, in a public demonstration, the crowd appeal of their unofficial leader. He has stayed the course because of his splendidly exceptional talent, unlike the "negro" who is now "broken" (66). Crowd control is a by-word for success.

As he contemplates "the darkness of the sea" under his boat, Santiago invokes the "great DiMaggio" (64), a god-like figure who popularizes the imperial project of conquering others through force of will. DiMaggio has triumphed in adversity—despite the bone spur in his heel—and led the Yankees to their 84th win of the season against the Washington Senators. He appeals to Santiago because, unlike the black baseball player, Jackie Robinson, he lives outside what Lisa Brock calls "the African cultural constellation" (25). Not only is DiMaggio "great," he appears to inhibit the spread of blackness in the wider baseball community.

The impact of Africa in *The Old Man and the Sea* is not only displaced by narratives of white power, it is also subsumed by a memory of adolescence. On the morning of his fishing trip Santiago is awakened by "the land breeze" that comes "very early" and is redolent with the "smell of Africa" in the "morning." The wilderness Santiago wants to remember—"the long golden beaches" "the high capes," "the great brown mountains," the sound of the surf, the native boats (*OMATS* 22)—is an example of what environmentalist critic William Cronon describes as the "romantic sublime," a form of subdued "primitivism" in which the "pristine sanctuary" is never "quite" what it appears. Cronon defines this type of wilderness as neither a "virgin place" nor an "uninhabited land," but one already contaminated by the presence of "civilization." Africa has been made safe for people like Santiago: its beaches tamed not by boys who sail from Tenerife on square-rigged ships, but slave masters and slave ships. The young lions he sees at dusk are his pets; he loves them as he loves Manolin, but only because they lack all semblance of adult desire and predatory aggression, natural attributes. Santiago's beach, as Cronon might put it, "hides its unnaturalness behind a mask that is all the more beguiling because it seems so natural" (76-80).

This version of Africa has no meaning for the people of Cuba nor does it reveal the way in which slave societies were willing and able to come to terms with the sea's meaning in the aftermath of their forced emigration. Santiago's Africa—virgin land, the game preserve as romantic retreat—is, in Cronon's words, a place where we "wipe clean the slate of our past and return to the tabula rasa that supposedly existed before we began to leave our marks on the world." The irony, as Cronon points out, is that only those "whose relation to the land (is) already alienated" are able to "hold up wilderness as a model for human life in nature." By imagining that their "true home is in the wilderness," they "forgive" themselves for "the homes" they "actually inhabit." The "flight from history" becomes an "antidote to the human self" (80).

We are given a clue on how Santiago's own "flight" will unfold the moment he smells the Trade Winds. These winds begin life in the equatorial regions of Africa and help create a system of currents that flow westwards to the Caribbean and feed eventually into the Gulf Stream. To the west of North Africa these winds form a river of seawater, the North Equatorial Current. In the 18th and 19th centuries this current was instrumental in facilitating the transportation of slaves from the sub-Saharan regions—the Gold Coast, the Bight of Benin, the Niger Delta—to the New World. The Atlantic waters that Santiago fishes are suffused, therefore, not only with the memory of slavery and the routes by which slaves might arrive in Cuba, but also with the high levels of mortality that occurred at sea and the trauma that accompanied a two-month-long voyage. "Cuba," says Herbert S. Klein, was "the largest slave colony ever created in Spanish America" and by the end of the 19th century "had become a major importer" of slaves "in its own right" (38, 197).

From the perspective of Santería, the sea emerged as an Africanized place, the natural domain of the orisha Olokun, a Yoruba sea god with male and female personifications that determine the sea's character. This sea is also rife with the spirit presences of the ancestors, whose lives and deaths must be acknowledged. Here are the souls of black folk who have the ability to rise up and walk on water, as they do in August Wilson's play *Joe Turner's Come and Gone*; here are the victims of slavery who "died bad" and demand recognition in Toni Morrison's novel *Beloved* (188). When Santiago ignores these presences he does so at his peril, especially as the dream that wakes him comes from a "breeze" with an African "smell" (*OMATS* 22). What Santiago does with this dream proves his undoing. He entertains a vision of Africa that is of no use in helping him complete the task to which he is firmly committed. He dreams of an Africa that seems attractive because of its cinematic and pictorial appeal. This is an Africa of boats and breezes from which slavery has been erased, as have the slave religions and the role they should occupy for any Cuban fisherman who looks to Africa for his inspiration.

We are reminded of this at a quiet moment when Santiago takes a "forward" position in the boat and, head bowed, dreams of a time when he saw the lions of Africa in "the evening off-shore breeze." "In the early dark" the lions come down onto the beach and in the dream he feels "happy" as the ship lies at anchor (*OMATS* 75). The dream, however, does nothing to pacify the marlin. Indeed, the Gulf Stream is the worst place to go to replace the heritage of African slavery with a vision of the sublime. Santiago is admonished: "the jerk of his right arm coming up against his face and the line burning out through the right hand." The fish jumps repeatedly. There is "a great bursting of the ocean." The speed of the line taken by the fish cuts his hands "badly" (76). We contrast this with the blood that comes "out from under the fingernails" when Santiago arm-wrestles the Negro from Cienfuegos. The strike exposes the folly of dreaming at sea.

Santiago does not know "what started" the fish (77). He can not explain the marlin's change from a fish that is "calm" and "strong" to one that appears to react aggressively to an image of Africa that lacks human presence and human remains (78). Because Santiago's sleeping position mimics the religious greeting known as *foribale* (salutation) in Santería, the jolt he receives comes as a warning to those who believe in virtual faiths. The thump disputes his romanticized vision of Africa as a place of tame wilderness, the colonized Africa of civilized recreation and safari. It's as if, in the darkness below, the fish takes on the personality of the rebellious slave, punishing the man who promotes that vision with a blow to the face. The action clearly illustrates the distance that has opened up between Santiago and Hemingway, who, throughout his time in Cuba, bore witness to the spiritual significance of its waters.

Hemingway shared his belief in channels of energy and streams of life with the Yoruba people who came to Cuba from Nigeria and the Western Sudan. For the Yoruba, spiritual life was governed by the God *Olodumare*, the "ultimate expression of force" who channelled his energy through a "divine current" a "blood" stream of "cosmic life" known as "*ashe*" (Murphy 8). These ideals appealed to Hemingway, who appears to have seen little difference between divine current and physical current. For Hemingway, the sea was a primordial place and the currents of energy circulating in the Atlantic were an embodiment of what the Yoruba saw as "the ultimate destiny of all creation" (7).

Hemingway's earliest writing about the Gulf Stream and the wandering fish that travel the globe to swim in it appears in his Esquire articles of the 1930s. In the most famous of these, "On the Blue Water: A Gulf Stream Letter," written in April 1936, Cuba is portrayed as the meeting place of transoceanic streams and currents that have been in motion since men first "went on (them) in boats" (*BL* 228). In another article, written in August 1934, "Out in the Stream: A Cuban Letter," Hemingway describes the fish that live hundreds of fathoms below the surface and travel thousands of miles in response to the flow of "current" and "counter current." The words "connected" "connection," and "circuit" suggest that the fish "follow" "the warm currents of all the oceans." The sense of connection to this wilderness endows the fisherman with a state of feeling that transcends mere "hunting" (*BL* 171, 172). In "On The Blue Water" Hemingway knows that the fish are more than physical specimens. They are "strange and wild things of unbelievable speed and power and [a] beauty . . . that is indescribable." The act of being "fastened to the fish as much as he is fastened to you" generates a divine energy, an appreciation of the cosmic life in the sea (231).

In "On the Blue Water," Hemingway writes that "the Gulf Stream and the other great currents are the last wild country there is left." And because all factual knowledge of the sea is at best provisional, "no one knows" the actual domain of the "unexploited." When the fish strikes, the primal "scream" of the reel creates an unimaginable "thrill," one "that needs no danger to make it real." The fish that takes the line may leave you "at the end of five hours" with nothing but "a straightened-out hook." Throughout this period, the fisherman has direct contact with the supernatural and is required to acknowledge the simplest of questions: "who can say what you will hook sometime?" (*BL* 228-230).

Hemingway's answer—a giant marlin or swordfish compared "to which the fish we have caught are pygmies" (*BL* 230)—brings to mind a spiritual role model whose "great weight" is reminiscent of the Yoruba God, *Olodumare*, "owner" and source of "all destinies" and the "pulse of life and death . . . incarnated in the world as force" (Murphy 7-8). In Santería, this force is dramatized through orishas of great power and extravagance that express their meaning in theatrical terms. Hemingway, in a similar vein, describes how a great fish "throws a column of spray like a shell lighting" and its "shoulders smash out of the water" as it "bursts" into life. The use of military imagery suggests Hemingway's willingness to rise to the challenge of the "indescribable" ("On the Blue Water," *BL* 231-232). Here, what is "strange and wild" from a western perspective is instantly recognizable from an African one. If the sea is a theater, the fish is an emissary of Chango, a warrior deity whose life principle is one of "force" and whose "dance posture" evokes a state of physical "aggression" through "violent acrobatics" (Murphy 42-3; Bailey 49). Chango, whose early life was spent at sea, is a ruler of thunder, lightning, and explosive fire reminding us of the marlin's "speed" and "force." Hemingway, "fastened" to the fish, is connected "intimately" to its "savage power." The "friction" of the line "against the water" generates, he says, a new awareness of the life below him ("On the Blue Water," *BL* 231, 229). In terms of Santería, the line is alive with "divine current" a conductor whose "receptivity" puts the fisherman firmly in touch "with spiritual beings" (Murphy 8).

Santiago, on the other hand, resists the spiritual instruction of water. He lets "the current do a third of the work," but is loath to recognize supernatural circuitry (*OMATS* 276-7). As the fish runs from the boat and performs its acrobatics in the water, the speed of the line cuts his hand. His back is burned and he loses feeling in his left hand; the effect is similar to an electric shock. The surge of explosive energy combines temporary paralysis—"There was a moment when I could not find you" (78), he tells the hand—with heightened awareness. Santiago is pulled "down" (76), as he has been on other occasions, into a praying position. The word "friction" (77) is used to signify the electromagnetic power that fish can generate when they travel on what Hemingway in "Out in The Stream" calls "certain circuits" (*BL* 172).

Hemingway was probably aware of the Gulf Stream's electromagnetic properties, discussed by oceanographer Henry Chapin in his study of the Gulf Stream, *The Ocean River*. Co-authored with Frederick G. W. Smith and published by Charles Scribner's Sons (Hemingway's publisher) in 1952, the same year as *The Old Man and the Sea*, *The Ocean River* "gives a good picture of the state of understanding about the Stream in Hemingway's time," says Susan Beegel. "It's hard to imagine he was not aware of it," she adds, especially because Hemingway's library at the Finca shows he kept up with Chapin's work, owning a copy of a later book, *The Sun, the Sea, and Tomorrow: Potential Sources of Food and Energy from the Sea* (Brasch and Sigman item 6163) and subscribing to *Sea Frontiers*, a journal of oceanography begun by Chapin in 1954. Chapin's interest in electromagnetism and sea currents recurs throughout his writing. In *The Ocean River* he puts it thus:

Currents of water in their passage through the salt water generate electricity, though in very small amounts. . . . Sea water, itself an electrical conductor, develops an electric current in its passage across the earth's magnetic field, and the greater the speed of the stream, the greater the electricity produced. (144)

Hemingway's apparent decision to experiment with the idea of an electric shock in *The Old Man and the Sea* invites us to consider the supernatural charge that water possesses in African religion. If Santiago is aware of this charge he doesn't let on. The fish shocks him and wakes him up but there is no spiritual awakening. Blood seeps from Santiago's hand and he immerses it in salt water to cleanse the wound. But in doing this, he misses once again an important opportunity to acknowledge the sea before the sharks arrive. In *African Magic in Latin America*, Migene Gonzalez-Wippler describes blood as an important offering given to the orishas to "replenish their powers." Blood offerings, he explains, are "the most important and indispensable" form of energy because they are "released" as "living energy" and, as such, able to nourish "the spiritual world" (Gonzalez-Wippler 200-1). Santiago's rinsing of his bleeding hand lacks devotion. With the hand "bled . . . clean" (*OMATS* 92), Santiago does not acknowledge the owners of fortune, *Los Ibelli*, the divine twins of Santería, nor does he intend to propitiate the spiritual world with sacrificial blood. Later in the novella, the marlin's spilled blood will settle like a dark cloud in the sea and bring sharks, perhaps because it has not been returned to the sea with sacred intent—the traditional custom in Santería—to "replenish" the energies lost with the death of the marlin and the discharge of electrical power (Martinez 34).

As the recipient of current, Santiago draws energy out of the water but prefers to recognize other "conductors" (Murphy 8). When he says that "it would be wonderful" to fish "with a radio" (*OMATS* 45), he signals his interest in networks of power and information that originate in the United States. His need to be stimulated by American broadcasts reassures him far more than Old World "circuits." The irony is considerable. Baseball, as expressed through the medium of the World Series, allows him to avoid any contact with Africa and its "human line of continuity with the past" (Murphy 9).

For Nadine Gordimer, Cuba and Africa have a shared "African bloodstream" and a relationship whose long history is based on "trade, ideas, values and culture" (7). In Santería the "bloodstream" of the sea commemorates that relationship in ceremonies that dramatize "the moral *ashe* of the ancestors" and the powers the sea bestows on the orishas (Murphy 11). The sea is a place of ceremonial instruction where the orishas "guide" and "admonish" as they see fit. In return, "the community of the present" can "look to the past for moral example" (Murphy 10). It is strange, therefore, that when Santiago takes a blow in the mouth and receives an indication that an offense has been committed, he is indifferent to the sign. The risk he takes in refusing to propitiate the orishas of the sea is close to willful.

At least Santiago is consistent throughout the novella. When he starts his journey he rows "out over that part of the ocean that the fisherman called the great well." The well goes to a depth of "seven hundred fathoms where all sorts of fish congregated because of the swirl of the current made against the steep walls of the floor of the ocean." The well is both oceanographic site and historical deposit where the "wandering fish" have fetched up, their journey shaped by a maritime process that belongs to an ancient world (*OMATS* 25). "The great well" has a special significance in Santería. Migene Gonzalez-Wippler, in his book, *The Santería Experience*, says that the presence of Yemaya is always much "stronger in very deep waters." In Santería, "anything that falls within these waters is lost forever . . . unless Yemaya is offered a prize in exchange for her bounty." Yemaya's "demands" are always "modest" and pennies or syrup or candles, for example, are normally "enough" to propitiate her. "The value of the gift" is always secondary to the particular "faith" that underlies it (Gonzalez-Wippler 8-9).

Santiago is not prepared to "please" Yemaya with simple gifts. The sea, to him, is whimsical. Its personality is lunar-"feminine," which makes "la mar" emotionally unstable. She kills the terns and sea swallows for no good reason and is inconsiderate to the small birds with their "sad voices" "who are made too delicately for the sea." She is "kind and very beautiful," but unpredictable and cruel. The sea's mind can not be fathomed. She "gave or withheld great favours," we are told, "and if she did wild or wicked things it was because she could not help them" (*OMATS* 26).

Santiago's sea is fickle, ruled by chance and "the wild or wicked things" (26). Because the sea is emotional it is best understood in references that imply control: Darwinism, baseball scores, bats, knives. Rather than fathom the ways of the sea by propitiating Eleggua (the trickster deity) or Chango (controller of force), Santiago describes the sea as a woman unable to help herself and indiscriminate in the way she chooses to bestow her "favours" (26). Ignoring the protection of Olokun, the orisha of sea depths in African folklore, Santiago subjects the sea to a mythology based on personal control. The problem is that the ability to dominate physically bears little relationship to the protection given the slaves who arrived on their terrible journey to the New World. Santiago's offense could not be worse. At moments of crisis, he purposely avoids the deep-sea gods and the help available from them through acts of propitiation.

In Hemingway's work, those who have offended the sea rarely escape its retribution. Like the orishas in Santería, his sea is "fierce" and "generous," yet willing to "criticise the behaviour of the living and hold them to the highest moral standards," should they offend (Murphy 9). The sea has a moral and providential presence in the novel. Yet, at the end of his journey, Santiago is keen to exonerate himself. If the fish is lost, at least he has managed to kill "many sharks" and ruin "many others." If he has failed he has done so in an epic quest, one that allows him to live briefly in the shadow of Joe DiMaggio. If he goes "too far" outside the circle prescribed by DiMaggio it is only because, as he tells himself, baseball is his sustenance and he does not want to "think" beyond it (*OMATS* 106). Santiago shares DiMaggio's "pain"; his movements are restricted, his hands torn and bloodied from the fight. But he also emulates DiMaggio's strength. "Do you believe the great DiMaggio would stay with a fish as long as I will stay with this one?" he wonders—as if he has come of age in the *Ligas* and the *galanos* have become the *Tigres of Detroit*. Sometimes the fetishism knows no bounds: "I must be worthy of the great DiMaggio who does all things perfectly," he says a little earlier (64).

In *The Old Man and the Sea*, the quest for human perfectibility in baseball is not transferable to the spiritual landscape of the Caribbean. The popular idea of the stadium as a "church" where the primacy of Yankee life is affirmed by a theology of rules, scores, and batting averages, the play of demi-gods, and the papacy of managers like Adolfo Luque, comes undone in a black Atlantic. Santiago worships America from afar. He can not attend Yankee Stadium or witness for himself the "sacred memory" of ceremonial space (Chidester 222). The way he worships is virtual yet all-consuming, the product of radio programs, magazine articles, newspapers, and the same kind of cultural diplomacy that all American governments have lent their support to since World War II.

From *The Hemingway Review* 26 no. 1 (Fall 2006): 46-61. Copyright © 2006 by The Hemingway Society. Reprinted by permission of The Hemingway Society.

Notes

1. The video of this interview, "A Day with Hemingway, A 'Sato' Cuban," was made available to the author in VHS format by Guidmar Venegas Delgado, c/o Cuban State Television, at the 10th International Ernest Hemingway Colloquium, Havana, Cuba, 23-25 May 2005.

2. One of the earliest uses of mythic tropes in a reading of *The Old Man and the Sea* can be found in a letter written by Malcolm Cowley to Ernest Hemingway on 3 August 1952 (quoted in Fuentes 391).

Works Cited

Bailey, James A. *The Yoruba of Southwestern Nigeria and Santería in the South-eastern United States: History, Culture, Rituals and Ceremonies of an Afro-Cuban Cult.* New Bern, NC: Godolphin House, 1991.

Beegel, Susan. E-mail to author. 6 July 2004.

Brasch, James D. and Joseph Sigman, comps. *Hemingway's Library: A Composite Record.* New York and London: Garland, 1981.

Brock, Lisa and Digna Castañeda Fuertes, eds. *Between Race and Empire: African-Americans and Cubans before the Cuban Revolution.* Philadelphia: Temple UP, 1990.

Chapin, Henry and Frank G. Walton Smith. *The Ocean River: The Story of the Gulf Stream.* 1952. London: Victor Gollancz, 1953.

_____. *The Sun, the Sea, and Tomorrow: Potential Sources of Food, Energy, and Minerals from the Sea.* New York: Scribner's, 1954.

Chidester, David. "The Church of Baseball, the Fetish of Coca-Cola, and the Potlatch of Rock 'n Roll." In *Religion and Popular Culture in America.* Eds. Bruce Forbes and Jeffrey Mahan. Berkeley: U of California P, 2001. 219-237.

Cronon, William. *The Trouble with Wilderness; or, Getting Back to the Wrong Nature.* New York: W.W. Norton, 1995.

Duany, Jorge. "Reconstructing Cubanness: Changing Discourses of National Identity on the Island and in the Diaspora during the Twentieth Century." In Fernández and Betancourt. 17-43.

Fernández, Damian J. and Madeleine Camara Betancourt, eds. *Cuba, The Elusive Nation: Interpretations of Identity.* Gainesville: UP of Florida, 2000.

Firmat, Gustav Peret. *Life on the Hyphen: The Cuban-American Way.* Austin: U of Texas P, 1994.

Fuentes, Norberto. *Hemingway in Cuba.* Trans. Consuelo E. Corwin. Secaucus, NJ: Lyle Stuart, 1984.

Gonzalez-Kirby, Diana H. "Santería: African Influences on Religion in Cuba." *Negro History Bulletin* 48 (July-September 1985): 39-44.

Gonzalez-Wippler, Migene. *African Magic in Latin America.* New York: Doubleday, 1973.

_____. *The Santería Experience.* Englewood Cliffs, NJ: Prentice Hall, 1982.

Gordimer, Nadine. "Back to the Laboratory." *The Guardian* [London]. 25 January 2003. 7.

Grimes, Larry. Conversations with the author. 7-12 June 2004.

Hemingway, Ernest. *By-Line: Ernest Hemingway.* Ed. William H. White. 1967. Harmondsworth: Penguin, 1970.

_____. *Ernest Hemingway: Selected Letters, 1917-1961.* Ed. Carlos Baker. London: Granada, 1981.

_____. *The Old Man and the Sea.* 1952. London: Jonathan Cape, 1953.

Hemingway, Hilary and Carlene Brennen. *Hemingway in Cuba.* New York: Rugged Land, 2003.

Herskovitz, Melville Jean. *Cultural Anthropology*. New York: Knopf, 1955.

Kinnamon, Keneth. "Hemingway and Politics." In *The Cambridge Companion to Hemingway*. Ed. Scott Donaldson. Cambridge: Cambridge UP, 1996. 170-197.

Klein, Herbert S. *The Atlantic Slave Trade*. Cambridge: Cambridge UP, 1999.

Martinez, Juan A. "*Lo Blanco-Criollo* as *lo Cubano*: The Symbolisation of a Cuban National Identity in Modernist Painting of the 1940s." In Fernández and Betancourt. 277-292.

Martinez, Rafael and Charles V. Wetli. "Santería: A Magico-Religious System of Afro-Cuban Origin." *American Journal of Social Psychiatry* 2/3 (1982): 32-38.

Morrison, Toni. *Beloved*. New York: Knopf, 1987.

Murphy, Joseph M. *Santería: African Spirits in America*. Boston: Beacon, 1988.

Murray, Margaret Alice. *The Witch-Cult in Western Europe: A Study in Anthropology*. Oxford: Clarendon, 1921.

Payne, Chris. "A Vatican for Film Makers." *The Guardian* [London]. 28 November 2003. 10-11.

Rogosin, Donn. *Invisible Men: Life in Baseball's Negro Leagues*. New York: Atheneum, 1983.

Rosenberg, Emily S. *Spreading the American Dream: American Economic and Cultural Expansion, 1890-1945*. New York: Hill and Wang, 1982.

Stephanson, Anders. *Kennan and the Art of Foreign Policy*. Cambridge: Harvard UP, 1989.

Talese, Gay. "The Silent Season of a Hero." *Esquire*. July 1966. Rpt. in *Fame and Obscurity*. New York: Ivy, 1993. 224-264.

Thomas, Hugh. *Cuba: The Pursuit of Freedom*. 1971. London: Picador, 2001.

Tunstall, Jeremy. *The Media are American: Anglo-American Media in the World*. London: Constable, 1978.

Tygiel, Jules. *Jackie Robinson and His Legacy: Baseball's Great Experiment*. New York: Vintage, 1984.

Wagnleitner, Reinhold. "Propagating the American Dream: Cultural Policies as Means of Integration." *American Studies International* 24.1 (April 1986): 60-84.

Williams, Walter L. "American Imperialism and the Indians." In *Indians in American History*. Ed. Frederick E. Hoxie. Arlington Heights, IL: Harlan Davidson, 1988. 231-251.

Wilson, August. *Joe Turner's Come and Gone: A Play in Two Acts*. 1988. New York: Penguin, 1992.

Zoss, Joel and John Bowan. *Diamonds in the Rough: The Untold History of Baseball*. London: Macmillan, 1989.

The Importance of Being Ernest_____

Louis A. Renza

> If you stand right fronting and face to face to a fact, you will see the sun
> glimmer on both its surfaces, as if it were a cimeter, and feel its sweet edge
> dividing you through the heart and marrow, and so you will happily con-
> clude your mortal career.
>
> —Henry David Thoreau, *Walden*

Like two bookends, Ernest Hemingway's *In Our Time* and *A Move-able Feast*, two collections of short prose, chronologically frame the official beginning and end of his literary career. Moreover, despite their generic dissimilarities, the two collections bear a certain topical relation to each other. *A Moveable Feast* comprises autobiographical sketches about the period in Paris when Hemingway actually wrote the stories and interchapters that would become *In Our Time*. *In Our Time* inaugurates a literary career that would endow these later sketches about his past life in Paris (and most notoriously, about his famous literary acquaintances there) with a virtually guaranteed public value—in other words, would justify and thus with hindsight motivate their very writing.

Beyond this loose symmetry of topic, the two collections also raise a persistent issue and perhaps even a continuing problem for Hemingway criticism in our time. The later collection reinforces the critical tendency to regard Hemingway's fiction in "referential" terms. In the first place, "Hemingway" as established public persona mediates our apprehension of Nick Adams in *In Our Time* as pure fictive character, so that we tend to read this early collection as simultaneously tracing the reconstructed story of Hemingway's own education into the violence of nature, modern social relationships, and war stripped of romantic pretensions. In the second place, the stories and very title of *In Our Time* invite us to construe them as symbolic representations of violence endemic to "our time." One way or another, then, this collection attracts referential readings to which *A Moveable Feast* contributes, as when it reveals (and serves to corroborate a well-known critical interpretation) that a major story in *In Our Time*, "Big Two-Hearted River," "was about coming back from the war but there was no mention of the war in it."[1] Conversely, critical discussions of *A Moveable Feast* typically focus on the truth-value or distortions of Hemingway's often vengeful depictions of Stein, Fitzgerald, and other literary contemporaries, for this reason also deeming it a minor or uneven work in his literary canon.[2] Permeated by the sense of "outside" reference, the two works at the beginning and end of Hemingway's literary career remain vulnerable to post factum judgments about their metaphorical relevance, autobiographical accuracy, and, at least in our critical time, complicity with discredited ideologies such as a naive existential code, macho heroics, unresolved anxieties of literary influence, intentional fallacies or, as the following remarks illustrate, illusions about the power of writing to elicit self-present experiences: "Then I went back to writing and I entered far into the story and was lost in it. I was writing it now and it was not writing itself."[3]

Yet both works also evince at least minimal protests against their apparent referential frames. For example, Hemingway openly suggests in his preface to *A Moveable Feast* that the reader may prefer to regard "this book . . . as fiction." And in a passage from the omitted section of "Big Two-Hearted River," Nick Adams reflects that "The only writing that was any good was what you made up, what you imagined. That made everything come true."[4] To be sure, in light of much biographical evidence showing the correlation between his fictional materials and actual experiences (or vice versa, how he constructed a public persona along the lines of his fictional protagonists), such claims may seem misleading or even disingenuous. But at least in the case of *A Moveable Feast*, his referential writing indeed veers toward becoming fiction. The tenor of his memoirs, after all, suggests that he writes them to reassert his literary credentials as an original writer at the expense of former peers who, either then or in the intervening years, had threatened, at least to his way of thinking, the public's acceptance of these credentials.[5] As one could argue in the case of Wordsworth's *The Prelude*, more than *what* he writes about himself and these artistic acquaintances, Hemingway's *act* of vocational reassertion constitutes the primary subject of *A Moveable Feast*. If nothing else, his work unconsciously tracks his literary as well as physical and psychological decline, and expresses his nostalgic desire "to recollect how he learned to write" in "those first four years when he won the name of an original artist."[6] Moreover, the early text, the "original" writing of which he here recollects, necessarily leads him to adopt a fictional relation to writing about it now. For how can Hemingway recollect his learning to write the stories of *In Our Time* without trying to position himself as a writer willfully repressing the identity and literary self-consciousness he has accrued as a successful author since the writing of his inaugural collection of fiction?

One could also argue that *A Moveable Feast* uses autobiographical materials as pretexts for repeating what necessarily remains out of reach: the interior or private scene of writing *In Our Time*. In writing this later work, Hemingway projects writing *as* a project, both at the time of writing the stories of *In Our Time* and writing these sketches attempting to imagine that former scene of writing. First, *A Moveable Feast* not only thematically refers him back to the time when he wrote this former work, it structurally duplicates *In Our Time* as a collection of short, snapshot-like pieces of prose narrative. More important, in the past as he recollects it, he desired to write "'the truest sentence that you know,'" that is, to construe writing not as "about" but as virtually synonymous with the empirical consistency of the things to which it was referring at that particular moment. For Hemingway, writing "truly" comes to mean recovering the experience of his former desire to write truly. It means to recover his former *sense* of writing this earlier collection of stories as a series of representational events in which imagined perceptions—as he seeks to reimagine *them*—occurred with all the sensory force and particular thereness of actual perceptions:

Some days [writing] went so well that you could make the country so that you could walk into it through the timber to come out into the clearing and work up onto the high ground and see the hills beyond the arm of the lake. A pencil-lead might break off in the conical nose of the pencil sharpener and you would use the small blade of the pen knife to clear it or else sharpen the pencil carefully with the sharp blade and then slip your arm through the sweat-salted leather of your pack strap to lift the pack again, get the other arm through and feel the weight settle on your back and feel the pine needles under your moccasins as you started down for the lake.[7]

Reference here gives way to the self-referential act of writing associated with its materials ("pencil-lead"), which then returns to a referential sense of physical, personal agency ("the sweat-salted leather of your pack strap" within the written scene) that in effect collapses or makes interchangeable the perceptual immediacy of the referential scene disclosed through writing, the material medium of this particular writing, and the psychological ambience or scene of writing itself: "and you would . . . sharpen the pencil carefully with the sharp blade and then slip your arm through the sweat-salted leather."

Hemingway thus defines writing as a desirable and perpetually reproducible concrete project in and for itself—as a metaphorical version of *hunger*, which quite clearly constitutes the "central image" and dominant trope of *A Moveable Feast* as a whole.[8] For this reason, he stops writing a section of "Big Two-Hearted River" at the point where a scene in the process of representation continues to stimulate his imaginative appetite to write more: "When I stopped writing I did not want to leave the river where I could see the trout in the pool. . . . But in the morning the river would be there and I must make it and the country and all that would happen. There were days ahead to be doing that each day."[9] By focusing on the scene of writing *In Our Time*, a completed work in the past, *A Moveable Feast* in effect purports to convert both it and itself into projects still in process and interchangeably infused with the ambience of physical hunger.

But certain kinds of "hunger" can also dilute this focus. Hemingway treats his hunger as a trope replete with the torque of negative and positive consequences—"a *moveable* feast"—in relation to his no less tropological past Parisian scene of writing *In Our Time*. On the one hand, hunger stimulates the healthy desire *to* write truly, or, the same thing, to represent things in a way that stimulates his desire to be with their concrete thereness. Thus he learns "to understand Cézanne much better"—the painter whom he also invoked in *In Our Time*'s omitted section of "Big Two-Hearted River" as his-alias-Nick's artistic alter ego—"and to see truly how he made landscapes when I was hungry."[10] Physical hunger here becomes synonymous with hunger for and "in" his writing: "But [hunger] also sharpens all of your perceptions, and I found that many of the people I wrote about had very strong appetites and a great taste and desire for food." On the other hand, hunger also stimulates his desire to write according to public economic standards of success, thus frustrating the very possibility of writing "truly." Monetary pressures tempt him to write journalism or do easy writing; to gamble on horse races or not write at all; or to complain about his financial troubles ("I was disgusted with myself for having complained about things"), which can lead him to compromise his artistic dedication: "And the next thing you would be compromising on something else."[11]

Hemingway applies both aspects of hunger to his entire Parisian experiences. "Paris" serves as a metaphorical occasion or inscribed scene of writing for isolating *now*, as he writes *A Moveable Feast*, whatever interferes with his desire to construe writing as a physically appetitive or hungry act. In this sense, Hemingway takes care in choosing literal scenes for writing the stories of *In Our Time*. Bad cafés with "the smell of dirty bodies and the sour smell of drunkenness" evoke no imaginative hunger, but instead mark the hedonistic distractions of Paris that would reduce rather than conduce to the concentration of such desire. But Paris also proffers the "good" or "pleasant café, warm and clean and friendly," where he can begin writing, for example, "The Three-Day Blow."[12]

Moreover, he personifies this "good" scene of writing in the figure of Hadley, his first wife with whom he lived in Paris while he was in fact writing (and to whom he eventually dedicated) *In Our Time*. First, her notorious loss of his story manuscripts actually renews his vocational incentive ("I was going to start writing stories again") and leads him to formulate a new theory by which he can imagine his writing perpetually evoking the equivalent of hungry responses: "that you could omit anything if you knew that you omitted and the omitted part would strengthen the story and make people feel something more than they understood."[13] Second, in believing in his work *as* an original project before he becomes known, she not only protects his vocational dedication from sexual hedonistic distractions in Paris, she also signifies the possibility of an intimate versus impersonal audience for this work.[14] She frees him, that is, to write as if in terms of an *unknown* intimate audience—to experience writing as an imaginary, constantly unconsummated liaison with internalized muse-like figures, such as the woman he sees while actually writing in the "good café that I knew on the Place St.-Michel": "I've seen you, beauty, and you belong to me now, whoever you are waiting for and if I never see you again, I thought. You belong to me and all Paris belongs to me and I belong to this notebook and this pencil."[15]

Adopting the persona of a literary apprentice, Hemingway uses his recollections of Paris in *A Moveable Feast* primarily as imaginative space in which to encounter the "beauty" of his writing itself, which is to say writing understood as an act in process, coterminously sponsored by his imaginative internalization of its intimate audience. But the self-addressed "you" he uses throughout these sketches as a strategy to invoke such an audience willy-nilly turns into "people" or readers of his text who tempt him into thinking *about* his writing as he writes it—that is, as an abstract as opposed to bodily activity: "When I was writing, it was necessary for me to read after I had written. If you kept thinking about it, you would lose the thing that you were writing before you could go on with it the next day. It was necessary to get exercise, to be tired in the body."[16] In short, this readerly self-consciousness introduces the context of canonical comparison, the question of his writing's public value according to prevailing literary-marketplace standards, into his desired scene of writing. In one sense, the writers he portrays so reductively serve as figurative alter egos of *his own* potential relation to writing.[17] In another sense, they break into his scene of writing as "outside" influences. Indeed, Hemingway here regards his own literary career since *In Our Time* as exerting a public influence on his desired project of original writing. *A Moveable Feast*, after all, essentially tells the story of his fall from this original project largely as the result of his own ambition or surrender to the ideology of public literary fame, especially associated with the writing of novels. Thus, in writing his earlier collection of stories, he remains haunted by pressures to write the novel, the muse for which he will associate with "the other" woman who eventually takes him from the primary muse of *In Our Time*, his wife Hadley: "I knew I must write a novel. But it seemed an impossible thing to do when I had been trying to write paragraphs that would be the distillation of what made a novel. . . . I would put it off though until I could not help doing it."[18]

In literally pertaining to the issue of physical-sexual size, Hemingway's notorious portrayal of Fitzgerald's anxiety over "a matter of measurements" metaphorically pertains to Hemingway's own sense of writing a condensed "physical" prose ("paragraphs" in lieu of novels), not unlike the physically tactile art or statues in the Louvre he uses to assuage Fitzgerald's anxiety. But Hemingway himself tends to measure his writing against the work of Russian novelists like Dostoyevski: "In Dostoyevski there were things believable and not to be believed, but some so true that they changed you as you read them." To resist this particular and generally unavoidable sense of textual or generic comparison, he uncritically cites Evan Shipman's unambitious but still hungry standard for writing: "'We need more true mystery in our lives, Hem,' he once said to me. 'The completely unambitious writer and the really good unpublished poem are the things we lack most at this time. There is, of course, the problem of sustenance.'"[19]

Hemingway, whose published comments elsewhere and even in *A Moveable Feast* tend to support critical assumptions about his virtually pathological literary ambition, turns out to harbor a latent wish at least to *write* without any sense of literary competition. He wishes, in other words, to write his works as "my own business," or as if in some private or secret scene of writing: "I was learning very much from [Cézanne] but I was not articulate enough to explain it to anyone. Besides it was a secret." At best, he shares his "secret" writing only in a post factum manner, and even then only with intimate doubles, those not associated with the public "literary" life. Until he meets Fitzgerald, who interrogates him directly about his writing, "I had felt that what a great writer I was had been carefully kept secret between myself and my wife and only those people we knew well enough to speak to."[20]

But despite his efforts to maintain a private scene of writing, Hemingway in the end cannot avoid simultaneously desiring the public fate of his activity. Like Fitzgerald but according to his own physically immediate criterion for writing the stories of *In Our Time*, Hemingway too succumbs to "the charm of [the] rich," namely to a view of his work endorsed by personifications of prevailing sociocultural powers. In reading aloud portions of his finished novel for "their" approbation, he surrenders his internal sense of its writing for "their" external relation to it. The publication of this novel marks the point in his career when he no longer becomes able to write without transforming private act into public product, in other words when his own writing becomes "a matter of measurements" or subject to the internalized surveillance of canonical expectations *as* he writes.

In short, like his sense of present-versus-past experiences of skiing in *A Moveable Feast*, Hemingway's experience of writing the stories collected in *In Our Time* "was not the way it is now": "the spiral fracture had not become common then, and no one could afford a broken leg. There were no ski patrols. Anything you ran down from, you had to climb up. That gave you legs that were fit to run down with." Imaginatively invoking "the way" it *was* to write these stories, he thus writes his memoirs to recover his present vocational "hunger": for his pre-patrol, pre-public, or private relation to writing construed as self-referential physical activity with potential physical consequences ("That gave you legs"); for a past paradisal scene of writing when "[t]here was no certainty" about the public value of *In Our Time*, but the writing "was as good and the happiness was greater" precisely because "no novel had been written."[21]

But in the first place, writing as a private psychophysical event remains an illusory goal—an unrealizable desire—because the linguistic medium precludes even as it engenders the possible perceptual coincidence between word and thing. In the second place, writing about one's past also forces one to encounter the abstract or self-alienated appearance of its facticity, its pastness per se. Even as it enables the possibility of recovering such hunger, then, Hemingway's *Feast* project constantly threatens to become sheer fantasy. How can he write now as if he were yet to write this earlier collection of short fiction? How can he reread its stories as if they were not yet completed—not yet existing signifiers precisely of a career responsible for his fall from writing "truly"?

Most interpretations of *In Our Time* construe it as an embryonic Bildungsroman, a collection of stories and interchapters teleologically unified around the theme of Nick Adams's evolving education from a boy averting his gaze from the violence or disorder of life, the tenor of the first story, "Indian Camp," to a young man who largely from his experience in World War I—the implicit experiential background of "Big Two-Hearted River"—comes to recognize violence or chaos as the primary condition of life "in our time."[22] Irony provides the narrative ligature for Hemingway's arrangement of stories and flash-forward interchapters. Taken separately or together, their very brevity and imagistic abruptness suggest photographic or prosthetic substitutions for life, the discontinuity or fragmentation of modern experience becoming shorn of socially sanctioned illusions about its ultimate coherence. For example, in "Indian Camp" Nick avoids looking at the Indian woman in labor: "Nick didn't look at it. . . . Nick did not watch. His curiosity had been gone for a long time." In the interchapter immediately following this story, the narrator cannot avoid witnessing the chaos implicit in a war evacuation scene where "a woman [was] having a baby with a young girl holding a blanket over her and crying. Scared sick of looking at it."[23]

Given its ironic formal and thematic cohesion, critics have reason to view *In Our Time* either as an embryonic novel or what Forrest Ingram would term a "short story cycle" comprised of "a set of stories linked to each other in such a way as to maintain a balance between the individuality of each of the stories and the necessities of the larger unity."[24] But to maintain this critical view, one must downplay the fact that barely half of the stories and only one of the interchapters literally concern Nick Adams. Second, the composition of *In Our Time* remains tentatively novelistic at best, and in this sense requests us to reflect on its status *as* a text. More important, certain of its stories effectively undercut its representational status as a (modern) novel by seeming to duplicate the way *A Moveable Feast* later frames this collection's scene of writing.

One could argue that the last story in this collection, the two parts of "Big Two-Hearted River," not to mention its omitted section "On Writing," inscribes the issue of writing per se—of writing literature "in our time" and Hemingway's particular writing of *In Our Time*. The traditional interpretation of this story, of course, argues that combined with the staccato simplicity of Hemingway's style, Nick's deliberate acts and focus on minute details serve to "banish [the] evil spirits" of Nick-alias-Hemingway's haunting war experiences.[25] But in "On Writing," Nick metaphorically equates his love of fishing and bullfighting with writing, and explicitly confesses his ambition "to be a great writer. He was pretty sure he would be."[26] According to one critic, then, "Big Two-Hearted River" contains a "metaphoric level" which casts "Nick's fishing trip as an attempt by Hemingway to write, perhaps for the first time, about the artist and the process of his art."[27] Catching small trout at first, then larger ones, "places a demand on all of Nick's fishing skill. The parallel to the artistic process is clear. Like the artist, Nick the fisherman has his limits"; thus Nick's refusal to fish the swamp where "the fishing would be tragic" metaphorically signifies Hemingway's own recognition at the time of writing *In Our Time* that he is not yet ready to meet "the ultimate test for the mature artist": namely, to write "tragedy."[28]

But the story also concerns something other than Nick's recognition of limits or his patient ambition to be "a great writer" along traditional aestheticist lines. Right from the beginning, Nick regards his fishing trip as an *escape* from the *demand* to write: "Nick felt happy. He felt he had left everything behind, the need for thinking, the need to write, other needs." Just as in *A Moveable Feast* where Hemingway associates his act of writing with its material ambience and "the sweat-salted leather of your pack strap," so "Big Two-Hearted River" concerns Nick's attempt to secure a private "camp," a private scene where the project of writing becomes interchangeable with the sense of hunger: "He was very tired. That was done. He had made his camp. He was settled. Nothing could touch him. It was a good place to camp. He was there, in the good place. He was in his home where he had made it. Now he was hungry."[29]

More than referring to itself, however, "Big Two-Hearted River" suggests that "Nick Adams" has authored the preceding stories and interchapters in the collection as well—its omitted section specifically informs us that he has written "My Old Man." Like a prefatory *A Moveable Feast*, this last story constitutes a retrospective, "self-referential" revision of *In Our Time* from a work readable as condensed representations of collective experience "in our time" to a work exercising Hemingway's private anxieties about becoming "a great writer." But the greatness these early stories strive to envisage has nothing to do with externally imposed criteria for literary success that would turn writing into competitive or "serious" work rather than an experience of private play: "[Writing] was really more fun than anything. That was really why you did it. . . . It wasn't conscience. It was simply that it was the greatest pleasure."[30]

As with his later autobiographical sketches, other stories in *In Our Time* variously reflect the obstacles to construing writing as private "fun." That is, "Big Two-Hearted River" allows us retroactively to re-gard each story as inscribing the desire for its writing to evince radically contingent acts of signification—of signifying percept-ridden imag-ined events exempt from the pressures of established if also heteroge-neous literary formulations. In other words, each story paradoxically seeks to withdraw from its public identity *as* writing, by shedding, for example, the section "On Writing" itself from "Big Two-Hearted River." In *A Moveable Feast*, Hemingway represents himself as having read "after-work books" so as not to think about the story (or its poten-tial literary value) he was still in the process of writing.[31] In "The Three-Day Blow," Nick and Bill's discussion of minor writers (Wal-pole, Hudson, and Chesterton) as if they wrote "classic" works at once ironically exposes the arbitrary aspect of personal literary standards, and also inscribes Hemingway's desire to regard literature as a non-competitive activity, as writing altogether free from the context of offi-cial literary evaluation. In this overdetermined scene (of writing), Nick and Bill at first juxtapose discussing writers with discussing baseball, a "fun" game but nevertheless a competitive sport; then they turn to fish-ing, a noncompetitive activity and, as endorsed by "Big Two-Hearted River" later, a metaphor for Hemingway's ideal writing: "'There isn't any comparison,' said Nick. 'How did we ever get talking about base-ball?'"[32]

The relationship between Nick and Bill exists in marked contrast to Nick's later hermeticism. Personal intimacy, especially between voca-tional peers, can puncture the writer's sense of private literary space. In short, Nick's intimate relationships mark the point of Hemingway's testing his own vocational dedication to writing "truly." In "The End of Something," Marjorie, Nick's girlfriend, "loved to fish. She loved to fish with Nick," which dependence indicates her failure to understand the writer's or Nick's need to exclude all sense of others while writing. When Nick and Marjorie set up and leave behind their "fishing" lines to eat together (thus sharing a metaphorical hunger), the situation prevents Nick from a direct physical experience of fishing, that of feeling a trout "taking line out of the reel in a rush and making the reel sing with the click on"—experiencing the act of *writing* about this scene as no less a radically particular perceptual event. In the same allegorical vein, their fishing where "there was nothing of the [old lumber] mill left except the broken white limestone of its foundations" possibly alludes to the modernist literary situation in which past values of writing (or an inherited literary tradition) clearly no longer apply or are "broken." Of vocational necessity, then, Nick, here a surrogate for the modern apprentice writer, rejects Marjorie's desire to romanticize this place in the manner of Victorian novelists: "'[The ruin of the old mill] seems more like a castle,' Marjorie said. Nick said nothing."[33]

Yet even as it inscribes Hemingway's attempt to reject intimately familiar, hence imminently influential criteria synonymous with past modes of writing, criteria that would deny the sense of writing as personal "fun" ("'It isn't fun any more,'" Nick tells Marjorie in the "end"), *In Our Time* also tracks his rejection of alternative literary models available in the modern world. To fish or write in his own private camp or scene of writing, Hemingway's Nick Adams, his surrogate Adamic (or original) writer in "Big Two-Hearted River," moves beyond "the burned-over country" around the abandoned town of Seney—beyond T. S. Eliot's modernist literary topos of "The Waste Land."[34] Suggested by its very title ("Elliot"), its allusion to the couple's sexual infertility, and the formal manner ("Mr. and Mrs.") by which the narrator refers to the poet husband and his wife who painstakingly types his "very long poems," "Mr. and Mrs. Elliot" satirizes the Eliotic writer's aesthetic quest for a pure "formalist" writing: Mr. Elliot "wanted to keep himself pure so that he could bring to his wife the same purity of mind and body that he expected of her." In other words, the story represents the modern "abstract" artist—potentially Hemingway himself in this "self-referential" work—whose all-consuming project for a self-contained art results in a referentially frustrated muse and thus lacks any physical connection to life. Like the picador and his bull-maimed, bleeding horse awaiting the action of the vital bull in the following interchapter, Mr. Elliot produces an art that at best remains uncertainly related to life: "The bull could not make up his mind to charge."[35]

Conversely, modern realistic art, art that purports to represent the chaotic realities of modern life, tends to traffic in sociopolitical agendas that make it no less abstract, no less subject to publicly authored ideals rather than private perceptions. Like the boy in "The Revolutionist" who ends up "in jail near Sion," metaphorically near yet so far from the utopian community or Zion promised by his revolutionary activities, so the politicized modern writer remains trapped within social ideals that prevent him—the boy prefers artistic "reproductions" to originals, painters of benign religious subjects to Mantegna's more graphically violent ones—from recognizing the presocial or "original" force defining Hemingway's desired experience of writing.

Yet neither does *In Our Time*'s ironic exposé of such idealisms as egregiously unrepresentative of one's brute experience of modern life automatically result in his realizing this vocational desideratum, for *In Our Time* also immediately calls to mind an autobiographical precedent that threatens to make Hemingway construe his own writing of these stories in the context of "reproductions." In representing the education of Nick Adams, *In Our Time*, whether taken as a whole or metaphorically focused in one story, "The Doctor and the Doctor's Wife," allusively doubles as the fictional counterpart to *The Education of Henry Adams*. Just as by the end of Hemingway's text Nick learns that past notions of order no longer work in the chaos of modern life, *The Education* tracks Henry Adams's uneasy surrender of past notions of ordered existence, for him especially symbolized by the medieval Virgin, to a realization of modern chaos, the release of new "supersensual" forces symbolized by the technological dynamo. Condensed and disguised so as to seem utterly farfetched—Hemingway cannot allow writing to become an explicit issue *in* his writing lest it also become subject to canonical demands—this internalized inscription nevertheless also applies to Hemingway's story. In "The Doctor and the Doctor's Wife," Nick's doctor father, who happens to be named Henry, backs down from a physical confrontation with Dick Boulton, an American Indian half-breed. So too, Henry Adams backs down from—admits failure in the face of—the chaos synonymous with brute nature in *The Education*.[36] Yet where Adams's narrative ambivalently betrays its nostalgia for the spontaneous order inspired by the Virgin as opposed to the reactionary modes of order proposed by modern patriarchal science in the face of (and also ironically contributing to) the forces unleashed by the Dynamo, Hemingway's Henry Adams receives no such inspiration from his "Virgin," the Christian Scientist wife whose fundamentalist Christianity instead drives him to masculine solitude (hunting alone) and even intimations of a solitary suicide: "'Remember that he who ruleth his spirit is greater than he that taketh a city,' said his wife. . . . Her husband did not answer. He was sitting on his bed now, cleaning a shotgun."[37]

In Our Time continues this internalized disaffiliation from modernist writing by outlining a return to an albeit equally revised tradition of American regionalist writing.[38] On the one hand, for example, Nick abandons his reading in nature, "sitting with his back against a tree," and goes off with his father to hunt "black squirrels" in a place Nick knows they reside, rather than return to his mother. With this move, Hemingway metaphorically abandons American writing associated with Thoreau ("sitting" in nature) and affiliates his project with that of the modern American Adams: "'All right,' said his father. 'Let's go there.'" But this affiliation also remains equivocal, for in having Nick and his father leave together only to hunt "black squirrels," the story indicates its resistance to the desire of Adams's text to evoke as well as disclose the chaos of modern life as a whole. Hemingway, that is, resists the universalistic claims of modernist literary writing, just as *In*

Our Time ultimately resists the internationalist ideology of modernism when it has Nick return not only to America but to the region-specific Michigan woods in the last story.

With Nick's return, moreover, Hemingway reverses the direction and in effect positions himself before the rural-to-cosmopolitan movement defining the latent Bildungsroman of Sherwood Anderson's collection of stories, *Winesburg, Ohio.* In particular, "My Old Man," a story clearly beholden to Anderson's "I Want to Know," constitutes an extended narrative pun through which Hemingway inscribes Anderson himself as "my old man" or immediate literary father within the act of writing *In Our Time.*[39] In this story, he places Anderson in Europe because of his modernist expatriate position, or the way Anderson's *Winesburg* collection exhibits nostalgia for yet final rejection of rural American society: "He'd tell me about . . . the old days in the States before everything went on the bum there." But in alluding to Anderson's subsequent failure as a full-fledged modernist writer (alias European jockey), Hemingway reinterprets this older writer's project not as blocking but as opening up American literary space yet to be explored.[40] At the very least, like the potential literary rivals he treats as his own vocational options in *A Moveable Feast,* Hemingway here regards Anderson as staking out the danger zones facing any would-be American writer in the modernist era who strives to determine his own relation to writing: "And he'd say, 'Joe, when we've got a decent stake, you're going back there to the States and go to school.'"[41]

By having his protagonist go back to Michigan, Hemingway indeed goes back to the American school or tradition of writing, the exemplary figure of which for him was—precisely under the influence of Anderson—Mark Twain.[42] Many critics, of course, have frequently remarked on Hemingway's stylistic and thematic indebtedness to Twain's *Huckleberry Finn.* Couldn't one regard Nick's uncanny encounter with Ad and Bugs in "The Battler" as Hemingway's revised, ironic reading of Huck and Jim's escape from all forms of social slavery to the American mythic territories of personal freedom?[43] In this sense, "The Battler" traces Hemingway's encounter with Twain as former American literary "champion." In depicting Nick's hungry repast with the two men and his ultimate expulsion from their firelit camp, the site of a still influential but distanced literary past, Hemingway seems to clear a space for the "mounting" significance of his own text: "Looking back from the mounting grade before the track curved into the hills [Nick] could see the firelight [of the two men's camp] in the clearing."[44]

But here again, just as with Adams, Thoreau, and Anderson in the aforementioned stories, so Hemingway links his collection not primarily with Twain's major work of fiction but with his literarily lesser though still canonical work written around the same time, the autobiographical *Life on the Mississippi*.[45] Not only "The Battler" but both the first and last stories in *In Our Time* redound to "camps" or, as we have seen, metaphorical scenes of writing. More specifically, "Indian Camp" and "Big Two-Hearted River" strategically allude to Twain's depictions of the Mississippi River region "before and after" the Civil War in *Life*: from the apprentice writer-alias-pilot's former antebellum relation to an endlessly original or Emersonian American nature, the metaphorical significance of the river in part 1 of his work, to the established writer's postbellum loss and recovery of such nature in part 2. In Twain's work, the frontier aspect of American nature endows his very act of writing with frontier or original status, hence his transformation of Chicago, synecdoche of a postbellum industrialized American society, into an endless "novelty"; hence the way he ends his revisitation to the Mississippi region "on the upper river" in Minnesota where, while "modern" boats are manned "with not a suggestion of romance about them anywhere," he can still experience scenes such as "a black night" when he encounters "dense walls of foliage that almost touched our bows on both sides; and here every individual leaf, and every individual ripple stood out in its natural color, and flooded with a glare as of noonday intensified. The effect was strange, and fine, and very striking."[46]

Referentially ending in a yet unsettled or "strange" American nature, Twain's *Life* textually ends on a recapitulation of Indian legends; in other words, it entertains the dream of an American or "Indian" mode of writing indissociable from this original nature. Once framed in the revisionary context of "Big Two-Hearted River," Hemingway's "Indian Camp," the beginning of *In Our Time*, marks the termination of precisely this dream. In this Michigan "camp" or misprision of Twain's metaphorical (Minnesota) scene of writing Life, Hemingway finds an American nature irreversibly permeated with the superior urban indifference about its value manifested in Anderson's *Winesburg*, and with the modernist scientific perspective of nature's "supersensual" status expressed in Henry Adams's *Education*. When first rowing to the Indian camp over a lake in Twain-like darkness, Nick's "Uncle George [Willard?] was smoking a cigar in the dark. . . . [He] gave both the Indians cigars." Lacking an available "anaesthetic" with which to operate, Henry the doctor seeks to repress registering the Indian woman's labor pain: "'her screams are not important. I don't hear them because they are not important.'" The doctor's "Caesarian" incision and the jackknife (or *pen*knife) instrument he uses to perform it metaphorically adumbrate the modern American writer's scientific or realistic—hence alienated—relation to nature, here represented in a scene wherein the latter reproduces itself in human form through the act of childbirth. This disengaged relation to nature also redounds to the event of writing itself. For the modern writer, the value of writing no longer resides in one's apprehension of its referent about to become a new, all but sensory event in the particular moment of its occurrence within the *act* of writing (the Indian woman's labor), but rather in its abstract, separable quality as a *socially* original performance (the doctor's Caesarian operation). Its value "in our time," in other words, accrues from its status only as a written, public, and therefore publishable *product*, perforce bypassing the private experience of writing per se, and which Hemingway here again associates with the activity of fishing: "'That's one for the medical journal, George,' [Nick's father] said. 'Doing a

Caesarian with a jack-knife and sewing it up with nine-foot, tapered gut leaders.'"[47]

No one "in our time" can escape this abstract and public contamination of American nature, especially not the Indian husband who represents the lost and so now self-destructive illusion of living an aboriginal relation to nature: "He had cut his foot very badly with an ax three days before. He was smoking a pipe. The room smelled very bad." If his suicide, like Nick's averted gaze, thematically indicates an inability to face the stark, socially disorienting (and in his case, deracinated) implications of modern life ("'He couldn't stand things, I guess'"), in our present context it reversibly suggests his unwillingness to surrender the Twain-like ideal of an unmediated relation to nature. By itself, this ideal cannot result in Hemingway's recovery of Twain's "river" position in writing *Life*, not even in his own "river" story of vocational declaration, "Big Two-Hearted River." But in exposing it as an ideal at the very beginning of *In Our Time*, Hemingway can imagine recovering, if not an original American nature as metaphor of writing, at least an original relation to writing as metaphor of such nature.

But his misprision of Twain does not mitigate the extent to which other kinds of influence also haunt his project to write an American prose as if for the first time. For example, "Soldier's Home" concerns the deleterious effect actual American society "in our time" has on Hemingway's desire to return "home," or to write in a radical American grain. The American social ethos, in this story made experientially imminent through Krebs's relation to his parents and especially his mother, leads him to question the very value of his vocation in terms of social definitions of work, ambition, success; it also tempts the apprentice writer. Krebs's main pleasure is to read "about all the engagements he had been in," "really learning about the war," and "to lie" about "everything that had happened to him," or to translate it into attractive conventional terms ("Now he would have liked a girl if she had come to him and not wanted to talk. But here at home it was all too complicated"), hence to destroy its private originality to himself: "Krebs acquired the nausea in regard to experience that is the result of untruth or exaggeration. . . . In this way he lost everything."[48]

Potential invasions of Hemingway's American scene of writing lurk everywhere. Like Krebs, he can try passively to resist them, simply declare them *non*influential: "He had tried so to keep his life from being complicated. Still, none of it touched him." But "Soldier's Home" ironically discloses how this strategy leaves Krebs in a negative or spectatorial relation to life, which is to say that it subliminally frames the act of writing as impotent inactivity unrelated to "real" experience: "He would go over to the schoolyard and watch Helen [Krebs's younger sister] play indoor baseball."[49] Writing, that is, becomes a mere self-referential or private ("indoor") game that he can only fantasize doing through Helen, a childish muse.

But if "Soldier's Home" inscribes Hemingway's self-imposed test for vocational integrity in the face of antithetical cultural odds, other stories in *In Our Time* exercise the consequences of his vocational dedication as itself a potentially disruptive influence on his scene of writing. Both "Out of Season," if only in an allusive sense, and "Cross-Country Snow" suggestively concern a male character's ambivalent dissatisfaction and resignation at the prospect of his spouse's pregnancy. In the first story, the man manifests guilt for such feelings: "'I'm sorry I talked the way I did at lunch. We were both getting at the same thing from different angles.'" Whatever its allusions to Hemingway's actual relation to Hadley at the time of writing *In Our Time*, the story plainly concerns the man's guilty flirtation with and second thoughts about fishing "out of season": "'We're probably being followed by the game police by now. I wish we weren't in on this damn thing.'"[50] As metaphor of writing, this potential fishing violation unconsciously traces the writer, here in the guise of the young husband, musing about violating social norms (for example, writing what Stein would term "inaccrochable" stories[51]), or even allowing his vocational dedication to take priority over—by using as materials for writing—his intimate relations to others.

But the man's sense of guilt in "Out of Season" also devolves on the violation of social norms *endemic* to the act of writing. For as we have seen in the case of *A Moveable Feast* and in certain stories from *In Our Time*, vocational dedication for Hemingway is synonymous with determining a private scene of writing that requires the assiduous purgation of all public influences. First, to write "truly" is to incur the guilt of running counter to living or seeing life in conventional and/or "literary" terms. Second, such a project entails the potential guilt of using autobiographically intimate experiences with others for private vocational purposes. Moreover, having occurred in his past, these experiences could only introduce an "outside" source—the sense of *his own* influence—into his act of writing. Finally, insofar as it concerns the possibility of writing fiction that never quite gets written, such writing also abuses the conventional notion of fiction writing itself.

Such vocational issues permeate the themes of uneasy heterosexual relationships and ambivalence over female pregnancy that occur in Hemingway's inaugural collection of fiction. Marriage, that is, inscribes the demand for conventional projects of writing: writing as storytelling essentially projected for the judgment and participation of others rather than for the writer's experience alone. Pregnancy connotes the inevitable loss of this experience (the baby in term) to the world (upon its actual birth) at publication. Far from extolling the joys (or unconsciously revealing the patriarchal selfishness) of male camaraderie, "Cross-Country Snow" shows Nick Adams striving rigorously to forget the vocational implications of his wife's pregnancy and instead dwell on skiing, metaphor for writing *without* such implications, with his friend George, Nick's alter ego or the writer's internalized private audience in writing: "George and Nick were happy. They were fond of each other. They knew they had the run back home ahead of them." But the thought of his social obligation raised by his wife's pregnancy constantly intrudes: in the ski lodge, "Nick noticed that [the waitress's] apron covered swellingly her pregnancy." Except as fantasy, this surrogate writer's ideal scene of writing as pure play remains just that, a fiction of writing fiction free from public determinations. Nick gives an affirmative answer to George's question, "'don't you wish we could just bum together? Take our skis and go on the train to where there was good running . . . and not give a damn about school or anything'?" but then can't promise George that they will ever "'go skiing again'" together.[52]

What awaits Nick when he goes back to the States with Helen to have the baby are mountains too rocky for him to ski, too crowded with timber and too far apart.[53] What awaits Hemingway when he completes the stories of *In Our Time* with his muse are the relatively fixed, yet widely various and impersonal public criteria that will inevitably make it more difficult, if not impossible, for him to regard his future writing as emanating from a "good running" private scene such as he seeks to secure in writing these very stories. And so if he imagines the success of *In Our Time* as he writes *In Our Time*, he also tries to imagine ways of disarming his internalized demand for literary success ahead of time. For example, he projects the disastrous results of adopting a literary-competitive ethos in "The Battler," the last story Hemingway in fact wrote for this collection. The story tells of Ad Francis's fallen status as a professional fighter due to his scandalous romance with his manager "sister" who "'looked enough like him to be twins'"; but with boxing as metaphor of writing, it subliminally tells of the professional writer who, having already entered the competitive literary arena, surrenders his project entirely to the vocational self-image reflected by the ideology of public fame and fortune (the destructive attraction of the "sister")—precisely the fate Hemingway later tries to mitigate in *A Moveable Feast*.[54]

In a story like "Out of Season," he also senses that trying to avoid the competitive literary marketplace may possess no less vocationally disastrous consequences. If, as previously suggested, this story deploys the husband as Hemingway's surrogate writer, the variability of a text's unconscious displacements allows for another interpretation more in accord with the major exigency of Hemingway's particular allegorical project: his desire to write what he is writing "now" within a private scene of writing, the inscription of which desire he simultaneously needs to suppress as he writes. One could argue that in "Out of Season," not the husband but the unlikely drunken guide Peduzzi, the story's invested point of view, represents the writer who, the value of his talents perceived only by himself ("Nobody spoke or gave any sign to [Peduzzi's greetings] except the town beggar"), risks self-delusion for writing "out of season," that is, not in accord with publicly endorsed notions of writing. Wanting to alleviate the sense of isolation he experiences with his unconventional project, the Hemingway writer desires at least a limited sympathetic audience for it, here in the guise of the foreign couple Peduzzi wants to take fishing. But such an audience may not exist ("He had called the young gentleman caro several times and nothing had happened") except as self-evident illusory wish: "He was through with the hotel garden, breaking up frozen manure with a dung fork. Life was opening out." At best it remains a momentary illusion: in "Cat in the Rain," a woman, again the story's assumed point of view and self-disguised figure of the Hemingway writer, remains subject to her husband's indifference (the writer's public audience) and only receives sympathetic attention from the "padrone" of the hotel (the writer's private audience) who retrieves her desired "'poor kitty out in the rain'" (the vital yet, like the small cat subject to the elements, canonically pressured "minor" project of writing) and gives her "a momentary feeling of being of supreme importance."[55]

Either way, with an imagined or imaginary audience, *In Our Time* seems to track, as Hemingway himself suggests in *A Moveable Feast* when he informs us about the omitted fate of Peduzzi, a literarily suicidal venture. This early work suspects its likely potential audience of introducing socially authored literary demands into its scene of writing, hence of working to deny its dream of becoming a series of radically original acts of writing. And so Hemingway seeks to occlude audience altogether, or, the same thing, to repress ahead of time his own literary ambition by writing the stories of *In Our Time* in a manner that defines them to himself as *preparatory* gestures *toward* writing them, that is, as if before becoming subject to public consumption, evaluation, influence. His compressed narrative praxis in these stories (in "Big Two-Hearted River," for example, where "nothing" happens[56]) foreshortens the occasions for registering their origins in his own past experience (or influence) and especially his sense of writing a "literature" that would be vulnerable to canonical scrutiny. The sense of omitted information in this story and others like "Out of Season" suggests their prenarrative or only embryonic literary formulation. The interchapters amount to distillations of novels—of "major" literary writing.[57] Stories like "A Very Short Story" exhibit narrative impatience, or all but signify their wish to resist literary-generic identification altogether. Above all, *In Our Time* as a whole outlines a novel that from Hemingway's position—this is its phenomenological definition— never gets written, not even as a proto-narrative portrait of the artist as a young man in the process of writing this very collection of stories.

These stories represent verbal photographs of "our time" largely through a central character named Nick Adams. Thanks to the revisionary function of the last story, "Big Two-Hearted River," they also retroactively reflect the (still referentially understood) autobiographical outlines of Hemingway-alias-Nick Adams's development as a literary artist. But for Hemingway this already muted artistic "autobiography" also entails a performative function: namely, to effect a particular relation to writing that would frame it as free from or as if occurring before the sense of its resulting in narrative cohesion, fictional *or* autobiographical. This function paradoxically requires him to disguise such a project from himself lest it become vulnerable to established narrative and/or public literary criteria—the reason for his unlikely identifications with *non*-Nick Adams figures such as the woman in "Cat in the Rain," Peduzzi in "Out of Season," or even more improbably, the Indian husband in "Indian Camp" whose omitted and narratively marginal presence nevertheless retroactively usurps the reader-alias-Nick's perceptual attention.

One could interpret each of the stories from *In Our Time* according to these three mutually exclusive levels of significance. For example, an early story like "A Very Short Story" formally enacts as well as thematically represents (1) an anonymous young man's experience of the pathetic anonymity or repeatability of modern love relationships, and (2) the young writer's temptation to abandon his career (turning it into "a very short story") after his first and failed relationship with the muse. But Hemingway's own rereading of *In Our Time* through *A Moveable Feast* allows us as well to regard this story as (3) part of a nonteleological sequence of stories attempting to expose and avert whatever threatens to make his act of writing them subject to public referential interpretations or literary comparisons. In this sense, "A Very Short Story" reflects *any* moment in the act of writing when Hemingway experiences the kind of vocational self-doubt about writing "truly" that he registers more directly in his later collection: "sometimes when I was starting a new story and [I] could not get it going . . . I would stand and look out over the roofs of Paris and think, 'Do not worry. You have always written before and you will write now. All you have to do is write one true sentence.'"[58]

About "our time," *In Our Time* also struggles to be about itself. About its own writing, it resists becoming *mere* writing—desires to refer to life without the sense of its own textuality. And so it steers a course between representational reference and self-reference. As a collection of stories precisely in the process of resisting its literary associations and potential canonical ambitions, it particularly resists becoming a novel, which would drag it into the public domain or make its writing not seem "fun any more." Such writing paradoxically *works* to remain "fun." Thus, Hemingway's muted metaphorical connections between fishing and writing in "The End of Something," "The Three-Day Blow," "Out of Season" and "Big Two-Hearted River," even his repetitive and terse style which "make[s] us more conscious of the signifying function" or activity per se, indicate strategies to defer his writing's sense of meaning *to himself*.[59] Or rather, since language can never escape meaning, Hemingway's narrative and stylistic strategies help him focus on quasi-referential details of the world that one might experience as if prior to their accruing public meaning.

But to write about things as if only at the level of one's desire for physical interaction with them *here and now* requires the destruction of self as an established identity: that is, how one tends to present oneself or represent this experience to others in the act of writing. It is to become like the woman in "Cat in the Rain," separate from others like her husband who use literature to repress life ("'Oh, shut up and get something to read'") rather than seek to possess it originally: "'If I can't have long hair or any fun, I can have a cat'"—in other words, write "short" works as if in the process of eluding canonical demands of any kind, and therefore of disclosing privately determined experiences of life. But like Nick in the act of skiing, to write this way is also to become wholly subsumed by the experience of one's own body: "The rush and the sudden swoop as he dropped down a steep undulation in the mountain side plucked Nick's mind out and left him only the wonderful flying, dropping sensation in his body."[60] It is, in short, by committing a kind of perceptual suicide through writing that one gets oneself into a radically original relation to things.

In the end, of course, Hemingway could not sustain the preconceptual vision of writing he desires to effect in *In Our Time* and desires to desire again in *A Moveable Feast*. After the public literary acclaim accorded *In Our Time* and two subsequent novels, Hemingway adds "On the Quai at Smyrna" to this collection in 1930 and retroactively revises it as indeed a "novel" representative of experience "in our time." From that point on until *A Moveable Feast*, writing becomes wholly a matter of public literary performance. In this late collection, he realizes that Peduzzi's no longer omitted fate was his, or that vocational honesty always required that he obliterate public self-identity in a private "garden of Eden" or scene of writing. But even at the beginning of his career and first major collection of stories, Hemingway had inscribed the consequences of failing to do so in the barely discernible figure of the Indian husband: that trace of himself as a would-be aboriginal American writer who, committed to invoking the suddenly disclosed thereness of experience through razor-sharp writing, could not bear to see his conception born and borne into the world.

Notes

1. Ernest Hemingway, *A Moveable Feast* (New York, 1986), 76.

2. See, for example, Arthur Waldhorn, *A Reader's Guide to Ernest Hemingway* (New York, 1972), 212-13; and Kenneth S. Lynn, *Hemingway* (New York, 1987), 586, 278-80 (on Hemingway's self-serving distortions of Fitzgerald).

3. Hemingway, *Moveable Feast*, 6.

4. Ernest Hemingway, "On Writing," in *The Nick Adams Stories* (New York, 1972), 237.

5. Paul Smith, "Impressions of Ernest Hemingway," *Hemingway Review* 6 (Spring 1987): 4, suggests that one of the motives for Hemingway's *Feast* memoirs was to settle an old score with Gertrude Stein for her unflattering portrait of him in *The Autobiography of Alice B. Toklas*. Also see Lynn, *Hemingway*, 322, and Waldhorn, *Reader's Guide*, 216-19.

6. Paul Smith, "Impressions," 6.

7. Hemingway, *Moveable Feast*, 12, 91.

8. Waldhorn, *Reader's Guide*, 214.

9. Hemingway, *Moveable Feast*, 76-77.

10. Hemingway, *Nick Adams Stories*, 240; *Moveable Feast*, 69.

11. Hemingway, *Moveable Feast*, 100, 7, 61, 72.

12. Ibid., 3, 5.

13. Ibid., 74-75.

14. A letter from Hadley to Hemingway before they got married clearly suggests this belief and also the private intimacy with which she shared it with him. Quoted in Peter Griffin's biography, *Along with Youth: Hemingway, the Early Years* (New York, 1985), she comments on his (pre-*In Our Time*) "enormous power of living and how inside intuition stuff comes through to you very, very often and gives you new food for tho't. . . . I have it too—not in the same degree—it's really the best gift I know of so don't tell anyone I said I had it. . . . But the great beauty of it is ideas just appearing in your mind that make you understand the way things are" (157-58).

15. Hemingway, *Moveable Feast*, 6. Paul Smith, "Impressions," notes that this unknown woman "was his muse, exciting him to the creative act of writing" (7).

16. Hemingway, *Moveable Feast*, 25.

17. In *A Moveable Feast*, Hemingway criticizes Stein for needing "to have publication and official acceptance," for lacking vocational discipline or abjuring "the obligation to make her writing intelligible" (17), for reducing literature to a matter of personalities (28), and for all these reasons being unwilling to write or, as in the case of his story "Up in Michigan," approve of "inaccrochable" stories (15-16). But Hemingway represents himself as vulnerable to the same problems, as when he finds himself complaining about there being "no demand for" his work (75), gets distracted from his work by his attraction to horse racing (61-62), resists using conventional narrative practices, as with his "theory" of omitting narrative information from readers, and of course effectively discusses Stein as well as Ford Madox Ford, Eliot, and Fitzgerald, among others, in terms of largely reductive anecdotes about their personalities in this very text.

18. Ibid., 75-76.

19. Ibid., 191, 133, 138, 146.

20. Ibid., 13, 150.

21. Ibid., 199, 208.

22. A number of critics have maintained this "unified" view of *In Our Time*: for example, Philip Young, "Adventures of Nick Adams," in *Hemingway: A Collection of Critical Essays*, ed. Robert P. Weeks (Englewood Cliffs, 1962), 97; Wirt Williams, *The Tragic Art of Ernest Hemingway* (Baton Rouge, 1981), 30-31; and David Seed, "'The Picture of the Whole': *In Our Time*," in *Ernest Hemingway: New Critical Essays*, ed. A. Robert Lee (Totowa, 1983), 19-20. Robert E. Gajdusek, "Dubliners in Michigan: Joyce's Presence in Hemingway's *In Our Time*," *Hemingway Review 2* (Fall 1982): 48-61, argues that the topical, thematic, even teleological unity of Joyce's earlier collection of stories exerted a discernible influence on Hemingway's construction and arrangement of the stories in *In Our Time*.

23. Ernest Hemingway, *In Our Time* (New York, 1958), 23, 19.

24. Forrest L. Ingram, *Representative Short Story Cycles of the Twentieth Century: Studies in a Literary Genre* (The Hague, 1971), 15.

25. Malcolm Cowley, "Nightmare and Ritual in Hemingway," in Weeks, ed., *Collection of Critical* Essays, 48. Corroborated by Hemingway himself in *Moveable Feast*, this "wound" or "war-trauma" theory of Hemingway's Nick Adams stories, especially "Big Two-Hearted River," was extended by Young, "Adventures of Nick Adams," 103-6, and has become a commonplace in Hemingway criticism, although it has recently become contested, especially by Lynn. See Frederick Crews's review of Lynn's biography in the *New York Review of Books*, 13 August 1987, 30-37.

26. Hemingway, *Nick Adams Stories*, 234-38.

27. B. J. Smith, "'Big Two-Hearted River': The Artist and the Art," *Studies in Short Fiction* 20 (Summer 1983): 130. For all his understanding of the story's "self-referential" implications, Smith still tends to construe its "metaphoric level" as self-referential or autobiographical in origin; that is, for him the story reflects Hemingway's attempt to come to terms with the "wound" he received not so much in the war but in Hadley's loss of his early manuscripts. See also Keith Carabine, "'Big Two-Hearted River': A Reinterpretation," *Hemingway Review* 1 (Spring 1982): 39-44.

28. B. J. Smith, "'Big Two-Hearted River,'" 131.

---

29. Hemingway, *In Our Time*, 179, 186-87.

30. Hemingway, *Nick Adams Stories*, 237-38.

31. Hemingway, *Moveable Feast*, 27, 25.

32. Hemingway, *In Our Time*, 51, 55.

33. Ibid., 36, 38.

34. Cowley makes this Eliotic connection in "Nightmare and Ritual," 49-59. Philip Young, *Ernest Hemingway: A Reconsideration* (University Park, Pa., 1966), 183, notes how Hemingway borrowed the Eliotic principle of the "objective correlative" in discussing his aesthetics of writing in *Death in the Afternoon*. In contrast to Lynn's biographical reduction of this story to Hemingway's thinly disguised satirization of Eliot's personal life (*Hemingway*, 246-47), I would contend that in both *A Moveable Feast* (111-12) and in *In Our Time*, Hemingway evokes in order to purge "Eliot" understood as synecdoche of modernist writing and/or the way it affects Hemingway's relation to his own acts of writing.

35. Hemingway, *In Our Time*, 113, 112, 110, 115.

36. See, for example, the chapter titled "Chaos" in Henry Adams, *The Education of Henry Adams* (Boston, 1973), especially 288-89.

37. Hemingway, *In Our Time*, 29.

38. James M. Cox, "Regionalism: A Diminished Thing," in *Columbia Literary History of the United States*, ed. Emory Elliott (New York, 1988), 776-77, provocatively suggests that in *In Our Time* "Hemingway moves to recover both realistic representation and naturalistic determinism," and does so by expanding the Nick Adams stories via interchapters or "very short stories, the hallmark of 'minor' [American] regional writing."

39. Although Hemingway publicly proclaimed that his story didn't derive from Anderson's, critics at the time and today all agree that it does. See Lynn, *Hemingway*, 140, 222, and 306.

40. Hemingway, *In Our Time*, 168. In *A Moveable Feast*, Hemingway praises Anderson's stories but "was prepared to tell Miss Stein how strangely poor his novels were, but this would have been bad too because it was criticizing one of her most loyal supporters"—Stein, of course, being for Hemingway a preeminent exemplar of modernist writing (28).

41. Hemingway, *In Our Time*, 168.

42. In *Hemingway*, Lynn maintains that Hemingway's early friendship with Anderson in Chicago "almost surely" resulted in a "heightening of [Hemingway's] consciousness about *Huckleberry Finn*," since Anderson admired Twain and thought this novel "a masterpiece . . . in a class by itself" (140).

43. Young makes this "ironic" connection between Ad/Bugs and Huck/Jim in "Adventures of Nick Adams," 101; also see his *Reconsideration*, 228-41. Young's observations, however, are mitigated by his literal and static—nonstrategic or nontropological—sense of literary influence.

44. Hemingway, *In Our Time*, 71-72, 79.

45. As far as I know, no extant biographical evidence exists to show that Hemingway ever read Twain's *Life on the Mississippi*, or for that matter Adams's *The Education of Henry Adams*. Neither work appears in his personal collection of books as com-

piled by Michael S. Reynolds, *Hemingway's Reading, 1910-1940: An Inventory* (Princeton, 1981). But it seems safe to assume that Hemingway was acquainted with both works by the time he wrote *In Our Time*. *The Education*, published posthumously in 1918, received the Pulitzer Prize in 1919, and exerted considerable influence on many American writers in the early twenties. See, for example, Sherwood Anderson, *A Story Teller's Story* (Cleveland, 1968), 275; and Louis Kronenberger, "The Education of Henry Adams," in *Books That Changed Our Minds*, ed. Malcolm Cowley and Bernard Smith (New York, 1939), 43-57. In 1944, Hemingway alluded to his acquaintance with Adams's less well-known companion volume to *The Education, Mont-Saint-Michel and Chartres* (Carlos Baker, *Ernest Hemingway: A Life Story* [New York, 1969], 405-6). Similarly, Hemingway's friendship during his early apprenticeship years with Anderson, a Twain devotee, not to mention with Stein, who in *Everybody's Autobiography* (New York, 1973), 257, extols *Life on the Mississippi*, surely indicates the probability of Hemingway's acquaintance with the Twain work. Ultimately, however, my discussion of his stories in dynamic relation to the specified works of Twain and Adams borrows from Harold Bloom's notion of poetry, which I here interpolate also to mean prose narratives: "the meaning of a [prose narrative] can only be . . . *another [prose narrative] . . . not itself*. And not a [narrative] chosen with total arbitrariness, but any central [narrative] by an indubitable precursor, even if the ephebe *never read* that [narrative]" (*The Anxiety of Influence* [New York, 1973], 70).

46. Mark Twain, *Life on the Mississippi*, ed. James M. Cox (New York, 1984), 416, 404. For a further discussion of Twain's "self-referential" concerns in *Life*, see my essay, "Killing Time with Mark Twain's Autobiographies," *ELH* 54 (Spring 1987): 157-82.

47. Hemingway, *In Our Time*, 15, 17, 19.

48. Ibid., 100, 99, 94-95, 90-91.

49. Ibid., 101.

50. Ibid., 129-30. Lynn, *Hemingway*, 200-204, reads the story's husband and wife "dispute" as reflecting Hemingway's "conflicted feelings" about Hadley's pregnancy around the time he was writing *In Our Time*.

51. Hemingway, *Moveable Feast*, 15-16.

52. Hemingway, *In Our Time*, 144, 143, 145-47.

53. Ibid., 146.

54. Ibid., 77. Lynn, *Hemingway*, 273, loosely suggests that "The Battler" refers to Hemingway's desire to gain "the literary championship of the world." Hemingway, of course, frequently indulged in this writing as boxing metaphor; see, for example, the quotation cited by Lynn regarding his competitive view of certain Continental writers (549).

55. Hemingway, *In Our Time*, 126, 134-35, 120.

56. Young, "Adventures of Nick Adams," claims that unless one sees Nick's "routine" as "desperately protecting his mind against whatever it is that he is escaping," then the story seems "pointless" (105-6).

57. Cox, "Regionalism," regards the compressed interchapters as "displacing the 'major' convention of the novel" (777)—a position I would maintain occurs in the "self-referential" undertow of the stories themselves.

---

58. Hemingway, *Moveable Feast*, 12.

59. Peter Schwenger, *Phallic Critiques: Masculinity and Twentieth-Century Literature* (London, 1984), 50.

60. Hemingway, *In Our Time*, 121, 139.

RESOURCES

Chronology of Ernest Hemingway's Life_____

1899	Ernest Miller Hemingway is born to Clarence and Grace Hemingway on July 21 in Oak Park, Illinois.
1917	Hemingway works as a reporter on the *Kansas City Star*.
1918	Hemingway serves in Italy as an ambulance driver for the American Red Cross and is wounded on July 8 near Fossalta di Piave. He has an affair with nurse Agnes von Kurowsky.
1919	Hemingway is discharged from the American Red Cross and returns to the United States.
1920	Hemingway works as a reporter for the *Toronto Star*.
1921	Hemingway marries Hadley Richardson and moves to Paris.
1922	Hemingway reports on the Greco-Turkish War for the *Toronto Star*.
1923	*Three Stories and Ten Poems* is published in Paris. Hemingway's son John is born.
1924	The short-fiction collection *in our time* is published in Paris.
1925	*In Our Time*, which adds fourteen stories to the earlier collection of vignettes, is published in the United States.
1926	*Torrents of Spring* and *The Sun Also Rises* are published by Charles Scribner's Sons.
1927	*Men Without Women*, which includes "Hills Like White Elephants," is published. Hemingway divorces Hadley Richardson and marries Pauline Pfeiffer.
1928	Hemingway moves to Key West, where his son Patrick is born. Clarence Hemingway commits suicide on December 6 in Oak Park, Illinois.

1929	*A Farewell to Arms* is published.
1931	Hemingway's son Gregory is born.
1932	*Death in the Afternoon* is published.
1933	The short-story collection *Winner Take Nothing* is published.
1935	*Green Hills of Africa* is published.
1937	*To Have and Have Not* is published. Hemingway returns to Spain as a war correspondent on the Loyalist side.
1938	Hemingway writes scripts for the film *The Spanish Earth*, and *"The Fifth Column" and the First Forty-nine Stories* is published.
1940	Hemingway divorces Pauline Pfeiffer and marries Martha Gellhorn. *For Whom the Bell Tolls* is published. Hemingway buys a house, Finca Vigía, in Cuba, where he lives throughout most of the 1940s and 1950s.
1942	Hemingway's edited volume *Men at War: The Best War Stories of All Time* is published.
1944	Hemingway takes part in the Allied liberation of Paris with a partisan unit; he meets Mary Welsh.
1945	Hemingway is involved in a serious car crash; he divorces Martha Gellhorn.
1946	Hemingway marries Mary Welsh.
1947	Hemingway receives the Bronze Star.
1950	*Across the River and into the Trees* is published.
1951	Grace Hall Hemingway dies.
1952	*The Old Man and the Sea* is published.

1953	*The Old Man and the Sea* receives the Pulitzer Prize for Fiction.
1954	Hemingway is awarded the Nobel Prize in Literature.
1960	Hemingway moves to Ketchum, Idaho; he is hospitalized for various ailments, including depression.
1961	Hemingway commits suicide on July 2 in Ketchum, Idaho.
1964	*A Moveable Feast* is published.
1970	*Islands in the Stream* is published.
1972	The short-story collection *The Nick Adams Stories* is published.
1985	*The Dangerous Summer* is published.
1986	*The Garden of Eden*, an unfinished novel, is published.

Works by Ernest Hemingway

Long Fiction

The Sun Also Rises, 1926
The Torrents of Spring, 1926
A Farewell to Arms, 1929
To Have and Have Not, 1937
For Whom the Bell Tolls, 1940
Across the River and into the Trees, 1950
The Old Man and the Sea, 1952
Islands in the Stream, 1970
The Garden of Eden, 1986
True at First Light, 1999

Short Fiction

Three Stories and Ten Poems, 1923
in our time, 1924
In Our Time, 1925
Men Without Women, 1927
Winner Take Nothing, 1933
"The Fifth Column" and the First Forty-nine Stories, 1938
The Snows of Kilimanjaro, and Other Stories, 1961
The Short Happy Life of Francis Macomber, and Other Stories, 1963
The Nick Adams Stories, 1972
The Complete Short Stories of Ernest Hemingway, 1987

Drama and Poetry

Today Is Friday, 1926 (play)
The Fifth Column, 1938 (play)
The Spanish Earth, 1938 (documentary film script)
The Collected Poems of Ernest Hemingway, 1970
Eighty-eight Poems, 1979
Complete Poems, 1983

Nonfiction

Death in the Afternoon, 1932
Green Hills of Africa, 1935
Men at War: The Best War Stories of All Time, 1942 (editor)

Voyage to Victory: An Eye-Witness Report of the Battle for a Normandy Beachhead, 1944

Two Christmas Tales, 1959

The Wild Years, 1962

A Moveable Feast, 1964

By-Line: Ernest Hemingway, Selected Articles and Dispatches of Four Decades, 1967

Ernest Hemingway, Cub Reporter: "Kansas City Star" Stories, 1970 (Matthew J. Bruccoli, editor)

Ernest Hemingway: Selected Letters, 1917-1961, 1981 (Carlos Baker, editor)

Ernest Hemingway on Writing, 1984 (Larry W. Phillips, editor)

The Dangerous Summer, 1985

Dateline, Toronto: The Complete "Toronto Star" Dispatches, 1920-1924, 1985

Hemingway at Oak Park High: The High School Writings of Ernest Hemingway, 1916-1917, 1993

The Only Thing That Counts: The Ernest Hemingway/Maxwell Perkins Correspondence, 1925-1947, 1996 (Matthew J. Bruccoli, editor)

Bibliography

Aldridge, John. "*The Sun Also Rises*: Sixty Years Later." *Sewanee Review* 94.2 (1986): 337-45.

Astro, Richard, and Jackson J. Benson, eds. *Hemingway in Our Time*. Corvallis: Oregon State University Press, 1974

Baker, Carlos. *Ernest Hemingway: A Life Story*. New York: Charles Scribner's Sons, 1969.

_____. *Ernest Hemingway: Critiques of Four Major Novels*. New York: Charles Scribner's Sons, 1962.

_____. *Hemingway: The Writer as Artist*. Princeton, NJ: Princeton University Press, 1972.

_____, ed. *Ernest Hemingway, Selected Letters*. New York: Charles Scribner's Sons, 1981.

Balassi, William. "The Trail to *The Sun Also Rises*: The First Week of Writing." *Hemingway: Essays of Reassessment*. Ed. Frank Scafella. Oxford: Oxford University Press, 1991.

Beegel, Susan, ed. *Hemingway's Neglected Short Fiction*. Tuscaloosa: University of Alabama Press, 1992.

Benson, Jackson J., ed. *New Critical Approaches to the Short Stories of Ernest Hemingway*. Durham, NC: Duke University Press, 1990.

_____. *The Short Stories of Ernest Hemingway: Critical Essays*. Durham, NC: Duke University Press, 1975.

Berman, Ronald. *Fitzgerald, Hemingway, and the Twenties*. Tuscaloosa: University of Alabama Press, 2001.

_____. *Modernity and Progress: Fitzgerald, Hemingway, Orwell*. Tuscaloosa: University of Alabama Press, 2005.

_____ *Translating Modernism: Fitzgerald and Hemingway*. Tuscaloosa: University of Alabama Press, 2009.

Brasch, James D., and Joseph Sigman. *Hemingway's Library: A Composite Record*. New York: Garland, 1981.

Brenner, Gerry. *Concealments in Hemingway's Works*. Columbus: Ohio State University Press, 1983.

_____. *The Old Man and the Sea: Story of a Common Man*. New York: Twayne, 1991.

Bruccoli, Matthew J. *Scott and Ernest: The Authority of Failure and the Authority of Success*. New York: Random House, 1978.

Burgess, Anthony. *Ernest Hemingway and His World*. New York: Charles Scribner's Sons, 1978.

Burgess, Robert F. *Hemingway's Paris and Pamplona, Then, and Now: A Personal Memoir*. Lincoln, NE: iUniverse, 2000.

Burwell, Rose Marie. *Hemingway: The Postwar Years and the Posthumous Novels*. New York: Cambridge University Press, 1996.

Comley, Nancy, and Robert Scholes. *Hemingway's Genders: Rereading the Hemingway Text*. New Haven, CT: Yale University Press, 1994.

Curnutt, Kirk. *Ernest Hemingway and the Expatriate Modernist Movement*. Detroit: Gale Group, 2000.

Davidson, Arnold E., and Cathy Davidson. "Decoding the Hemingway Hero in *The Sun Also Rises*." *New Essays on The Sun Also Rises*. Ed. Linda Wagner-Martin. New York: Cambridge University Press, 1987.

Donaldson, Scott. *By Force of Will: The Life and Art of Ernest Hemingway*. New York: Viking Press, 1977.

_____, ed. *The Cambridge Companion to Ernest Hemingway*. New York: Cambridge University Press, 1996.

_____. *Fitzgerald and Hemingway: Works and Days*. New York: Columbia University Press, 2009.

Eby, Carl P. *Hemingway's Fetishism: Psychoanalysis and the Mirror of Manhood*. Albany: State University of New York Press, 1998.

Falco, Joseph M. *The Hero in Hemingway's Short Stories*. Pittsburgh: University of Pittsburgh Press, 1968.

Fantina, Richard. *Ernest Hemingway: Machismo and Masochism*. New York: Palgrave Macmillan, 2005.

Fenton, Charles Andrews. *The Apprenticeship of Ernest Hemingway: The Early Years*. New York: Farrar, Straus and Young, 1954.

Fleming, Robert E. *The Face in the Mirror: Hemingway's Writers*. Tuscaloosa: University of Alabama Press, 1994.

Flora, Joseph M. *Ernest Hemingway: A Study of the Short Fiction*. Boston: Twayne, 1989.

_____. *Hemingway's Nick Adams*. Baton Rouge: Louisiana State University Press, 1982.

Gajdusek, Robert E. *Hemingway in His Own Country*. Notre Dame, IN: University of Notre Dame Press, 2002.

Gurko, Leo. *Ernest Hemingway and the Pursuit of Heroism*. New York: Crowell, 1968.

Hatten, Charles. "The Crisis of Masculinity, Reified Desire, and Catherine Barkley in *A Farewell to Arms*." *Journal of the History of Sexuality* 4 (July 1993): 76-98.

Hays, Peter L. *Ernest Hemingway*. New York: Continuum, 1990.

Hemingway, Ernest. *By-Line: Ernest Hemingway, Selected Articles and Dispatches of Four Decades*. Ed. William H. White. New York: Charles Scribner's Sons, 1967.

Hemingway, Gregory. *Papa: A Personal Memoir*. Boston: Houghton Mifflin, 1976.

Hemingway, Leicester. *My Brother Ernest Hemingway*. Cleveland: World Publishing, 1962.

Josephs, Allen. *For Whom the Bell Tolls: Ernest Hemingway's Undiscovered Country*. New York: Twayne, 1994.

Justice, Hilary K. *The Bones of the Others: The Hemingway Text from the Lost Manuscripts to the Posthumous Novels*. Kent, OH: Kent State University Press, 2006.

Kert, Bernice. *The Hemingway Women*. New York: W. W. Norton, 1985.

Killmann, Hans-Joachim. *Ernest Hemingway's Short Story Technique: A Study*. Frankfurt: Selbstverlag, 2005.

Lamb, Robert P. "Hemingway and the Creation of Twentieth-Century Dialogue." *Twentieth Century Literature* 42.4 (Winter 1996): 453-81.

Larson, Kelli A. *Ernest Hemingway: A Reference Guide, 1974-1989*. Boston: G. K. Hall, 1991.

Lee, A. Robert, ed. *Ernest Hemingway: New Critical Essays*. Totowa, NJ: Barnes & Noble, 1983.

Lewis, Robert W. *A Farewell to Arms: The War of the Words*. New York: Twayne, 1992.

Meyers, Jeffrey. *Hemingway: Life into Art*. New York: Cooper Square Press, 2000.

_____, ed. *Hemingway: The Critical Heritage*. Boston: Routledge & Kegan Paul, 1982.

Moddelmog, Debra. *Reading Desire: In Pursuit of Ernest Hemingway*. Ithaca, NY: Cornell University Press, 1999.

Monteiro, George, ed. *Critical Essays on Ernest Hemingway's A Farewell to Arms*. New York: G. K. Hall, 1994.

Nagel, James, ed. *Ernest Hemingway: The Writer in Context*. Madison: University of Wisconsin Press, 1984.

Nahal, Chaman Lal. *The Narrative Pattern in Ernest Hemingway's Fiction*. Rutherford, NJ: Fairleigh Dickinson University Press, 1971

Nelson, Raymond S. *Ernest Hemingway: Life, Work, and Criticism*. Fredericton, NB: York Press, 1984.

Ott, Mark P. *Sea of Change: Ernest Hemingway and the Gulf Stream*. Kent, OH: Kent State University Press, 2008.

Raeburn, John. *Fame Became Him: Hemingway as a Public Writer*. Bloomington: Indiana University Press, 1984.

Reynolds, Michael S. *Critical Essays on Ernest Hemingway's "In Our Time."* Boston: G. K. Hall, 1983.

_____. *Ernest Hemingway*. Detroit: Gale Group, 2000.

_____. *Hemingway: The American Homecoming*. Cambridge: Blackwell, 1992.

_____. *Hemingway: The Final Years*. New York: Norton, 1999.

_____. *Hemingway: The 1930's*. New York: Norton, 1997.

_____. *Hemingway: The Paris Years*. Cambridge: Blackwell, 1989.

_____. *Hemingway's First War: The Making of "A Farewell to Arms."* Princeton, NJ: Princeton University Press, 1976.

Rovit, Earl H. *Ernest Hemingway*. Boston: Twayne, 1986.

Rudat, Wolfgang. "Hemingway's *The Sun Also Rises*: Masculinity, Feminism, and Gender-Role Reversal." *American Imago* 47.1 (1990): 43-68.

_____. *A Rotten Way to Be Wounded: The Tragicomedy of The Sun Also Rises*. New York: Peter Lang, 1990.

Ryan, Frank L. *The Immediate Critical Reception of Ernest Hemingway*. Washington, DC: University Press of America, 1980.

Scafella, Frank, ed. *Hemingway: Essays of Reassessment*. Oxford: Oxford University Press, 1991.

Smith, Paul. *A Reader's Guide to the Short Stories of Ernest Hemingway*. New York: Macmillan, 1989.

_____. ed. *New Essays on Hemingway's Short Fiction*. New York: Cambridge University Press, 1998.

Spilka, Mark. "The Death of Love in *The Sun Also Rises*." *Ernest Hemingway: Critiques of Four Major Novels*. Ed. Carlos Baker. New York: Charles Scribner's Sons, 1962.

_____. *Hemingway's Quarrel with Androgyny*. Lincoln: University of Nebraska Press, 1990.

Stephens, Robert O., ed. *Ernest Hemingway: The Critical Reception*. New York: B. Franklin, 1977.

Strong, Amy L. *Race and Identity in Hemingway's Fiction*. New York: Palgrave Macmillan, 2008.

Strychacz, Thomas. *Dangerous Masculinities: Conrad, Hemingway, and Lawrence*. Gainesville: University Press of Florida, 2008.

_____. "Dramatizations of Manhood in Hemingway's *In Our Time* and *The Sun Also Rises*." *American Literature* 61.2 (1989): 245-60.

Wagner-Martin, Linda. *Hemingway and Faulkner: Inventors/Masters*. Metuchen, NJ: Scarecrow Press, 1975.

_____. ed. *Hemingway: Eight Decades of Criticism*. East Lansing: Michigan State University Press, 2008.

Weber, Ronald. *Hemingway's Art of Non-Fiction*. New York: St. Martin's Press, 1990.

Young, Philip. *Ernest Hemingway*. Minneapolis: University of Minnesota Press, 1952, 1959, 1966.

_____. *Ernest Hemingway: A Reconsideration*. University Park: Penn State University Press, 1966.

Young, Philip, and Charles W. Mann. *The Hemingway Manuscripts: An Inventory*. University Park: Penn State University Press, 1969.

CRITICAL INSIGHTS

About the Editor

Eugene Goodheart is the Edytha Macy Professor of Humanities Emeritus at Brandeis University. He has written extensively on nineteenth- and twentieth-century literature and modern literary and cultural theory. He is the author of eleven books, including *The Skeptic Disposition: Deconstruction, Ideology, and Other Matters* (1984, 1991), *The Reign of Ideology* (1997), *Does Literary Studies Have a Future?* (1999), *Darwinian Misadventures in the Humanities* (2007), and a memoir, *Confessions of a Secular Jew* (2001, 2004). His many articles and reviews have appeared in, among other journals, *Partisan Review, Sewanee Review, New Literary History, Critical Inquiry*, and *Daedalus*.

About *The Paris Review*

The Paris Review is America's preeminent literary quarterly, dedicated to discovering and publishing the best new voices in fiction, nonfiction, and poetry. The magazine was founded in Paris in 1953 by the young American writers Peter Matthiessen and Doc Humes, and edited there and in New York for its first fifty years by George Plimpton. Over the decades, the *Review* has introduced readers to the earliest writings of Jack Kerouac, Philip Roth, T. C. Boyle, V. S. Naipaul, Ha Jin, Jay McInerney, and Mona Simpson, and published numerous now classic works, including Roth's *Goodbye, Columbus*, Donald Barthelme's *Alice*, Jim Carroll's *Basketball Diaries*, and selections from Samuel Beckett's *Molloy* (his first publication in English). The first chapter of Jeffrey Eugenides's *The Virgin Suicides* appeared in the *Review*'s pages, as well as stories by Edward P. Jones, Rick Moody, David Foster Wallace, Denis Johnson, Jim Shepard, Jim Crace, Lorrie Moore, Jeanette Winterson, and Ann Patchett.

The Paris Review's renowned Writers at Work series of interviews, whose early installments include legendary conversations with E. M. Forster, William Faulkner, and Ernest Hemingway, is one of the landmarks of world literature. The interviews received a George Polk Award and were nominated for a Pulitzer Prize. Among the more than three hundred interviewees are Robert Frost, Marianne Moore, W. H. Auden, Elizabeth Bishop, Susan Sontag, and Toni Morrison. Recent issues feature conversations with Salman Rushdie, Joan Didion, Stephen King, Norman Mailer, Kazuo Ishiguro, and Umberto Eco. (A complete list of the interviews is available at www .theparisreview.org.) In November 2008, Picador will publish the third of a four-volume series of anthologies of *Paris Review* interviews. The first two volumes have received acclaim. *The New York Times* called the Writers at Work series "the most remarkable and extensive interviewing project we possess."

The Paris Review is edited by Philip Gourevitch, who was named to the post in 2005, following the death of George Plimpton two years earlier. Under Gourevitch's leadership, the magazine's international distribution has expanded, paid subscriptions have risen 150 percent, and newsstand distribution has doubled. A new editorial team has published fiction by Andre Aciman, Damon Galgut, Mohsin Hamid, Gish Jen, Richard Price, Said Sayrafiezadeh, and Alistair Morgan. Poetry editors Charles Simic, Meghan O'Rourke, and Dan Chiasson have selected works by Billy Collins, Jesse Ball, Mary Jo Bang, Sharon Olds, and Mary Karr. Writing published in the magazine has been anthologized in *Best American Short Stories* (2006, 2007, and 2008), *Best American Poetry*, *Best Creative Non-Fiction*, the Pushcart Prize anthology, and *O. Henry Prize Stories*.

The magazine presents two annual awards. The Hadada Award for lifelong contribution to literature has recently been given to William Styron, Joan Didion, Norman Mailer, and Peter Matthiessen in 2008. The Plimpton Prize for Fiction, given to a new voice in fiction brought to national attention in the pages of *The Paris Review*, was presented in 2007 to Benjamin Percy and to Jesse Ball in 2008.

The Paris Review won the 2007 National Magazine Award in photojournalism, and the *Los Angeles Times* recently called *The Paris Review* "an American treasure with true international reach."

Since 1999 *The Paris Review* has been published by The Paris Review Foundation, Inc., a not-for-profit 501(c)(3) organization.

The Paris Review is available in digital form to libraries worldwide in selected academic databases exclusively from EBSCO Publishing. Libraries can contact EBSCO at 1-800-653-2726 for details. For more information on *The Paris Review* or to subscribe, please visit: www.theparisreview.org.

Contributors

Eugene Goodheart is the Edytha Macy Professor of Humanities Emeritus at Brandeis University. He is the author of eleven books of literary and cultural criticism as well as a memoir, *Confessions of a Secular Jew* (2001, 2004).

R. Baird Shuman, Professor Emeritus of English at the University of Illinois at Urbana-Champaign, has taught at the University of Pennsylvania, Drexel University, San José State University, and Duke University. He has published critical studies of Clifford Odets, William Inge, and Robert E. Sherwood. The editor of the thirteen-volume encyclopedia *Great American Writers, 20th Century*, he lives in Las Vegas, Nevada.

Petrina Crockford is a writer living in Western Colorado.

Jennifer Banach Palladino is a writer and independent scholar from Connecticut. She has served as the contributing editor of *Bloom's Guides: Heart of Darkness* and *Bloom's Guides: The Glass Menagerie* for Facts On File, Inc., and is the author of the forthcoming volumes *Bloom's How to Write About Tennessee Williams* from Facts On File, Inc., and *Understanding Norman Mailer* from the University of South Carolina Press. She has also composed teaching guides to international literature for Random House's Academic Resources division and has contributed to numerous literary reference books for academic publishers such as Facts On File, Inc., and Oxford University Press on topics ranging from Romanticism to contemporary literature. Her work has appeared in academic and popular venues alike; her fiction and nonfiction have appeared under the *Esquire* banner. She is a member of the Association of Literary Scholars and Critics.

Robert C. Evans earned his Ph.D. from Princeton University in 1984. In 1982 he began teaching at Auburn University Montgomery, where he has been named Distinguished Research Professor, Distinguished Teaching Professor, and University Alumni Professor. External awards include fellowships from the ACLS, the APS, the NEH, and the Folger, Huntington, and Newberry Libraries. He is the author or editor of more than twenty books and of numerous essays, including recent work on twentieth-century American writers.

Matthew J. Bolton is an English teacher and the academic dean of Loyola School in New York City. He earned his Ph.D. in English literature in 2005 from the Graduate Center of the City University of New York, where he wrote his dissertation on Robert Browning and T. S. Eliot. He received the T. S. Eliot Society's Fathman Young Scholar Award for work related to his dissertation. In addition to his doctorate, Bolton holds master's degrees in teaching and in educational administration from Fordham University. His research and writing center on connections between Victorian and modernist literature.

Carlos Baker was the Woodrow Wilson Professor of Literature at Princeton University. His books on Shelley and Hemingway have been influential in defining the fields of study on those authors. He wrote and edited numerous volumes of fiction and nonfiction, including *Shelley's Major Poetry: The Fabric of a Vision* (1948), *Hemingway: The Writer as Artist* (1952), *Forty Years of Pulitzer Prizes* (1957), *Hemingway and His Critics: An International Anthology* (1961), *Ernest Hemingway: Critiques of Four Major Novels* (1962), *Coleridge: Poetry and Prose* (1965), *Modern American Usage: A Guide* (with Jacques Barzun, 1966), *Ernest Hemingway: A Life Story* (1969), *Ernest Hemingway: Selected Letters, 1917-1961* (1981), *Echoing Green: Romanticism, Modernism, and the Phenomena of Transference in Poetry* (1984), and *Emerson Among the Eccentrics: A Group Portrait* (1996).

Hilary K. Justice is Associate Professor at Illinois State University. Her publications include *The Bones of the Others: The Hemingway Text from the Lost Manuscripts to the Posthumous Novels* (2006) and essays in *The Hemingway Review* and *American Literary Scholarship*.

Ron Berman is Professor of English Literature at the University of California, San Diego. His publications include *Public Policy and the Aesthetic Interest* (1992), *The Great Gatsby and Modern Times* (1994), *The Great Gatsby and Fitzgerald's World of Ideas* (1996), *Fitzgerald, Hemingway, and the Twenties* (2001), and *Fitzgerald-Wilson-Hemingway* (2003).

Neil Heims is a writer and teacher living in Paris. His books include *Reading the Diary of Anne Frank* (2005), *Allen Ginsberg* (2005), and *J. R. R. Tolkien* (2004). He has also contributed numerous articles to literary publications, including essays on William Blake, John Milton, William Shakespeare, and Arthur Miller.

George Cheatham is Professor of English at Greensboro College, where he also serves as Assistant Dean of Faculty.

Scott Donaldson taught English at the College of William and Mary, where he retired as Louise G. T. Cooley Professor of English. He has written widely and extensively, and his book publications include *Poet in America: Winfield Townley Scott* (1972), *By Force of Will: The Life and Art of Ernest Hemingway* (1977), *Fool for Love: F. Scott Fitzgerald* (1983), *John Cheever: A Biography* (1988), *Archibald MacLeish: An American Life* (1992), *Hemingway vs. Fitzgerald: The Rise and Fall of a Literary Friendship* (1999), and *Edwin Arlington Robinson: A Poet's Life* (2007).

Mark Spilka is Professor Emeritus of English and Comparative Literature at Brown University, where he served as editor of *Novel: A Forum on Fiction*. His books include *Love Ethic of D. H. Lawrence* (1955), *Dickens and Kafka* (1963), *D. H. Lawrence: A Collection of Critical Essays* (1963), *Virginia Woolf's Quarrel with Grieving* (1980), *Hemingway's Quarrel with Androgyny* (1990), and *Eight Lessons in Love: A Domestic Violence Reader* (1997).

Diane Price Herndl is Director of Women's Studies and Professor of English at Iowa State University. She has contributed essays to journals such as *Signs: Journal of Women in Culture and Society*, *PMLA*, *The Hemingway Review*, and *Narrative*. With

Robyn Warhol-Down, Mary Lou Kete, Lisa Schnell, Beth Kowaleski-Wallace, and Rashmi Varma she served as coeditor of *Women's Worlds: The McGraw-Hill Anthology of Women's Writing* (2008), and with Robyn R. Warhol she edited the volume *Feminisms: An Anthology of Literary Criticism and Theory* (1991). Her book *Invalid Women: Figuring Feminine Illness in American Fiction and Culture, 1840-1940* was published in 1993.

A. Robert Lee is Professor of American Literature at Nihon University, Tokyo. Among his many publications and edited volumes are *Black Fiction: New Studies in the Afro-American Novel Since 1945* (1980), *Ernest Hemingway: New Critical Essays* (1983), *Herman Melville: Reassessments* (1984), *Edgar Allan Poe: The Design of Order* (1987), *First Person Singular: Studies in American Autobiography* (1988), *The Modern American Novella* (1989), *A Permanent Etcetera: Cross-Cultural Perspectives on Post-war America* (1993), *Other Britain, Other British: Contemporary Multicultural Fiction* (1995), *Beat Generation Writers* (1996), *Making America, Making American Literature: Franklin to Cooper* (with W. M. Verhoeven, 1996), *Designs of Blackness: Mappings in the Literature and Culture of Afro-America* (1998), *Loosening the Seams: Interpretations of Gerald Vizenor* (2000), and *Multicultural American Literature: Comparative Black, Native, Latino/a, and Asian American Fictions* (2003).

Philip Melling is Professor of American Studies at Swansea University, where he is the founding head of the American Studies Department. His books include *Vietnam in American Literature* (1990), *Fundamentalism in America* (1999), and *America in the 1920s* (2004). He has also contributed essays to edited volumes such as *Critical Essays on the Myth of the American Adam* (2001) and *The Legacy of the Vietnam War* (2007) and to journals including *The Hemingway Review.*

Louis A. Renza is Professor of English at Dartmouth College. He has contributed essays to a number of critical volumes, including *Autobiography: Essays Theoretical and Critical* (1980), *Critical Terms for Literary Study* (1990), *The American Face of Edgar Allan Poe* (1995), and *Hemingway: Seven Decades of Criticism* (1998). His books include *"A White Heron" and the Question of Minor Literature* (1984) and *Edgar Allan Poe, Wallace Stevens, and the Poetics of American Privacy* (2002).

Acknowledgments

"Ernest Hemingway" by R. Baird Shuman. From *Dictionary of World Biography: The 20th Century*. Copyright © 1999 by Salem Press, Inc. Reprinted with permission of Salem Press.

"The *Paris Review* Perspective" by Petrina Crockford. Copyright © 2008 by Petrina Crockford. Special appreciation goes to Christopher Cox and Nathaniel Rich, editors for *The Paris Review*.

"The First Forty-five Stories" by Carlos Baker. From *Hemingway: The Writer as Artist* by Carlos Baker. Copyright © 1952 Princeton University Press, 1956 2nd Edition, 1980 renewed in author's name. Reprinted by permission of Princeton University Press.

"The Personal Stories: Paris and Provence, 1926-1927" by Hilary K. Justice. From *The Bones of the Others: The Hemingway Text from the Lost Manuscripts to the Posthumous Novels* (2006) by Hilary K. Justice. Copyright © 2006 by Kent State University Press. Reprinted by permission of Kent State University Press.

"Recurrence in Hemingway and Cézanne" by Ron Berman. From *The Hemingway Review* 23, no. 2 (Spring 2004). Copyright © 2004 by The Hemingway Society. Reprinted by permission of The Hemingway Society.

"'Sign the Wire with Love': The Morality of Surplus in *The Sun Also Rises*" by George Cheatham. From *The Hemingway Review* 11, no. 2 (Spring 1992). Copyright © 1992 by The Hemingway Society. Reprinted by permission of The Hemingway Society.

"Frederic Henry's Escape and the Pose of Passivity" by Scott Donaldson. From *Hemingway: A Revaluation* (1983) edited by Donald R. Noble. Copyright © 1983 by Whitston Publishing Company. Reprinted by permission of Whitston Publishing Company.

"Three Wounded Warriors" by Mark Spilka. From *Hemingway's Quarrel with Androgyny* (1990) by Mark Spilka. Copyright © 1990 by University of Nebraska Press. Reprinted by permission of University of Nebraska Press.

"Invalid Masculinity: Silence, Hospitals, and Anesthesia in *A Farewell to Arms*" by Diane Price Herndl. From *The Hemingway Review* 21, no. 1 (Fall 2001). Copyright © 2001 by The Hemingway Society. Reprinted by permission of The Hemingway Society.

"'Everything Completely Knit Up': Seeing *For Whom the Bell Tolls* Whole" by A. Robert Lee. From *Ernest Hemingway: New Critical Essays* (1983) edited by A. Robert Lee. Copyright © 1983 by Rowman and Littlefield. Reprinted by permission of Rowman and Littlefield.

"Cultural Imperialism, Afro-Cuban Religion, and Santiago's Failure in Hemingway's *The Old Man and the Sea*" by Philip Melling. From *The Hemingway Review* 26,

Redemption, 23, 29, 178, 276
Referential writing, 307, 309
Regeneration (Barker), 240, 242
Reiteration, 139-140, 144, 151
Religion, 198, 224, 269, 286, 290, 293, 296, 300
Remorse, 183
Renner, Stanley, 114-115, 117, 120, 123
Responsibility, 88, 173, 183
"Revolutionist, The" (Hemingway), 319
Rewald, John, 140, 154-155
Reynolds, Michael S., 114, 135, 179, 185, 201
Richardson, Hadley, 9, 23, 102, 104, 107, 115, 128, 132, 134, 207, 217, 221, 225, 229, 234, 236, 311, 325, 332-333, 335
Rinaldi (*A Farewell to Arms*), 26, 40, 183, 189, 194, 196, 241, 243, 245, 248
Rituals, 27, 80, 86, 276, 288, 291
Rivers, W.H.R., 241
"Road at Chantilly" (Cézanne), 154
Road motifs, 139, 146, 148
"Rocks at Fontainebleau" (Schapiro), 146
Roderick Hudson (James), 72
Rogosin, Donn, 292
"Romantic Lady, The" (Arlen), 214, 236
Romero, Pedro (*The Sun Also Rises*), 38, 157, 167, 169, 211, 214, 219, 231
"Rose for Emily, A" (Faulkner), 52-53, 56, 59, 65
Rosenberg, Emily S., 284
Rosenfeld, Isaac, 228
Route tournante, 145, 151
Rovit, Earl, 28, 32
Russell, Bertrand, 148

Santería, 286-287, 289, 291, 295, 298, 300, 302
Santería Experience, The (Gonzalez-Wippler), 301
Santiago (*The Old Man and the Sea*), 5, 43, 45, 283-284, 288, 290, 292, 294, 296, 299-300, 302
Sarason, Bertram, 133
Sassoon, Siegfried, 254
Satire, 38, 218
Schapiro, Meyer, 139, 146, 154-155
Schatz ("A Day's Wait"), 88
Schwenger, Peter, 242
"Sea Change, The" (Hemingway), 94, 108, 134
Self-inflicted wounds, 189, 208, 244, 253
Self-pity, 206, 211, 219, 231
Self-referential work, 309, 314, 316, 319, 325, 330, 333, 335
Selfhood, 223, 227, 229
Selfishness, 230, 233
Selflessness, 221, 224, 229, 231-232
Sentimental Education, The (Flaubert), 146
Seven African Powers (Santería), 287
Sex roles, 208, 224
Sexual intercourse, 41, 97, 180, 200
Sharks, 283, 289-290, 300, 302
Sheldon, Barbara (*The Garden of Eden*), 223, 237
Sheldon, Nick (*The Garden of Eden*), 223, 237
Shipman, Evan, 312
"Short Happy Life of Francis Macomber, The" (Hemingway), 11, 73
Showalter, Elaine, 243
Silence, 241, 243, 247
Simmons (*A Farewell to Arms*), 186, 190
"Simple Enquiry, A" (Hemingway), 94
